Industrial Dislocation

Over the past decade there has been much discussion on the decline and depression of heavy industry in its traditional heartlands. This is no stark contrast to the rapid growth in this area in the Newly Industrialized Countries (NICs) of the Far East. The shipbuilding industry has become symbolic of this dislocation.

Much of the literature written on this has concentrated on the alternatives available to the depressed areas. In *Industrial Dislocation: The Case of Global Shipbuilding*, however, the author emphasizes how this situation arose and how both NICs and AICs have coped with it. Todd argues that these two points are central to understanding this subject. He examines the key factors of industrial life cycles, the international division of labour and the energy crises of the 1970s. Although the author is at pains to point out that the latter cannot be held solely responsible for this dislocation. Rather the book emphasizes that the processes of industrial maturity (and in particular Japanese attitudes towards them), the removal of barriers to entry and the lengthening product life cycle encouraged new companies at a time when hard-pressed traditional producers were falling at the twin hurdles of declining competitiveness and dwindling markets. The other crucial factors in this equation were the actions and reactions of the respective governments. This took the form of rear-guard action in the traditional areas and the state promotion in the NICs. In conclusion, Todd considers the present situation and offers an outlook for the future. The book is logically laid out and presents detailed discussions of various sample countries. It also contains a very useful glossary for more specialized vocabulary. *Industrial Dislocation: The Case of Global Shipbuilding* is an effective illustration of how and how not to succeed in the shipbuilding industry.

Daniel Todd is Professor of Geography at the University of Manitoba, of which he has been a faculty member since 1975. He has written extensively on heavy industry, publishing *The World Shipbuilding Industry* in 1985.

Industrial Dislocation

The case of global shipbuilding

Daniel Todd

London and New York

First published 1991
by Routledge
11 New Fetter Lane, London EC4P 4EE

Simultaneously published in the USA and Canada
by Routledge
a division of Routledge, Chapman and Hall, Inc.
29 West 35th Street, New York, NY 10001

Typeset by NWL Editorial Services, Langport, Somerset
Printed and bound in Great Britain by
Biddles Ltd, Guildford and King's Lynn

British Library Cataloguing in Publication Data

Todd, Daniel
   Industrial dislocation: the case of global shipbuilding.
   1. Shipbuilding industries
   I. Title
   338.4762382

ISBN 0–415–04213–5

Library of Congress Cataloging in Publication Data
has been applied for

Contents

List of tables

List of figures

Preface

In the progression from birth to senescence, industries experience different forces which compel the relocation of production. Inception hinges on technical innovation and it follows that an industry's best chances for consolidation occur where the conditions conducive to experimentation coincide with an endowment of far-sighted venture capitalists ready, able and willing to support the innovation in its formative years. For its part, maturity finds the industry replete with standard technologies and sited wherever marginal cost efficiencies are realised. Cost competitiveness now overrides technical innovation as the benchmark of enterprise success. Finally, the onset of senescence condemns the industry to eroding viability regardless of location; for neither technical edge nor price competitiveness suffice to counter the evaporation of demand for that industry's product. After enduring a long phase of maturity, the contemporary shipbuilding industry is confronted with the pressures imposed by this progression: it is devoid of significant technical innovation, subject to an intense cost-price squeeze, and fails to prosper signally because of a glaring mismatch between the supply of shipbuilding capacity and the demand for the shipping needed to sustain it. The industry has succumbed to the dictates of technical advance which have left it exposed to the kind of cost competition that requires summary plant excision in some places at the same time as new capacity is being brought on stream elsewhere. In keeping with both its protracted evolution and latter-day convolutions in location, the shipbuilding industry offers itself as a quintessential candidate for scrutiny. It serves, in short, as a touchstone for global industrial trends, setting off the problems of industrial heartlands against those arising in the parts of the earth which have only just taken up the banner of industrialisation.

Situated as they are in an industry seemingly permanently poised on the brink of entry into the senescence stage, today's shipbuilders broadly fall into two camps. On the one hand, the longstanding producers in the advanced industrial countries (AICs) of Western Europe and North America – the inheritors of the innovation traditions of the industry's birthplace – find themselves in the unenviable position of having to come to terms with approaching senescence while simultaneously competing with galvanised upstarts in the newly industrialising countries (NICs). On the other hand, the new producers – determined to make the best of a manufacturing base only just conferred on them – will stop at nothing to enlarge their share of the world shipbuilding market. Paradoxically, therefore, both camps are stepping up efforts to compete in a highly uncertain global shipping market. Holding the ring, as it were, is Japan: the pre-eminent maritime power by virtue of its commanding stature in shipbuilding and shipping. Straddling the global maritime world with a foot in both camps, this colossus acts as the cornerstone linking the fortunes of old and new producers alike. It forcibly entered the international shipbuilding scene in the 1950s, carved out a role for itself as dominant supplier and basked thereafter in the glow of assured superiority. In essence, Japan officiated as the pioneer NIC for much of the postwar era, blazing a trail for the current NICs to follow. Over the last decade, however, its market share has been assailed by an offensive mounted from the neophyte producing countries. These inroads are the natural corollary of the interplay of technical and cost factors which conspire to promote shipbuilding investment in hitherto virgin venues. In particular, Japan perceives itself to be increasingly under siege as a result of encroachments on the world market prosecuted by South Korea and neighbouring East Asian incipient competitors.

This book examines the forces leading to these dislocations, using the Japanese example as the linchpin upon which all the forces are writ large. How Japan's hand is forced by the pressures exerted through the need to overcome the impasse in technology in the first place, while encountering the challenge of frenetic NIC competition along with a measure of AIC revival in the second place, is a matter of fundamental concern to the future of global maritime activities. Accosted on all sides, Japan's shipbuilding enterprises have looked searchingly at ways to ameliorate their forbidding prospects. It is on such diversification strategies, adopted in Japan and the other AICs, that great stress will be laid in the main body of the book. These strategies roam the spectrum from offshore drilling-rig construction, power-plant fabrication, railway rolling stock manufacturing to fish farming and the conjuring up of entire artificial islands dedicated to tourism, and all of them will be accorded a place in what follows. For good measure, considerable attention is devoted to the incursions undertaken by shipbuilding enterprises into defence contracting, ship repair and ship operation: those more conventional alternatives taken up by shipbuilders as diversification ploys. To begin with, however, attempts will be made to enlist the aid of the statistical record for the purposes of illustrating the rise of Japan and its partial eclipsing of the traditional European ship producers. Occupying a substantial portion of Chapter 1, that discourse is supplemented with an outline of the circumstances besetting these AIC producers as well as an adumbration of the factors surrounding inchoate shipbuilding in the NICs. The 1970s heralded a period of severe dislocations for existing shipbuilders, dislocations that were compounded both by the appearance of new producers and by the massive upheavals in shipping consequent upon the disruption of oil supply and the throttling of economic growth. Collapse of demand for shipping coupled with a newly enlarged shipbuilding sector ushered in an extended period of unsettling times for the world's shipyards; a period of crisis proportions which has persisted almost to the present day and which has left a battered and bruised industry in its wake.

Casualties in profusion littered the shipbuilding landscape, but the survivors were compelled to make the best of what was very evidently a stricken industry. Chapter 2 evinces how they came to grips with the straitened conditions that prevailed after 1975 and, moreover, how they continue, while still in the throes of restructuring, to strive for a larger share of a market mired in uncertainty. The urgency of their efforts has received considerable impetus from the appearance on the world scene of new competitors, led by South Korea. The most recent parvenu, China, promises not only to saddle Japan and the other AICs with yet more pressing competition, but even bodes ill for the likes of South Korea and Taiwan: NICs which have witnessed sharp cost increases in the last few years. The lot of the individual enterprise during these trying times comes into focus in Chapter 3. The shipbuilding denizens of Japan, Western Europe and North America constitute the initial object of interest, for it is they that feel most imperilled by the destabilising supply situation which still obtains in global shipbuilding. Subsequent attention, however, is directed to NIC firms that have drawn heavily on the strategies and forms of organisation evolved by the key AIC enterprises exposed to the rigours of competition and bearing the brunt of its vicissitudes. As models, the actions of these latter turn for the most part on the question of survivability. In the first place, that requires boosting competitiveness in shipbuilding, a process demanding the eradication of excessive overheads (i.e. rationalisation) while invoking government – and especially its defence agencies – to participate as an ally in the battle to claw back market share or shore up activity levels outside the mercantile sphere. In the second place, the firms have no option but to resort to diversification. Firms may sanction diversification within the marine sector – as is elucidated in Chapter 4 – or they may prefer to opt out of marine-related activities and settle for the presumed security afforded by other branches of economic activity. This latter aspect is the purview of Chapter 5, as are the repercussions of conglomerate forms of organisation on the inception and fostering of shipbuilding. The chapter suffices to drive home the fact that, while the curtailment or demise of a mature industry in the AICs is often cloaked in the guise of conglomerate reorganisation, that same apparatus can quite readily be turned to shipbuilding promotion, and not least in the NICs.

The note of optimism that creeps into Chapter 5 becomes almost a clarion call in Chapter 6: the review of the emerging shipbuilding enterprises in the NICs. Theirs is a condition of hope and growth notwithstanding the dire global situation, local structural problems aplenty and the stumbling of more than a few enterprises. Espoused by their governments as vital and necessary ingredients in industrialisation programmes geared to nothing less than national transformation, they can and do revert to state help in overcoming barriers to entry. Furthermore, the neophyte shipbuilders have no compunction in calling upon their government patrons to obtrude in the market so as to guarantee a customer base if all else fails. As the concluding chapter makes abundantly clear, the practitioners of shipbuilding in the AICs and NICs share many concerns and hold in common many characteristics, but they differ profoundly in outlook. The former are the outcome of a gruelling weeding-out process whereas the latter are the products of freshly conceived national strategies for growth and development, and rejoice in a much more sanguine outlook in consequence. Japan, subscribing to the AIC camp but with recent memories of the NIC experience, combines both viewpoints. This, together with its commanding role in shipbuilding, ensures that the ways and means adopted by Japanese shipbuilders to safeguard their operations will invariably determine the course of all other shipbuilders around the world in the foreseeable future.

Acknowledgements

Any book with pretensions of global relevance, such as this one, is beholden to a vast number of sources for its facts and its inspiration. To attempt to name them all would be both tedious and wearing on the reader's patience, so I will not indulge the pastime here. Instead, I will make do with a select group deserving of special thanks. They are, in no particular order, Zhang Lei (Chinese Academy of Sciences), Yen Ruohichi (Evergreen Group), Shoichi Yokoyama (Ehime University) and John Kerr (British Maritime Technology). As far as institutions are concerned, I am indebted to the libraries of the University of Manitoba and the London School of Economics, to say nothing of material disseminated by Lloyd's Register of Shipping and a host of other organisations with maritime affiliations. Grant assistance to enable me actually to visit sites of shipbuilding activity was made available by my own University of Manitoba (in conjunction with the Social Science and Humanities Research Council) and the Pacific Cultural Foundation in Taiwan.

1 Climax and débâcle

One can be forgiven for assuming that shipbuilding inhabits a world of everlasting crisis. The pronouncements issuing from the industry certainly conspire to give such an impression. A one-time purveyor of gloom, distraught at the impending demise of the US shipbuilding industry, warned that America's then biggest shipbuilder, Bethlehem Steel Company, rejoicing in half of the industry's capacity, would soon be forced to close its Sparrows Point shipyard.[1] Yet, more than three decades after that solemn proclamation, and a host of emulations also intimating the most dire of outcomes, both Bethlehem and the Sparrows Point yard survive. Admittedly, that survival is predicated on government intervention which takes the form of naval programmes that fill much of the void left by nonexistent demands for merchant tonnage, but its upshot is an assemblage of plant, assets, capital and skills which constitutes a recognisable shipbuilding enterprise and gives sustenance to a community of people that rely on it for their livelihoods.[2] Even so, naval programmes are susceptible to their own brand of instability, replete with periodic and dreaded downturns in demand; downturns which excite outbursts from an industry anxious about the prospect of imminent collapse. As one observer, commenting on the situation obtaining in 1987, so pithily put it: 'US shipbuilders have weathered many tough business downturns in the past. But this year, analysts say, the Navy's shrinking budget may deep-six some of them.'[3] In due deference to the prediction, a sprinkling of yards actually closed in 1987, but the major players – Newport News, Litton with its Ingalls yard, General Dynamics and Bath Iron Works – discovered that the Navy could find further business to tide them over, while a number of second-rank suppliers, Bethlehem included, succeeded in prising enough contracts from the government to prolong their naval workload and, in some cases, preserve their existence. As perhaps the least competitive of the world's major shipbuilding industries, survival of the

US industry hints at the perseverance of shipbuilders notwithstanding adverse circumstances of the first order. It hints, for example, at the presence of reasonably bountiful times to leaven the bouts of severe depression: in other words, at the prevalence of a business cycle to which the industry is subjected. More to the point, it conjures up the thought that structural mechanisms must be operating not just to pitch observers of the industry into paroxysms of despair but, paradoxically, to forestall their predictions before they have reaped the grim reward of total industry failure. To be sure, it was a near run thing for the US industry in the mid-1950s, as it was for the UK industry of the early 1960s, the European industry in the late 1960s and the entire global shipbuilding industry for much of the 1970s and a goodly portion of the 1980s to boot. The business cycle characterised by daunting troughs interspersed with episodic crests began to take on a new complexion during those years. Industry depression tended to plumb new depths with each successive crisis, in part as a result of the steady augmenting of capacity in the intervening good times by the existing producers themselves, and partly following from the entry of producers domiciled in countries hitherto devoid of even the appurtenances of a shipbuilding industry. Indeed, the original producers soon perceived themselves as being in a bind: their own problems associated with overcoming the mismatch between supply and demand were compounded by the bursting onto the scene of NIC suppliers who rapidly grasped the ways and means of competitive shipbuilding. Unsurprisingly, the intensity of the vociferous pleas for help emanating from AIC shipbuilders rose in direct proportion to the introduction of new shipbuilding capacity in the NICs. Evaporating demand consequent upon the energy crisis triggered by OPEC in 1973 arrived at the exact moment that this unwelcome addition to capacity was beginning to make its presence felt on the AIC producers. A tenacity, springing partly from desperation and partly from recognition of definite competitive advantages, infused NIC producers and incited them to redouble their efforts to utilise what was essentially brand-new plant. In consequence, unrelenting rivalry between shipyards – and the states championing them – became the order of the day in global shipbuilding.

DESPONDENCY: THE CATCHWORD OF THE TIMES

Outcries from European shipbuilders, agitated at the prospect of severe retrenchment, did not surface until the early 1960s when the UK industry was forced to undergo a phase of painful cutbacks. Truth to say, the first glimmerings of trouble had been plain to see since 1956 when

Japan usurped Britain as the pre-eminent ship producer, but excision of capacity was delayed until 1962 when corporate bankruptcy became an alarming reality rather than an impending possibility. An extended period of industry shrinkage, mitigated by a hotchpotch of government bail-outs, take-overs, subventions and other support measures, was to follow in the wake of this trade recession.[4] Yet, neither piecemeal dollops of state aid nor intermittent phases of demand resurgence availed to stem the secular decline of the British industry. Spurring the contraction of UK shipbuilding, of course, was the OPEC-triggered upheaval in trade patterns which stamped most of the 1970s and, fearing for the very survival of the industry, the British Government resorted to nationalisation. Harland and Wolff (H&W) of Belfast was acquired in 1975 while the assets of most of the mainland yards were secured two years later and transformed into a monolithic entity, British Shipbuilders (BS). Under the less-interventionist political climate of the succeeding decade, the former was returned to the private sector in 1989 while the latter was gradually wound-up, with its units either having reverted to private ownership by 1989 or been withdrawn from production in the preceding years. A king's ransom had been expended in the meantime. In the 15 years of active state interest, H&W absorbed more than £1 billion in government subsidies. Despite pruning its work-force from 9,500 in 1975 to 3,800 by late 1988, each remaining job cost the state about £16,000 a year. Its vital role in the Northern Irish economy, where between 33 and 44 jobs depended directly or indirectly on every 100 H&W jobs, ensured continuing government support even though the firm's losses in the year ending in March 1987 amounted to no less than 74 per cent of its turnover.[5] Not to be outdone, BS ingested £1.3 billion in state support during the 1977–88 period, and it had done its utmost to justify unrelenting subsidies partly on the palpable need to restructure the yards to make them more competitive and partly on the grounds of the pivotal place accorded many of those yards in peripheral regional economies.[6] Nevertheless, the relic structure of BS, the private enterprises remaining in shipbuilding after the corporation's demise, held title to capacity that aggregated to but a fraction of the 1977 level and employed a combined work-force just a shadow of that available on the inception of BS.

If only moderately successful in staving off the collapse of UK shipbuilding, the government intervention exercise was of salutary benefit to a clutch of other European governments who, before the decade of the 1970s was out, found themselves confronted with compelling reasons for interfering in their own shipbuilding industries. At first they could afford to take a more sanguine outlook, equipped as they generally were with newer industrial facilities than the British while being spared the ingrained obstacles to better industrial practices which afflicted the older UK industry.[7] Some, such as Sweden and the Netherlands, had appeared to prosper signally on the tanker boom. Some, such as Denmark and West Germany, had diversified into building a variety of ship types while keeping an eye on the overall trend to larger vessels and accepting the necessity to respond with suitable investment in production facilities. Some, most notably Norway and Finland, had chosen to specialise and, accordingly, had carved out niche ship markets for themselves. Others – and France, Poland, Spain, Italy and Yugoslavia stand out – attempted to leapfrog the competition by adopting 'dirigiste' policies for underwriting their own industries. Poland, indeed, only envisaged shipbuilding as a serious proposition in the late 1940s, and, abiding by the dictates of its command economy, single-mindedly set about instituting an industry on a broad front.[8] Given such diverse approaches to shipbuilding, it is hardly surprising that some performed better than others, and the less fortunate began to feel the strains soon after the British reversal. The French industry, for example, had long struck observers as being generally unprofitable and, since 1951, had lived off subsidies made available under the government's Aid Act. Enforced mergers, judicious disbursing of naval orders and generous provision of export credits had all vouchsafed French shipbuilding a measure of protection unmatched elsewhere in Western Europe. Nevertheless, only yard rationalisation, government directed plant modernisation and managed orderbooks contrived to guarantee shipbuilding in France by the end of the 1960s.[9] For its part, West Germany had subjected its shipbuilding industry to a slimming exercise in the early 1960s, when the 10,000 jobs shed were generally overlooked in the aura of expansiveness then pervading the country's economy. Remarkably prescient misgivings as to German competitiveness in comparison with Japan forced the government's hand in the late 1960s and led to another attenuation programme. Its inevitable accompaniment of 10,000 lay-offs provoked greater notice and stir than had been the case with the earlier rationalisation.[10]

Individual cases aside, all European ship producers were united in being caught unawares by the severity and harshness of the altered circumstances brought on by the radical disruption of shipping in the 1970s. Discrete upsurges in oil prices in 1973 and 1979 which effectively pushed up the cost from just over $1 a barrel to over $30 a barrel also sufficed to scuttle the oil carrying trades. From an unprecedented boom in September 1973, the tanker market slid into the depths of a Stygian slump.[11]

To begin with few took it really seriously. They expected the depression to last only three, or at the most five years. By 1978, it was obvious to all that this was no ordinary slump for there was still a 30–40% oversupply of tanker capacity. By 1982, rather than getting better, it had got far worse; 60–70% of the fleet was surplus to demand.

While the shipping firms may have affected an air of unconcern during the period immediately following the explosion in oil prices, their actions contradicted such pretended normality and it was the builders who bore the weight of the real response. In the aftermath of the first oil price upsurge, somewhere in the region of 60 million dwt (deadweight tonnage) of tanker tonnage on order round the world was summarily cancelled but still in excess of 100 million dwt of the existing fleet remained unemployed. The large tanker which had provided the 'bread and butter' work for many new or revamped shipyards changed overnight from being a profitable resource to becoming a glaring liability. Table 1.1 reveals that the momentum to boost numbers of large vessels during the 1966 to 1976 period was suddenly halted. The tempo of deliveries suffered a severe jolting in the 1977–82 period, with only the upper end of the size scale, that is, vessels realising the full benefits of economies of scale in transport, managing to maintain the trappings of a relatively stable output, and even that stability was more illusory than real since the number of routes capable of sustaining such vessels began to wither away. Smaller supertankers, however, sustained

Table 1.1 Changing fleet of large tankers

Years and composition	Size ('000 dwt) of vessels delivered					
	200–50	250–300	300–50	350–400	400+	Total
1966–8						
Number	7					7
Tonnage ('000 dwt)	1,422					1,422
1969–72						
Number	103	37	1	1		142
Tonnage	22,883	9,613	332	372		33,201
1973–6						
Number	144	257	35	20	20	476
Tonnage	33,570	69,423	11,244	7,445	8,886	130,568
1977–82						
Number	4	19	12	9	15	59
Tonnage	923	5,123	3,882	3,287	6,817	20,032

Source: Intertanko data, cited in *Far Eastern Economic Review*, 5 February 1982

Table 1.2 The importance of tankers in shipbuilding

As of last day of	Tanker tonnage on order (million dwt)	Percentage of all tonnage on order	Percentage of existing tanker fleet (in previous July)
1971	45.31	54.2	47.1
1972	57.75	66.8	54.9
1973	97.56	75.7	84.6
1976	17.12	32.5	10.2
1977	10.28	30.0	5.9
1978	6.59	25.5	3.8
1979	8.75	30.9	5.0
1980	9.83	28.4	5.6
1981	7.17	20.3	4.2
1982	4.81	16.5	2.9
1983	5.01	15.4	3.2
1984	5.62	18.3	3.8

Source: Lloyd's Register of Shipping, various *Annual Reports*

swingeing slashes in production from the onset of the crisis as ship-owners rushed to cut their losses. At that juncture, the tanker market was absolutely vital to the world's shipbuilders. From constituting 19.5 per cent of the world fleet in 1949, the share taken by tankers had climbed to 30.3 per cent by 1959, to 36.6 per cent by 1969 and had levelled off at 39.8 per cent by 1973. Table 1.2 demonstrates that, at the end of 1971, tanker contracts accounted for 54.2 per cent of all new-building orders taken by shipyards. This proportion soared to 75.7 per cent at the zenith of the boom two years later. After the climactic upheaval in shipping that was manifested through a precipitous decline in freight rates, the tally of virtually 100 million dwt of tankers on the order-book had shrunk to just over 17 million in 1976; a decline reducing the relative share of new buildings attributable to tankers from three-quarters to scarcely one-third. The situation was to deteriorate steadily thereafter, oscillating in tonnage terms around the 5 million dwt mark by the early 1980s and accounting, in relative terms, for a 15–18 per cent share of a vastly deflated new-building market. Put otherwise, the tanker order book had been dramatically transformed from its 1973 position where it aggregated to an amount fully equal to 84.6 per cent of the fleet of tankers then trading to a position barely a decade later where it composed between 3 and 4 per cent of the extant tanker tonnage. Worse still, tankers constituted a diminished share of the world fleet by this later date; that is to say, 35.2 per cent in 1984 or a total representing a slippage of almost five percentage points on the 1973 ratio.

Of course, as well as dragging down tanker demand, the energy crises sufficed to curtail overall trade growth. For example, in 1978 seaborne trade was estimated at 16.9 billion tonne-miles whereas a decade later it was put at 15.2 billion tonne-miles. In truth, blame for most of that decline can be laid squarely at the door of declining crude oil shipments, but other trades – grain, coal, iron ore and general dry cargo – had not expanded to fill the void created by faltering oil demand.[12] In other words, the deleterious impact of the collapse in tanker construction could not easily be amended by shipbuilders switching their attention to other carrying trades. That apparent remedy merely resulted in intense price competition among the yards for other static or eroding ship markets. European governments, concerned to safeguard their ship-builders in the main to prevent excessive localised unemployment, applied a battery of interventionist tools against this backdrop of decaying demand. However, the manner of the intervention underwent a sea-change as the period stretched from the 1970s into the 1980s and the industry's problems stubbornly persisted.[13]

In the 1970s, the desire to protect unemployment came to the fore far more clearly. At the beginning of the acute phase the market down-turn was still seen as a cyclical fluctuation to be bridged by Keynesian policies of government support. The 1980s have been characterised by attempts to withdraw from the giant subsidies of the earlier period, by strategies based on a much more pessimistic and realistic view of the industry's future.

In a nutshell, the revised viewpoint arose from a belated appreciation of the structural changes in world shipbuilding imposed by Japan and the NICs following in its train. No longer would it be viewed as a growth industry temporarily checked by aberrant market forces; rather, it would be dismissed in the Western AICs as a prime candidate for eventual extinction along with the other unwanted appendages of 'rustbelt' technology. That process of attitude conversion, from attempting to preserve shipbuilding to acquiescing to its virtual elimination, was a gradual one, however, occupying the bulk of the 1960s and all of the 1970s. A remnant of sympathy for preserving a smattering of shipyards remains to this day, although more likely than not it is couched in the rubric of the strategic requirements of the state.

Ironically, Japanese shipbuilding emerged badly scarred from the first energy crisis. As the contributor of the lion's share of the world's supply of large tankers, it took the brunt of the cancellations and was left with by far the largest mass of redundant capacity. Some figures clearly underscore its parlous situation. In 1973 it had received 37.9 million dwt in shipping orders, 33.1 million of which emanated from overseas. A year later, only 13.6 million dwt was booked, 9.4 million originating with overseas buyers. The 1973 orders were dominated by large tankers, some 54 VLCCs (very large crude carriers) and 41 ULCCs (ultra large crude carriers, see Glossary for capacities), but in 1974 just 11 VLCC orders were taken and all those occurred in the first quarter. So long as the industry could depend on tankers for its staple business, it had little to fear from European competitors. Thanks to a 10 per cent cost advantage in ULCC construction and a 5–7 per cent edge in VLCC production, Japanese shipbuilders had hitherto boasted bulging order books beyond the wildest dreams of their European counterparts.[14] But owing to the disappearance of this market, the yards were forced to turn their giant drydocks, purpose-built for tanker construction, to the production of LNG (liquid natural gas) carriers – an expedient exemplified by the experiences of Kawasaki Heavy Industries (KHI) at Sakaide – and a variety of much smaller dry cargo vessels (e.g. the action pursued by Sumitomo at Oppama): types which the Europeans had pioneered (e.g. the French with LNG carriers) and in the construction of which they remained fully competitive.[15] Grasping the nettle of the abruptly changed circumstances, the Japanese implemented a major overhaul of their industry, resorting to a slate of support measures in which the government enjoined the producers to rationalise capacity and augment competitiveness. Soon all governments were pumping subsidies into shipbuilding in the belief that such action was the only recourse remaining to them in discharging an obligation to their constituents. That obligation rested on the preservation of at least some semblance of a shipbuilding industry in the face of a powerful Japanese industry set on riding out the turmoil by trespassing into ship markets that it had previously largely left untouched. This action was lent a further degree of credibility by the sudden advent of a phalanx of NICs – led, noticeably, by South Korea – hungry to enter as serious contenders what fragmented markets remained. Consequently, shipbuilding subsidies were running at about $5 billion per year by 1983, a sum equivalent to one-quarter of the prices realised on all annual new buildings.[16]

Frustratingly, however, shipbuilding profitability remained as elusive as ever. From a peak post-1973 level of Y353,000 per cgrt (compensated gross register tonnage) in 1981, average Japanese ship prices descended to Y176,000 in 1987 and Y160,000 in the first half of 1988.[17] Accusations and counter-accusations flew thick and fast: the Europeans lambasted the Japanese for failing to close proportionately as much shipyard capacity as they had done and went on to denigrate them for using artificial prices to drum up ship orders. For their part, the

Japanese denied any wilful misconduct on the pricing issue and retorted, by way of rebuttal, through taunting the Europeans with the example of their own subventions which seemingly were all that was keeping the best part of the European shipbuilding industry from expiry. Both Europeans and Japanese delighted in castigating South Korea. The European Commission, for example, arraigned the Koreans for allegedly selling ships at prices well below building costs, whereas Japanese shipbuilders claimed that their counterparts in South Korea had never been profitable and were aggressively and irresponsibly seeking extra market share solely on the strength of cross-subsidies transferred from other corporate earnings. Paradoxically, in the light of this onslaught, confirmation of the dire straits afflicting Korean shipbuilders was soon forthcoming notwithstanding the constant rejection by the builders themselves of overtures from the Europeans and the Japanese requesting their co-operation in measures aimed at redressing the global situation. In 1987 Hyundai Heavy Industries (HHI) registered a miserly Won 32 million ($43,200) profit on sales of Won 963 billion and its accumulated debts, together with those of the other three big Korean producers – Daewoo, Samsung and Korea Shipbuilding and Engineering (KSEC) – amounted to a staggering Won 3.7 trillion.[18] Other less controversial newcomers to the shipbuilding scene were also exhibiting sure signs of distress. William Wei, chairman of the China Ship Building Corporation (CSBC) of Taiwan in 1986, decried the 40 per cent fall in new-building prices in the preceding two years, holding it responsible for losses of $31 million on his company's 1985–6 sales of $240 million.[19] Closer to the West European heartland, the Polish Government declared that, whereas the 1987 output of the Lenin Shipyard in Gdansk was valued at 39 billion zlotys ($150 million), some 5 billion zlotys in subsidies were required to underwrite that production. It subsequently displayed little compunction in cutting its losses by announcing the closure of the yard.[20] Further up the Baltic, Finland's highly respected Wärtsilä Marine enterprise, renowned for its cruise ship and icebreaker expertise, could not avoid the ignominy of government take-over in 1989: a bail-out likely to result in the eventual suppression of its shipbuilding facilities.[21] Spain, which had basked in its standing as a European low-cost producer, was not spared the pains of contraction either. Major builder Astilleros Españoles (AESA) recorded losses of Ptas 27 billion in 1985 and, in conjunction with Astano, shed 13,500 jobs between 1984 and 1987. The third state-owned Spanish shipbuilder, Bazan, was instructed in 1986 to dispense with 4,500 of its workers over the next three years.[22] In short, the problems upsetting West European and Japanese shipbuilders in the 1970s were

merely the harbingers of more pertinacious obstacles from which no
shipbuilding enterprise anywhere could escape.

All these instances of stress and plight give credence to the notion
that oversupply is the fundamental drawback touching every shipbuilder
regardless of its relative competitiveness. This stance was adopted by
J. G. Davis, chairman in 1987 of the International Maritime Industries
Forum. Starting from the premise that there 'has been – and remains –
an oversupply of ships, of shipbuilding capacity, and of finance' which
has only served to effect a situation where 'too many ships are chasing
too little cargo', he goes on to apportion prime culpability to the
shipyards.[23]

> The most persistent weakness in shipping has been excess shipbuild-
> ing capacity. Governments, for social and political reasons, have been
> reluctant to allow large sections of their national shipbuilding indus-
> tries to close, and consequently have persisted in providing subsidies
> and cheap credit to attract new orders. There are now encouraging
> signs that the sheer cost of continuing such assistance is causing gov-
> ernments to think again.

The valedictory part of the quotation alludes, of course, to the portents
of exhaustion about to overtake even government coffers but, more
positively, it also hints at a possible revival in shipbuilding fortunes
resulting from anticipated upsurges in shipping markets in the 1990s.[24]
Should it so transpire, that revival will be greeted with wondrous
acclamation by shipyards inured to the crushing burdens of debt. Yet,
tales of woe overshadow and belie previous periods of expansion in the
1960s and early 1970s when a significant section of the global shipbuilding industry became accustomed to reasonably propitious returns.
Equally, they belittle the favourable conditions impinging on some
NICs which induced them to participate in ship production. Past growth
episodes thus would warrant some attention if only to herald what
future revival may have in store for the industry. Assuredly, they are
deserving of attention in addition for the insights they offer into the
shipbuilding attitudes prevailing in the NICs as opposed to those
current in the AICs.

EXPANSIONISM: AN EMBLEM OF TIMES PAST

The first flush of a new-building boom occurred in the events leading up
to, and following, the 1956 Suez crisis when the opportunity was seized
by Japan to satisfy the world's newly discovered need for larger and ever
larger tankers. In the months extending from April to September 1955,

for example, tankers accounted for 83.1 per cent of the tonnage ordered in Japan (i.e. verging on 2 million grt (gross register tonnage)), most of which derived from principals registered in Panama, the USA and Liberia. Before long, the tanker market beckoned all shipbuilders eager to profit from a fortuitous juxtaposition of circumstances; that is to say, the emergence of the large tanker product innovation just at the opportune moment of a massive uplift in the demand for oil. Once the first tanker boom had subsided, a fresh one was in the offing, and thereafter throughout the 1960s and early 1970s the secular trend appeared to condone expectations of an insatiable thirst for oil and increasing numbers of vessels to carry it. Furthermore, since the product innovation of the large tanker turned on bulk economies in transport coupled with production economies in ship construction, there seemed to be no restraints on drawing out the successful formula through progressively larger ship sizes. Because augmenting ship size conflated with scale economies in plant operations, process innovations were introduced into shipbuilding which called for very large construction facilities laid out on spacious uncluttered sites. Table 1.3 monitors the trend to larger tankers both in the years preceding the 1973 oil crisis and those immediately following it. The disruption of that year interrupted the enlargement trend and, after a brief hiatus of disarray, severed ship-building from its growth catalyst. As the table evinces, the wind was effectively knocked out of the sails of Japan's drive to bigger ships and, after 1975, the country lost its long-held, annually renewable title as source of the world's biggest tanker. To be sure, the late 1970s witnessed a final flourish of ULCC building, but this was abruptly curtailed by the second oil crisis. The French belatedly entered the fray with a bevy of giants and to them falls the honour of bringing the curtain down on mammoth vessels (the 'Prairial' of 1979, for example, attained a record 274,838 grt or 555,000 dwt).[25] By the same token, a clutch of NICs began to enter the lists during the twilight era of the ULCC. Taiwan burst onto the scene in 1978 with the 231,629 grt (gross register tonnage, 445,000 dwt) 'Burmah Endeavour', the same year that Brazil launched the 140,646 grt (279,749 dwt) 'Henrique Dias' and South Korea put into the water the 125,249 grt (264,572 dwt) 'Saffron', while Portugal floated out the 163,348 grt (323,097 dwt) 'Nogueira' in the succeeding year. Spain had enthusiastically adopted supertanker building several years earlier whereas the traditional northern European shipbuilding nations had broached the 100,000 grt threshold in their tanker building efforts a good decade before. In true pioneering fashion, Japan broke the 100,000 dwt barrier in 1958 and the 100,000 grt barrier in 1966. Oddly, part of the impetus for the Japanese penchant for large tankers had American roots.

Table 1.3 The enlargement trend in tankers

Year	Largest vessel (gross tonnage)	Place of launch	Other significant vessels		
1950	22,000	UK			
1951	20,600	UK			
1952	21,800	UK			
1953	26,000	West Germany			
1954	30,000	Netherlands			
1955	31,000	UK			
1956	51,400	Japan			
1957	51,398	Japan			
1958	69,100	Japan			
1959	40,800	Japan			
1960	72,266	Japan			
1961	65,740	USA			
1962	74,869	Japan			
1963	58,211	Sweden			
1964	62,195	Japan			
1965	96,500	Japan			
1966	107,957	Japan			
1967	105,245	Japan			
1968	149,609	Japan	104,772 West Germany	104,561 Netherlands	103,148 Denmark
1969	149,623	Japan	{127,158 West Germany {114,270 Italy	127,158 Netherlands 113,760 Denmark	126,543 UK 113,656 Sweden
1970	140,012		131,495 Sweden	125,424 Denmark	118,415 France
1971	184,855		143,686 Denmark	127,777 France	
1972	235,000		{163,795 Spain {138,472 France	143,686 Denmark	140,462 Norway
1973	238,207	Japan	155,000 West Germany		
1975	238,517	Japan	191,006 Spain	178,515 Sweden	176,100 West Germany
1976	275,276	France	211,359 Japan		
1977	273,550	France	234,638 Japan		
1978	245,140	Sweden	{231,629 Taiwan {125,249 South Korea	172,147 UK 118,500 Japan	140,646 Brazil
1979	274,838	France	189,416 USA	163,348 Portugal	

As well as utilising flow-line series-production techniques initiated in US wartime shipyards, the Japanese benefited from the presence in their midst of Daniel Ludwig. This doyen of the American shipping scene attached great importance to the tanker and valued the economies of scale inherent in it. National Bulk Carriers, founded in 1936, affixed his loyalty to this class of vessel. After toying with tanker construction in his native land (at his Welding Shipyard in Norfolk, Virginia), Ludwig cast around for a site capable of giving him more than the 30,000 dwt then at his disposal. Conveniently, the former Kure Naval Dockyard in Japan possessed a building dock dating from 1912 which could be turned to the production of vessels reaching 150,000 dwt. Armed with a ten-year lease of the site, National Bulk Carriers brought with them the assembly-line methods and techniques of prefabrication of large ship sections which they had learned during the war. Employing about 2,000 workers, Ludwig's company proceeded by leaps and bounds to knock out a series of tankers beginning with the 38,000 dwt 'Petro Kure' in 1952. By 1959 the organisation was in a position to produce its first 'century' ship, the 103,000 dwt 'Universe Apollo'. Its second vessel in the 'century' class, a 106,400 dwt tanker of 1960, accorded Ludwig the laurels for producing the world's largest ship at the dawn of the new decade. On the termination of the lease and Japanese reluctance to renew it, Ludwig's facilities were absorbed into Kure Zosen, the other inheritor of the old naval yard.[26] By then, however, his example had been followed by shipbuilders across Japan. Through judicious application of best-practice process technology and formulation of incremental innovations in the supertanker product, the Japanese shipbuilders entered tanker building with a vengeance.[27] A string of product innovations issued from Japanese shipbuilders in the 1960s, most prominently the 'economical' hull form of Ishikawajima–Harima Heavy Industries (IHI), the bulbous and cylindrical bows of Nippon Kokan (NKK), a general reduction in the thickness of steel plate and, on the propulsion front, the introduction of advanced admission data and reheat cycles in marine turbines, to say nothing of the application of turbo-charging techniques to utilise exhaust gas energy in marine diesels. The Ministry of Transport (MoT) concluded that, as a direct result of improvements in shipbuilding techniques, the man-hours required to produce one gross ton of tanker dipped from 100 in 1958 to 40 in 1964 while, in the same time horizon, the amount of hull steel required for the identical unit output plunged from an index value of 100 to 64.[28] The complementary process innovations effected a radical change in shipyard lay-out to accommodate the production of large standard ships built in prefabricated blocks. As early as the 1949–54 quinquennium, the yards were reporting that the adoption of block building, prefabrication of parts and welding combined to cut material consumption by 17 per cent. After a suitable gestation period, block fabrication by welding was able to accomplish a 30–40 per cent paring of labour costs and was instrumental in slashing tanker construction times from about seven months to scarcely four months. Orders for tankers of up to 45,000 dwt in the middle years of the 1950s triggered a rash of expansion schemes for existing premises. Thus NKK lengthened its No.5 berth at Tsurumi, Mitsubishi Nippon took its Yokohama No.5 berth in hand, Hitachi Zosen enlarged its Innoshima No.3 slip, Mitsubishi Heavy Industries (MHI) extended its Kobe No.1 slip, Harima did likewise to its Aioi No.1 berth, leaving Ishikawajima, Kawasaki and Mitsubishi Shipbuilding and Engineering to execute comparable capacity bolstering exercises respectively in Tokyo, Kobe and Nagasaki.[29] This expedient proved inadequate, however, failing to keep pace with the growing size of tankers. Shipbuilders were left with little choice but to invest heavily in building docks initially equal, and latterly superior, to the one at Kure embracing the Ludwig undertaking. Their determination was reinforced by the evident need to incorporate straight-line production principles in the construction of large ships, principles for which existing yards were patently ill-prepared. New sites with ample room to handle an 'I' line consisting of a steel landing lot, shot blast area, strengthening boiler shop, marking and cutting shop, processing shop and welding shops, became much sought-after assets.

In the beginning, a shortage of suitable building docks inhibited expansion plans. The MoT was alive to the disturbing fact that as late as 1962 there were but two facilities in the country capable of building vessels of a size greater than 100,000 dwt; a poor showing when contrasted with the eight in the UK, six in Sweden, five in West Germany and four in the Netherlands. Unable to meet rising demand, some shipyards resorted to constructing tankers in two halves on different berths and connecting them together only after the parts had been separately launched. Indeed, MHI went so far as to perfect the so-called two-portion building method for this purpose.[30] In due course, though, makeshift measures of this nature could be dispensed with. The Chiba yard of Mitsui, rejoicing in a 85,000 dwt-capacity building dock, was merely the augury of a stream of huge plants, each successively newer one vying to exceed in size all that had gone before. Chiba's commissioning in 1962 on a 'greenfield' site spurred hasty emulation: Mitsubishi Shipbuilding and Engineering plumped for two 150,000 dwt-capacity drydocks at Nagasaki, Hitachi Zosen opted for a 160,000 tonner at Sakai (Osaka) whereas IHI upped the ante by receiving MoT approval for a pair of 160,000 dwt-capacity docks in Yokohama. This last project involved the laying out of a totally new shipyard on reclaimed land at a budgeted cost of Y8.5 billion; a seemingly better bargain than the equally new Sakai yard which cost Hitachi Zosen some Y16 billion. Fearful of being overtaken by events, Mitsui immediately began enlarging its new Chiba dock to 130,000 dwt. This first flurry of activity was boosted in 1965 with a second round of expansion. Kawasaki was authorised to build a new yard at Sakaide containing two 150,000 dwt-capacity drydocks and costing Y10 billion. Hitachi extended the capacity of a dock at Innoshima from 50,000 to 130,000 dwt. MHI upgraded its Nagasaki docks to 200,000 dwt standard. Sasebo Heavy Industries pushed ahead with a plan to convert its No.4 building dock from 220,000 to 500,000 dwt capacity. In short order, IHI absorbed Kure Zosen and implemented a scheme to alter its No.2 building dock into a 400,000 dwt monster; Mitsui raised the capacity of its Chiba dock yet again, this time to 500,000 dwt; while the 1969 merger of Sumitomo Machinery and Uraga Heavy Industries, creating Sumitomo Heavy Industries (SHI), actuated a plan to set out a 300,000 tonner in the Oppama district. For its part, NKK reclaimed 80 hectares from the sea at Tsu, just south of Nagoya, and transformed the site into a model shipyard complete with a 1 million dwt-capacity building dock.

The upshot of this frenzy of investment in capital plant was an endowment, by the beginning of the 1970s, of 13 building docks able to handle ships of 200,000 dwt and over, with six of them equal to the task of turning out half-million ton behemoths. As if that were not enough, the heretofore middling and modest shipbuilders succumbed to the fever of expansion and clamoured to join the ranks of the supertanker builders or, failing that, aspired to become manufacturers of the larger bulkers which were beginning to rival the smaller VLCCs in size. Several of them decided to set up completely new shipyards. For example, Osaka Shipbuilding initiated an Oshima site for new buildings of up to 150,000 dwt, Sanoyasu Dockyard committed Y15.8 billion to reclaim land at Mizushima for a yard capable of accommodating 80,000 grt vessels, Namura Shipbuilding erected one at Imari City of comparable dimensions, while Kanasashi Zosensho set aside Y16 billion for a 150,000 dwt-capable yard on reclaimed land at Toyohashi City. Others exercised the option of remodelling existing sites. Hayashikane Shipbuilding, for instance, rebuilt its Nagasaki yard to deal with 40,000 grt ships instead of those limited to 12,000 grt; Kurushima Dockyard added an 80,000 dwt-capacity building dock to its Onishi yard whereas Hakodate Dock chose to install a 300,000 dwt-capacity building dock on reclaimed land adjacent to its existing Hakodate shipyard.[31] This wealth of facilities afforded shipbuilders the opportunity to realise significant economies of scale in the fabrication of large vessels, especially when those vessels could be built in batches rather than single units. It was calculated that when the cost of building a 55,000 dwt tanker was accorded an index value of 100 per ton, the equivalent cost for a vessel of 100,000 dwt reduced to 78, a 150,000 tonner registered 70, a 200,000 dwt tanker cost 67, but shipbuilders able to avail themselves of giant docks could produce 300,000 dwt VLCCs for as little as 45 per ton and 500,000 dwt ULCCs for a paltry 35 per ton.[32] With these structural assets, Japan's already dominant share of the world tanker market began to swell even more. According to the Association of West European Shipbuilders (AWES), Japan alone produced 13,441,000 dwt of tankers in 1967–70 compared with the 16,276,000 dwt produced by all the traditional European shipbuilders put together. In other ship types equally touched by considerations of economies of size, the disparity in favour of Japan was still more pronounced. Hence, AWES members could manage to produce only 8,005,000 dwt of bulkers during that same period in marked contrast to Japan's tally of 13,602,000 dwt.[33]

After an initial languorous reaction to the Japanese preoccupation with large-ship construction, the Europeans – admittedly unevenly – responded with alacrity by instituting their own drydock programmes. Sweden was first off the mark. The Götaverken concern abandoned its old Arendal yard in Gothenburg, constrained by limited space, for a spanking new £14 million replacement of the same name, opened in 1963 and centred on two building docks each capable of accommodating 150,000 dwt vessels. In hot pursuit of Japanese best-practice technology, the new Arendal facility functioned on the straight production line principle, possessed a plate yard operated by remote control (using closed circuit TV), and relied on partly covered building docks (a building hall) which used innovative sliding planes to project the completed part of the vessel out of the hall as each prefabricated section was welded to it. Taken up with gusto by Kockums and manifested in that enterprise's 750,000 dwt-capacity drydock in Malmö, the production line approach to shipbuilding was forthcoming with a flood of VLCCs: indeed, Malmö was able to refine building times for a 255,000 dwt ship down to an astonishing 40 days. Another firm, Eriksberg in Gothenburg, not only inaugurated its own 500,000 dwt-capacity building dock, but concluded an arrangement with Setenave in Portugal (in which it took a 12.5 per cent stake) whereby even bigger vessels – up to 1 million tons – could be tackled. Under the arrangement, Setenave also supplied much-needed hull parts to the Swedish firm; providing, at one fell swoop, a cheap fabrication source for Eriksberg and a means for overcoming capacity restraints hindering expansion at the Swedish site. At the end of 1970, for example, the first Setenave-built tanker forepart was towed from Setubal to Gothenburg for incorporation into the ship's more complicated aft section.[34]

Fellow Scandinavian producer, Denmark, was not overly dilatory in jumping on the bandwagon either. The Lindö yard of Odense Staalskibsvaerft was prepared for the construction of 100,000 dwt tankers soon after opening in 1961 and by the end of the decade was inducting a 650,000 dwt-capacity dock into service for building their larger offspring. At about the same time, H&W in Belfast and Verolme United at its Rozenburg yard near Rotterdam were each engaged in creating docks of 1 million tons capacity while Howaldtswerke in Hamburg was breaking ground on a 750,000 dwt-capacity facility. Even Italy, encumbered by a shortage of large yards, was pressing its largest site, Monfalcone, into series production of 253,000 dwt VLCCs. The Fincantieri yard was obliged to make use of the semi-tandem principle; that is to say, to practise a system whereby the stems of the vessels were built separately on a berth restricted to 140,000 dwt but, after launching, were transferred to a building dock, some 350m long by 50m wide, whereupon block assemblies were joined and final outfitting was executed. Similarly circumscribed, but just as determined to participate in VLCC output, the Uljanik Shipyard at Pula, Yugoslavia, widened its largest berth from 32m to 50m, installed a battery of 150-ton lift-capacity cranes and embarked on the construction of vessels weighing up to 300,000 dwt in two halves for subsequent connecting after separate launches.[35] An even more dramatic response was to come from Spain where Astilleros Españoles SA (AESA) was founded in 1969 with the VLCC market very much in mind. Alert to the opportunities afforded by the uplift in shipping freights consequent upon the closure of the Suez Canal in 1967, the government had conceived the Accion Concertada plan to bring Spanish shipbuilding to the world's attention. Liberal provision of export credits and generous tax concessions complemented the formation of AESA and gave it the flow of orders needed to tide it over the early years.[36] A merger of Astilleros de Cadiz, Sociedad Española de Construcción Naval and Compañia Euskalduna, the newly founded enterprise immediately set about establishing a 'greenfield' yard at Puerto Real near Cadiz expressly designed to attack this market. It boasted an order book of two 410,000 dwt ULCCs and six 260,000 dwt VLCCs before formally opening in 1974. To be sure, by that juncture, even the Americans had given it to be understood that they wished seriously to engage in VLCC construction. Indeed, two shipbuilders had already commenced VLCC production; namely,

Seatrain Shipbuilding in Brooklyn (with room for vessels of up to 225,000 dwt) and Bethlehem Steel at Sparrows Point (350,000 dwt capacity); three others were prosecuting yard expansions – Avondale of New Orleans and Sun of Chester pushing up to 400,000 dwt and Newport News stretching to 600,000 dwt – while three more were in process of formulating plans (Todd Shipyards for a 400,000 dwt-sized dock in Galveston, General Dynamics for an upgrade in Quincy's capacity to 225,000 dwt and Ingalls with a projected dock at Pascagoula for vessels of 265,000 dwt).

All this concerted activity did not go unnoticed in the larger world outside shipbuilding. In fact, its combination of surging investment, soaring demand and apparent profitability sparked entry of VLCC construction by NICs previously little inclined to give shipbuilding much credibility. At government instigation, the solitary yard in South Korea enjoying any pretensions to shipbuilding, KSEC, undertook to remodel its facilities in 1972 upon receipt of an order from Gulf Oil of the USA for six tankers. By the same token, the Hyundai conglomerate charged into shipbuilding by committing itself to a monster shipyard at Ulsan designed specifically to turn out five 259,000 dwt vessels each year. Pointing to these ventures, the government outlined grandiose plans to boost South Korea's 1973 annual capacity of 250,000 grt of shipping to 1.9 million by 1976 and 9 million by 1985. Almost concurrently, the government of Taiwan announced its intention to enter the fray, promising that the world's second-largest building dock would be open for business before the end of 1975. Sadly for their proponents, these ambitious projects were only just under way when the tanker market plummeted and, in so doing, scotched any prospects of their future profitability. Nothing deterred, the NIC governments resolved to make the best of a disquieting situation by urging their shipbuilding charges to accumulate market share. If denied profits, they reasoned that their new shipbuilding assets would at least be good for earning foreign exchange and stimulating the programme of national industrialisation. In any event, high costs of servicing the borrowed capital used in shipyard erection mandated an instant and complete utilisation of these assets. Circumstances thus impelled NIC producers into active and aggressive participation in latter-day shipbuilding. Yet, condemned to strive for orders and struggle for survival, the lot of new and remodelled yards alike was not an enviable one. Some comparative indicators of the outcome of that uneasy and uncertain rivalry are presented in the next section.

COMPARISONS IN RELATIVE SURVIVAL

A conventional means of assessing the relative importance of shipbuilding nations in these times of adversity is to peruse activity levels from a comparative-static point of view. In practical terms, that entails contrasting the contemporary leading producers with their equivalents of some fixed antecedent period, and remarking on obvious deviations in rank order that have cropped up in the interim. Figure 1.1 acts as a point of departure for such an exercise. In bar-graph form, it superimposes the main producers (as gauged from the gross tonnage of vessels in hand) of December 1988 on those of a decade earlier.[37] Immediately striking is the fact that the top six producers of 1978 have all suffered absolute declines in the amounts of tonnage building, and some (e.g. Brazil, France and the UK) by considerable margins. By way of contrast, the then lesser lights have conspired to augment their

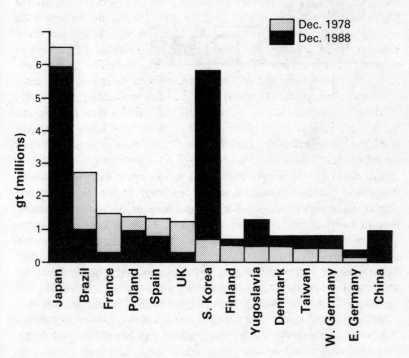

Figure 1.1 Shipbuilding league table, 1978 and 1988

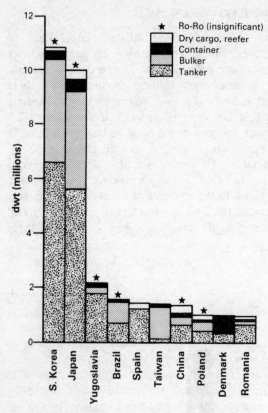

Figure 1.2 Shipping on order at the end of 1988

activity levels; none more so than South Korea which has zoomed up the world shipbuilding league positively to rival Japan as the leader. Structural insights into the ship-type composition of contemporary new-building orders (valid for the end of 1988) held by the top ten producers can be gleaned from Figure 1.2. What is abundantly clear from the graphs therein displayed is that, despite the horrendous adjustment problems occasioned by the energy crises of the 1970s and the resulting devastation wreaked on the tanker market, the world's ship producers remain wedded to tanker construction for the bulk of their workload. In the instance of South Korea – which had actually usurped Japan as the country garnering most orders – no less than 61 per cent of that imminent workload was ascribable to tankers. Japan, for its part, depended on tankships to the tune of 57 per cent of its impending activity, Yugoslavia relied on tankers for 86 per cent of its order book,

Brazil for 45 per cent and Spain for 86 per cent. Truth to say, bulkers had also crept into the reckoning, accounting for 51 per cent of the Brazilian workload, 82 per cent of that pertaining to Taiwan and 35 per cent apiece for South Korea and Japan; but for the most part bulker construction was unequivocally overshadowed by tanker contracts. The remaining primary ship types – container, dry cargo and reefer, and Ro-Ro – emerged as insignificant contributors to the weight of tonnage on order, although that evident inconsequence belied their importance to shipyard viability (as, for example, high-value units) or, indeed, to individual shipbuilders with a vested interest in their production. The figure, for instance, is sufficiently discerning to identify Denmark as a shipbuilding nation with a disproportionate involvement in the provision of container vessels.

It stands to reason, of course, that shipbuilding nations might deliberately cultivate an element of specialisation in their offerings; specialisation, that is, in anything but low value-added ships which present few hurdles to entry by yet more producers determined to contest an already crowded market. That way, they can acquire a degree of immunity from market crashes affecting the mainstream activity common to them all; namely, tanker building. Moreover, specialisation may be conducive to comparative advantage whereby the producer either gains a reputation for excellence in a particular class of ship or commands attention by virtue of the competitive prices it can charge for that ship type, and, in consequence, is allowed to affirm its dominance of a global market niche. Conceivably, a few producers may risk all by concentrating their resources in the comparative advantage area to the exclusion of almost everything else. Finland falls into this category. Apart from a trio of conventional reefers, its new-building activity during the first quarter of 1989 was restricted to 13 coasters, 10 passenger vessels and a clutch of research ships (including icebreakers): all special-purpose ships the construction of which the Finnish industry had paid particular attention to over the years. Generally speaking, however, the big-volume shipbuilding nations are far less specialised. Figure 1.3 hints at their relative specialisation in 1984. A compilation of Lorenz curves, the figure's interpretation rests on the distance separating the curve representative of a given country from the 45° line. The farthest curve from the line is tantamount to the most specialised producer whereas, in reverse, the curve closest to the line is symbolic of the most diversified producer. At the extremes, a curve overlapping the 45° line would denote a producer retaining a workload taken up with an equal mix of ship types, but one adhering to the left vertical and upper borders of the graph would betoken an industry entirely confined to the

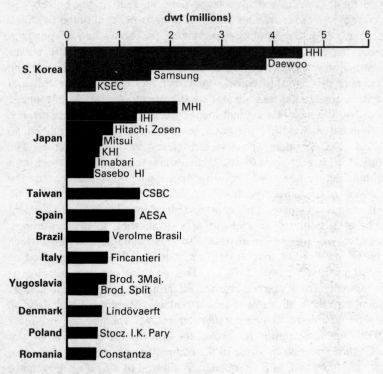

Figure 1.3 Shipbuilding specialisation, 1984

production of a single ship type. All things considered, Poland appears to be the least specialised of the major producers in 1984 while Brazil appears as the most specialised. West Germany and South Korea occupy the middle ground, but Japan's curve suggests that an inordinate amount of its workload is restricted to a single ship type. In point of fact, 68.4 per cent of Japan's workload is focused on its prime ship class in contrast to 70.8 per cent for Brazil, though the second most important ship type preoccupies Japanese shipbuilders only to the extent of 8.7 per cent of the aggregate work in hand whereas it takes up 26.5 per cent of the Brazilian workload. Using Poland as a yardstick, the same producers are compared on the basis of their 1988 activity in Figure 1.4. Now, Japan vies with Poland for the title of most diversified of the major producers, while South Korea and West Germany have symbolically shifted to the left unabashedly to rival Brazil as highly specialised producers. The reshuffling of the configurations hints at the relative

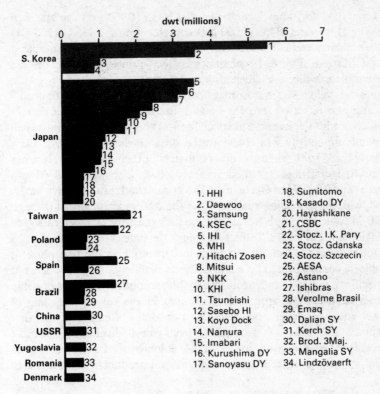

Figure 1.4 Shipbuilding specialisation, 1988

instability endemic to shipbuilding activity in a number of countries, underscoring perhaps the versatility of the shipyards composing the production capabilities of the likes of Japan and West Germany. The stability of Poland and Brazil, however, points in the other direction, suggesting that shipyards may be intentionally established around fixed objectives: specialisation in a very limited range in the case of Brazil but an expectation of orders for a wide variety of types in the case of Poland. The former may be a faithful reflection of NIC entry into shipbuilding via labour-intensive, low value-added series production of one or two types whereas the latter manifests an industry tailored to the export (to the USSR) of a gamut of standard ship types, varying in size and complexity, for which the yards are comprehensively equipped. The Gdansk yards, for example, initiated a veritable cornucopia of standard ship classes in the 1960s and 1970s of which the numerous B40 (10,200 grt) and B41 (5,700 grt) cargo vessels, B437 (6,400 grt) reefers, B26 (2,900 grt) trawlers, B438 (7,200 grt) container ships, B436 (10,200 grt) timber carriers and B69 (13,100 grt) fish factory ships are but a sample.[38]

Adopting a Polish benchmark as the quintessence of diverse shipbuilding, indices of concentration can be computed which give a numerical value to the Lorenz curves exhibited in the figures.[39] Allotting an index of zero for Poland, the magnitude rises in correspondence with the increase in specialisation and would reach unity if all shipbuilding activity was concentrated on a single ship type. In 1984, Brazil scored 0.79, while the others, matching their progressively more diversified offerings, revealed values of 0.47 (Japan), 0.36 (South Korea) and 0.20 (West Germany). The ground had shifted somewhat by 1988, with the gradation running from the 0.80 index of Brazil through the 0.74 value for South Korea and the 0.63 value for West Germany to the 0.08 index of Japan. Table 1.4 extends the index coverage to nations excluded from the figures. Its purpose is twofold: in the first place, it enables a comparison to be made between significant ship producers at a specific time – 1984 and, again, 1988 – but, secondly, it renders possible a comparative-static appraisal of changes in the relative standing of those same producers between the two dates. Regarding the first purpose, an array of producers, from most diversified to most specialised, is displayed in the 1984 column of the table. Several countries emerge therein as more specialised producers than Japan; to

Table 1.4 Indices of concentration, 1984 and 1988

Country	Index value	
	1984	*1988*
Poland	0.00	0.00
Denmark	0.02	0.37
Netherlands	0.09	0.09
China	0.17	0.51
West Germany	0.20	0.63
Spain	0.35	0.46
South Korea	0.36	0.74
Italy	0.43	0.38
East Germany	0.45	0.66
Japan	0.47	0.08
UK	0.57	0.68
Sweden	0.61	0.70
USA	0.62	0.78
Yugoslavia	0.64	0.63
Finland	0.64	0.63
Taiwan	0.77	0.63
Brazil	0.79	0.80

wit, the UK, Sweden, the USA, Yugoslavia, Finland, Taiwan and, of course, Brazil. Conversely, Denmark, the Netherlands and China join Poland as diverse producers. Four years later and the upper end of the spectrum unites the USA, South Korea and Sweden along with Brazil, but the lower end now attaches Japan and the Netherlands to Poland. The second purpose directly addresses changes in relative standing and, as the table clearly reveals, some considerable alterations in index magnitudes have occurred between 1984 and 1988. China leapt from 0.17 to 0.51 and East Germany from 0.45 to 0.66 in the one direction, for example, leaving Japan to drop from 0.47 to 0.08 and Taiwan from 0.77 to 0.63 in the other. In contrast, the staunch adherents to a constant pattern include not only Poland and Brazil, but also the Netherlands at the diverse end of the scale and Finland at the specialised end.

Fluctuating degrees of specialisation are simply the outward revelations of adjustments in global comparative advantages. Evidently, some ship classes are more liable to require specialist attention than others and are thus susceptible to production by a narrow band of constructors able and willing to devote the requisite resources to them. Others, by comparison, are less demanding in their production requirements and therefore more inclined to find favour with constructors across the board. The coefficient of localisation is a sort of index of concentration amended to monitor geographical specialisation.[40] By its lights, a coefficient value approaching unity equates with a ship type likely to be taken up by very few producers who dominate global output. Absolute unity implies that the entire output of a ship type emanates from a unique source. On the other hand, a coefficient hovering around zero is symptomatic of a ship type widely dispersed in its sources of supply, with no single supplier hogging more than a small fraction of the output. A glance at Table 1.5 suffices to elicit the finding that all eight ship types are moderately dispersed in their sources of supply, but that an appreciable trace of spatial concentration has taken

Table 1.5 Localisation coefficients, 1984 and 1988

Ship type	Coefficients for	
	1984	*1988*
Tankers	0.31	0.31
Bulkers	0.16	0.33
General cargo vessels (>2,000 gt)	0.37	0.26
General cargo vessels (<2,000 gt)	0.46	0.36
Container ships	0.49	0.33
Liquid gas and chemical carriers	0.31	0.46
Large fishing vessels	0.46	0.60
Miscellaneous vessels	0.22	0.53

place between 1984 and 1988. For example, the most localised class in 1984, container ships, registered a coefficient value of 0.49, but by 1988 two classes recorded values substantially in excess of that figure: apparently the producers of large fishing vessels and miscellaneous vessels experienced an upheaval in the intervening years which had the effect of forcing their coefficients upwards from 0.46 to 0.60 in the first instance and from 0.22 to 0.53 in the second. Moreover, the numerically important bulker category had witnessed a doubling in localisation and the combined category embracing LPG (liquefied petroleum gas), LNG and chemical carriers had also undergone a tendency towards spatial concentration. From the opposite perspective, though, both categories of general cargo vessels, to say nothing of container ships, had submitted to a trend enforcing a more geographically diffuse pattern of supply. Spurning both tendencies, tanker supply remained firmly anchored to a 0.31 coefficient for both years; indication in itself that tanker production was scattered throughout the shipbuilding world and, hence, vital to a host of producers, but not so commonplace as to be dismissive of pockets of expertise or producers replete with economies of scale. This last conclusion could have been drawn only if the coefficient had been lower or had evinced a predilection for oscillations.

The question of what constitutes an appropriate degree of specialisation is a compelling one, and is particularly acute at the shipyard level. As such, it will return to distract our attention in subsequent pages. The fundamental fact remains, however, that specialisation will avail the producer little or not at all if it cannot prevent serious underutilisation of shipbuilding capacity. In the final analysis, capacity utilisation requires the retention, if not the extension, of market share. Shift-and-share analysis offers a perspicuous means of inferring the relative abilities of shipbuilding nations to retain market share, and is resorted to here with that object in mind.[41] The analysis compares the 1984 workload of a country, expressed in tonnage building and on order, with its 1988 workload, presented in the same manner, after due allowance is made for the country's footing in the overall global workload. The resultant shift values, suitably transformed to graphical form in Figure 1.5, convey an impression of comparative gainers and losers. The gainers are united in as much as each of them flaunts a positive shift value, the magnitude of which indicates the amount of tonnage won by the country over and above what it should have managed if it had maintained its original share of the global workload. Capping them all is South Korea which, between 1984 and 1988, captured an extra mass of business worth in the range of 4.9 million dwt of new buildings. Yugoslavia is revealed as the next disproportionate gainer, with a windfall of 1.5 million dwt,

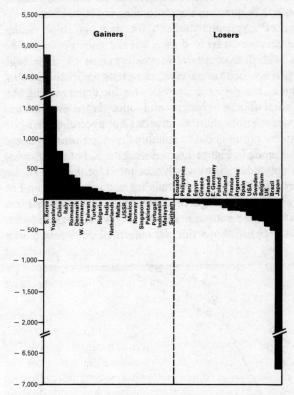

Figure 1.5 Relative gainers and losers, 1984–8

while China and Italy each disport gains in excess of half-a-million tons.
A further group, embracing Romania, Denmark, West Germany,
Taiwan, Turkey and Bulgaria bask in enhanced market shares worth
between 400,000 and 100,000 dwt of additional new construction
business. In contradistinction, countries encumbered with negative
shifts are not so fortunate. The magnitude of the negative shift gives a
measure of the shortfall in national workload relative to the country's
original share of the global workload: it is emphatically, therefore,
indicative of an erosion in market share. The principal loser by far under
these arrangements is Japan. Almost in exact counterpoise to South
Korea, it must grapple with a shortfall verging on 5.8 million dwt.
Burdened with shortfalls in the 500,000 to 100,000 dwt range, Brazil, the
UK, Belgium, Sweden, the USA, Spain, Argentina, France and Finland
have also suffered from sliding market shares between 1984 and 1988.

Should these abrading trends continue unchecked, the competitiveness of each of the countries in question begins to hang in the balance.

The marshalling of aggregate statistics for national shipbuilding industries is a valid exercise so far as it goes, but it does not go so far as to come to grips with the comparative performance of individual shipbuilding enterprises. For that purpose, data must be distilled so as to demonstrate which enterprises are responsible for underpinning the principal national shipbuilding industries and, once that is established, then going on to infer whether those enterprises are upcoming firms or members of the hapless group about to stumble down the slippery slope of decline. A start is made in Figure 1.6. Enlisting the aid of bar graphs, it discloses those shipbuilding firms which accounted for the bulk of the work in hand recorded by the major shipbuilding countries at the end of 1983.[42] To assist clarity, only large companies merited incorporation into the figure; that is, those with at least 500,000 dwt of work in hand. Not unexpectedly, the figure shows that the enterprises of South Korea

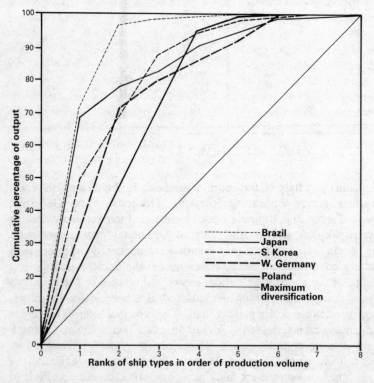

Figure 1.6 Leading shipbuilders, December 1983

were pitted against those of Japan in vying for the top positions in the world shipbuilding stakes. Two in particular, HHI and Daewoo, matched the leading Japanese shipbuilders; so much so, indeed, that HHI unambiguously won the crown as the world's biggest single shipbuilder. Yet, an extraordinary tally of 16 Japanese shipbuilders qualified for inclusion in the figure, as opposed to but four from South Korea. No fewer than 11 of the Japanese firms presided over workloads exceeding 1 million dwt (with IHI, MHI and Hitachi Zosen exceeding 3 million dwt, Mitsui and NKK holding more than 2 million and KHI and Tsuneishi garnering in excess of 1.5 million). The other producers had no choice but to settle for only three or less leading shipbuilders worthy of the name. Thus, Taiwan's respectable presence in the new-building league was almost single-handedly the work of CSBC, Spain's commercial shipbuilding was shouldered for the most part by AESA and Astano, Poland's by three complexes belonging to the monolithic state shipbuilding organisation and Brazil's by a trio of private concerns led by the IHI-affiliated Ishibras. Yet, the short space of a half-decade has been ample time to effect some drastic changes on the leading enterprises.

As Figure 1.7 evinces, the number of shipbuilders from Japan qualifying for consideration on the grounds of a minimum of 500,000 dwt of work in hand has shrunk to less than half the total of 1983: testimony in itself to the partial eclipse of the Japanese industry by its counterpart in South Korea. Attesting to the perseverance of the latter, meanwhile, is the finding that not only did the four main builders remain in play at the end of 1988, but the two dominant players – HHI and Daewoo – had contrived to lengthen their lead over the big Japanese shipbuilders. Totalling 4.6 million dwt and 3.9 million dwt, respectively, the workloads of HHI and Daewoo positively towered over the best that the Japanese could muster; namely, the 2.2 million dwt proffered by MHI. To be fair to the Japanese, workload totals have diminished throughout the shipbuilding world as revival eluded the business cycle and vanishing orders, instead, pitched activity levels lower in December 1988 than was the case in December 1983.[43] Few shipbuilders managed to retain the absolute levels enjoyed at the earlier date, and there has been a general thinning of the ranks in Figure 1.7 as a result. The notable exception is Italy, whose state-owned Fincantieri organisation has blossomed to pull in 830,010 dwt of work in hand at the end of 1988. Reasons for the rise of shipbuilding enterprises and, on the other side of the coin, explanations for their fall, are many and varied. However, as stated above, the intent here is merely to introduce the movers and shakers among their number. Subsequent chapters will assume the task

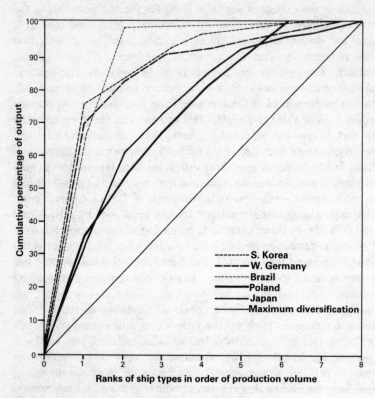

Figure 1.7 Leading shipbuilders, December 1988

of pursuing the factors which cause them either to embrace the industry wholeheartedly or elect to withdraw from it.

SUMMARY

In appraising contemporary shipbuilding, one cannot avoid the barrage of informed and not-so-informed opinion which foretells dire outcomes for the industry at best or evokes a cataclysmic ending for it at worst. Much of that opinion is informed by the recent history of the industry in the Western AICs: a grounding which gives the predictions an aura of veracity while somehow managing to overlook non-Western experience or, indeed, the cardinal changes which have recently taken place in Western shipbuilding. Yet, the fact remains that shipbuilding every-where is dogged with significant structural problems, and one hardly need resort to outlandish claims of impending disaster to acknowledge the grave quandaries confronting the industry which they bring in their train. In the preceding pages, much attention has been directed to defusing the more extreme speculations in the light of cold, hard facts. Unravelling of those facts suffices to provide an outline of the dimensions of the problems coming to bear on ship producers but also touches on the opportunities that may exist and the producers that may turn them to good account. By no stretch of credibility can it be said that the producers have experienced a smooth passage since the mid-1970s: on the contrary, the business environment has been too charged with uncertainty to confer anything but moderate returns, scant returns or no returns at all to every producer persisting with shipbuilding. Some solace can be taken, though, from the examples of expansion antedating that time and possibly from the conditions of today which may presage an industry-wide revival. On the whole, then, one is tempted to go along with measured views which recognise strains on the one hand while holding to the standpoint that these can but herald the promise of better things to come on the other. Typical is the assertion that, whereas domination 'of the world's shipbuilding industry is becoming a liability for Japan and South Korea', yet 'neither wants to withdraw from shipbuilding' because 'both think it will be worth dominating in the 1990s'.[44] This sentiment not only imbues Asian producers with a mission that is manifested through a determination to persevere with the industry, but it also continues to influence Western advocates of shipbuilding. Ever wary, chastened and vigilant of Asian competition, this sentiment instils in them the confidence doggedly to persist in arguing for the retention of some industrial capacity often in the face of overwhelming disenchantment, pessimism and downright indifference. How these Asian and Western parties have navigated the industry through the perilous shoals of an inopportune business climate is the subject of the next chapter.

2 Shipbuilding as a stricken industry

Despite the patent anguish of shipbuilders and the internecine bickering between them that has typified international exchanges in global shipbuilding in recent years, the real villain of the piece is the protracted condition of oversupply. Like it or not, all shipbuilders and their protective governments have been obliged to come to terms with this villain because they have all played a part first in cultivating it and latterly in perpetuating it. Long after the energy crisis of 1973 pitched shipbuilders into persistent problems which could only be overcome through concerted actions aimed at redressing the excess supply situation, shipbuilders continued to assure themselves that natural forces would effect a return to equilibrium between demand and supply. They arrived at the conviction that it behoved them in the meantime to engage in cut-throat competition on the understanding that the competitors would be the ones to fall by the wayside while their particular facilities would somehow avoid the pitfalls so glaringly abroad in the world. Any shipbuilder capable of coercing governments to forge an artificial demand for ships through price-support schemes, credit measures and downright conjuring up of orders on national account would clearly benefit in the new, competitively charged environment, and soon all shipbuilders were calling for government aids as a matter of course. While rationales steeped in unemployment-mitigation platitudes were invoked, the hard-headed approach investing such entreaties resorted to justifying public intervention on the grounds of countercyclical short-term expediency. In other words, the crisis could only be made intelligible to policy-makers and the world at large as a temporary upset in the business cycle and, adorned with a multitude of plausible submissions each bound up with the peculiar local circumstances of the time, shipbuilders leapt to defend their competitive positions through political means. In practical terms, the shipbuilders were lobbying for – and receiving – an industrial policy which hinged on three types of clauses: those reserving domestic markets for domestic suppliers, those offering subventions to underwrite export contracts and those dedicated to forgiving tax liabilities. Quite frequently, the upshot was a package forthcoming with elements of all three. Of course, support was only won at a price, and that price was increasingly exacted by politicians and bureaucrats who took on the roles of paymasters and salvors of last resort. This levy assumed the form of obtrusion into the affairs of shipbuilders, effectively removing decisions regarding rationalisation, diversification and general restructuring out of the reach of the builders themselves. Ultimately, shipbuilders came to resemble powerless bystanders, buffeted by forces unleashed by governments initially determined to cushion them from global downturns but latterly set on forcibly adjusting them to government-concocted programmes geared to extricating public bodies from such intervention. Political intervention, perforce, lent itself to government interpretations of which yards were deserving of bail-outs and which not; an outcome not always in tune with the restructuring moves propounded in logical adjustment plans. What is more, government intervention really pitted state against state, with the winnings falling to the country either blessed with the deepest pockets or imbued with the keenest ideology and the longest staying power in favour of state support for the industry.

In the end, shipbuilders and governments alike were forced grudgingly to acknowledge that traditional business-cycle views of the oversupply predicament were inapt foundations for adjudicating the futures of this industry. The long secular path of growth in ship output, peaking in 1975 as the last of the pre-oil crisis orders fed through, vanished in the confusion that clouded shipbuilding thereafter. Never again would output approach the dizzy levels of the salad days of the early 1970s; rather, it would swing viciously in response to short-term alarms and mini-recoveries. Figure 2.1 encapsulates the heady period of expansion, beginning rather modestly in the early 1950s, but succumbing to virtual exponential rates of growth in the succeeding decade.[1] Output climbed tenfold in the 25 years after 1950 and new-building capacity sustained a commensurate explosive growth as berths, docks and entire new yards were piled one on top of the other in an orgy of plant proliferation. The OECD, for example, held that shipbuilding capacity, which had grown in step with – or in anticipation of – world output, attained in 1975 an aggregate size equal to 39 million grt or 25 million cgrt.[2] Yet, on the brink of the second energy crisis in 1979, annual output scarcely equalled 11.5 million cgrt: a level sufficient to utilise less than one-half of the capacity in place in 1975. While it is true to say that

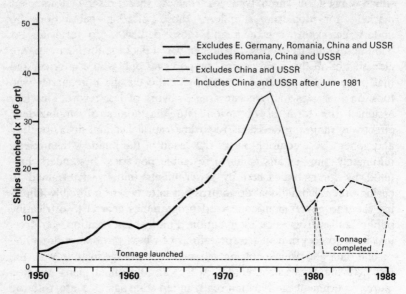

Figure 2.1 World ship production, 1950–88

some capacity had been extinguished in the brief interlude between 1975 and 1979, much of it remained in readiness for instant application to ship production and, in so doing, acted as a drain on the costs structure of the yards (forcing up overheads) as well as a continual inducement to them to entice orders out of the market almost regardless of profitability. The events of the 1970s imposed a new set of circumstances on the industry. It was as if the business cycle had run up against a massive discontinuity and was attempting to find a new stable track from a much less elevated jumping-off place. In obedience to the provisional nature of that disconnected stabilisation process, shipbuilders responded inadequately, and consistently failed to match capacity to output. Some were driven to the wall as a result of that inadequacy whereas others became the overt wards of government. In any event, sliding ship prices, eroding viability, a continuing stream of bankruptcies and persistent meddling by governments became the hallmarks of the age. All this took place against a backdrop of declining activity which, while affecting some countries worse than others, united almost all of the AIC producers in a painful course of industrial contraction.

Table 2.1 Output in the aftermath of the apogee

Year	Annual tonnage launched ('000gt) in				
	Japan	*South Korea*	*West Germany*	*Brazil*	*Denmark*
1975	17,987	441	2,549	389	961
1976	14,310	689	1,792	426	957
1977	9,943	455	1,390	572	636
1978	4,921	424	600	698	360
1979	4,317	479	385	467	229
1980	7,288	629	462	615	227
1981	8,857	1,229	669	549	364
1982	8,247	1,530	722	455	434
1983	7,071	1,201	651	359	525
1984	9,408	2,515	528	460	393
1985	9,354	2,740	594	401	392
1986	7,750	2,596	461	316	295
1987	4,236	2,291	223	41	263
1988	4,555	3,395	519	269	277

Source: Lloyd's Register of Shipping data

Table 2.1, which displays the performance of a select group of principal producers through the years following the zenith of output, intimates that the tendency towards contraction was qualified, on the one hand, by substantial oscillations in activity from year to year and, on the other, by the encroachment of NICs pushing for a larger share of a dwindling market. South Korea and Brazil together defy the trend afflicting the AIC producers (Japan, West Germany and Denmark) which saw their output totals whittled down to but a fraction of their 1975 levels of production. In 1979, for example, West Germany only managed to launch 15 per cent of the tonnage of four years earlier, while Japan and Denmark each achieved 24 per cent. By way of contrast, South Korea's 1979 performance exceeded the earlier level by 9 per cent whereas Brazil boosted its 1979 output by a margin fully one-fifth as much again as that prevailing in 1975. However, a degree of flux is evident even within that grave picture of diminished AIC activity relative to the earlier 1975 standard. In short, a bimodal pattern is discernible, with minor pinnacles of activity occurring at the beginning of the 1980s and again a few years later. South Korea, intent on expansion and using all means at its disposal to ensure it, is not exempt from these oscillations, although it is able to amass contracts at the expense of the others. The Brazilian record sounds a cautionary note, however. Brazil, too, was bent on carving out an export market for its ships, but unlike South Korea, virtually foundered in the mid-1980s. The industry is deserving of exoneration, though, since the collapse occurred through no fault of its own, but as a result of colossal debt- servicing problems undermining the national economy. Shipbuilding underwent a spell of drastically reduced activity in which the woes of the international ship market compounded local difficulties. It was only beginning to surface from those uncongenial conditions in the late 1980s. Brazil aside, the emergence of neophyte producers in the 1970s, and especially the forceful appearance of South Korea, set the seal on the dawning AIC realisation that market forces alone would not suffice to right the imbalance between shipbuilding supply and demand. Unreconstructed advocates of free-market mechanisms for solving shipbuilding oversupply were roundly criticised and, for a time, their views were overturned. Despite official pronouncements from the likes of the OECD supporting the universal withdrawal of building subvent- ions, the NIC challenge only served to drive AIC shipbuilders further into the arms of government. Ironically, intrusion of the NICs not only laid to rest the credibility of self-righting mechanisms, but it eventually persuaded several former proponents of state support among the AICs to abandon their stand on the basis of the hopelessness of their cause in the face of such thrusting inchoate competition. Thus, the climate of opinion reverted to a species of free enterprise or, at least, non-intervention: put candidly, if the enterprise could not stand alone without government props, it must reconcile itself to not standing at all. In the light of these happenings, the first purpose of this chapter is to sketch in the industrial context of shipbuilding; a context which accords it the status of a mature sector. Subsequently, the focus of attention will divert to consideration of the responses of AIC producers to straitened circumstances; responses which are, in truth, influenced by recognition of the industry's role as a mature sector in the global scheme of things.

INDUSTRIAL MATURITY

Mention of shipbuilding occupying the mature stage in its industrial life-cycle presupposes that it has already advanced through adolescence and at some unspecified point will venture into the ultimate stage, that of senescence. As a denizen of the mature stage, the industry is largely devoid of product innovation, has by and large fixed on a well-known body of knowledge concerning production and, in consequence, presents few barriers to entry apart from those associated with economies of scale. A finer grasp of the implications of maturity awaits assessment of the industry life-cycle concept as a whole, and that is the task to which we now turn. To begin with, it is worth stressing that the inception of any industry rests on the formulation of a product which promises rewards to those enterprises willing to risk losses during the transition period from product conception to market acceptance. For the sake of convenience, the point of departure initiating the complete cycle is termed the 'conception' stage. It encompasses, quite simply, all that is necessary in the way of trials and tribulations to devise a potential product. The materialising of that potential product as a prototype rather than a 'paper' design distinguishes the second or 'birth' stage. The expression 'childhood' stage has been coined to represent the market preparation phase. At this juncture, the budding enterprise is fully engaged in devising a variety of prototypes as offshoots of the original innovation in hopes of hitting upon a model which merits further development. For the duration of the childhood stage, production plant is scarce and most of the effort depends on human capital; that is to say, the skills ingrained in the kernel of workers – including those in the tight-knit circle around the innovator – which has a vested interest in the anticipated success of the start-up enterprise. To test the waters of market reception, it is vital that the enterprise progressing through childhood be located in a place conducive to good and easy contact relations with would-be customers. That way, feedback from trial marketing efforts can be conveniently incorporated into product design. Besides, product enhancement calls for uncomplicated access to specially trained engineers and craftsmen, preferably those with experience of activities bearing some resemblance to the task at hand. Skilled workers of this ilk are likely to be found in large and diverse labour pools: the same locations, indeed, that masquerade as major market centres. Fortuitously, then, the twin locational criteria of market accessibility and ability to tap skilled and resourceful labour coincide to offer a limited number of choice sites for a precocious enterprise attempting to force the pace in product development.

In due course, the enterprise gambles on a preferred prototype, converting it into a marketable item with an extended production run. Quantity production, in turn, requires a revamping of process technology. Rather than the assemblage of odd, non-standard jigs and tools prevalent hitherto, the firm can take the plunge, so to speak, and invest in product-specific machine tools. The implementation of quantity production of either a single product or a narrow range of products effects a transformation of the enterprise, propelling it into the 'adolescent' stage. Attention to the demands of production comes to the fore. It lends itself to the substitution of machinery and equipment for skilled manpower and, eventually, nudges the firm into the mature stage. As aforementioned, maturity stamps its presence on the firm by enforcing a regime in which both products and processes are practically standardised. To all intents and purposes, innovation has been eschewed other than in a cosmetic market segmentation sense on the product side or in respect of the furtherance of economies of scale on the process side. Yet, besides radically altering the scope, scale and outlook of the enterprise, maturity brings with it another fundamental change; namely, liberation of the enterprise from the fetters binding it to a limited selection of sites which blend the peculiar market and labour requirements of novice enterprises. Gone is the need to be close to major markets because product development as a corporate activity has all but disappeared. In the same vein, the need to locate the production unit within easy reach of pools of skilled labour has largely vanished in the pell-mell rush to replace manual dexterity with the limitless application to the tasks in hand resident in the mechanical adroitness of production plant. As well as reducing the quality of labour, standard process technology rejoices in the added property of reducing its quantity, since, by dint of augmented productivity, fewer workers are required to produce a given level of output. At one fell swoop, the enterprise can dispense with expensive labour-intensive methods along with the work-forces required to operate them and, in their place, can make use of more cost-effective capital-intensive methods (e.g. mechanisation and automation) which are adequately served by cheaper, less-skilled work-forces.

In a phase of settled product and process technology, market success depends more on price competitiveness than product superiority and the firm has no option but to subscribe to cost minimisation as its primary objective. Accordingly, it forsakes high-cost sites for those revelling in factor-cost advantages. Since labour is the main factor-cost constituent during the operating life of an industrial establishment, the search for cost reductions gradually translates into a renouncing of AIC locations for the allurements of NICs blessed with cheaper labour. With some industries, that transference actually involves the closure of plants in the high-cost locations and the relocation of their divisible assets to cheap-labour sites. The wholesale closure of TV and other consumer electronics factories in the USA and their reappearance in the 'offshore' havens of East Asia and Mexico is a well-documented case in point.[3] The geographical shift in operations is marked by a metamorphosis of the enterprise. No longer bound to remain a local or even a national enterprise, the dictates of maturity can convert it into a multinational corporation obliged, on the one hand, to retain marketing and perhaps final-assembly functions in the AIC while, on the other, compelled to build up production plant further afield in the Third World's export processing zones. To be sure, firms need not penetrate into the remote recesses of the earth in order to gratify their lust for lower-cost locations. A body of opinion concurs with the view of Vernon that peripheral regions within AICs are ideally placed in the competitive global environment owing to their proximity to AIC core regions plus an endowment of cheaper factors of production. Such a combination serves to attract 'industry with standardised output and self-sufficient process'.[4] In this view, the firm's early history is entwined with the AIC core region, for, after all, that is where the rich assortment of labour skills and the chief customers are to be found. After breeching the maturity boom, however, the firm abandons production in the core region and chooses, instead, to utilise factory sites in peripheral regions replete with cheaper labour, land and rents (possibly made so as a consequence of regional policy). Alternatively, mature firms may elect not to embark on relocation at all, deciding that they would rather remodel their already amortised premises inherited from adolescent days. Of course, in preference to the recapitalisation involved in either relocation or revamping, the enterprise could opt to license its technology to incipient producers in the lower-cost havens. As a result, it would gain short-term benefits from the marketing of economically made items furnished by its offshore licensees. In the longer term, though, its technical edge would degrade: the combined outcome of the loss of production experience on its part and the securing of those skills by the neophytes as they invariably progress along the learning curve. The conscious decision to retreat from the rigorous demands of cost minimisation consigns the progenitor enterprise to eventual eclipse by the upstarts, but, in recompense, it paves the way for the transfer of returns – increasingly derived from licensing rents rather than output – to other fields judged to be more lucrative and within which the firm can again aspire to function as a begetter of new product lines. For their part, the upstarts in the NICs, eager to fill the shoes of the departing AIC enterprises, can find consolation in being spared the teething troubles accompanying product and process development, and, in consequence, can devote all their efforts to production tasks. As mature firms almost from their inception, the neophytes soon come into their own by tapping factor-cost advantages at the same time as they lunge for expansion on account of their declared need to trigger economies of scale. At all events, this thrusting dynamism might prove very intimidating to the remaining AIC producers; sufficient, indeed, to tip the scales in favour of their withdrawal from the industry. Long-established firms caught up in this dilemma, unused by now to product innovation and ill-suited to competing with neophytes on the score of production costs, are said to belong to the 'senescence' stage. The onset of senescence can be checked by the mature firm if it is able to retain a competitive edge via economies of scale or is capable of revival through a fresh burst of innovative activity which allows it to corner some niche market. Yet, the fact remains that many AIC mature firms are sorely tempted to desert their industry simply because the alternative course of vigorously competing is perceived to be beyond their capabilities. Rather than face up to this last eventuality, these firms seek the seclusion of government bail-out either as a stopgap measure or as a form of permanent receivership.

The evolution of modern shipbuilding is brimful of aspects bearing strong comparison with the tenets of industry life-cycle thinking as outlined above. It also evinces aspects which are markedly at odds with those tenets. Essentially conceived round the pioneering efforts of marine engineers concentrated on the Clyde and Thames in Britain during the early part of the nineteenth century, a spate of enabling technologies led to the metal-hulled screw-driven vessel powered by a simple or compound steam engine.[5] Relying during its adolescence on hand tools taken up from tinsmithy and boilershop practice current in the 1850s and 1860s, the industry's standardisation on steel hulls and reciprocating engines by the end of the century was instrumental in introducing special tools for manufacturing heavy metal sections. Nevertheless, the industry could hardly be categorised as mature at that stage in its evolution. It continued to depend on disproportionately large numbers of skilled workers, many contracted to perform crafts-style jobs on a temporary basis, in order to produce custom-built ships. Its enterprises, moreover, were imbued with attitudes dismissive of mechanisation. For the most part they put their trust in small-scale, labour-intensive operations geared to turning out multiple prototypes ('one-off' ships) rather 'than increase fixed costs by using more capital-intensive methods', and they justified this behaviour on the argument that it gave them the flexibility to shift 'the burden of market uncertainty on to labour through periodic layoffs'.[6] The early twentieth century, and especially the years spanning the First World War, heralded the innovations commensurate with maturity; namely, standard ships in the product line, and a host of process innovations centred on welding, prefabrication, straight-line yard lay-outs and other methods in tune with production economies (though, note, nothing resembling mechanised assembly lines, let alone automation). The British led the way in standard ship design, admittedly embracing it as a dire necessity in the struggle to counter the depredations of German U-boats. For example, Austin of Sunderland was charged with formulating the 'D' and 'H' classes of coal carriers while Tyne Iron Shipbuilding came up with the 'C' class.[7] The Americans, however, were the harbingers of the new-model shipbuilding process technologies. The government's Emergency Fleet Corporation encouraged the formation of three yards which acted as assembly sites for inputs supplied by widely dispersed steel fabrication plants.[8] Scratch labour forces, subjected to only a rudimentary training in shipyard practices, proved perfectly adequate for the exacting business of producing standard ships in unprecedented numbers.[9] Yet, once the wartime contingency had evaporated, progression into maturity took an inordinate amount of time as ship-builders resisted adoption of the innovations and refused to countenance genuine quantity production. They pointed to the atomised nature of the market, full of small shipping firms with specific trading and therein ship requirements, as justification for their rejection of the methods learned by their more enlightened brethren during the war. The postwar recession and the virtual extinction of multiple-ship contracts merely convinced them of their wisdom in eschewing innovation. Shipbuilding thus defied the conventional industry life-cycle, and individual enterprises stubbornly persisted then, and partly to this day, in adhering to methods more in keeping with batch production than mass production. They also condoned practices requiring heavy dosages of skilled labour rather than unskilled workers and went along with its corollary of frequently resorting to outside, ancillary contract labour in order to top up the shipbuilding work-force proper. It was only the exigencies imposed by the Second World War and the hasty espousal of all the symbols of maturity by the US industry which set the scene for the confirmation of shipbuilding as a postwar mature industry in the Western AICs. The war demonstrated very emphatically that with volume production of standard products – most conspicuously illustrated through the Liberty ship programme – nothing would prevent shipbuilding from achieving production economies of the kind usually associated with the mass-production automobile industry. Indeed, as a direct result of learning economies the man-hour index for work required to build a Liberty ship fell from 100 in December 1941 to 45 in December 1944: a remarkable feat when it is acknowledged that 97 per cent of the labour intake in shipbuilding had no previous experience of the industry.[10] Japan, already owning a major shipbuilding industry, proceeded to rebuild it in the light of lessons learned from this experience.[11] Its new-found strength rested on adoption of best-practice Western process technology adapted to achieve economies of scale. The full fruits of these endeavours became apparent once Japanese shipbuilders adjusted the standard ship to the circumstances of the times and evolved the VLCC.

The Japanese example reveals that technology transfer rather than relocation of mature enterprises from the pioneering shipbuilding centres was the medium through which factor-cost advantages were realised in global shipbuilding (although, one must not overlook Ludwig's enterprise which, in transferring from the USA to Japan, serves as the grand exception to the rule). While a modicum of relocations were contemplated in like fashion to that of Ludwig, these were generally acted out against a national backdrop rather than an international one. In other words, firms deliberating on the prospects opened up through relocation tended to confine their attention to alternative sites within Western AICs. For example, as early as the beginning of the century a clutch of firms on the Thames departed for cheaper locations elsewhere in the UK (e.g. Yarrow to the Clyde and Thornycroft to Southampton) fully alive to the fact that failure to do so would result in closure (as borne out by the record of the Thames Iron Works).[12] The relatively few multinational initiatives prosecuted in recent years have, like the Swedish-Portuguese venture mentioned in the previous chapter and the Japanese-NIC schemes dealt with in later chapters, entailed the retention of existing production facilities in the home AIC at the same time as new capacity was being founded in the lower-cost haven.[13] Part of the reason for this state of affairs can be laid at the feet of governments. NIC governments have encouraged the securing of foreign technology for the use of new domestic shipbuilders which effectively became 'national champions' and therefore ineligible for exposure to the perceived ignominy of direct foreign control. Conversely, AIC governments have jealously preserved home capacity in the name of job protection or national defence and, consequently, have looked askance at firms wishing to trade domestic capacity for new plant overseas. It is safe to say, then, that enterprise relocations, particularly of the multinational kind, have not been characteristic of shipbuilding and this, too, flies in the face of conventional life-cycle thinking.

What is not in dispute, however, is the affinity between the central features of contemporary shipbuilding and those characteristic of maturity in the classic industry life-cycle. The traits of oversupply, dormant or inconsequential innovation, heightened price competition and deteriorating or zero profitability – all emblematic of global shipbuilding – are traits representative of any industry sunk in the mature stage and seemingly irrevocably bent on commencing senescence. The enterprises themselves bear the brunt of this feeble outlook. They are stuck with a surfeit of plant capacity, frequently burdened with a heavy organisational superstructure resulting from previous merger and take-over activities and are constrained to fend off competition in the existing stagnating markets from vibrant nascent NIC enterprises determined to make inroads.[14] Governments have aided and abetted the defensive concentration strategy and, in consequence, have inadvertently contributed to the ills of mature firms. Excess capacity and prodigal administrative overheads not only saddle enterprises with additional costs, but they weaken the corporate ability to respond with alacrity to the limited market opportunities which still exist. By all accounts, forced concentration bridles the competitive instincts of the mature company, delays needed restructuring and cultivates a reliance on state bail-outs. In short, it promotes rigidities in market structures. All AIC shipbuilding industries have been affected to varying degrees by these symptoms of rigidity and it has come to pass that all resort to some form of state involvement in order to sustain their operations. By virtue of their longstanding dominance in the global market, the Japanese shipbuilders have reckoned on less direct state support than most of the others. Nevertheless, the Japanese state is a far from disinterested onlooker and continues to play a decisive, if unobtrusive, role in the affairs of the industry. It is appropriate, then, that we evaluate its intervention within a frame of reference which envelops the overall retrenchment of this, the world's largest single shipbuilding industry.

THE RESPONSE OF THE HEAVYWEIGHT

The nurturing of the Japanese shipbuilding industry was deemed from Meiji times to be a legitimate purpose of government, both to affirm the country's strategic interests and to project its economic power. After the Second World War the former goal largely disappeared, leaving the latter to come to the forefront. It will repay us to step back and briefly survey the history of the government-business alliance; for the relative success of modern intervention is made intelligible only on appreciation of the deep roots of the symbiotic relationship between the state and the shipbuilders. The First World War was the watershed for Japanese shipbuilding. Hitherto, it had grown as a protected infant industry, sheltered from the harsh competition afforded by UK builders but fully prepared to tap the reservoir of British and other Western technology from within its secure bastion.[15] For the first time, however, outside markets beckoned to supplement the greatly enlarged domestic demand for shipping, and Japanese builders acquired a taste for expansion. Initially, all the signs and portents looked promising, not the least of them being an apparent labour-cost advantage. According to a survey conducted by the US National Foreign Trade Council in 1918, wages for skilled shipyard workers in Japan ranged from £0.16 to £0.18 for a ten-hour day in contrast to the £0.45–0.57 applying to Britain for a nine-hour work day and the £1.21 obtaining for an eight-hour day in the USA. Equivalent wage scales for semiskilled labour were £0.15 in Japan, £0.40 in Britain and £0.92 in the USA; whereas unskilled labour commanded a princely £0.13 in Japan, £0.38 in Britain and £0.92 in the USA. Consequently, the number of shipyards capable of producing steel vessels of over 1,000 gt leapt from six in 1913 to 45 in 1918, with a corresponding surge in the number of slipways from 17 to 135.[16] In tune with this expansion, the work-force quadrupled from 26,000 to 107,000 and the government, encouraged by the putative signs of well-being, responded in kind in 1917 by withdrawing the safety net offered by subsidies. Unfortunately, this was to prove premature. Inadequately equipped to cope with the return of Western competition after the war and totally unprepared for the rigours of the trade downturn following 1921, the industry underwent a salutary coming of age in which it avoided ruin by barely a whisker. Capacity withered away to 23 yards comprising 83 slips by 1924. The 612,000 gt of vessels launched in 1919 had fallen back to 72,000 gt in 1923 and the work-force had slipped in proportion to 46,000. Mindful of the industry's plight and desirous of a strong shipbuilding sector for strategic reasons, the government tipped the scales in favour of revival. A series of support measures, capped by a scrap-and-build scheme, burst onto the scene in the 1930s and was codified through the Shipbuilding Industry Law of 1939. These measures were efficacious in restoring viability to the industry. It was related, for instance, that in the three business years preceding the Ship Improvement Plan (scrap-and-build scheme) of 1932, the eight major shipbuilders all recorded consistent losses; but they all effected a dramatic about-face in the succeeding business year and reported reasonable profits. From a low of 29,000 in 1931, employment in shipbuilding rose to 132,000 in 1939 and output climbed from 101,000 gt to 333,000 gt; an improvement in its turn dwarfed by wartime expansion. In 1944 the industry attained an unprecedented output of 1.73 million gt of cargo vessels as well as 205,000 displacement tons of warships, and required the services of 334,000 workers to bring it about.

Planned shipbuilding

The return of peace brought a new slant to government involvement. Gone were the military imperatives and in their place came 'planned shipbuilding' (keikaku zosen) in the Keynesian mould. From 1947 the government would set annual tonnage targets and authorise its credit agency (the Japan Development Bank, JDB, after 1951) to advance long-term low-interest loans to shipping firms prepared to order vessels in conformity with the targets. From 1950, it would insist that all contracts for new buildings be submitted for official permission to proceed. Initially, too, a public shipping corporation was founded with the object of subsidising shipowners to the tune of 70 per cent of the costs of new ships through the medium of loans repayable over ten years. Planned shipbuilding constituted the backbone to the industry's rebirth, ensured permanent activity in the main yards and guaranteed a fall-back position should export markets fail to meet expectations. It was carefully conceived from the outset as a joint government and industry initiative.[17]

> Each year the government – that is to say, the MoT in consultation with its industry advisers in the Shipping and Shipbuilding Rationalization Council – decides on the tonnage of ships to be built, by type (tankers, ore carriers, liners, and so on), and allocates production contracts and the ships among the applicant domestic shipbuilders and shipowners. The selected shipping lines receive preferential financing and in turn are subject to close government supervision.

All in all, the annual programmes accounted for 85 per cent of all ships built for domestic shipowners during 1950–4, some 40 per cent for the succeeding quinquennium, 51 per cent for the 1960–4 period and 71 per cent for the second half of the 1960s. By then, of course, the industry had successfully transformed itself into an exporter of the first order. Prior to 1948 its only exports to speak of were 45 freighters delivered to the USA at the end of the First World War in exchange for good quality steel, and six tankers and eleven other vessels supplied to the USSR under a deal struck in 1937. The postwar breakthrough came with the construction by Mitsui and Harima of a pair of tankers for Norwegian principals. A flood of orders followed, partly stimulated by an inability of other producers to meet surging Korean War demands and partly fuelled by the incentives given to Japanese shipbuilders by their government. One such, the raw sugar ship linking scheme of the early 1950s, allowed shipbuilders holding export contracts to import sugar and sell it at a handsome profit on the domestic market. The proceeds so garnered covered any deficits incurred in securing the export orders at below-cost prices.[18] Competitors' prices could thus be undercut, and when allied with the promise of quick delivery times, afforded an unbeatable package which pushed Japan to the position of leading shipbuilder by 1956. The 148,000 gt of output recorded for 1949 had multiplied to 1,746,000 gt by 1956, virtually a twelve-fold increase. By way of contrast, UK output, which stood at 1,267,000 gt in 1949, had increased by a mere 9 per cent to 1,383,000 gt in 1956. As early as 1953 the export ratio obtaining for Japanese output had reached 36 per cent in comparison with the 28 per cent registered for the UK, and Japan was able to bolster its position over the succeeding years by offering better deferred payment terms than many of its competitors bound by OECD regulations. Since its formation in 1961, the OECD had lent its support to the West European Shipbuilding Informal Contact group (later AWES, see Glossary) which had attempted to co-ordinate production among member countries and seen fit to work towards the establishment of minimum ship prices and maximum subvention levels. Considering such interference as troublesome and unwarranted, Japan's builders' association studiously ignored the pleas for effective co-operation even after the country elected to join the Organisation in 1964. Complacent as a result of their 50 per cent share of world export orders in 1963, the Japanese builders wished to retain the effective combination of flexible financing and facilities accustomed to cost-efficient output which had been so rewarding in terms of advancing their market share.[19]

The shipbuilders paid a high price for this export success, however. Initially plagued with low labour productivity and expensive materials charges, their competitiveness appeared highly questionable in 1950.[20]

> The volume of labour required for shipbuilding operations in Japan is about double that required in England and some North European countries. On the other hand, wages in Japan are about one-third of those in these countries. Thus, personnel expense stands almost equal. Hence, prices of steel materials, accounting for more than 20 per cent of the ship (total cost) prove a decisive factor. Having to depend upon imports for iron ore and high-quality coking coal, Japanese iron works find it impossible to manufacture steel materials at the same unit prices as iron mills in England or Northern Europe.

Cheap labour was a factor-cost advantage, but only if it could be reinforced through enhanced productivity. Hence, the government resolved to encourage the industry to invest in improved process technology. Despite a precarious financial standing (the builders were all losing money in the early 1950s), the industry effected a revolution in shipbuilding method. Adoption of block building did much both to upgrade labour productivity and speed building times. The improvement is vividly evidenced by the finding that while each worker produced an average 3.7 gt of shipping in 1951, his successor managed to produce 55.6 gt in 1968: an upheaval which owed everything to the augmentation of the capital-to-labour ratio by a factor of 24 during that period.[21] Thus, with a virtually constant work-force (97,000 in 1952 and 95,000 in 1963), the industry was able to make use of productivity improvements to more than double output between the early 1950s and the early 1960s. Simultaneous radical improvements in steelmaking technology served drastically to reduce Japanese disadvantages on the score of steel inputs. In terms of sheer capacity growth alone, Japanese steelmakers had clawed their way into the upper ranks of the world's producers. Several steelmakers enjoyed privileged links with shipbuilders and participated in this frenzy of growth to the full. For example, NKK built a duplicate blast furnace at Kawasaki in 1958, a second one at Tsurumi in 1960, a plant at Mizue in 1962 and a larger mill at Fukuyama beginning in 1965.[22] For its part, Kawasaki Steel (an affiliate of KHI) built two large mills at Chiba and Mizushima, respectively in 1953 and 1966, while Sumitomo opened two mills in the 1960s; namely, Wakayama and Kajima. Nevertheless, Japanese materials costs were still 15 per cent higher than those enjoyed by the UK as late as 1959, even though unit labour costs were 45 per cent lower. But it was labour that had become the telling factor. When averaged for the 1960–5 period, the man hours required per weighted steel ton of shipbuilding output stood at 70 for Japan; a remarkable showing when contrasted to the 82 for Sweden, 155 for West Germany, 164 for the USA and 187 for the UK. In so far as total costs were concerned, however, Japan had bettered the UK (1959 index value of 97 as against the UK's 100) and was vastly superior to Sweden (141) and the USA (175), although it still trailed West Germany (90) and the Netherlands (92). In the pivotal tanker market, though, it reigned supreme. For example, the most competitive European yards could build a 19,000 dwt tanker for £58 per dwt at this time, but the Japanese could turn one out for £57 per dwt. The Europeans could shave costs to £56.75 for a 32,000 dwt vessel, £50 for a 47,000 dwt ship and £49.50 for a 65,000 tonner whereas the Japanese could match them size for size with £55, £49 and £48. As the 1960s unfolded, incremental innovations, best exemplified by the VLCC and building dock, allowed Japan to consolidate its cost competitiveness and to greatly amplify its edge in the matter of fast delivery times. Reputedly, its yards could build a 60,000 dwt vessel in 6–8 months in contrast to the 9–12 months needed by builders in West Germany, Sweden and Denmark; the 13–18 months required of yards in the Netherlands, Norway, France, the UK and USA; and the 19–24 months typical of yards in Italy and Spain. The absence of demarcation disputes among the work-force membership, together with the flexible nature of the labour process as practised in Japan which made workers interchangeable, proved to be a godsend. Moreover, the widespread use of temporary and subcontract labour (reminiscent of the UK industry in its prime) offered the builders a dispensable reserve in times of cutbacks. Of the 110,000 workers employed in the 24 main yards during 1959, for instance, no fewer than 22,000 were subcontract workers and a further 13,000 were solely engaged on short duration contracts.[23]

This rather agreeable state of affairs vindicated the government's stewardship of the industry which had continued apace since 1947. In line with the formulation of national industrial policy via a set of 'visions' delineated for carefully selected industries, the state had entered the ring to prevent interfirm competition during the rebuilding phase; a ploy conducted to stop the firms from endangering the main objective of export competitiveness. Planned shipbuilding was also undertaken to nurture the expansion of the firms, with the government acceding to their requests for subsidies to aid investment in new yards as well as furnishing tax concessions for investment in a whole host of process technologies and virtually anything connected with export activity.[24] Only with the added punch of corporate stature, the government reasoned, would Japan's shipbuilders be able to outmanoeuvre outside competitors. With the revision of the Anti-monopoly Law, the previously dismembered zaibatsu were gradually allowed to reunite. This reversion to conglomerate structures directly or indirectly affected a number of shipbuilders, but none more so than the ex-Mitsubishi yards. The old MHI, deprecated as an agent of imperialism, was broken up during the Allied occupation into three distinct shipbuilding enterprises: the Eastern Japan (later Mitsubishi Nippon) Heavy Industries, the Central Japan (later Shin Mitsubishi) Heavy Industries and the Western Japan Heavy Industries (later Mitsubishi Zosen). It resurfaced in 1964 on the merger of these three. Previously, in 1960, its giant counterpart, IHI, had been fashioned from the merger of Ishikawajima Jukogyo and Harima Zosensho; the resultant firm going on to absorb Nagoya Shipbuilding in 1964, Usuki Iron Works in 1965 and Kure Zosen in 1968.[25] Within a year of this last occurrence, Sumitomo Machinery and Uraga Heavy Industries combined into what was to become SHI. Consummated with a view to affirming horizontal integration, these major mergers overshadowed several moves in which sizeable shipbuilders gobbled up smaller yards. Hitachi Zosen, for example, brought Maizuru Shipbuilding under its wing while Mitsui took over Shikoku Dockyard and forged ties with Hashihama Shipbuilding, Osaka Shipbuilding and Fujinagata Shipbuilding.[26] A little later, its affiliate, Setoda Zosen, merged with Takuma Shipbuilding to form Naikai Zosen round a much enlarged shipyard at Setoda-cho near Hiroshima. Nor were mergers aimed only at horizontal integration; for the instigators made great play of the benefits arising from the 'internalising' of the entire shipbuilding production chain. Kawasaki Dockyard (subsequently restyled KHI), for instance, had established an ironworks at Kakogawa and went on to supplement it, first, with the Hamano Iron Works for propeller manufacture and, in 1964, with the Kyushu Works of Kita-kyushu for the fabrication of ship frames. By the beginning of the 1970s and the inauguration of the huge building docks, all of the major shipbuilders had brought on stream an immense tail of back-up activities. The example of IHI will answer for them all. Its Tokyo Shipbuilding and Crane Works dealt with steel structures, the Yokohama No.1 Works handled pressure vessels, the Aioi Shipbuilding and Boiler Works made boilers, pipes and storage tanks; leaving engines, compressors, fans, winches, cranes, deck machinery, casting and forging products and sundry other components to be shared among the Tokyo Turbo Machinery and Casting Works, the Yokohama No.2 Works, the Nagoya Works, the Aioi Diesel Engine Works, the Shingu Branch Works and the Kure Machinery Works.

The turnabout in fortunes

We come at length to the awful decade of the 1970s with its aura of expansionism shattered by forces outside the ken of the burgeoning shipbuilders. Beset by enormous problems, the builders found themselves teetering on the edge of bankruptcy by the latter years of the decade. Table 2.2 provides one measure of the altered circumstances. Assessed initially for half-yearly terms and then for annual terms, the time series indicates that the operating profits for the top ten shipbuilders ascended within five years to a level three times what they had been in 1965. They had more than doubled again by early 1973. However, the climax had been reached and they began to falter thereafter. In the full year terminating at the end of March 1978, operating profits had fallen to a figure barely 62 per cent of those obtaining for the year ending March 1973. An alternative means of grasping the change-over is presented through a run of net profit-to-sales ratios. The 2–3 per cent range of the mid-1960s had practically doubled by 1971, but began to deteriorate almost immediately afterwards. Ratios slumped to below 2 per cent (apart from a brief revival in 1973–4) for the rest of the 1970s, dipping to a meagre 0.6 per cent for 1978. While there is some dispute as to the precise implications

Table 2.2 Returns of ten top Japanese builders

Period ending	Sales (Y. million)	Operating profits (Y. million)	Net profits (Y. million)	Net profit-to-sales ratio (%)
9. 1965	396,623	22,981	8,704	2.2
3. 1966	421,801	23,595	8,448	2.0
9. 1966	453,021	28,841	12,315	2.7
3. 1967	533,903	32,067	14,047	2.6
9. 1967	584,450	39,774	19,684	3.4
3. 1968	649,925	39,972	18,044	2.8
9. 1968	659,159	47,740	20,618	3.1
3. 1969	697,401	52,238	24,936	3.6
9. 1969	803,212	65,595	30,395	3.8
3. 1970	894,008	69,894	34,626	3.9
9. 1970	862,757	72,293	33,968	3.9
3. 1971	912,304	81,067	37,753	4.1
9. 1971	968,858	86,876	47,047	4.9
3. 1972	1,002,807	98,021	15,445	1.5
9. 1972	1,043,443	106,506	18,028	1.7
3. 1973	1,121,094	123,982	16,983	1.5
9. 1973	1,231,922	156,405	27,489	2.2
3. 1974	1,323,714	130,350	28,211	2.1
9. 1974	1,531,910	132,881	23,340	1.5
3. 1975	1,700,784	109,745	24,662	1.5
3. 1976	3,244,792	199,568	57,216	1.8
3. 1977	3,558,623	247,794	61,876	1.7
3. 1978	3,823,951	172,855	25,096	0.6

Source: Zosen, October 1978, p. 23

of these ratios for inferring comparative profitability, their crumbling following the peak of the early 1970s lends irrefragable support to the feeling that the industry was being overtaken by events of disastrous dimensions.[27] Corroborative evidence is afforded by the record of shipbuilding employment. Figure 2.2 displays the total work-force employed by the shipbuilders for each year from 1970 to 1980. In addition, it charts for the same period the aggregate number of workers, designated as 'ancillary workers', which were engaged by the builders either on temporary tasks or subcontracts. Whereas direct shipyard employment rose from 158,186 in 1970 to a maximum of 184,198 in 1974 and subsequently declined to 112,602 in 1980, employment of ancillary workers climbed from 76,348 in 1970 to 89,706 in 1974 and fell back to 51,608 in 1980. In other words, the early 1970s witnessed the builders mount an expansion of direct employment which registered a 16 per cent gain over 1970. Their employment of ancillary workers more than kept

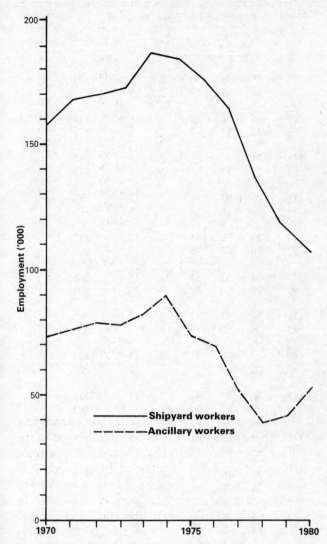

Figure 2.2 Japanese shipyard work-force, 1970–80

pace, amounting to a 17 per cent gain. In sharp contrast, the later 1970s saw direct employment slip by 39 per cent but ancillary employment drop by almost 43 per cent. There is the suggestion in these latter figures, therefore, that ancillary workers may have taken the brunt of the

Table 2.3 Fluctuating Japanese shipyard capacity

Year	Berth/dock size range ('000gt)						Total
	0.5–3	3–5	5–30	30–100	100–150	>150	
1969							
building	100	25	55	30	3	5	218
repair	70	18	49	10	2	7	156
1970							
building	97	26	56	26	3	6	214
repair	78	21	53	11	2	7	172
1971							
building	111	24	60	28	2	8	233
repair	83	21	53	12	3	7	179
1972							
building	112	25	67	34	2	13	253
repair	89	23	58	14	4	8	196
1973							
building	113	26	78	41	2	13	273
repair	92	26	62	15	3	10	208
1974							
building	120	32	67	54	2	13	288
repair	91	27	60	17	3	10	208
1975							
building	135	34	73	42	3	13	300
repair	85	26	60	19	3	10	203
1976							
building	149	27	80	41	3	13	313
repair	85	26	60	19	3	10	203
1977							
building	148	26	81	41	3	13	312
repair	85	27	61	19	3	10	205
1978							
building	154	24	79	41	3	13	314
repair	87	24	65	19	3	10	208
1979							
building	155	24	79	40	3	12	313
repair	88	24	70	14	2	10	208
1980							
building	152	38	38	25	0	10	263
repair	85	25	64	19	2	10	205
1981							
building	153	38	38	25	0	10	264
repair	88	25	62	21	2	10	208

Source: Zosen, October 1979 and October 1980

cutbacks and, in so doing, partially sheltered the permanent work-force from summary dismissal. The fact remains, however, that a cut in direct labour of massive proportions was inflicted; a cut, it should be stressed, that left the 1980 direct work-force at a size just equal to 71 per cent of its 1970 level.[28]

In view of the Japanese penchant for capacity investment and given the natural reluctance of erstwhile expansionist firms to suppress plant, the sensitivity of shipyard physical facilities and paraphernalia to the sea-change in corporate viability is much less acute. Table 2.3 traces the aggregate trend for the years spanning the cataclysm. The table makes a distinction between building and repair plant before further distinguishing the plant by size. It allows us to infer that in 1969, for example, only eight of 218 building facilities (that is, less than 4 per cent) were of a stature sufficient to construct vessels of 100,000 gt or more. By 1975, some 16 docks conformed to this category, a doubling in number if not in proportion (they now equalled about 5 per cent of the enlarged total of 300 facilities). In slavish response to the crash in VLCC demand, no further additions to the number of large facilities were enacted after 1975. At the same time, plans to commission yet larger monster docks were quashed.[29] Paradoxically, however, the crackdown did not extend to smaller building berths and docks, which continued to proliferate until 1978 when 298 were counted. Indeed, the total of 16 large docks only diminished by a single unit through to 1979, although a good one-third of the big facilities remaining after that year were expunged during 1980 as a result of government-imposed rationalisation. It is highly significant, nevertheless, that the 264 building berths and docks extant in 1981 represented an aggregation some 21 per cent greater than the 1969 tally even though it was a 16 per cent shortfall on the record 1978 level. Repair facilities had also increased in harmony with the boosted ship production of the early 1970s. Between 1969 and 1973 their number grew by one-third, but subsequently – and in marked contra-distinction to new-building plant – the total remained tolerably steady. It had occurred to the shipbuilders to diversify into ship repair once the bottom fell out of the new-building market since the need for periodic overhaul of vessels in service appeared inviolate, and this partly accounted for the relative stability of repair facilities in the second half of the 1970s. However, government eagerness to expunge building capacity had the effect of encouraging the yards to redeploy former new-building plant as repair plant. As such, they retained the option of restoring it to construction activities should an upturn in market conditions so warrant. Truth to say, some shipbuilding plant was switched to ship repair for keeps. Mitsui, for instance, transformed its Fujinagata

Works on Osaka Bay into a plant dedicated to ship repair, offshore structures, container manufacturing and land machinery and, at one fell swoop, suppressed a shipbuilding tradition extending back 290 years.[30]

Most of the plant excision fell on new-building facilities, however. After a spell of dithering, the MoT, exercising the authority of government, brought in a rationalisation programme with the full co-operation of the industry. Yet, a number of yards came to grief even prior to the inception of the scheme in 1978. IHI was first off the mark, closing its Nagoya yard in 1974. This facility, 33 years old at the time, had built 228 vessels of 1,644,000 gt, but was handicapped in having to make do with a cramped lay-out. Its tasks were taken over by the newly built Chita yard.[31] However, 1977 was the bumper year for yard failures. Mie Shipbuilding, a newcomer dating from 1969, went bankrupt during that year with outstanding liabilities of Y20 billion; heretofore the worst case of insolvency in the industry since its revival after the Second World War. That dubious honour was soon lost, though, as Hashihama Shipbuilding failed in December with liabilities of Y43 billion. This firm had over-reached itself in creating a 120,000 dwt-capacity building dock at Tadotsu which, while costing Y16 billion, had come on stream when the prospects of gaining orders to fill it were just about non-existent. Hard on its heels, Watanabe Zosen announced debts of Y10 billion and proceeded to dismiss its work-force and cease operations. All told, 11 shipbuilders sought the protection of the bankruptcy courts in that year (including Okayama Shipbuilding and Nishii Dockyard), some destined never to reopen their gates.[32] Hakodate Dock, reeling under the twin blows of a 28.4 per cent sales decline and an accumulated loss of Y13.7 billion, almost went to the wall in 1978 but was rescued in the nick of time by its parent organisation, the Fuyo (Fuji Bank) zaibatsu. Usuki Iron Works narrowly escaped dissolution with estimated debts of Y30 billion, while Ichikawa Shipbuilding, Shinhama Dockyard and Tokushima Zosen were not so lucky, since circumstances forced them to cease trading. Yamanishi Zosen and Imai Shipbuilding were also casualties of 1978. The most spectacular collapse of that year, however, occurred when Sasebo Heavy Industries admitted to grave financial difficulties. Blaming a combination of disappearing demand for tankers and adverse currency fluctuations, the company found itself with a scant backlog of new-building work and little in the way of diversified activities to tide it over. Its achievement was to remain afloat despite debts of Y100 billion and the evident reluctance of its creditors to acquiesce to a stay-of-execution. Severe pruning of overheads, including the dismissal of one-quarter of its 6,000 strong work-force, eventually paid off. Yet, acceptance of the rescue plan meant that the firm effectually lost its independence, falling under the sway of Hsiao Tsubouchi, the president of Kurushima Dockyard.[33] An adept at accumulating vulnerable yards (he already ruled over Kochi Jukogyo, Uwajima Shipbuilding and Kishigami Zosen as well as Kurushima), Tsubouchi was instrumental in restoring confidence in the yard, and new orders were the material result. Furthermore, panic and fear engendered by the prospect of losing its major employer actuated local authorities in Sasebo to press for government backing for the bail-out engineered by Tsubouchi. This was not withheld, since both the Japanese and US governments wished to retain Sasebo as an important naval ship repair centre. As a token of government solicitude, orders for naval auxiliaries were lodged with the yard.

Rationalisation

Stopgap measures introduced by the government had scarcely been able to stem the lurch into financial insolvency which was sweeping through the industry. A directive of 1976 urging the 67 significant shipbuilders to co-operate in cutting activity to a level equivalent to 72 per cent of the 1973 peak by 1977, and 67 per cent by 1978, had been, by and large, ignored by the industry. With the dawning of 1978 it was obvious that decisive and meaningful action alone would prevail. Consequently, subsidies were restored to shipowners after a hiatus of three years. Some Y71 billion was committed to the JDB for the express purpose of subsidising interest payable on loans for ships ordered in Japan. The interest borne by domestic shipowners was driven down to a mere 2.8 per cent and, in combination with an upgraded loan ratio of 75 per cent, effectively trimmed one-fifth off the price of buying a Japanese new building.[34] Demand stimulation in an era of depressed freight rates and surplus shipping bordered on the irresponsible, however, and it was the supply side which received most government attention. Determined to redress the oversupply situation at its roots, that is, in the shipyards themselves, the government enacted the Law Concerning Special Measures for the Stabilisation of Specific Industries in July 1978 and nominated shipbuilding (and textiles) for systematic and phased eradication of excess production capacity. After due process of consultation with the Shipbuilders' Association of Japan (SAJ), it was agreed that 35 per cent of the capacity on hand in 1974 capable of building 5,000 gt vessels and larger would be withdrawn from use. The MoT, through the joint government and industry advisory body, the Shipping and Shipbuilding Rationalisation Council, assigned targets for all affected builders. Expressed in terms of cgrt, the intent of the targets was to apportion the cuts as equally as possible among enterprises of comparable footing. All told, 3.4 million cgrt of the nominal 9.8 million cgrt would be extinguished. Under the umbrella of the Financial Institutions for Specific Depressed Industries, loans were made available to firms to assist them in plant suppression. A special fund worth Y36.8 billion administered by the Designated Shipbuilding Enterprises Stabilisation Association was set aside for the shipbuilders. An additional sum of Y14.2 billion was reserved for the medium and smaller shipbuilders; that is to say, those deemed particularly vulnerable to the snares brought on by retrenchment. In fact, this group was spared the worst of the cuts under the rationalisation formula. While the seven majors (defined as those able to build 1 million gt per annum) were expected to cut their joint capacity by 40 per cent and the 17 quasi-majors (those able to produce between 100,000 and 1 million gt) received an injunction to reduce their aggregate capacity by 30 per cent, the 16 medium builders (each producing between 10,000 and 100,000 gt) were requested to chop their total capacity by 27 per cent and the score or so of smaller builders (individually constructing from 5,000 to 10,000 gt in a year) were advised to cut theirs by just 15 per cent. Supplementary measures, such as the Law on Special Measures Concerning the Stabilisation of Employment of Workers Related to Specified Depressed Industries or Specified Depressed Areas and the Law on Provisional Measures towards Smaller Enterprises in Areas Related to Specified Industries, added a regional policy aspect to the grand programme of shipbuilding restructuring. Through them, steps were taken to subsidise the costs of labour redundancy; steps which were specially aimed at the smaller shipbuilders and allowed for worker retraining and relocation. As a sop to all builders, a scrap-and-build scheme, inspired by its predecessor of 1932, was inaugurated; and an organisation, the Association of Ship Scrapping Promotion, was established to grant subsidies to shipbuilders willing to undertake ship demolition in their erstwhile ship construction facilities.[35]

Undoubtedly, the industry profited by the rationalisation programme in as much as the oversupply problem was partly relieved. The overall target was more than met, since some 3.6 million cgrt was withdrawn from new-building activity by 1981. Employment of direct and indirect shipyard labour had eroded from its 1973 peak of 253,000 to about 162,000 by the end of 1979 in part because of the systematic elimination of 60 building berths and docks. In the words of one observer, the 'industry was in a good deal better shape as a result and, with an additional million tons of domestic orders from the scrap-and-build plan in 1979, the leading firms were making profits again by 1980'.[36] A closer scrutiny of the cutbacks, however, discloses the fact that, notwithstanding the attention to equitable treatment professed by the Council in meting out the cuts, some enterprises suffered disproportionately in comparison with their peers. A not inconsequential number abandoned new building altogether. Table 2.4 reveals that none of the major and quasi-major builders was forced to relinquish new-building activity, but Table 2.5 shows that Imai Shipbuilding, Kochiken Zosen, Fukuoka Zosen (a subsidiary of Usuki Iron Works) and Kochi Jukogyo (a subsidiary of Kurushima Dockyard) of the medium group gave up the struggle, as did Setouchi Zosen, Higaki Zosen, Kagoshima Dock, Shinhama Dockyard, Ujina Zosensho and Geibi Zosen from the set of smaller builders. After the plan's implementation, some firms were no longer capable of constructing vessels greater than 5,000 gt. They included Niigata Engineering, Honda

Table 2.4 Rationalisation 1978–81: 1st tier

Japanese shipbuilder	New building capacity (cgrt)		b/a (%)
	(a) Before	(b) After	
Majors			
MHI	1,326,126	804,250	60.6
IHI	1,175,378	714,182	60.8
Hitachi Zosen	889,100	532,686	59.9
KHI	709,224	433,741	61.2
Mitsui	623,413	378,908	60.8
NKK	539,091	313,375	58.1
SHI	427,284	248,498	58.2
Quasi-majors			
Sasebo	322,186	245,620	76.2
Hakodate	309,000	59,740	19.3
Sanoyasu	173,626	118,763	68.4
Namura	177,548	118,763	66.9
Osaka	76,553	60,900	79.6
Oshima	118,763	118,763	100.0
Kanasashi	167,592	118,763	70.9
Nipponkai	111,605	70,078	62.8
Onomichi	132,671	88,359	66.6
Kasado	145,273	99,720	68.7
Hayashikane	196,884	102,238	51.9
Kurushima	190,681	169,826	89.1
Imabari	192,039	206,215	107.4
Koyo	200,424	127,907	63.8
Usuki	80,809	48,654	60.2
Hashihama	117,857	117,857	100.0
Tsuneishi	181,784	181,784	100.0

Table 2.5 Rationalisation 1978–81: 2nd tier

Japanese shipbuilder	New building capacity (cgrt) (a) Before	(b) After	b/a(%)
Medium group			
Shin Yamamoto	48,812	32,155	65.9
Narasaki	68,401	5,822	8.5
Tohoku	48,478	48,478	100.0
Nakai	69,510	48,478	69.7
Imai	58,590	–	0
Kanawa	35,278	35,278	100.0
Kanda	83,671	61,028	72.9
Shikoku	33,066	29,082	88.0
Uwajima	35,278	35,278	100.0
Watanabe	48,265	34,403	71.3
Kochiken	35,278	–	0
Fukuoka	28,346	–	0
Mie	51,830	46,651	90.0
Kyokuyo	34,183	25,020	73.2
Minaminippon	35,155	48,812	151.8
Kochi	75,722	–	0
Smaller builders			
Shimoda	21,721	21,721	100.0
Miho	40,324	34,769	86.2
Setouchi	23,125	–	0
Taihei	28,098	20,855	74.3
Higaki	14,986	–	0
Asakawa	18,456	14,896	80.7
Kagoshima	22,005	–	0
Ishikawajima S&C	13,862	13,862	100.0
Niigata	13,862	13,859	100.0
Honda	13,862	13,859	100.0
Hashimoto	13,862	13,859	100.0
Yamanishi	18,764	15,901	84.7
Nakamura	13,862	13,859	100.0
Shinhama	13,862	–	0
Ujina	24,486	–	0
Kurinoura	27,849	23,675	85.0
Miyoshi	13,862	13,859	100.0
Towa	18,764	15,901	84.7
Ube	13,862	13,862	100.0
Geibi	16,230	–	0

Zosen, Hashimoto Zosensho, Miyoshi Zosen, Nakamura Zosen and Narasaki Zosen; the last of which had previously warranted respect as a medium-sized builder.[37] Thus, while it is true to say that the various builders' groups were subjected to a rationalisation plan which accorded

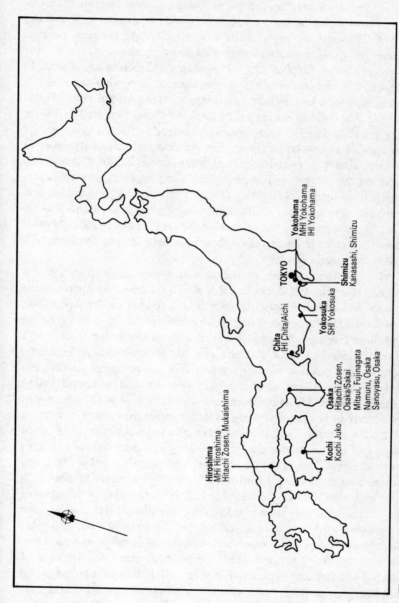

Figure 2.3 Japanese yards deleted during 1978–81

the heaviest blows to the largest and the lightest cuts to the smallest, the averaging of the cutbacks by group served to mask many anomalies. As far as the majors were concerned, no builder was cut by more than 41.9 per cent while, by the same token, none avoided cuts of at least 38.8 per cent.[38] The disparity between the least affected and the most ravaged among the quasi-majors was somewhat more pronounced. On the one hand, Oshima Shipbuilding, Hashihama Shipbuilding, Tsuneishi Shipbuilding and Imabari Shipbuilding escaped altogether (and the last gained approval to expand its capacity) whereas, on the other, Haya-shikane Shipbuilding witnessed its capacity sliced by a hefty 48.1 per cent and Hakodate Dock was positively savaged with the removal of 80.7 per cent of its new-building capacity. An enormous disparity becomes evident with the medium group, since some builders completely departed the industry, others evaded any significant cutbacks, yet others emerged unscathed (Tohoku Zosen, Kanawa Dock and Uwajima Shipbuilding) and one, Minaminippon Zosen, was authorised to increase its capacity by half as much again. A similar situation obtained with the smaller builders, although none actually gained the Ministry's assent to expand capacity.

Most of this capacity reduction was accomplished through the closure of berths and docks in yards which continued to operate their remaining facilities because the owners believed the surviving plant was better suited to the new-building requirements of the age (i.e. was newer and more lavishly equipped or was of a size more fitting to deal with vessels of less than VLCC dimensions). Not all yards were so fortunate, however, as several were utterly deprived of any vestige of shipbuilding activity. Figure 2.3 pinpoints sizeable yards – those of at least 20,000 gt capacity – deleted from the roster of active new-building sites. As would be expected, they mostly belong to larger enterprises which had grown to sustain a multi-plant, multi-site organisational structure. The seven majors, of course, conform to this category, and their various reactions merit attention. One of the victims, the Hiroshima shipyard of MHI, was turned over completely to offshore work. It had begun in 1944 as a two-berth yard and had graduated to 120,000 dwt tankers by the onset of the shipping crisis in the mid-1970s. Another MHI facility, the Yokohama yard, was also sacrificed on the altar of rationalisation. Slightly smaller than its sister yard, Yokohama likewise possessed two building berths. Together, they represented some 408,000 cgrt of deleted new-building capacity. The other MHI facilities affected, Kobe and Koyagi, each lost a berth which, in combination, added 113,000 cgrt to MHI's quota earmarked for suppression. In carrying the load, these yards allowed the Shimonoseki, Nagasaki and Nagahama centres to continue untouched by the plan (the last two sited in proximity to each other). IHI also elected to delete two sites, one of which also happened to be in Yokohama. This yard boasted a single 150,554 cgrt-capacity dock. The other choice, Chita, was a modern VLCC-building centre with a 226,149-cgrt capacity dock. The company's Tokyo yard lost a 39,460 cgrt-capacity berth, but Aioi and Kure emerged unscathed. Mitsui, meanwhile, chopped its Fujinagata yard and erased a building position apiece at Chiba and Tamano. Hitachi Zosen closed its Mukaishima yard, deleted its building dock at Sakai, cut a berth at Maizuru and preserved intact its Innoshima and Ariake yards. SHI chose to cease building at Kawama and Yokosuka, while leaving unimpaired its building facilities at Oppama and reducing those at Uraga. For want of obvious sites to delete, KHI and NKK retained use of all their yards. None the less, the former expunged a berth at its Kobe yard and a dock at Sakaide while the latter eradicated a berth at Tsurumi and a berth and a dock at Shimizu. Less bountifully endowed with multi-plant sites, the quasi-majors had correspondingly less opportunity to axe entire yards. None the less, Kurushima Dockyard contrived to concentrate its losses on the Hashihama shipyard which was closed outright as a new-building centre. Osaka was the hapless sacrificial lamb for both Sanoyasu Dockyard (now restyled Sanoyas Corporation) and Namura Shipbuilding, losing two shipyards in consequence of the rationalisation plan.

While reduction in capacity to a level scarcely reaching two-thirds of that obtaining in 1974 was laudatory, it was certainly insufficient to stay aligned with the drastic drop in output. Table 2.6 makes it clear that while the 1974 output registered 113 on the index scale (compared with

Table 2.6 Japanese output composition

Year	Ships completed ('000gt)	Index (1973 =100)	Domestic market	Export market	Domestic-to -export ratio (%)
1973	15,014	100	4,922	10,092	48.8
1974	17,009	113	2,713	14,296	19.0
1975	15,757	105	2,642	13,115	20.1
1976	15,864	106	3,540	12,324	28.7
1977	13,000	87	1,984	11,016	18.0
1978	7,323	49	1,416	5,907	24.0
1979	5,371	36	2,148	3,223	66.6
1980	5,948	40	2,687	3,261	82.4
1981	8,180	54	2,689	5,491	49.0
1982	7,859	52	2,517	5,342	47.1
1983	6,512	43	2,144	4,368	49.1

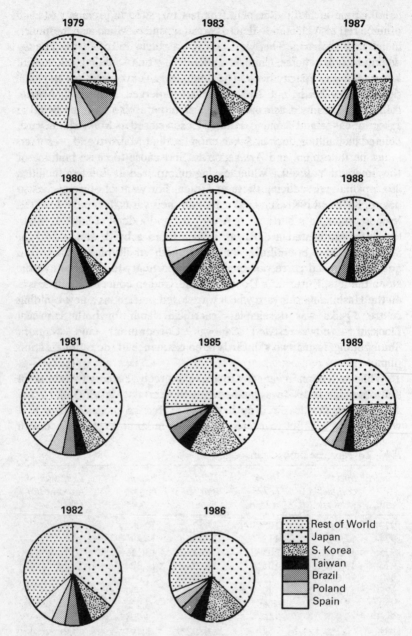

Figure 2.4 World order-book shares, 1979–89

a 1973 base of 100), the output totals for 1978, 1979 and 1980 had plummeted to 49, 36 and 40; and by the early 1980s had only hesitantly clambered back to about half the level of a decade earlier. Put bluntly, whereas MoT initiatives had cut capacity to around the 75 mark, output hovered a good 20 points lower and thus the overcapacity problem persisted. Not only had depressed shipping markets failed to recover fully, but Japan's dominance of ship exports also appeared to be faltering. As late as 1977, domestic ships were equivalent to just 18 per cent of the builders' export production, but in the succeeding two years – and partly as a result of government stimulation – domestic ships took the lion's share of a much depleted production total. Even in the early 1980s when production had picked up from its 1979 nadir, the share appropriated by domestic shipping was running at twice the level of the mid-1970s.

This evident decline in competitiveness owes far more to the incursions made by NICs into what had hitherto been a virtual Japanese preserve than it does to any disturbance wreaked by the hasty retirement of shipbuilding plant. Figure 2.4 is perspicuous on this point; namely, that the rise of South Korea, no matter what it has done to undermine Western AIC shipbuilding, has definitely served to dent the Japanese share of world order books. Data for tonnage on order in March of each year from 1979 to 1989 is rearranged to elicit the interesting finding that Japan's share remained buoyant in the 35 to 43 per cent range through to 1986 when it underwent a dramatic slump to 24 per cent. At the same time, the rising producers (South Korea, Taiwan, Brazil, Poland and Spain) watched their combined share ascend from about 26 per cent at the end of the 1970s to 31 per cent by 1984 and 40 per cent by 1988. South Korea was by far the biggest contributor to this surge: its modest 3.2 per cent of 1979 being transformed into a weighty 25.8 per cent by 1989. Table 2.7 is instructive in revealing just how far South Korea has come in rivalling Japan for control of export markets. Assessing work in hand at the end of March of each year from 1984 to 1989, it shows that Korean activity soared almost six-fold to reach nearly 6.5 million gt, a level sufficient to wrest the leading position from Japan. This latter, boosting activity by a modest 8 per cent over the same period, had to be content with an order-book of 6 million gt at the end of March 1989. What is more telling, though, is the growth of export tonnage. South Korea's grew 5.82 times to a level of 5.5 million gt; that is, some 600,000 gt more than Japan's total. Interestingly, the export tonnage of Japan grew by a factor of 1.29; a performance rather better than what it achieved on the aggregate export plus domestic tonnage score. The startling decline in the ratio of domestic-to-export tonnage from 79 per

Table 2.7   Export dependency: Japan and South Korea

Year (as of 31 March)	Total order book ('000gt)	Domestic market (A)	Export market (B)	A/B (%)
Japan				
1984	5,562	1,784	3,777	47.2
1985	5,837	1,941	3,896	49.8
1986	5,672	2,229	3,443	64.7
1987	4,947	2,189	2,758	79.4
1988	5,473	1,101	4,371	25.2
1989	6,008	1,107	4,901	22.6
South Korea				
1984	1,082	135	946	14.3
1985	2,294	119	2,175	5.5
1986	2,471	255	2,216	11.5
1987	4,463	705	3,759	18.8
1988	6,105	1,037	5,067	20.5
1989	6,486	976	5,510	17.7

cent in 1987 to 25 and 23 per cent in 1988 and 1989 suggests that the revival in Japan's export competitiveness occurred suddenly towards the end of the decade (and is explainable, in part, by Japanese shipowners rushing to invest in 'open registry' tonnage so as to benefit from cheaper crews and operating costs). While creeping upwards, South Korea's domestic-to-export ratio never exceeds 21 per cent: testimony, if such be needed, to the country's unswerving loyalty to export-oriented shipbuilding.

Stung by this onslaught from its neighbour, the Japanese industry (incited by its government guardian) responded with an offensive of its own. Falling ship prices after 1981 induced the government three years later to insist on screening all prices entailed in shipbuilding permits in an attempt to keep them at an acceptable level. In the year before, the MoT had recommended that the 33 main builders stick to a 4.4 million cgrt ceiling on output; that is, agree to use no more than 74 per cent of nominal capacity. Coincident with the attempt to redress the vexed over-capacity problem, the government used its considerable powers to stimulate domestic demand. For example, it set aside Y100 billion in the 1985 fiscal year for the 41st shipbuilding programme, anticipating orders amounting to 1.35 million gt. Despite such interference, the unrelenting pressure on shipbuilders continued. Truth to say, ship prices had recovered in 1980–1 from the below-cost slump dating from 1976, but this was soon seen in its true colours: a fleeting respite from a propensity to slide. By 1985, ship prices had eroded an extra 40 per cent and their subsequent rallying brought them in 1987 only to a standard equivalent to that prevailing in 1973.[39] Nor did the ship scrapping scheme offer much relief. Although extended to 1986 with subsidies of up to Y2,840 per grt of shipping scrapped, the government could only lay claim to 2.8 million grt of vessels demolished by July 1985: a tally far below the 4 million grt target set for fulfilment by 1982.[40] Basically, the high worker cost in Japan of labour-intensive shipbreaking prevented its ready adoption by shipbuilders faced with competition from a well-established demolition industry in Taiwan. In all honesty, ship-building prospects appeared reasonably propitious for a while. After all, the 123-ship ordering spree undertaken by the maverick Sanko Group, a domestic tanker operator determined to assemble a huge bulker fleet, seemed to augur good times. Within a three-month spell in 1983, for instance, ship prices surged upwards by 20–30 per cent. The medium-sized builders in particular benefited from the business injected by Sanko, for the shipowner had put its faith in handy-sized (20,000–40,000 dwt) and Panamax-sized (70,000–80,000 dwt) ships. The gamut of builders appreciating the windfall which occupied 19 per cent of the nation's capacity included Kurushima Dockyard, Minaminippon Zosen, Kanasashi Zosensho and Sasebo Heavy Industries as well as such luminaries as IHI, MHI and Mitsui. However, the sensational collapse of Sanko in 1985, and the prolonged circumstances of its bail-out, undermined the financial soundness of several of these builders. By all accounts, the yards lost about Y18 billion as a direct consequence of Sanko's defaulting on its new-building and repair contracts. As if that was not enough, the bail-out of Hong Kong's Tung Group hard on the heels of the Sanko difficulties necessitated a wholesale cancellation of orders placed with Japanese shipbuilders. As 1987 dawned, average losses in the region of 15 per cent on all new-building contracts summed up the parlous state of the industry. Mitsui Engineering and Ship-building (MES) recorded losses of Y3.34 billion in the 1986 fiscal year, compared with Y2.8 billion in the previous year; the net loss of KHI climbed to Y15.56 billion from Y3.65 billion in fiscal 1985; IHI suffered a turnaround in fortunes, registering a net loss of Y21.27 billion rather than the net income of Y4.75 billion listed for the preceding year; while Sasebo Heavy Industries disclosed a net loss of Y1.38 billion in contrast to the previous year's net income of Y119 million. Clearly, loss-making new-building contracts were rebounding to undermine the entire business viability of the enterprises.

The upshot of this unsettled state of affairs was a renewed bout of rationalisation. Resolved to lay to rest once for all the oversupply

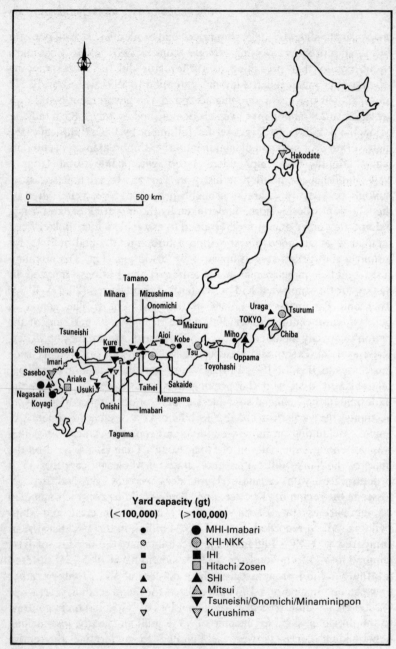

Figure 2.5 Location of Japanese shipbuilders

situation which continued to feed shipbuilders' fears – a restlessness not ameliorated by the need to keep a vigilant eye on Korean competition – the MoT lent to its intervention an air of grave and magisterial purpose. The Temporary Measures Law Concerning Operation Stabilisation of Designated Shipbuilding Industries was passed in April 1987 and enforced over the year that followed. In the first place, a cartel arrangement was imposed on the industry which set limits on the amount of capacity to be utilised. In fiscal 1988, for example, the output ceiling was fixed at 2.4 million cgrt.[41] Secondly, shipbuilders were thoroughly shaken up, with the 44 of 1987 being reorganised into eight groups. Thirdly, financial support was made available to the shipbuilders to enable them to accomplish these ends. Some Y30 billion was allowed for disposal of unneeded land and equipment while compensation worth up to Y50 billion could be tapped to cover liabilities arising from the rationalisation. The structure of the groups as they existed in mid-1989 is detailed in Table 2.8 whereas their physical spread, as etched on a map of Japan, is evident from Figure 2.5. Shake-out of the shipbuilders went hand in hand with further depletion of production capacity. Building berths and docks were cut from 73 to 47 in an exercise sufficing to chop 23.6 per cent off the 6.03 million cgrt surviving from the forerunner plan of 1978. Actual contraction thus easily exceeded the 20 per cent target, or 4.8 million cgrt, which the Ministry had thought ought to be necessary. Work-force reductions were intended accompaniments of this restructuring. One year after its inception, SAJ members could count on 30,000 permanent workers, a far cry from the 130,000 on their books in 1974, and this reduced employment base effectively capped output at 3 million cgrt notwithstanding the nominal capacity of 4.6 million cgrt. All told, yards capable of producing vessels of at least 5,000 grt saw their work-forces shrink from a total of 160,000 in 1974 to 36,000 in 1988, while employment in all shipyards regardless of size had contracted from 273,900 to about 65,000. At the group level, several yards were taken out of shipbuilding altogether and either closed or put into ship repair. For example, Nipponkai Heavy Industries (Mitsui group) and the Innoshima yard of Hitachi Zosen were converted to ship repair while Osaka Shipbuilding of the SHI group suffered a similar fate and Tohoku Shipbuilding (KHI–NKK group) was closed. In fact, the Designated Shipbuilding Enterprises Stabilisation Association bought up five redundant shipyards for Y10.7 billion in fiscal 1987. Other yards did not escape violation, being deprived of single berths or docks; while yet others were sharply cut back: Hayashikane Shipbuilding (SHI group), for instance, was shorn of two berths and prevented from building any

Table 2.8 Japanese shipbuilding groups

Builder	Capacity ('000gt)	Builder	Capacity ('000gt)
MHI–Imabari		*SHI*	
MHI Kobe	48.0	SHI Oppama	210.0
MHI Shimonoseki	19.8	SHI Uraga	16.8
MHI Nagasaki	152.0	Oshima	80.0
MHI Nagahama	11.2	Sanoyas	80.0
Imabari/Imabari	15.9		386.8
Imabari/Marugama	90.0	*Mitsui E & S*	
Koyo	75.0	MES Chiba	213.0
Miho	8.0	MES Tamano	76.3
	419.9	Shikoku	10.8
KHI–NKK			300.1
KHI Kobe	49.0	*Tsuneishi –*	
KHI Sakaide	300.0	*Onomichi –*	
NKK Tsurumi	55.0	*Minaminippon*	
NKK Tsu	154.1	Tsuneishi	121.9
	558.1	Hashihama	91.0
IHI		Onomichi	58.0
IHI Tokyo	20.0	Kanda	20.0
IHI Aioi	91.0	Minaminippon	19.9
IHI Kure	346.0	Usuki	13.0
	457.0	Kurinoura	8.2
Hitachi Zosen			332.0
HZ Ariake	250.0	*Kurushima*	
HZ Maizuru	61.0	Shin K./Onishi	97.8
Namura	80.0	Shin K./Taihei	8.7
Naikai	19.8	Sasebo HI	225.0
	410.8	Kanasashi	30.0
		Hakodate	22.0
			383.5

Source: Lloyd's List, 14 July 1989, p.8

vessel greater than 5,000 grt in the remnants of them. At all events, group formation was the signal to implement a division of labour among the remaining new-building facilities. The Hitachi Zosen group, for example, decided to assign all significant merchant work either to the parent firm's Ariake yard or to Namura Shipbuilding in Osaka, to allocate small merchant vessels to Naikai Zosen at Setoda and to consign its warship contracts to the Maizuru yard. NKK, for its part, chose to confine merchant shipbuilding to the Tsu site while the yard at Tsurumi was reserved exclusively for naval vessels and Shimizu was given over to ship repair.

Government insistence on the group structure not only effected a massive concentration in the industry, but it altered the relative importance of some of the builders. This is exemplified through the experiences of Kurushima Dockyard and Tsuneishi Shipbuilding.[42] With a total capacity of 383,500 gt (Table 2.8), the Kurushima group rivalled SHI (386,800 gt) in size and was almost treading on the heels of the smallest of the big four; namely, Hitachi Zosen (410,800 gt). Less impressive in size, the Tsuneishi-centred group was, with some 332,000 gt of newbuilding capacity, still placed ahead of MES, a longstanding major which mustered 300,100 gt. Under its dynamic president, Hsiao Tsubouchi, the Kurushima organisation had manoeuvred the MoT into acceding to its growth via an increase in the tonnage limit privileges of Hakodate Dock. In return for guaranteeing the continuance of an ailing yard in the unemployment-hit community of Hakodate in an equally depressed Hokkaido, the MoT had overruled SAJ objections to Tsubouchi's expansion plans for Hakodate Dock (although, to be sure, this company was drastically reducing its new-building presence at its alternative Hokkaido location, Muroran). As a result of this stratagem, Kurushima accounted for no less than one-fifth of Japanese shipbuilding output by 1985. It had overreached itself, however, and was soon plunged into bankruptcy. A bail-out fashioned by five banks restored the company to a semblance of its former glory, albeit now with a bank delegate as its president and a name amended to Shin Kurushima Dockyard Company. Undeterred by its uncongenial experiences, the reorganised firm was to press ahead with shipbuilding operations in Onishi and Taihei on its own account, while controlling a number of other shipbuilders dotted around Japan, most notably Sasebo Heavy Industries. The group had not managed to avert fresh difficulties, however, since one of its number, Kanasashi Zosensho, was declared bankrupt in 1988.[43] Moreover, at the end of 1989 Hakodate Dock voiced an intention to extricate itself from the group: an exercise not liable to mitigate Kurushima's difficulties. The events surrounding the surge in Tsuneishi's fortunes were less momentous, but perhaps more rewarding for the enterprises concerned. When combined with Onomichi Dockyard and Minaminippon Zosen, the group containing Tsuneishi Shipbuilding had production assets amounting to 13.1 per cent of Japan's and 5.3 per cent of the world's shipbuilding capacity. Ensconced in the Inland Sea industrial belt, Tsuneishi and Onomichi appropriated most of the new-building functions of the group, claiming a costs structure 15–20 per cent better than majors such as MHI and 5–10 per cent better than the competition in South Korea. Extensive use of subcontracted labour (1,000 out of 1,713 workers at Tsuneishi in 1988), lower wages than those obtaining with the majors and lower R&D costs to boot, all contrived to confirm the group's presence as a force to be reckoned with. The revival in ship sales was so encouraging, indeed, as to induce Tsuneishi Shipbuilding into opening a new 33,000 cgrt-capacity building dock at Tsuneishi. Its partner, Onomichi Dockyard, expanded a berth at Onomichi from 88,359 cgrt capacity to 97,988 cgrt capacity at the same time.

To be sure, the majors also felt conditions were sufficiently auspicious to seek MoT approval for capacity expansions in 1989. Buoyed by the rise in ship prices that was occasioned both by the industry-wide capacity restraint and the move towards more even relations between Japanese and Korean builders, IHI announced that it wished to bolster the capacity of its Tokyo No.1 berth from 15,000 grt to 22,600 grt and thereby allow the facility to handle passenger vessels and 'Freedom 32' standard bulkers. This intention was all the more remarkable as the berth had previously been dedicated to warship construction. While admittedly only a small step in the opposite direction from that taken by the majors since 1978, this modest expansion plan complemented the same firm's preparation of its Kure shipyard for a return to large-vessel construction, and heralded the formulation of plans of similar scope on the part of other shipbuilders.[44] For the first time in three years, IHI conceded that it felt able to pay a dividend to its shareholders on the strength of a pre-tax profit of Y12.9 billion earned for the fiscal year ending in March 1988. With the exception of Hitachi Zosen, the other majors could take hope from similar indicators of a reversal in their sagging fortunes. Ship sales at KHI, for example, rose 30.2 per cent on the previous year to reach Y52.4 billion in March 1988, while those at SHI were lofted upwards by as much as 46.5 per cent to attain Y41.8 billion. Pre-tax profits of Y13.7 billion were recorded by KHI, an about-face on losses of Y6.3 billion in the previous year; whereas SHI's pre-tax profits of Y2.4 billion was a welcome change-over from losses of Y1.4 billion recorded in the preceding period.[45] The 10 per cent appreciation of the Won, in conjunction with wage increases bordering on 20 per cent, drastically pared down the Korean competitive edge in ship prices during 1987 and 1988 and, in consequence, go a long way towards explaining the resurgence of Japanese sales. By the end of 1988, break-even costs for constructing a medium-sized VLCC were estimated at $67 million for South Korea, $75 million for Japan and of the order of $75–90 million for Western Europe. Allowing a slight differential in acknowledgement of superior Japanese quality, the bids proffered to shipowners by Japan's builders were converging on those tendered by the Koreans. The Japanese triumphed in terms of parsimonious and efficient use of manpower – the famed 'kanri' system

– and were far superior to the Koreans on the score of computerised design and manufacturing (CAD/CAM), to say nothing of just-in-time parts scheduling, superb quality control and punctuality in ship deliveries. When all is taken into account, the situation obtaining for Japanese builders was far from reassuring, however. Whereas cargo vessel prices had risen substantially from a low of Y173,000 per ton in early 1987 to Y194,000 per ton in early 1989, the revised price still fell short by a considerable margin of the SAJ-estimated break-even price of Y240,000. For a handy-sized bulker, that shortfall translated into a loss to the builder of at least $6 million.[46] In other words, the industry in Japan – despite significant shrinkage and remodelling – was still bedevilled by problems preventing ready viability. Beset by comparable difficulties, shipbuilding in the Western AICs underwent its own, albeit fragmented, rationalisation and has emerged far smaller and scarred with a demeanour much less optimistic than its Japanese counterpart. It is to the Western experience that we now direct our comments.

REACTIONS IN WESTERN SHIPBUILDING

To tell how matters stood in Western European shipbuilding in the mid-1970s one can do no better than point to the aggregate share of world output appropriated by its producers. While Japan luxuriated in a 49.7 per cent share of world ship completions in 1975, the Western Europeans had to make do with a 36.3 per cent share. That proportion had suffered a decline by 1978, to 32.8 per cent; but so too had Japan's, which had sank to 34.7 per cent. However, while the latter's picked up immediately afterwards, to equal 49.6 per cent in 1981, the Western European share continued to dwindle, and managed no better than 22.2 per cent in 1981.[47] By then, of course, disquiet was rampant throughout Western shipbuilding circles and AWES was voicing great alarm at the deterioration in European competitiveness. Notwithstanding its mobilisation of political support, AWES watched helplessly as the situation continued to worsen. Of the 15.2 million gt of shipping on order around the world in 1984, the members of AWES were able to garner just 13.9 per cent of the market whereas Japan cornered 55.4 per cent. One celebrated firm of shipping consultants had the temerity to forecast that the Western European share of global output in 1990–4 would settle at 8 per cent, leaving Japan with 40 per cent and South Korea with 20 per cent.[48] The virtual collapse of shipbuilding industries in individual countries appeared to bear out the gloomy prognosis. In 1975, for example, West Germany was responsible for 7.3 per cent of world ship completions; a percentage which fell to 4.2 per cent in 1981 and 3 per

cent in 1985, but rallied to 4.8 per cent in 1988. Since the Federal
Republic must be credited the most successful of the long-standing
European producers, its record was not matched by the other traditional
shipbuilding nations. Corresponding figures for Spain are 4.7, 4.6, 3.1
and 1.5, while those for France are 3.4, 3.0, 1.1 and 0.7 and the percentages applying to the UK are 3.4, 1.3, 1.0 and 0.6. Worst of all,
Sweden's respectable share of 6.4 per cent in 1975 dipped to 2.7 per cent
in 1981 and then almost expired, with the industry accounting for a mere
1.1 per cent in 1985 and a minuscule 0.2 per cent in 1988. Employment
ebbed in line with waning market shares. The work-force in the West
German industry, for example, dropped by 19,200 or 41 per cent
between 1975 and 1982; that of Sweden declined by 15,700 or fully two-
thirds; while employment in the Netherlands, Belgium and Denmark
withered in each case by about one-third. Japan's work-force was also
pruned during this period (recall Figure 2.2), but the 37 per cent
shrinkage undergone between 1975 and 1982 was substantially less in
relative terms than that endured by either Sweden or West Germany and
only a mite worse than the contractions enforced elsewhere in Europe.

Institutional counteraction

As a blatant example of a languishing industry, shipbuilding after the
mid-1970s provoked official concern and wide-ranging government
intervention. Public interference was already endemic to the European
industry, of course, but its plight was now of such enormous dimensions
as to prompt anew a spate of support measures. At the supranational
scale, attempts were made both to restore order to a situation verging
on incessant disorder and to provide a cushion of price supports so as to
retain at least a vestige of business viability. Previous endeavours by the
OECD to limit competition between producers on the basis of credit
concessions and government subsidies were very obviously now
honoured more in the breach than in the observance, and the onus of
attention shifted to the European Community.[49] The EEC took up the
gauntlet with alacrity, choosing to fight on behalf of its shipbuilding
charges on two fronts. The first was aimed at co-ordinating an orderly
marketing agreement with the main threat, Japan, and the accent was
placed on ship pricing and bilateral capacity reductions in order to bring
it about. The second was concerned with divining a way to harmonise
competition and industrial restructuring among the European producers themselves. This second front achieved more concrete results than
the first. Manifested in the Fourth Shipbuilding Directive of the
Commission of the European Communities which appeared in 1978 and

overturned previous injunctions echoing the exhortations of the OECD, the EEC agreed to the provision of crisis aid by European governments provided that the aid was allied with capacity withdrawal.[50] Acknowledging prevailing national subsidy schemes, the Directive set a ceiling on aid of 30 per cent of ship end costs. Simultaneously, the Commission appealed to the industry to delete 46 per cent of its capacity and 50,000 of its workers. Its entreaties to the Japanese, seeking relief from the fierce competition emanating from that country's yards, were generally rebuffed. The attempt to share the pains of retrenchment with the Japanese were hardly more rewarding. Truth to tell, the Japanese pressed ahead with capacity removal – as can be educed from the foregoing account – but this was not accomplished in parallel with European cutbacks and, consequently, failed to mollify EEC uneasiness. The succeeding Fifth Directive of 1981 professed that a further 30 per cent reduction in capacity was warranted and advocated what in the event proved to be an abortive scrap-and-build scheme. The Sixth Directive, which superseded it in 1987, began the aid abatement process by dropping the ceiling a notch to 28 per cent and, in 1989, by easing it down to 26 per cent.[51] These upper limits were arrived at after a comparison of average production costs in EEC yards and preponderant world ship prices was undertaken: the ceilings, in short, faithfully reflected the cost differential between Western European shipbuilders and competitive Asian producers after due allowance was made for the latter's ability to take advantage of veiled government support. A combination of factors – wage rises and currency appreciation in the Far East along with productivity improvements and cheaper steel inputs in the EEC – persuaded the Commission to cautiously lower the ceilings as the 1980s progressed. In spite of this glimmer of improvement, however, the Commission persisted with its view that the Western European industry would need to undergo yet more slimming during the four-year span of the Sixth Directive. Figures of one-third of remaining capacity and 40 per cent of the remaining work-force were bruited abroad.

Within the loose framework of the Directives, national governments operated a legion of industry-specific policies. They included exemptions and rebates of taxes, R&D support and domestic and export credit schemes, as well as direct production subsidies.[52] By one account, the aggregation of direct subsidies to yards and shipowners together with interest subsidies to both of them, resulted in a total subventions package which amounted to about 24 per cent of the ship price of a West German-built vessel for the home market in 1981. The comparable figure for France was much higher, estimated at 57 per cent; while Spain

(50 per cent), Italy (41 per cent) and the UK (39 per cent) were all significantly higher than the German comprehensive subsidy level. Italy was interesting in that it discriminated between regions in disbursing aid. Thus, yards were generally eligible for direct subsidies of up to 25 per cent of ship contract prices, but those hailing from the depressed Mezzogiorno region could rely on direct subsidies of 30 per cent. While not made so explicit, regional concerns have still managed to exercise other governments into favouring certain shipyards. A celebrated 1983 incident in Denmark, for example, exposed the government predilection to take up the cudgels on behalf of a troubled yard in a district with a fragile employment base. In this instance it granted a contract for railway ferries to Nakskov Skibsvaerft, a builder sited in job-scarce Nakskov on the island of Lolland, rather than to the builder tendering the lowest bid, Lindö in Odense (although, in the event, Nakskov closed in 1987).[53] Most conspicuously, however, state commitment was expressed through state ownership of production assets. On occasion, the state nationalised shipbuilders preparatory to restructuring them. Wholesale nationalisations of the bulk of the British and Swedish industries occurred in 1977. Government incursions in West Germany, in contrast, were piecemeal: HDW, for example, was controlled by the Salzgitter state steel undertaking (with the residual 25 per cent held by the Land of Schleswig–Holstein) while the Bremen Land was a minority shareholder in Bremer Vulkan. In fact, the Länder of Schleswig–Holstein, Niedersachsen, Bremen and Hamburg were particularly prominent in agitating for shipyard restructuring. Pointing to a 40 per cent erosion in the shipbuilding work-force between 1976 and 1986 (reducing the level to 44,000), they successfully negotiated Federal transfer payments of DM350 million to cover shipyard labour redundancy expenses and DM500 million to subsidise the creation of replacement jobs for displaced workers. They were also instrumental in forcing the enterprises to countenance reorganisations which rested on mergers and the removal of surplus plant. Schleswig–Holstein, for example, mediated in apportioning capacity cuts among yards located in eight of its communities: Kiel (HDW and Paul Lindenau), Lübeck (Flender Werft and O&K), Rendsburg (Werft Nobiskrug and Krögerwerft), Flensburg (Flensburger Schiffbau), Husum (Husumer Schiffswerft), Wewelspleth (Schiffswerft Hugo Peters), Lauenburg (Hitzler) and Büsum (Büsumer Werft).[54]

The outlook for state acquisition in France, meanwhile, was more favourable owing to the industry's long history of dependence on demand which either was directly conjured up by the government to occupy the yards or was indirectly fostered through state manipulation of private shipping markets. In 1981 the Compagnie Générale d'Electricité was nationalised outright, and one of its subsidiaries, Alsthom–Atlantique, fell right into government hands. With it came a significant marine engineering presence and a major shipyard, Chantiers de l'Atlantique in Saint Nazaire.[55] From this base the government imposed an industrial reorganisation. Two groups were formed in a bail-out engineered in 1983 which was to oversee a reduction in capacity of 30 per cent together with the shedding of 5,000 jobs. The first group, anchored on Alsthom–Atlantique, also embraced Dubigeon Normandie in Nantes. The second group, ostensibly independent, was an amalgamation of the Empain–Schneider yards in Dunkirk and La Ciotat with the CNIM yard at La Seyne (see Glossary). Styled NORMED, the group was in reality a ward of the state by virtue of the Schneider interest succumbing to the state Banque de Paris et des Pays Bas, to say nothing of the 15 per cent stake held by the Usinor state steel company. Despite government aid, NORMED was doomed to failure in 1986. Its last remnant, the La Ciotat yard, was earmarked for closure in 1989 in the face of intense worker opposition. This yard, more noteworthy than most, had pioneered the construction of LPG carriers in 1955 and, for many years thereafter, had thrived on their subsequent adoption. As late as 1978 it employed 6,200 workers, but that total had eroded to 3,700 in 1981 and, with the demise of new building in 1989, the outlook appeared bleak for what remained of the shipyard workforce: ship repair, it was calculated, would gainfully occupy no more than 200 or 300 of them. In effect, restructuring catapulted the remnants of French shipbuilding into the arms of the state in the 1980s, with the indirect control of earlier years being replaced by overt control.

Smacking of state control by stealth, the restructuring of the industry in the Netherlands was brought about by the failure of a major builder. The impending demise of a large part of the industry attendant upon the downfall of the RSV Group left the state with no choice but to intervene in order to pick up the pieces. Founded in 1971, RSV combined several longstanding yards with wide-ranging assets and capabilities. Grossly overextended at the time of the energy crisis, it lingered on and attempted to recoup its fortunes, only to succumb to bankruptcy at the end of 1982 despite the best efforts of the government. Throughout its existence, the organisation had benefited from the extension of credits to finance exports, the advancing of subsidies to underpin capacity expansion and the granting of naval contracts partly to occupy that new and renewed capacity. In return for this support the government had amassed a 46 per cent holding in the group, but neither demand manipulation nor the complexion of the shareholding availed to save the firm in the end.[56] Ironically, costs associated with phasing out the supertanker building yards of Nederlandse Droogdok in Amsterdam, Verolme Botlek in Rozenburg and Rotterdamse Droogdok (RDM) in Rotterdam had contributed more than a little to the alarming deterioration of RSV's financial position. The government bail-out, instituted after the original organisation had been consigned to oblivion, restored 12,000 of the 17,000 jobs and reconstituted several yards as separate entities. Bereft of significant merchant shipbuilding, the survivors pinned their hopes on naval work. In regulating naval contracts, the government continued to assume ultimate control over the yards' destinies. The temporary nationalisation in all but name of Burmeister and Wain (B&W) in Denmark during 1979 and 1980 bears comparison with the Dutch experience, although the Copenhagen yard avoided the fate of RSV and was resuscitated as a viable constructor of large merchant vessels.[57] Defying the predictions of its detractors, the rehabilitated firm recorded profits of DKr31.7 million in 1987 and DKr81.5 million in 1988.

Wholesale state acquisitions in Sweden and the UK succeeded all too well in rationalising capacity but, in so doing, virtually rationalised the shipbuilding industry out of existence. The process was taken farthest in the former. The Swedes had experience of state bail-outs prior to the massive nationalisation experiment. In 1971 government action staved off collapse at Götaverken and in 1975 the looming dissolution of Eriksberg (despite that firm's earlier rationalisation expedient which required the excision of its Lindholmen yard) forced the state's hand once again. In the immediate aftermath of the shipbuilding crisis, the state effectively controlled Eriksberg and Götaverken as well as Uddevallavarvet which had been jointly rescued by the government and Eriksberg as long ago as 1963. The establishment of a more far-reaching state shipbuilding organisation, Svenska Varv, was merely the logical progression of the bail-out imperative. Swedyards (i.e. Svenska Varv) lost SKr2.242 billion in its first year and SKr2.149 billion in 1978 in spite of the admirable labour productivity displayed by Swedish shipyards. As Table 2.9 reveals, their ratio of cgrt of output per worker topped that of Japan by a margin of 17 per cent (interestingly, almost an exact inverse of the situation prevailing in the 1960s), exceeded that of West Germany by 41 per cent, and was superior to British productivity by a whopping factor of 3.67! Sadly, high productivity could not defray other expenses and Swedish prices, in consequence, were pitched one-quarter higher than those prevailing in East Asia. Götaverken Arendal, for example, was building 155,000 dwt tankers for stock (subsequently to be auctioned) in lieu of constructing them for buyers, whereas Kockums

Table 2.9 Shipyard productivity, 1977

Country	Average number of shipyard workers in new building	Output (million cgrt)	Cgrt per worker
Sweden	16,200	0.89	55
Japan	160,000	7.44	47
West Germany	33,000	1.30	39
Denmark	11,000	0.42	38
France	26,400	0.69	26
Italy	20,400	0.39	19
Britain	45,000	0.66	15

Source: OECD and AWES estimates reported in *Fairplay*, 24 August 1978, p.61

was attracting orders only through the desperate ruse of offering ships at prices well below market rates. Fading demand for tankers in conjunction with finances perilously near to insolvency convinced Swedyards of the urgent need to delete capacity. Yards both within and without the group were grossly over-stretched in view of their vanishing financial reserves. Eriksberg, once employing 6,000, but by 1978 reduced to employing 1,500 completing a pair of 400,000 dwt ULCCs, was designated for closure in 1979. Kockums, a pioneer VLCC builder, disclosed at the same time that it would prune its labour force of 5,300 by one-fifth. Kalmar Varv, with losses of SKr500 million staring it in the face, let it be known that it was on the verge of collapse with 300 workers surplus to requirements. With no relief in sight, losses continued to mount at Swedyards, recording SKr867 million in 1979 and SKr1.461 billion in 1980. Nor were they assuaged by the belated decision of Kockums to join the state group, since this last major independent builder registered losses of about SKr550 million in the year preceding its integration in 1980. Deprived of any real choice, Swedyards initiated a plan to decimate the work-force while simultaneously jettisoning capacity. In the event, it cut manning levels from the 17,800 employed at the beginning of 1981 to 12,000 by 1984. As for capacity retirement, the Öresund and Sölvesborg yards were earmarked for closure whereas the Finnboda facility in Stockholm was slated for conversion entirely to ship repair at the cost of 200 of its 400 jobs. Closures did not end there, however. Table 2.10 offers an abbreviated account of the extinction of large merchant new-building yards in the country by the end of the decade. The situation obtaining at Kockums offers vivid testimony to the despair felt at the likelihood of ever restoring their viability. In the nine years after 1977 the yard sold its new buildings at an average price

Table 2.10 Swedish capacity cuts

Yard	Closure	Maximum ship size (dwt)	Employment	
			1975	1984
Eriksberg	1979	500,000	5,000	–
Öresundsvarvet	1983	130,000	3,300	–
Uddevallavarvet	1986	800,000	3,400	2,000
Finnboda[1]	1983	18,000	400	200
Sölvesborg	1983	8,000	300	–
Götaverken Arendal[2]	–	230,000	7,000	3,000
Kockums[3]	1988	600,000	5,300	3,000

Notes: 1. Survives in ship repair
2. Converted to offshore functions
3. Remains involved in naval construction

fully 20 per cent below cost and, of the 145 vessels at issue, no fewer than 40 per cent were repossessed by the state owing to their purchasers defaulting on payments.[58] At the end of the day, Celsius Industries (as Swedyards was renamed in 1987) found its activities restricted to naval work through its Karlskronavarvet and Kockums facilities (the latter a much reduced entity following its withdrawal from merchant new building). It was indulging in a spot of privatisation, returning the Finnboda ship repair yard to private ownership in December 1988.

While in equally despairing straits in the later 1970s, the UK industry was of a markedly different stamp from that of Sweden. Rather than consisting of a relatively small number of yards, mostly large and blessed with high labour productivity, the UK industry was constituted from an appreciably larger number of generally smaller yards burdened with low labour productivity. Its nationalisation was partly invested with an ideological hue; one which reflected that state orchestrated divisions of labour among the yards and a central design and marketing organisation could be forthcoming with a semblance of revival. It did not take long, though, for British Shipbuilders (BS) to be disabused of any hopes on that score. A dearth of orders had, by the early 1980s, turned the holding action into a rout. At the beginning of 1983, four of its major merchant ship new-building yards (Austin and Pickersgill, Sunderland Shipbuilders, Govan Shipbuilders and Smith's Dock) were working through their backlog with no fresh orders in sight, five yards of the small-shipbuilding division (Hall Russell, Ferguson–Ailsa, Goole Shipbuilding, Clelands and Henry Robb) were in an even worse state with scarcely any backlog left to keep them active, the two dedicated offshore yards (Scott Lithgow and Cammell Laird) were also fast running out of work, while the Kincaid branch of the engine division was but weeks away from completing all its workload.[59] Only the diversified yards, by now dealing almost entirely with defence contracts, elicited any uplifting signs in what was otherwise a prospect of unremitting gloom. Some 9,000 of the corporation's 64,500 workers were dismissed at this time in line with the run-down of activity. By 1984, BS had contrived to cut its original work-force by 25,000, but was still urgently casting around for other targets for deletion. A radical plan was mooted which called for a reduction in the establishment from 48,000 to 15,000. That labour reduction was to be aligned with the elimination of up to 40 per cent of merchant new-building capacity and the retirement of all warship-building capacity. This last expedient was to be accomplished through the privatisation of diversified yards which sought a future as independent entities competing with one another for the limited number of naval contracts available. Already, BS had elected to scrap most of its ship repair yards and it subsequently decided to abandon offshore activities as well. The two yards in question were released to the private sector: Scott Lithgow succumbing to Trafalgar House (who later closed it) and Cammell Laird to VSEL (who returned it to naval work). Starting in 1985, the corporation sold Yarrow, VSEL, Vosper Thornycroft and Swan Hunter to principals determined to survive on the strength of warship and other specialised new building. The smaller yards for the most part were closed outright. These measures, however drastic, scarcely dented the downward trend in the corporation's fortunes. For example, in 1985 BS garnered just 23,000 tonnes of new orders, barely one-tenth of the amount needed to attain a break-even point. By then the die was cast and the corporation had no choice but to extend the rationalisation process. New building was concentrated on the Govan yard in Glasgow and the newly constituted NESL (which lumped together Austin and Pickersgill and Sunderland Shipbuilders) in Sunderland. The last remaining major yard outside this hard core, Smith's Dock at Middlesbrough, was shut at this time and, along with it, went one of the last two engine building sites, the Wallsend works of Clark Kincaid, and the small Ferguson–Ailsa shipyard at Troon (although, hoping to restore shipbuilding, this last was purchased by the Perth Corporation).[60] Table 2.11 divulges the extent of the retreat from merchant new building. The writing was now on the wall for BS, for even the few surviving facilities were apt to incur losses. Despite £18 million invested in new plant, for example, Govan Shipbuilders still managed to record a loss in 1984 of £12.8 million. Two years later, its trading loss amounted to £13.9 million on a turnover of £36.6 million; a situation which deteriorated to a loss of £31.4 million on a turnover of a mere

Table 2.11 BS capacity cuts

Site	Merchant new-building capacity (dwt)	
	1977	1989
Ailsa, Troon	13,000	–
Appledore Shipbuilders	21,000	21,000
Austin & Pickersgill, Sunderland	75,000	–
Brooke Marine, Lowestoft	16,400	naval
Robb Caledon, Leith	23,750	–
Cammell Laird, Birkenhead	345,000	naval
Clelands, Wallsend	95,000	–
Ferguson, Port Glasgow	5,000	5,000
Goole Shipbuilding	18,600	–
Grangemouth Dockyard	5,000	–
Govan Shipbuilders	175,000	175,000
Hall Russell, Aberdeen	6,500	6,500
Scott Lithgow, Clyde	600,000	–
Smith's Dock, Middlesbrough	80,000	–
Sunderland Shipbuilders	258,000	–
Swan Hunter, Tyne	1,353,000	naval
VSEL, Barrow	350,000	naval
Vosper Thornycroft, Southampton	naval	naval
Yarrow, Clyde	naval	naval

£22.1 million in 1987.[61] NESL, for its part, was driven out of business as a result of the foundering of a major contract to build ferries. Not to be outdone, the two-yard Appledore–Ferguson subsidiary at Appledore in Devon and Port Glasgow on the Clyde succeeded in recording losses of £13.4 million in 1988 while the relic of the engine building division, Clark Kincaid in Greenock, lost £4 million during the same period. By this stage, the current of political opinion was running decidedly against BS, and politicians openly declared their lack of sympathy for its endeavours. The House of Commons empowered the UK Government to raise the ceiling of subsidies earmarked for BS to £1.7 billion provided that the corporation took steps to dissolve itself. Politicians, roundly critical of BS, arrived at the startling figure of £24,000 per year as the cost to the taxpayer of sustaining each of the corporation's residual 6,261 employees.[62] Abiding by the injunction to wind up operations, BS disposed of the Govan yard to Kvaerner for £6 million and was generally successful in restoring its other facilities to private-sector interests within the marine industries. Attempts to turn NESL over to the private sector failed, however, when the government rejected plans to reactivate Sunderland as a shipbuilding centre.[63] Apart from bowing to European Commission pressure to curtail shipbuilding overcapacity, the episode also signalled government willingness to tolerate severe localised unemployment as a regrettable consequence of refraining from rescuing NESL. The loss of 2,000 shipyard jobs in a community plagued with job shortages was not the full extent of the distress: some 500 jobs in local supplier firms and a further 3,500 in related service activities either disappeared with the extinction of the shipbuilder or were placed in jeopardy following the sharp drop in income circulation. Alternative work in incipient activities outside the sector were more in the nature of optimistic projections than concrete reality.[64]

Qualified revival

Government tutelage has not invariably led to the virtual demise of merchant shipbuilding. Elsewhere in Europe, state control of the industry has been tantamount to the furnishing of more persistent capacity safeguards and, dare one say it, to the provision of conditions which have repaid their sponsors through rebounding activity levels which offer the promise – if no more – of eventual profitability. Spain and Italy are cases in point. As intimated in the previous chapter, the lion's share of Spain's new-building operations are undertaken by three state enterprises, Astano, Bazan and, more particularly, AESA; this last being especially organised to tackle the Spanish onslaught on the VLCC market in the halcyon days of shipbuilding. Guided by the Division de Construccion Naval, the overseeing body for the yards, the government resolved that as much capacity as possible should ride out the storm of shipbuilding recession. In part, it was convinced of the justness of its cause as an adjunct of its sensitivity to the quandary facing local communities dependent on shipbuilding. This difficulty was brought home to it during the episode occasioned by the conversion of the Euskalduna yard at Bilbao from new building to ship repair. Entailing the loss of 1,500 jobs in the politically charged Basque region, the event caused such a stir among local workers as to provide the government with much food for thought. A chastened government appeared distinctly reluctant to impose future capacity curbs through wholesale yard closures. The government, instead, preferred to stoke up demand, offering incentives to Spanish shipowners to purchase domestically supplied tonnage, as well as presenting the yards with a huge veiled subsidy as it continued without demur to absorb their mounting losses.[65] A kernel of seven new-building yards were to be preserved at virtually all costs; namely, Vigo, Gijon, Santander, Sestao (Bilbao) and Desierto de Erandio in the North and Seville and Puerto Real in the South. In spite of such good intentions, production slipped steadily into a downward spiral for the best part of a decade from the late 1970s. The 1977 output of 1.1 million cgrt, for instance, dropped almost unremittingly to 0.25 million cgrt in 1986, with only a slight upswing in 1982 and 1983 to relieve the declining trend. To make matters worse, Spain's adherence to the EEC meant that its shipbuilding industry could not avoid contributing its share to the Community-wide capacity reduction programme on the one hand, while acceding to the Commission's more rigid industrial assistance terms as laid down in the Sixth Directive on the other. In respect of the latter, a transition period was granted to Spain until 1991, after which its aid must be compatible with that made available by other EEC producers. While not bound by the 26 per cent subsidy ceiling during the interim period, Spanish yards, none the less, must demonstrate not only that they are competing fairly on ship pricing, but also that they are taking steps to eradicate excess capacity. Compelled to initiate systematic restructuring at the urging of the EEC, the government proposed to compensate the yards to the tune of Ptas107.188 billion; an amount judged excessive by the European Commission.[66] The Olaveaga (Bilbao) and Cadiz yards of AESA were diverted to ship repair while the El Ferrol yard of Astano (a former VLCC builder once noted for owning the largest building berth in Europe) was switched entirely to offshore work. In the meantime, the Spanish Minister of Industry promised that, by 1990, the country's new-building capacity would be scaled back to a level just 60–5 per cent of the total extant in 1985 and, correspondingly, the employment base, which stood at 40,000 in 1980, would be whittled down to 18,500 by the end of the decade. His government's sagacious mix of subsidy and productivity enhancement was evidently paying off in so far as new building was concerned. AESA, for example, reported a surge in orders during 1988 which, in totalling 840,000 grt, amounted to a weight of impending activity sufficient to boost Spain to the second-ranking producer in Europe and the fifth in the world (recollect Figure 2.4). As, the country's principal shipbuilder, they could boast an 80 per cent capacity utilisation rate and a restructuring plan well on the way to completion (involving the shedding of 4,000 of the remaining 14,500 jobs and the stabilisation of capacity at 400,000 cgrt). While in truth a long way from profitability, AESA was openly contemplating the cessation of loss-making by 1991. A preoccupation with series building was proffered as partial substantiation of this view. The construction of nine 140,000 dwt tankers at Puerto Real and nine reefers jointly at Seville and Puerto Real would trigger learning economies of sufficient magnitude to shorten the 750,000 man hours of work on the first tanker to 650,000 by the last of the series, whereas man-hour cuts of the order of 12–15 per cent would occur in the progression from the first to the fourth of the reefers. The realisation of production economies on this scale would not only serve to diminish yard insolvency, but would invest the yards with a degree of competitiveness verging on East Asian levels.

Although starting from different antecedents, Italy's state ship-building has ploughed a similar furrow to that of Spain. The disparate state yards, accumulated over the years through periodic bail-outs, were thoroughly reorganised in 1984 and placed under the aegis of a monolithic state enterprise: Fincantieri–Cantieri Navali Italiani (hereafter known simply as Fincantieri).[67] Established round four divisions – merchant shipbuilding, naval shipbuilding, ship repairing and marine-engine building – Fincantieri imposed a division of labour among its facilities reminiscent of the one ordained by BS. Head-quartered in Trieste, the merchant shipbuilding division embraced the neighbouring Monfalcone yard, together with yards in Ancona, Castellammare di Stabia, Genoa (Genova Sestri), Livorno and Venezia Marghera. As with other European consolidated undertakings, Fincantieri failed to register any profits; in 1985, for instance, losses equalled L89 billion whereas in the following year they registered L59 billion and in 1987 reverted to L89 billion once again. Enjoined by the government to stem the losses and return the group to profitability, Fincantieri embarked on a restructuring plan from 1987. Dismissing the option of outright yard closures, it promised to shave 4,000 jobs from the work-force of 22,000 through natural wastage, early retirement and incentive schemes.[68] The achievement of a break-even status for the group was provisionally set for 1990. Such aspirations rested on parallel government schemes to drum up demand. In addition to the usual EEC subsidies afforded to Fincantieri, the government had stimulated demand through a shipping aid package. Under its terms, Italian shipowners were eligible for interest subsidies on domestically ordered tonnage. Up to half of the ship price could be covered by one or other form of subsidy. The potency of the scheme is incontrovertible: the order book of 89,640 dwt pre-vailing at the beginning of 1985, for example, was bolstered to 807,600 dwt one year later as a consequence of this package. The order windfall is also credited with saving the Genova Sestri yard from extinction at the end of 1985. A vestige of the shipping promotion package survives, as witness the circumstances pertaining to a 70,000 grt cruise liner building at the Monfalcone yard in 1989. The owners were not only entitled to the regular subsidies advanced under the Commission's Directive, but were in receipt of an extra subsidy – reputedly worth in the region of 15 to 17 per cent of the ship price – granted on the strength of the vessel's Italian registry and crewing. Supplementary to such demand stimulus, the state's own shipping organisation, Finmare, has on occasion directly intervened in the market to boost flagging shipyard business. The last spree, undertaken during 1987, allocated large sums for a fleet renewal programme which would occupy shipbuilding capacity through to 1991. Naturally, the state shipbuilder was the principal beneficiary of this initiative. Finmare companies, for instance, accounted for 54 per cent of the Fincantieri merchant new-building workload in January 1989; that is to say, 449,000 dwt of the 830,100 dwt in question.

SUMMARY

Rationalisation and cutbacks were the stuff of shipbuilding in the AICs after 1975. Japan, the dominant player, instituted a fundamental overhaul of its industry in the late 1970s and discovered that, notwithstanding the efficacy of this action, another restructuring was called for within a decade. The pressing need to redress the situation in the second half of the 1980s arose out of the gravity of the insolvency crisis afflicting Japanese shipbuilders; a crisis occasioned both by the continuing depression in shipping markets and, consistent with the tenets of industry life-cycle theory, the emergence of heightened competition from new shipbuilding industries, especially those in East Asia. Threatening circumstances were the catalyst for an out-and-out revamping of the industry's organisation, resulting, at government connivance, in its consolidation round eight groups. The Western Europeans, denied the comparative advantages enjoyed by the Japanese, were obliged to conduct their own painful rationalisation programmes while confronting unrelenting competition from this quarter and the rising NICs. All producers throughout the AICs had to enforce measures aimed at overstepping the obstacles littering the road to redemption. Japan saw its capacity drop substantially, and shed both plant and workers with apparent abandon. Cutbacks proceeded with comparable prodigality in Western Europe. Attempts to mitigate the worst excesses brought on by closures were subverted and then swept away by abysmal market conditions. The traditional producers of the UK, France and the Netherlands were compelled to accept the reduction of merchant new building to a scarcely discernible rump while the postwar parvenu, Sweden, deliberately turned its back on the industry altogether. Even West Germany, vested with a widely acknowledged engineering expertise on the one hand and a determination to remain a significant ship producer on the other, was unable to prevent capacity deletion in the decade and more following the first energy crisis. The 100 or so builders operating in the mid-1970s were transformed, as a result of closures and mergers, into a collection of 30 during these years. All governments resorted to hoisting the levels of subsidies, both direct and indirect, veiled or ostentatiously and truculently admitted. Yet, subsidies alone did not make for profitable business. The chairman of Bremer Vulkan, commenting on his firm's 1987 losses of DM168 million, blamed the long history of loss-making on corporate strategies designed to garner contracts which, while doomed from the outset never to bring profits, did suffice to bring work, prevent plant wastage and preclude the dissolution of experienced work-forces.[69] Unsaid but equally material, the ability to procure contracts, albeit wanting in terms of profitability, served to frustrate any move on the part of the shareholders which was meditated with the object of extricating the enterprise from shipbuilding.

A glint of light at the end of the tunnel appeared to beckon shipbuilders in 1988 and 1989, however. Thanks to rising ship prices, in part triggered by the amelioration of the gross oversupply situation in shipbuilding and partly owing to a modest uplift in shipping markets, some shipbuilders could actually point to restored profitability – a number of the Japanese groups being prominent on this score – while very many more could hold out hopes of becoming profitable. Attaching its consent to the builders' view that revival is at hand, the government allowed production ceilings to lapse in Japan during the latter part of 1989 (although officials were taking pains to assure the maritime world that effective capacity would be held at about 3 million cgrt).[70] However, the reawakening of dormant ambitions is not exclusively a Japanese phenomenon. A few instances from Western Europe spotlight this turnaround. In 1988, for example, a Dutch trampship operator, Spliethoff's Bevrachtingskantoor, ordered six 10,000 dwt vessels in the Netherlands for DFl180 million; an event breaking a 14-year spell during which the owner patronised Japan's Miho Zosensho. The shipowner cited as deciding factors the favourable prices (providing savings of DFl30 million in comparison with the Japanese alternative) and the ability to make use of a new $16 million covered shipyard at Harlingen belonging to Tille Scheepsbouw.[71] Another Dutch firm, Wilton Fijenoord, a one-time member of RSV and the inheritor of its former VLCC yard of Verolme Botlek (now devoted to ship repair), returned to profitability in 1988 and earned a tidy net income of DFl24.1 million.[72] In neighbouring West Germany, the Bremer Vulkan organisation slashed its losses to DM90 million in 1988 and was promising at least break-even figures for subsequent years. As if on cue, a bevy of Norwegian enterprises, consigned to ship repair for much of the 1980s, signalled their intention to re-enter new building and gave it to be understood that they considered the risks of so doing to be negligible.[73] Yet, one must be wary of undue optimism. The fact remains that Western European profitability, if and when it becomes paramount, will be inordinately indebted to state underpinning. In short, its incidence is firmly dependent on the continued provision of subsidies, and this is as true of the West German industry as it is of the others. According to estimates furnished by the Shipbuilding Council of America, the shipbuilders of West Germany received direct subsidies worth at least $1.1 billion between 1975 and 1987 and were earmarked to receive a further $370 million in such aids through to 1991. These subsidies allowed the yards to clinch orders – in one case investigated by the European Commission in 1989, for example, the HDW yard was alleged to be tempting Zim Israel Navigation with subsidies amounting to 30 per cent of the contract price for container vessels – and account in large measure for the resurgence of the West German order book.[74] It is sobering to reflect that without such props the yards would have their work cut out deflecting NIC and Japanese competition. To hammer that point home, one need look no further than to a recent new-building contract struck between a West German shipowner and a South Korean shipbuilder. Spurning a domestic builder because its unit price quoted for a batch of four container ships was DM80 million, the shipowner chose the Korean alternative on the basis of deliveries beginning in 1990 for DM53 million apiece.[75] Stripped of its niceties, this outcome speaks for the current predicament confronting Western shipbuilders. In short, when the gloves are off, as it were, and European and Asian shipbuilders resort to a straight fight for shipowners' business, all the signs continue to suggest that the former will be bested by the latter.

3 Industrial reorganisation and the enterprise

Peter Drucker is generally credited with delimiting concisely and comprehensively the goals that motivate corporate managements. These goals rest on the basic notion of enterprise survival and stress such aims as profitability, innovation, market standing and social responsibility.[1] In auspicious times, growth is the corporate watchword; inauspicious occasions, in their turn, are greeted with sombre appeals to belt tightening and retrenchment. The accent placed on the different goals varies according to the state of the economic environment, but beyond dispute is the fact that the mix of goals is constantly dedicated to safeguarding the survival of the corporation. Such goals are evidently as relevant to shipbuilding enterprises as to any other corporation, although their relative importance may diverge from the current preoccupations of other members of the corporate sector. For example, there was considerable heart-searching by shipyard managers at the social consequences of unemployment arising from cutbacks in the later 1970s. Other industries, spared both the depth of cuts and the extreme localisation of labour pools that were commonplace among shipbuilders, could afford to pay comparatively less attention to this issue. Again, the trend towards public ownership in shipbuilding during the 1970s – in part a legacy of its geographical concentration in unemployment blackspots – forced shipbuilding managers to be alive to the goal of social responsibility. This issue was touched on in the previous chapter where it was seen to lurk behind the reasons for piecemeal bail-outs of individual shipbuilders in a number of countries (to wit, Sasebo Heavy Industries and Nakskov Skibsvaerft, to give but two examples) and, indeed, may be held accountable for much of the inclination to indulge in wholesale nationalisation in other countries which had tried fragmentary bail-outs and found them wanting. The formation of BS in the UK, for instance, was justified on the grounds of preserving an industry, but nevertheless served to protect some of the more spatially isolated builders caught up in its net. Thus, in allocating orders among the yards to keep up activity levels, BS contrived to save the Troon yard from certain closure for an extended period and, in so doing, provided an uplift for the job-scarce Ayrshire district of Scotland. Moreover, when left with no choice but to close yards, the state enterprise may undertake to shepherd alternative activities to the moribund sites so as to absorb the surplus labour. Sweden's government, for example, ensured that regional investment grants were sufficiently generous to induce car makers Volvo and Saab–Scania to erect plants on former shipyard premises at Uddevalla and Malmö after Celsius Industries could find no further use for them.[2]

As was made abundantly clear in the last chapter, however, some goals must ultimately give way to others, and in shipbuilding the goal of profitability eventually usurped social responsibility for prime place: in other words, even the state was reluctantly obliged to withdraw support from perpetual loss-makers in the face of bitter work-force hostility. By the same token, the goal of innovation has of late been belittled by shipbuilders distracted by more immediate concerns of day-to-day survival. Besides, as befits their status of mature firms in a mature industry, many shipbuilders were already inclined to downgrade innovation. Only a clutch of prescient builders have persevered with R&D, appreciating that it is the well-spring of their future power within the market. A few examples speak for all. In Japan, MHI and IHI have devised the contra-rotating propeller, KHI has delved into screwless propulsion, while the industry as a whole has funded investigations into 'intelligent' ships equipped with robots and electronic control systems. In West Germany and elsewhere, builders have conceived 'ship of the future' projects which bring together a number of incremental innovations with the object of producing vessels which optimise ship operating costs through reduced manning, greater automation and more fuel-efficient propulsion.[3] Yet, common to all shipbuilders, not excepting Japanese and German ones, has been an acute awareness of harsh market circumstances, continuing with scarcely any relief since the mid-1970s, and the ensuing unremitting pressure on sales has given them all cause seriously to consider their future roles within the industry. This hostile economic environment has conspired to focus the minds of managements on one all-important goal; namely, that of profitability. Its absence, quite simply, calls in question the very survival of the enterprise in any prolonged period of faltering demand. Understandably, then, the obsession with profitability infuses the subject matter of this chapter, an attempt to grapple with changing industrial organisations against a background marked out by the enterprises themselves as being both deleterious to their existing interests and discouraging in respect of their future plans.

Striving for profitability during periods of business downturns can lead to two, seemingly opposing, corporate responses. On the one hand, firms can opt for rationalisation whereby total capacity is adjusted downwards in conformity with attenuated demand. In practice, this choice requires that surplus plant and labour are shed because the firm believes that the savings made through containing overhead costs are such as to outweigh any advantages incurred in retaining spare capacity while keeping a labour force waiting in the wings for better times. Short-term savings, in effect, are judged to be more important than the long-term ability to rapidly regain market share when rebounding business arises out of an eventual upswing in demand. On the other hand, firms can confront the adverse circumstances head-on, so to speak, and engage in strategies of 'extensive growth'; that is, they can duplicate their existing production processes by adding capacity and capturing a greater share of the market at a time when their competitors are preoccupied with rationalisation and, hence, indisposed to put up a stirring fight.[4] By concentrating on current technology and eschewing innovation, the expansionist enterprise evades the costly 'diversion' into R&D and, in consequence, can field more resources for meeting the object of capacity enlargement. Rather than resort to the expensive and time consuming act of creating new plant, this latter ploy can be more expeditiously achieved through acquisition of other enterprises or, in what amounts to the same thing, through the merger of like-minded enterprises. In times of recession, smaller firms may easily fall prey to larger aggressive companies, while their bigger counterparts may not be averse to take-over and merger overtures if they should foresee decline and bankruptcy as the most likely alternative outcomes for themselves. The first strategy, therefore, is a manifestation of partial withdrawal from the industry whereas the second is tantamount to horizontal integration.

Complicating the decision-making is the protracted stage of maturity within which shipbuilding enterprises find themselves; a complication, in fact, which may transform an outcome of partial withdrawal into one resulting in total disengagement from the industry. Divorced from a life-cycle perspective, a firm would rationally choose to scrap a plant, or indeed abandon the industry altogether, only when it determined that the plant or group of plants was no longer able to yield any surplus (profits) over operating costs. Premature closure would deny the firm any surpluses that the plant or group of plants might have earned, while delayed closure would merely exacerbate losses: so, evidently, timing of capacity adjustment is a critical factor. Given the gravity of the decision, firms would err on the side of caution and refrain from hasty decisions to suppress plant on the understanding that trade revival in due course would be bound to restore plant utilisation and profitability with it. However, real firms function within a dynamic matrix encapsulated through their industry life-cycle. In view of shipbuilding's long occupancy of the mature stage of its life-cycle, individual firms cannot afford to treat the business environment in the manner just outlined; that is, with a degree of equanimity and composure which turns on the assumption that demand will inevitably pick up and expresses itself through a reluctance to dispose of capacity. On the contrary, they must presume that fresh competitors will emerge even in a depressed market if for no other reason than ineffectual technical barriers to entry may pose as a lure to draw them into it. The chances that the firm's market will ever be restored to past glories granted such a scenario are exceedingly remote indeed. One only need reaffirm the characteristics of firms rooted in maturity to underscore the point.[5]

> A mature industry is one in which an earlier uncertainty has been re-placed by a stability in core concepts, a stability that permits process technology to be embodied in capital equipment or in engineering personnel and purchased in the marketplace. By this line of reasoning, the fundamental characteristics of a mature industry are the sta-bility of its technology and the ease with which it can be copied.

A combination of minimal technical barriers to entry and factor-cost advantages such as cheaper labour can induce new-firm formation which inevitably rebounds to haunt incumbent firms, diminishing the prospects of profitability which may have been entertained by them. Not to put too fine a point on it, overcapacity occasioned by ready entry of new firms could indefinitely prolong the loss-making environment within which extant producers are labouring. Even an eventual upturn in the trade cycle might not suffice to break the logjam of oversupply and so do little to allay the postponement of the return to profitability. Given such an admixture of shifting competitive conditions, incumbent mature firms are apt to be less sanguine about long-term prospects and therefore prone to scrap plant in the short term. Government sub-ventions or bail-outs might serve to deter them from carrying out these courses of action, but in their absence the propensity should be for the withdrawal of capacity. As was made crystal clear in the last chapter, removal of institutional supports in both Sweden and the UK led to headlong closure of plants, and the pattern was repeated on a smaller scale in France. Of course, if the firm is in a position to rely on corporate partners imbued with long-term visions, inured to intermittent episodes of loss-making and, more importantly, invested with a wealth of resources that can be called upon to sustain non-profitable activities in the meantime, the survival of the firm cannot be gainsaid. This last set of circumstances is particularly applicable to Japanese shipbuilders (although the same holds true for their peers in South Korea) and will receive due attention in the pages that follow. Moreover, if the firms have recently undergone a period of expansion – as Japanese builders did in the early 1970s and NIC emulators thereafter – the instinctive reaction of managements is likely to veer towards delaying capacity retirement. This predisposition to plant retention by comparatively new ship-builders is reinforced, of course, by the knowledge that cross-subsidies from other corporate affiliates may be available to tide the builder over spells of insolvency. Before venturing into the realms of Japanese industrial affiliations, however, it is necessary to address the issue of plant closure and its most arresting aspect, that of complete enterprise abandonment of the industry. Subsequently, it becomes expedient to deal with the broader question of horizontal integration and the forms of industrial organisation compatible with its accomplishment.

CAPACITY SUPPRESSION AND ENTERPRISE WITHDRAWAL

Somewhat perversely perhaps for a section dedicated to shipyard extinction, the following commentary starts on the note of parvenu shipbuilders. Yet, the verve and competition injected into the global ship market by these newcomers added precisely that ingredient needed to goad the world's crop of fading and jaded shipbuilders into action; an action, more often than not, made manifest through yard closures. Beleaguered on all sides by thrusting neophytes, many dispirited managements in the AICs felt that profitability would continue to elude them until some unacceptably distant time, pushed even further beyond reach with the consummation of every new-entry shipbuilder, and therefore they came at length to the conclusion that the industry was not worth persevering with. Others, slightly more bullish, elected to cut their losses and retain but a foothold in shipbuilding. The appearance of Malta Shipbuilding, doubtless, was perceived as one such nail in the coffin for established hard-pressed builders. Bequeathed with a ship-repair industry from the days when the island functioned as a major British naval base, the government decided to supplement the repair activity of Malta Drydocks (which, incidentally, requires subsidies amounting to 25–8 per cent of contract prices to attract business) with new building, and established a yard at Marsa equipped with a 120,000 dwt-capacity building dock to that end.[6] Employing 2,000 workers, the yard was engrossed for much of the 1980s constructing a series of 7,700 dwt timber carriers-cum-container vessels for the USSR. Plagued with teething troubles, Malta Shipbuilding relied on a Polish design – the ships are improved versions of the B352 class turned out by the Gdansk yard – and Polish equipment supply, including the main engines which are made in Gdansk. A loss-maker in debt to the government for $70 million, the yard nevertheless is acquiring hard-won experience and is sedulous in canvassing for other work requiring series production methods. It thus looms as a further competitor to AIC yards actively chasing those most desirable of new-building contracts, batch orders. Across the Mediterranean, Turkey is also a recent legatee of Soviet beneficence. Possessing a motley collection of small, generally poorly endowed yards, this country's industry has survived on the strength of domestic demand drummed up by government machinations and sustained by public subsidy. The slashing of that subsidy in the mid-1980s had dire repercussions for the yards, unused to the export market and, by all accounts, unable to bear comparison with best-practice shipbuilders elsewhere. Fortunately, AKP Sovcomflot stepped into the breach, placing orders for at least two dozen 4,000 dwt timber carriers with the Sedef Gemi yard.[7] This transaction, which caused considerable surprise in the rest of the shipbuilding world, acted at any rate as an augury of better times for the country's shipbuilders. The only builder to penetrate the export market prior to Sedef's coup was the state-owned Turkish Shipbuilding Industry's Pendik yard which had booked a contract for three 26,300 dwt bulkers from Poland, and this was joined in short order by the Madenci Gemi yard which logged a contract for four 5,700 dwt multipurpose cargo vessels from UK principals. Indeed, so much optimism infused Turkish shipbuilding that a shipowner, Um Denizcilik, proclaimed its intention in 1989 to found a new shipyard to produce 150,000 dwt tankers (the firm had previously declared an interest in purchasing H&W in Northern Ireland). Of course, these tentative beginnings pale in comparison with the rise of the NICs in the 1970s. As Figure 3.1 dramatically displays, both Brazil and South Korea began making major inroads during that decade. Divided into order-book totals and annual completions, the graphs distil the great strengths of these two producers, revealing their substantial impact on a global sector already saddled with severe overcapacity.[8] Giant strides were made by South Korea, with completions jumping

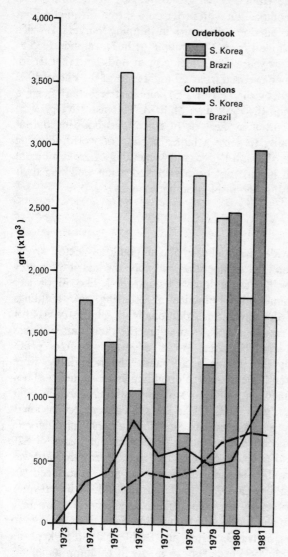

Figure 3.1 NIC producer persistence

from the minuscule 14,000 grt of 1973 to the respectable 814,000 grt of 1976: a trend which, after a temporary relapse, resumed its climb to reach 932,000 grt by 1981. Less impressive, to be sure, Brazil's growth was still appreciable, managing to more than double between 1975 and

1981 with an increase from 295,000 grt to 715,000 grt. Completions make an interesting comparison with order books. In a disquieting but accurate reflection of the global downturn in shipping markets, Brazil's order book steadily slipped from 3.57 million grt in December 1975 to 1.66 million grt some six years later. Decidedly at odds with that trend, South Korea's order book soared from 1.3 million grt at the end of 1973 to almost 3 million grt by the end of 1981, albeit after experiencing a hiatus in growth during the dark days of 1978. This assertive growth, both in augmenting output in the case of Brazil and boosting output together with the ability to seize a larger portion of world shipping orders in the instance of South Korea, was something of great moment to AIC builders, and it must not be overlooked when weighing their decisions to reorganise in the fashion outlined below.

The US special case

The US industry provides a model case of a shipbuilding sector largely cocooned from international competition, but none the less at the mercy of the global trade cycle because domestic shipowners, like shipowners everywhere, discontinued their practice of ordering new buildings during the tenure of the downturn. Additionally, this industry was for the most part run by conglomerates as an adjunct to their main business interests. As such, its managers were alive to diverse profit opportunities outside the marine sector and, understandably, were perhaps only indifferently wedded to shipbuilding in consequence. They exhibited little sentiment in pulling out of shipbuilding when, in their opinion, circumstances warranted it. The Sun Oil concern, for instance, determined in 1981 to phase out its Sun Shipbuilding subsidiary in Chester, Pennsylvania, after announcing that persistent losses of $20 million per year would no longer be tolerated. In the event, the yard was bought by the Capital Marine Corporation and resurfaced as Pennsylvania Shipbuilding in 1982, albeit shorn of half of its previous 4,000-strong work-force. By the same token, conglomerates are in a position to recognise the merits of shipbuilding operations relative to other, less-deserving activities. After all, Bethlehem Steel kept its Sparrows Point yard in 1986 even though it saw fit to dump its metals distributing, plastics and building products and reinforcing-bar operations.[9] Truth to tell, though, shipbuilding generally performs poorly in comparison with most other sectors which, in glaring contrast, parade higher profit margins before the investors of the world. Accordingly, it has been among the first to suffer at the hands of managers charged with corporate clipping.

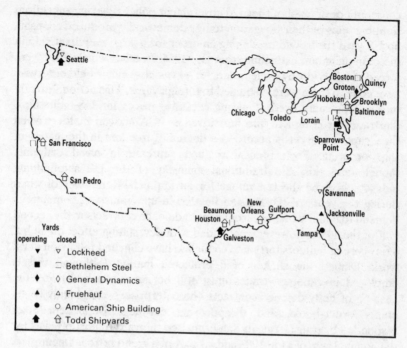

Figure 3.2 The demise of US multiplant builders

Figure 3.2 offers an insight into effects of corporate boardroom decisions taken with the object of scrapping redundant capacity. While two shipbuilding groups, Todd Shipyards and American Ship Building, are prominent exponents of rationalisation, the other multiplant operators, members of conglomerates to a man, displayed an equal or greater keenness to dissolve superfluous shipbuilding capacity. It would not be exaggerating to claim that, notwithstanding their alternative sources of income and latent potential to cross-subsidise new building, the conglomerates led the van in the wholesale repudiation of shipbuilding in the USA. Some 55 yards closed during the decade following 1978 and with them went 60,000 jobs. Besides, 14 shipbuilders continued in operation solely at the discretion of the bankruptcy courts after seeking the respite afforded by Chapter 11 protection. For many years, the shipbuilders could take solace from legislation which secured for them captive orders from shipping lines benefiting from the Operating Differential Subsidies granted by the government. That cosy relationship was scotched, however, with the passage of the Shipping Act of 1984.[10] As a consequence of an about-face in government policy relieving subsidised shipping lines of their obligation to buy domestically produced tonnage, no US yard succeeded in winning an order for a large merchant ship in the quinquennium extending from late 1984. In other words, they were forced to stand idly by while orders for 44 vessels which would otherwise have gone to them were disbursed to foreign yards. This action, brought on by shipowners tired of paying excessive prices for US-built ships, illustrates the complete uncompetitiveness of American builders when their captive market is accorded a degree of freedom in the matter of ship ordering. Protectionism reigned supreme in naval ordering, though, and this, the traditional mainstay of the US shipbuilding industry, became the last refuge for an appreciable number of yards during the years of the Reagan fleet build-up. Vanishing commercial demand together with the curtailment of defence contracts in the second half of the 1980s, however, rebounded with devastating effect on all but a tiny core of builders fortunate enough to have clinched follow-on naval work. Denied the shelter of a protected market (although vessels employed in cabotage trades must still be American built) and the cushion of hefty defence contracts, the enterprises were doubly hit by empty order-books and disappearing earnings. Bethlehem Steel responded by transferring its San Francisco shipyard to port officials for the nominal sum of $1 in 1983 and, as part of a grand retrenchment plan, excised its ship-repair sites at Baltimore, Boston and Hoboken. Closure of its Beaumont yard in August 1988 (reactivated by Trinity Industries in 1989) left Sparrows Point as its sole US new-building site. For its part, General Dynamics forsook its Quincy yard in favour of concentrating on submarine construction at Groton. Lockheed, another large defence contractor, deleted its Seattle complex; a facility registering losses in 1986 of $3.4 million.[11] A profitable venture manufacturing military landing craft at yards in Gulfport and Savannah was retained, however. Of the pure builders, Todd underwent the greatest shrinkage. Consigned to Chapter 11 bankruptcy in 1987 after disclosing a loss of $46.8 million for the previous year, the firm wallowed in the doldrums during the next two years, recording losses of $20.5 million in 1987 and $84.8 million in 1988. Banking on its prosperous Aro pneumatic-equipment manufacturing subsidiary and a duo of ship-repair facilities in Seattle and Galveston, the company was forced to shut down its last remaining new-building yard in September 1989. This, the San Pedro yard in Los Angeles, had sustained no less than 6,000 workers on naval contracts until well into 1983, but had become a costly embarrassment with the termination of that work.[12] The American Ship Building Company, which combined the Nashville Bridge Company's barge-building sites at Nashville and Ashland City in Tennessee with shipyards on the Great Lakes and in Florida, actually registered a profit of $3.2 million in 1986, although in truth this evident well-being derived more from the proceeds realised from the sale of the Lorain yard in Ohio than from shipbuilding proper. Stark reality overtook the firm in 1987 when, devoid of new-building contracts, it registered losses of $8.9 million.[13] The fact that the firm's last new buildings (five naval oilers erected at Tampa because of size limitations at the other yards) relied on parts fabricated at Lorain and Nashville prior to being towed to Florida speaks for the complexities involved in running multiplant operations. The need to transport the ships' main engines from even further afield – IHI in Japan – adds a new dimension to the spatial division of labour which circumstances forced on US shipbuilders.

Conglomerate retrenchment

Examples of large conglomerates withdrawing from shipbuilding in other parts of the world are somewhat scarce owing to the relative paucity of such business organisations outside the USA in the first place and, perhaps, because of the less vulnerable nature of non-American shipbuilding in the second.[14] One example which comes readily to mind, however, is that offered by Fried Krupp GmbH. Presented with a choice of persisting with a parlous shipyard operation or regrouping around other activities, the West German industrial concern opted for the latter course. Rather than continuing the fruitless pursuit of 'pouring good money after bad', it made the decision to extricate itself from shipbuilding so as to redirect assets to the machinery and plant-building sectors while, simultaneously, reserving sufficient resources for its mainstream steelmaking activities. As a result, the new-building arm, AG Weser in Bremen, was shut down in 1986 while the ship-repair arm, Seebeckwerft in Bremerhaven, was sold to Bremer Vulkan for incorporation into that firm's ship-repair division.[15] Valmet is another major industrial entity which tried in vain to transform its shipbuilding arm into a stable, profitable enterprise only to reverse its commitment and intimate that shipbuilding was expendable. It differed from the German concern, however, in being a state enterprise. As a forestry machinery to aerospace group, Valmet had seemingly profited from risking VLCC construction at a time when large-vessel new building was disdained by the rest of the Finnish shipbuilding industry. Indeed, it had found the capital necessary to lay out a new shipyard in Helsinki during the late 1970s: an investment strikingly at variance with shipbuilding cutbacks prevalent elsewhere in Europe, but not at odds with Finnish practice (for Wärtsilä had just completed its Perno yard and Navire was opening its Naantali yard).[16] In common with other Finnish builders, Valmet relied on the USSR for about 60 per cent of its workload; in the event, an over-dependence with troubling implications. When that market began to falter, so too did Valmet's interest in shipbuilding begin to recede. Finally, in 1986 the state firm transferred its Helsinki, Turku (Laivateollisuus) and Kotka shipyards to a newly minted organisation, Wärtsilä Marine Industries; whereupon they were assimilated into the Helsinki, Turku and Kotka yards of Oy Wärtsilä. Valmet retained a 30 per cent stake in the new company, with Oy Wärtsilä holding the balance of the shares and, along with them, control of shipbuilding, ship repair and marine-engine production. A parallel undertaking absorbed the paper machinery interests of these two firms, although in this case – and sealing Valmet's new orientation – the state enterprise assumed control and held 65 per cent of the shares.[17] For its part, Wärtsilä Marine was instructed to eliminate surplus capacity and reduce its work-force from 10,000 to 6,000. A loss of $51.2 million for fiscal 1987 spurred the process, and concrete signs of retrenchment included the Laivate-ollisuus new-building yard and the Kotka repair yard, both speedily axed. Unfortunately, losses were not stemmed by these actions, and in early 1989 the principal shareholder, Oy Wärtsilä, announced its intention of divesting from Wärtsilä Marine. Alarmed at the impending demise of this, the largest shipbuilder in Finland, the government intervened to effect a bail-out. Evidently, the residual responsibility attaching to Valmet's minority stake in Wärtsilä Marine was sufficient cause to initiate the government rescue operation. Despite this attempt to avert collapse, the shipbuilder formally declared itself bankrupt in late 1989 and was fulfilling its remaining obligations under the title of Masa Yards.

Yard closures

Krupp and Valmet, of course, were not alone in expressing a desire to quit the industry in the 1980s. A number of non-conglomerate shipbuilders, some of them single-yard undertakings, gave up the struggle to persevere with shipbuilding, and the instancing here of a select few will do justice to them all. The Rickmers Werft yard in Bremerhaven, for example, was closed (although its ship-repair operations were passed to Bremer Vulkan) while fellow West German yard Nobiskrug in Rendsburg also abandoned new building in favour of ship repair (reappearing as HDW Nobiskrug). Elsinore Shipbuilding in Denmark forswore new building for ship repair while Nakskov Skibsvaerft was wound-up; Horten Verft and Moss Rosenberg Verft in

Norway elected to give up new building, Trosik Verksted was liquidated and Anterlokken Floro declared bankrupt. The NORMED group in France went into liquidation while, in the same country, the Ateliers et Chantiers de la Manche suffered the ignominy of collapse and Dubigeon Normandie was merged into Chantiers de l'Atlantique and deprived of its Nantes shipyard. In Ireland, the Verolme Cork Dockyard was placed in receivership whereas Portugal's biggest yard, Lisnave, was shorn of its new-building function.

Suppression of entire shipyards catches the imagination because of the sheer magnitude of the dislocations which may thus be engendered, but in relative terms it is rare to 'find that scrapping and replacement decisions refer to whole plants; rather, the majority of such decisions deal with individual machines within plants'.[18] Transcribed for a shipyard context, this observation implies that managements will be much more disposed to scrap some berths and docks (especially where they can be 'mothballed' for eventual reactivation if need be) in any given yard while maintaining others in the same premises. Granted, this expedient tends to push up yard overhead costs, but it promises to restore the firm's market position in the first flowering of trade upswings and this prospect alone might outweigh the short-term benefits of exorcising unwanted facilities. Besides, the reserve capacity consists in the main of lumpy plant that is neither subject to rapid obsolescence nor easily replaced. This cautionary response not only preserves capacity for more auspicious occasions, but it suffices to safeguard a core of seasoned workers, again not easily recreated once dispersed. The wide-ranging actions of Japanese builders in sparing many yards while stripping them of excess construction facilities, both permanently and temporarily, was remarked upon in the last chapter, and a comparable process was widely practised in Europe at the same time. In the former instance, this practice was particularly prevalent among the major shipbuilders; that is, those enjoying membership of conglomerates, the modern-day zaibatsu. In view of the evident importance of these business organisations to the well-being of some of the world's pre-eminent shipyards, a digression delving into the substance of their operations is appropriate at this juncture.

EAST ASIAN CONGLOMERATES

Militarism and labour exploitation were only two of the many pernicious outcomes imputed to the traditional zaibatsu and, in deference to this checkered past, they were recast in modern times in a manner that purportedly placed them alongside US-style conglomerates and large industrial holding companies. Yet they continue to differ appreciably from their Western counterparts and it is misleading to suppose that they are one and the same thing. Their roots extend back to the early days of the Meiji Restoration when the old-established Mitsui and Sumitomo family trading enterprises assumed the trappings of Western corporate entities and adopted, at the behest of the government, responsibility for developing new lines of manufacturing. One of them, however, originated in a manner decidedly analogous to the incipient US corporations then being built by self-made entrepreneurs. The individual in question, Iwasaki Yataro, launched a shipping line connecting Tokyo with Osaka and Shikoku in 1870 which became the foundation stone for Mitsubishi. After alternating between support and penalty, the government ordered the line to merge into NYK in 1885; whereupon the Mitsubishi concern directed its energies into mining, banking and shipbuilding. Yataro was aided in this last course by the government's sale to him of the Nagasaki shipyard in 1881; an action preceded by the privatisation of the Ishikawajima shipyard (the precursor of IHI) in 1876 and repeated in 1887 with the transfer of the Hyogo yard to Kawasaki Shozo, the ancestor of KHI.[19] By the early years of this century, Mitsui, Sumitomo and Mitsubishi were firmly established holding companies with control vested in their core founding families. Besides displaying an aptitude for trading and its maritime offshoots, these organisations were especially prone to invest in producer goods of which shipbuilding was a paramount example. Together with Yasuda, the trio accounted for one-quarter of all paid-in capital and incorporated business in Japan by the onset of the Second World War. Formally dismembered at the conclusion of that war, the zaibatsu were quickly reassembled after revisions in the Antimonopoly Law, accomplished in 1949 and 1953, empowered them to do so. Significantly, though, they were reconstituted with banks as their centre-pieces rather than family-owned holding companies.[20] Indeed, several new bank-centred groups emerged at this time to vie with the originals; that is to say, the Fuyo or Fuji (in fact, the successor to the pre-war Yasuda zaibatsu), DKB, Sanwa, Tokai and IBJ groups. Stressing 'keiretsu' or vertical linkages between group companies on the one hand and 'kigyo shudan' or horizontal linkages on the other, the new-style zaibatsu soon eclipsed their 1945 predecessors in size and global market power. Unlike their forebears, however, they no longer function as centrally controlled conglomerates but participate in a loose structure in which the practising of mutual shareholding serves as the effective binding. An element of uniformity of direction is imposed through the Council of Presidents, a body to which all group members delegate managers. Such has been the dynamism and growth of Japanese industry that several concerns, previously devoid of group leanings, have grown to the stature necessary to generate groups of their own. Nippon Steel, Hitachi, Nissan, Toyota, Matsushita and Toshiba–IHI all fall into this category and, in so doing, rival both the original zaibatsu and the postwar bank-centred groups in dominating the Japanese economy.

Many of the contemporary zaibatsu are serious contenders in global shipbuilding: in fact, the seven major Japanese builders are all embedded in larger groups. As can be elicited from Table 3.1, the three original groups lay claim to MHI, MES and SHI. The bank-formed Fuyo, DKB and Sanwa each control a leading builder; respectively, NKK, KHI and Hitachi Zosen. The remaining major, IHI, is a principal constituent of the Toshiba–IHI industrial group. Nor is that all, for

Table 3.1 Maritime affiliates of zaibatsu

Group	Shipbuilding	Shipping	Ocean development
Mitsubishi	MHI	Nippon Yusen Tokyo Senpaku Kaisha Shinwa KK Taiheiyo Kaiun Co.	
Mitsui	MES	Shinyei SS Co. Fuji KK Inui Shipping Co. MOL*	(Mitsui Ocean (Devel. & (Engineering
Sumitomo	SHI Sanoyasu Dockyard	Nihonkai SS Co. Daiichi Chuo KK MOL* Kansai SS Co.	(Sumitomo (Ocean Devel. & (Engineering
Fuyo	NKK Hakodate Dock	Showa Line Hinode Kisen	(Fuyo Ocean (Devel. & (Engineering
DKB	KHI Niigata Engineering	Kawasaki Kisen Iino Kaiun Kisen Ocean Transport Co.	(World Ocean (Systems
Sanwa	Hitachi Zosen Naikai Zosen Namura Shipbuilding	Y–S SS Co.	(Toyo Ocean (Devel. & (Engineering
Toshiba–IHI	IHI Ishikawajima S & C		

Note: * Control shared by two groups.
Source: Abstracted from Dodwell Marketing Consultants, *Industrial Groupings in Japan* (Tokyo, 1978)

some groups have involvement in other not inconsequential ship-builders. Sumitomo, for instance, has links with Sanoyasu Dockyard (now Sanoyas Corporation), Fuyo with Hakodate Dock, and Sanwa with both Naikai Zosen and Namura Shipbuilding.[21] The groups extol the virtues of maritime activities not merely through their shipbuilding connections but also by courtesy of their holdings in shipping and, for good measure, offshore activities too. It can be educed from the table, for instance, that they feel constrained to fulfil their trading obligations by active participation in shipping lines. Such formidable lines as Nippon Yusen (NYK), MOL, Kawasaki Kisen ('K' Line) and Y–S Line are, in their various ways, common carriers for the groups. Similarly reflective of maritime involvement, and also a manifestation of their extensive mining and metallurgical interests, several of the groups have bothered to form dedicated offshore enterprises. The groups, additionally, have done their level best to embrace as many production sectors as possible and in this respect, of course, they bear comparison with Western conglomerates. It does not behove us to examine the extent of each full-blown group, but a brief insight into that pair of them in which shipbuilding features prominently will not go amiss. To that end, Figure 3.3 presents the manifold activities of the Mitsubishi group. Central to it is MHI, one of the three leading group companies. On its own, MHI entertains subsidiaries in the automotive industry, but its status as a core member of the group grants it access to affiliates in a host of fields ranging from shipping to real estate. By one count, the Mitsubishi group has representation in 13 manufacturing sectors alone; namely, food processing, textiles, pulp and paper, chemicals, pharmaceuticals, petroleum refining, glass and cement, iron and steel, metals, machinery, electrical and electronics products, vehicles, and scientific instruments.[22] Perpetually rivalling MHI for the honours of top shipbuilder, IHI enjoys privileged links with a collection of firms spun off by electronics giant Toshiba. As is revealed in Figure 3.4, it additionally reigns over a string of subsidiaries in its own right: in metallic products, machinery and real estate, to say nothing of shipbuilding (Ishikawajima Ship and Chemical Plant). What is more, it upholds with Toshiba an interest in power engineering through the Nippon Atomic Industry subsidiary. MHI and IHI owe their origins to shipbuilding initiatives and, despite many vicissitudes in their subsequent careers, continue to identify strongly with that industry. The other groups are more diffuse, however, and shipbuilding appears to occupy but one place among many in their respective portfolios of business interests.

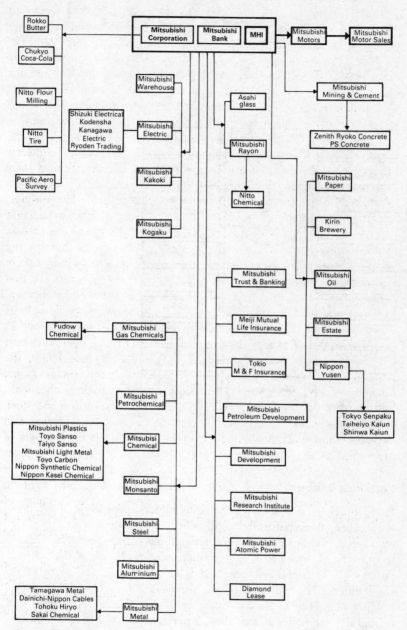

Figure 3.3 Mitsubishi group

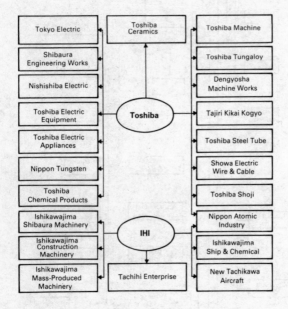

Figure 3.4 Toshiba–IHI group

Corporate linkages

Often overlooked is the fact that shipbuilders, regardless of whether they adhere to zaibatsu, frequently effect corporate linkages on their own behalf. Table 3.2 highlights shareholdings of Japanese shipbuilders in other firms drawn from the maritime sector. Of note is the relative paucity of horizontal linkages; that is to say, corporate ties between shipbuilders. The only link of any substance, in fact, is the majority holding that Hitachi Zosen retains in Naikai Zosen. Otherwise, the formal ties are paltry affairs: the 7.5 per cent stake of SHI in Sanoyas Corporation and the 3.2 per cent holding of NKK in Hakodate Dock. In

Table 3.2 Ownership links of Japanese shipbuilders

Shipbuilder owner	Shareholdings in Shipbuider (%)	Shipping/trading (%)
Hitachi Zosen	Naikai (53.2)	Ocean Transport (17.4)
		Y–S (5.9)
		Iino (2.4)
		Hinode (1.8)
IHI		Japan Line (8.5)
		Ocean Transport (3.3)
		Iino (3.2)
		Hinode (1.8)
		Nihonkai (1.0)
KHI		Kawasaki Kisen (7.3)
		Kawasho Corp. (3.3)
		Iino (2.3)
		Toa Oil (1.6)
MES		Fuji KK (14.5)
		Meiji Shipping (11.3)
		Shinyei (5.8)
		MOL (5.6)
		Inui (5.2)
		Nihonkai (1.0)
MHI		Japan Line (5.9)
		MOL (4.1)
Narasaki Shipbuilding		Narasaki Sangyo (3.7)
NKK	Hakodate (3.2)	Showa Line (5.4)
		Hinode (1.9)
Onomichi Dockyard		Shinyei (1.0)
Sanoyasu Dockyard		Kansai (1.7)
SHI	Sanoyasu (7.5)	MOL (3.3)
		Japan Line (2.9)
		Sumitomo Shoji (2.7)
		Daiichi Chuo (1.8)
Tsuneishi Shipbuilding		Fuji KK (3.4)

Source: Derived from Dodwell Marketing Consultants, *Industrial Groupings in Japan* (Tokyo, 1978)

truth, the contemporary upheaval in Japanese shipbuilding resulting in its remodelling into eight groups is likely to trigger profound changes in interfirm corporate linkages, including affirmation of ties through the swapping of shares and directors. Already the mould has been broken with the sinking of zaibatsu shipbuilding interests into the new functional groups: the KHI–NKK shipyard combine, for example, assembles a unit from DKB (i.e. KHI) with one from Fuyo (i.e. NKK).[23] Of much greater moment, at least heretofore, is the value attached by shipbuilders to shareholdings in shipping companies; a means presumably of influencing shipowner choices when it comes to deciding among suppliers for fleet additions or replacements. Five of the major builders, Hitachi Zosen, IHI, KHI, MES and SHI, have involvements in a spread of shipping firms, whereas two of them – MHI and NKK – confine their shipping incursions to just a couple of lines apiece. Interestingly, a clutch of smaller builders each find merit in sustaining a presence in a single shipping firm. There is circumstantial evidence to suggest that such linkages may be forthcoming with tangible benefits for the builders, or, to qualify that allegation, at least for the major builders. Consider MOL: a huge shipping company with attachments to MES, MHI and SHI. Of its 113 vessels either in service or on order in July 1989, some 19 per cent were supplied by MES, 14 per cent emanated from the yards of MHI and 6 per cent originated with SHI. In terms of supplier shares, a conservative benchmark of 14 per cent – a one-seventh share for each of the majors – might be expected regardless of corporate affinities; and evidently, whereas MES comfortably exceeds that percentage and MHI equals it, the same cannot be said for SHI. Seemingly, SHI's stake in the shipping line does not encourage MOL to lean disproportionately in its favour when engaging in ship procurement.[24] SHI is also disadvantaged in reference to Japan Line. Whereas fellow shareholders IHI and MHI each rejoiced in a one-fifth share of the 41 vessels operated by Japan Line in April 1989, the Sumitomo shipbuilder could only attain half that level. Corporate links are clearly no substitute for builder competitiveness in many cases: in short, they do not necessarily buy a captive market for the shipbuilder. This finding is reinforced by the situation applying to smaller builders, since a holding in the Kansei Steam Ship Company avails Sanoyas Corporation not at all when it comes to ship purchases and Tsuneishi Shipbuilding's stake in Fuji Kisen Kaisha is equally barren in fashioning orders for that shipyard. Offsetting these cases, however, are instances where ship-building-shipping links are decidedly beneficial to the first party. KHI, for example, benefited from its association with Kawasaki Kisen to the tune of a 43 per cent share of 'K' Line's July 1989 fleet of 58 vessels, NKK furnished no less than 56 per cent of Showa Line's July 1989 assemblage of 25 ships, while Hitachi Zosen provided a respectable 23 per cent of the Y–S Line fleet of 26 ships. It remains to be seen whether the recent restructuring of the shipbuilders into eight groups and further consolidation among the shipping lines (e.g. the merging of Y–S Line and Japan Line) will substantially alter the pattern of ordering.

As denizens of a former Japanese colony, South Korea's enterprises bear the imprint of the zaibatsu style of organisation. Indeed, the present-day chaebōl are often likened to the original zaibatsu in that they are controlled by entrepreneurs strategically placed to direct operations from the centre. Their main claim to distinctiveness lies in their inability to control the banks. Unlike their modern Japanese peers, the chaebōl must turn to government controlled credit institutions in order to find the bulk of their investment funds.[25] But like the pioneering Japanese entrepreneurs of a century ago, the latter-day Korean entrepreneurs adjusted their growth ambitions to coincide with the greater hankering for industrial expansion harboured by a succession of South Korean governments. Since officialdom at length came round to advocating shipbuilding as a target industry, then so too did the entrepreneurs oblige them by trespassing into that sector. Granted such a concurrence of ambitions, the fiscal means for accomplishing this task was not withheld. Three chaebōl embarked on shipbuilding with celerity once the government had made its wishes known. The three in question were Samsung, Hyundai and Daewoo. A fourth, Hanjin, was less avid in its display of enthusiasm for the sector and, indeed, was only persuaded to indulge in it after strong government representation. The scope of activities encompassed by Samsung, the largest of the chaebōl, is outlined in Table 3.3. Its shipbuilding branch, Samsung Shipbuilding (or SSHI, as it is now styled), was acquired in 1977 at government connivance and, by 1980, was reporting sales of $35.5 million which amounted to 0.96 per cent of the group total. A year later, the shipbuilding arm was basking in sales of $103.7 million and accounting for 2.03 per cent of the group total: an impressive increment in absolute terms but still answering for only a minute fraction of Samsung's overall business.[26] Thus, as with most of the zaibatsu, the significance of shipbuilding is generally overshadowed by other group activities in the chaebōl sphere. Tracing its beginnings to trade (1952), sugar (1953) and textiles (1954), Samsung had in fact come to shipbuilding late in the day in terms of its corporate evolution if not in respect of government interest in the sector. Uncomfortable at the idea of venturing into heavy industry, the group required some official prompting before sanctioning the diversification into shipbuilding. Hyundai, the second largest chaebōl, had fewer reservations about entering heavy industry in general and shipbuilding in particular. As Figure 3.5 makes clear, HHI is a pivotal element in the group. Its founder, Chung Ju Yung, began in the construction industry in 1950, consolidated his position via cement and ceramics in 1958 and motor vehicles in 1967, before plunging into shipbuilding in 1973 with the

Table 3.3 Samsung group firms

Sector	Firm
Shipbuilding	SSHI
Industrial machinery	Taesung Heavy Industries
Aerospace	Samsung Aerospace
Electronics	Samsung Electronics
	Samsung Electron Devices
	Samsung Electric Parts
	Samsung Telecommunications
Glassware	Samsung Corning
Chemicals	Samsung Petrochemical
Textiles and clothing	Cheil Wool Textile
	Cheil Synthetic Textiles
Foodstuffs	Cheil Sugar
Pulp and paper	Chonju Paper Manufacturing
Engineering	Korea Engineering
Trading	Samsung Co.
Construction	Samsung Construction
	Joong-ang Development
Publishing	Joong-ang Daily News
Retailing	Shinsegae Department Store
Insurance	Dongbang Life Insurance
	Ankuk Fire & Marine

object of creating from scratch the world's biggest shipyard: his construction arm was simultaneously learning how to build shipyards in the Middle East (ASRY). Three years later, he inaugurated a shipping line, now known as Hyundai Merchant Marine, and ensured that it acted as a good customer for his shipyard (89 per cent of the 57 vessels operated by this line in July 1989 were supplied by HHI).

A positive infant in comparison with the other two, Daewoo only emerged in 1967 as a trading company. By 1973, however, it had bought its way into textiles, insurance, construction and, most importantly from our viewpoint, heavy industry (Figure 3.6). The last acquisition, evinced in the formation of Daewoo Heavy Industries (DHI), spearheaded the establishment of Daewoo Shipbuilding (DSHM). Emulating the actions of the other groups, in turn responding to shifts in government priorities, Daewoo subsequently switched its attention to electronics (1974) and the automotive industry (1977). The last chaebōl to exhibit

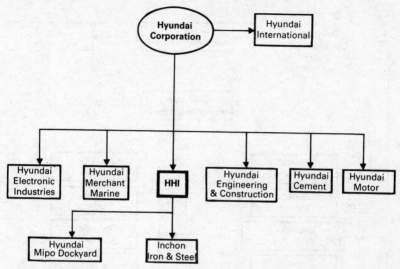

Figure 3.5 Essentials of Hyundai

leanings towards shipbuilding, Hanjin, was a transport-oriented group noted more for running the country's chief airline (Korean Air) and a container shipping line than for manufacturing aspirations. Its incursion into shipbuilding – a subject about which more will be said in later pages – was rendered feasible through the government bail-out of KSEC. Confirmed in 1989, Hanjin's penetration of the shipbuilding sector was upheld because of the affirmation of vertical integration between shipping and shipbuilding. Significantly, however, only Hyundai and Hanjin bothered to maintain shipping lines as adjuncts of their other units and, in this respect, they do not differ markedly from their Japanese confrères. The other South Korean groups have evidently discounted direct involvement in shipping, preferring to orientate their shipbuilding business to overseas markets and to the brisk custom stemming from autonomous domestic shipowning firms. This is not to say that they are dismissive of other vertical linkages: on the contrary, they cultivate robust vertical integration within the production side of the marine industries (an occurrence made conspicuously clear in succeeding chapters). In point of fact, while vertical linkages have long been held up to justify the conglomerate system in both Japan and South Korea, the possibility of achieving horizontal integration has also told heavily in its favour. The ability to link together large production units characterised by the use of 'massive

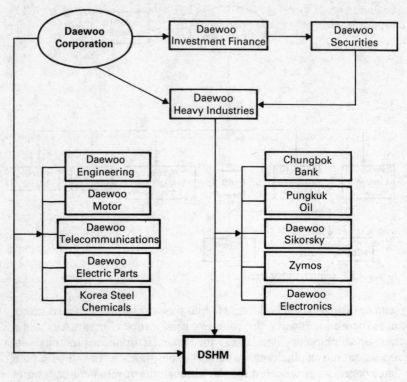

Figure 3.6 Daewoo group

capital equipment and a well-paid, permanent labour force, on the one hand, and the world of labour-intensive, small or medium units of production using cheaper labour on the other hand' is just as compelling for horizontal integration as it is for vertical integration.[27] The utilisation of ancillary workers by Japanese builders was touched upon in the last chapter and, equally endemic to the industry, is the careful discrimination among fixed plant by the builders to determine its most appropriate use. It is precisely because of this valued flexibility in apportioning plant that the leading shipbuilders in both Japan and South Korea keep shipyards of different sizes. Hitachi Zosen, for example, wields five widely different plant capacities in its four shipyards: a 19,800 gt berth at the Naikai Zosen subsidiary, a 21,000 gt berth at the Maizuru yard, a 40,400 gt dock at the same site, an 80,000 gt dock by courtesy of Namura Shipbuilding and a 250,000 gt dock at the

Ariake yard. IHI likewise sustains four increments of capacity, beginning with a 16,750 gt dock in Tokyo and progressing through a 91,000 gt berth at Aioi to, first, a 95,000 gt dock at Kure and, secondly, a 251,000 gt dock in the same premises. The newly constituted MHI–Imabari shipbuilding group is even more elaborate in its capacity gradations. Starting with the modest 8,000 gt berth available at Miho Zosensho, the capacities are adjusted upwards to harness the 11,200 gt and 15,900 gt berths retained at Nagahama and Imabari, through the 19,800 gt and 48,000 gt berths found in Shimonoseki and Kobe, to the 75,000 gt and 90,000 gt docks on hand in Mihara and Marugama, before culminating with the 152,000 gt Nagasaki dock. This range of facilities allows the group to take orders for vessels as small as 810 dwt ferries or as large as 258,000 dwt VLCCs.[28] Less profusely endowed with shipyards, the South Korean groups nevertheless have ensured that their building complexes are copiously furnished with an assortment of plant capacities. Most lavishly equipped is HHI, whose Ulsan yard boasts seven building docks and one slipway. In consequence, it was constructing in the third quarter of 1989 vessels covering the size spectrum from 3,700 dwt to 280,000 dwt. Reckoning on three building berths available at its Donghae Shipbuilding subsidiary in Ulsan as well as four docks and four berths on tap at its main Busan yard, KSEC at the same time was working on vessels occupying a spread in sizes from 4,250 dwt to 47,977 dwt but, if called upon, had sufficient capacity in hand to accommodate 150,000 dwt ships. While less institutionalised through huge group structures, the search for complementarity among different production units stamps other non-East Asian shipbuilding industries and frequently leads to formal approaches for enacting horizontal integration. This is an issue to which we now turn.

HORIZONTAL INTEGRATION

Concerted attempts at cementing horizontal integration through the blending of independent shipbuilders into a corporate whole were one facet of the first great merger frenzy in Western industrial capitalism: that which occupied the stage in the USA during the dying years of the last century and the dawning years of this century. Of the two noteworthy initiatives, one was a spectacular flop while the other was a modest success. The former, summed up through its grandiloquent title of the US Shipbuilding Corporation, was erected between 1899 and 1901 with Bethlehem Steel as a key player in its conception. Uniting Bethlehem and four other East Coast yards with the Union Iron Works in San Francisco, the new entity failed to find its feet and dissolved through bankruptcy in 1905. In recompense, most of the constituent units were restored to independent existence (one of which was Bath Iron Works), while Bethlehem emerged permanently enlarged with the addition to its corporate mantle of Union Iron Works and two other yards.[29] The second case, meanwhile, was effected through the combination in 1899 of a number of Great Lakes shipbuilders. The upshot, American Ship Building, avoided the crash and denouement of its contemporary, persisted as a builder of lakers until 1985 (latterly at Lorain) and, as related above, retains a foothold in the industry to this day. A fall-out from a benign business environment, these early US stabs at horizontal integration were echoed in the UK during the next rosy period for merchant shipbuilders, that following the First World War. At that juncture, several percipient builders judged it timely to expeditiously amass capacity. Convinced that rapid acquisition of existing yards would enable them to corner significant portions of the uplifting market, they mingled strategies of take-over with in situ additions to existing plant. The outstanding exponent of the art was the Northumberland Shipbuilding Company. Led by a band of London financiers determined to profit from the postwar boom, the firm – hitherto a modest builder of workhorse cargo vessels at Howden on Tyne – took a leaf from the book of one of its directors, Lord Furness, and chose the course of aggrandisement. This man, the scion of Christopher Furness who had built up Furness Withy and Company as a leading shipowner and shipbuilder (at Hartlepool), precipitated events by laying out a large shipyard at Haverton Hill on the Tees. Impatient at the delays incurred in creating new capacity, the Northumberland group quickly gained control of Doxford in Sunderland, Fairfield and Blythswood on the Clyde, Workman Clark in Belfast and Monmouth Shipbuilding at Chepstow, not to mention such vertically linked organisations as the Lancashire Iron and Steel Company and the Globe Shipping Company. Alas, under-financed, highly geared and singularly ill-adapted to ride out the new-building slump beginning in 1922, the Northumberland group fell from grace and ended up in receivership four years later.[30] A similar train of events overtook other consolidations of the time. One newly coined enterprise, Rennie Ritchie and Newport Shipbuilding, was formed with the express purpose of melding the capabilities of a Wivenoe yard (owned by R. Forresst) with two on the Clyde (William Chalmers of Rutherglen and Ritchie Graham and Milne of Whiteinch) and then progressing to bolster capacity with the aid of a 'greenfield' venture in Newport. The brave new group, capitalised for £500,000, was scarcely functioning, and certainly not flourishing, when it was forced into liquidation in 1922.

Other horizontal integrations were affirmed by leading shipbuilders eager to promote their hold on the market in an era of climbing demand. Emanating from the North East were initiatives put into effect by William Gray of Hartlepool, Palmers of Jarrow, Armstrong Whitworth of both Elswick and Walker and Swan Hunter of Wallsend. The first secured the Egis Shipbuilding Company in Sunderland and pressed ahead with a new yard at Graythorp on the Tees, the second bought up the Amble Ferro-Concrete Shipbuilding Company, Armstrong Whitworth snatched up the Willington Quay yard of Tyne Iron, whereas Swan Hunter welded together a combine of Grayson's of Liverpool, the North of Ireland Shipbuilding Company of Londonderry, Barclay Curle on the Clyde and Philip of Dartmouth. An outsider, J. Samuel White of Cowes, penetrated the district with its purchase of Ropner of Stockton-on-Tees. That other great fulcrum of the industry, the Clyde, was equally astir with acquisitions. H&W, the Belfast interloper, had been present since before the war (acquiring the London and Glasgow Engineering and Iron Shipbuilding Company of Govan) and enhanced its position through take-overs of Caird, Henderson, McMillan and Inglis. Lithgows, for its part, snapped up Robert Duncan, William Hamilton and Dunlop Bremner to form a lower Clyde group centred on Port Glasgow. Not to be overlooked is Vickers of Barrow which acquired Forth Shipbuilding of Alloa and the Dublin Dockyard. Almost without exception, all of these accretions were speedily retired once the bottom fell out of the market. Indeed, many shipbuilders took advantage of the National Shipbuilders Security, an anti-recession cartel formed in 1930 specifically to phase out surplus capacity, in order permanently to rid themselves of unwanted yards.[31] Intentionally or otherwise, the anti-recession cartels so popular with Japanese shipbuilders in the 1970s and 1980s bore all the hallmarks of this UK predecessor of the 1930s.

In a belated replay of this industry-wide move to horizontal integration, British shipbuilders again underwent the throes of consolidation in the second half of the 1960s. This time round, however, they were urged to merge by the government acting on the recommendation of a committee report authored by R. M. Geddes. Armed with a brief to evaluate the industry's prospects, Geddes canvassed the firms and arrived at the conclusion that, in its current form, the industry would admit of no competitive future without restructuring along the lines of horizontal integration. In effect, he was advocating the forging of external economies among geographically proximate yards, specialising in different market niches to be sure, but enjoying the mutual benefits of adherence to a group which provided centralised direction, research and marketing from a single headquarters. This proposal of regional groups was a stepping stone on the road towards nationalisation in 1977; it heralded, in addition, horizontal integration among a number of European shipbuilding enterprises. Geddes proposed that one yard in a regional group should be earmarked for sophisticated vessels such as passenger ships and warships which required extensive outfitting work and, hence, a large force of workers; another should be of sufficient size to handle large tankers and, therein, likely to be a building dock; while the rest would take care of smaller vessels. In combination, the six or so yards comprising the group would muster capacity capable of an annual throughput of about 500,000 dwt and summon the services of 8,000 to 10,000 workers to do it. Swan Hunter took up the challenge as group leader for the Tyne, receiving official blessing to acquire all other builders on that river. The resultant Swan Hunter and Tyne Shipbuilders set aside Wallsend for VLCCs and ULCCs, the Walker Navy Yard for container vessels, the Walker Neptune Yard for warships, the former Hawthorn Leslie yard at Hebburn for specialist vessels like LNG/LPG carriers and the ex-Readhead yard at South Shields for standard cargo ships. Subsequently, the Furness yard on the Tees was taken up as an adjunct tanker-building facility, while out-stations at Goole and Grangemouth dealt with coasters and other smaller types. Comparable groups emerged elsewhere: the amalgamation of Scotts and Lithgows constituted a lower Clyde axis while, on the upper reaches of the same river, John Brown, Fairfield, Yarrow, Connell and Stephen coalesced to fashion Upper Clyde Shipbuilders.[32]

It is noteworthy that Geddes disparaged vertical linkages and was dismissive of their relevance to his proposed groups, opining that the linkage chain in the UK was too inflexible and marred with inefficiencies to prosper under the auspices of unified organisations. Instead, he justified the groups on the basis of a spread of capability across all manner of yards and, thus, all possible ship markets. In short, Geddes was groping for organisations which, by dint of their dominant size advantage, would realise both technical economies of scale and pecuniary economies. A multiple-plant firm could not only achieve the former, as reflected in decreasing average costs with rising output, but should be well placed to relay pecuniary economies to its members by encouraging them to dip into a pool of accountants, planners, designers and marketing experts held in common for all of them. What is more, the group had other strings in its bow: it could 'manipulate demand and supply within the firm so that certain subsidiaries may be able to purchase inputs from one another thereby reducing excess capacity for the firm as a whole'; or, in view of its stature as a major enterprise, it could 'wrest price concessions from smaller firms' studded along its supply chain. Equally valuable, its large size would stand it in good stead when raising capital and bargaining for terms from financial institutions.[33] It behoved independent firms either to initiate take-over proceedings or welcome such overtures from others because it was self-evidently in their best interests so to do. As well as the potential economies recited above, horizontal merger brought other perceptible advantages to the firms taken up by it. For example, they would avoid the necessity of independently creating plant which could exacerbate the excess capacity problem, depress prices and prevent them from indulging to the full in their preferred specialisation.[34] These essentially defensive reasons for horizontal integration differ profoundly from the underlying pressures stimulating mergers in the earlier part of the century. The US instance was largely motivated by the desire to foment industrial concentration in a robust market whereas the British post-1918 flurry of acquisitions was actuated by the wish to avoid the entry barriers imposed by the lengthy period required to set up capacity from scratch.[35] In not so many words, it was pursued as part and parcel of 'extensive growth'. Put bluntly, horizontal integration was then construed by its practitioners as an offensive strategy, and only prolonged bouts of depression such as the episode extending from the early 1920s could effect a transformation whereby horizontal acquisitions were regarded primarily as defensive means of rebuffing disquieting conditions. Facets of both defensive and offensive rationales persist in shipbuilding to this day, although the former has increasingly come to the fore in tandem with the maturing of the industry. Let us embellish the point with a few salient examples.

Contemporary cases

Reminiscent of the US industry in several respects, shipbuilding in Canada survives mainly on the strength of government contracts. Shipbuilders unlucky in the lottery for state largesse face an uncertain future in the commercial market and endure, if they can withstand the absence of government business at all, on the basis of serving niche markets such as the Great Lakes and coastal trades, the needs of the fishing fleets and the demanding requirements of offshore and Arctic energy exploration and extraction. Fairly generous subsidies – at one stage worth 20 per cent of production costs plus 3 per cent for productivity gains – had not sufficed to fill the order-books for the yards.[36] Employment suffered severe shrinkage, slipping for example from the 16,888 recorded in April 1982 to the 9,400 registered in December 1983 as work began to run out. Elimination of direct subsidies in 1985 brought matters to a head, since several yards that had garnered some orders on the strength of the aid advanced to them were incapable of continuing without it.[37] The dearth of commercial orders forced no fewer than 15 yards to solicit the government for favourable treatment in the dispensing of contracts for an icebreaker, naval auxiliaries and a Ro-Ro ferry. The government share of the tonnage on order in Canadian shipbuilding, which had hovered in the 2–3 per cent range during the 1970s and early 1980s, shot up to 31 per cent in 1983, 62 per cent in 1985 and an overwhelming 96 per cent in 1986. Yet, the amount of new-building business at the disposal of the government was not equal to the task of sustaining so many yards and an industrial restructuring was long overdue. Except for the warship-oriented Saint John Shipbuilding, unassailable given its stranglehold on frigate contracts, the other yards could no longer afford to remain aloof from mergers and take-overs. In executing defensive horizontal integration, they aimed not only to cut overheads and allocate facilities to their best use, but, by such means, they hoped to retire obsolescent capacity once and for all. One proponent of such integration was Canadian Ship-building and Engineering (CSEL), a specialist in the production of lakers. Operating yards at Collingwood and Thunder Bay (Port Arthur), CSEL struck an alliance with Upper Lakes Shipping – a fellow member of the Power Corporation – which ran shipyards at St Catherines (Port Weller Dry Docks) and Pictou.[38] The newly enlarged group immediately deleted its main Collingwood establishment, preferring to assign its larger new buildings (up to 10,000 gt) to Port Weller and its smaller vessels to Port Arthur (6,000 gt) and Pictou (5,000 gt). An industrial-holding group, the Versatile Corporation, had entered upon a shipbuilding expansion of the horizontal-integration kind under the impression that sizeable orders were in the offing for vessels to be employed in the Arctic energy industry (the same reason, incidentally, which had induced Dome Petroleum to purchase the Davie firm, the one-time shipyard supplement of Canada Steamship Lines).[39] Apart from its original yards in North Vancouver and Victoria, the corpor-ation seized control of the Lauzon-based Davie yard in 1985 to add to its Montreal ship-repair yard (once owned by Vickers of Britain) and, thereby, was enabled to balance its Pacific operations with Atlantic interests and dominate the national industry to the tune of a 40 per cent share of its capacity. Alarming losses on these activities, however, impelled Versatile to abandon the industry; a resolve it began to meet in 1986 with the sale of its two Eastern yards to Marine Industries (MIL) of Sorel.[40] A state enterprise, MIL was mostly owned by the Quebec Government (65 per cent), but the French state-owned Alsthom–Atlantique group, operator of Chantiers de l'Atlantique, retained a minority (35 per cent) shareholding. In effect, MIL had pursued its own 'dirigiste' form of horizontal integration, securing for the province ownership and control of all the significant shipyards located within its territory. Setting the seal on Versatile's disillusionment with shipbuilding, the conglomerate sold its North Vancouver yard in 1989 to a Toronto investment and manufacturing company. During its latter stint as a Versatile unit, this yard had only built three ships, including a government icebreaker, and had been lured into loss-making contracts for assembling port cranes and mine conveyor systems.

The growth and development of the Yugoslav shipbuilding industry has also been invested with a concern for horizontal integration, albeit from the markedly different perspective of the linking together of state enterprises. Success attended this industry to a far greater extent than its Canadian counterpart, although, to be sure, much of this good fortune arose out of the factor-cost advantages incident to a country bordering on NIC status. Selecting shipbuilding for active promotion in the 1960s, the government transformed the exiguous and inchoate sector into a force to be reckoned with. Indeed, ships soon assumed the position of chief export earner for Yugoslavia. While each shipbuilding enterprise was given a free-hand in running its everyday operations, a division of labour was enforced by the controlling body, Jadranbrod, in order to avoid duplication of facilities and excess overheads. To this end, the Titovo Shipyard in Kraljevica was restricted to vessels of 5,000 dwt or less, the Bijela yard was effectively limited to those in the 15,000 dwt class, Trogir was permitted to handle ships up to 70,000 dwt, the 3 Maj Shipyard at Rijeka could accommodate vessels of 150,000 dwt, the Split site pushed that margin up to 170,000 dwt and, at the pinnacle, Uljanik Shipyard at Pula was reserved for the largest class of vessels, those of 400,000 dwt. Floored by the market recession of the late 1970s, the industry struggled through the first half of the succeeding decade plagued with debt problems and intermittent work stoppages. In default of overseas orders, recourse was made to a domestic fleet renewal plan in an attempt to fill the berths. By 1986 the outlook was distinctly promising: new-building prices fixed by Jadranbrod were said to rival South Korea's; at any rate, they sufficed to inveigle orders from abroad. In addition, the group of yards had amassed experience of a kind capable of matching the likes of Finland in the production of specialised ships. An order for a large ferry from Finland placed with the Split yard, together with orders for products tankers from the USSR lodged with

Split, Uljanik and 3 Maj, attested to this competitiveness.[41] However, this hive of activity did not come about without exacting ravaging side-effects on the industry. Excessive domestic inflation inflamed the poor industrial relations and exposed the ship pricing mechanism for what it was: an artificial expedient which set prices well below break-even point and, on that score, was in the end untenable. Moreover, the dependence of Jadranbrod yards on imports of materials – steel plate from Czechoslovakia and EEC stainless steel for products tankers, for example – required high levels of outgoings that the hard-pressed economy could ill afford. Attempts to correct the situation and cut the dependence on foreign suppliers were frustrated, in turn, by the shortage of investment capital needed to upgrade plant. The longstanding goal of the 3 Maj Shipyard to raise the local content of its licence-made Sulzer marine diesel engines was thwarted owing to this restraint. Impediments notwithstanding, Jadranbrod endeavours to put on a brave face and, taking solace from low labour costs, insists on maintaining the yards on an export footing. Typical is the Uljanik Shipyard: in the entire span of years from 1971 to 1988 only a meagre 4 per cent by tonnage of its output has been diverted to domestic shipowners. Of late, Uljanik along with 3 Maj and Split have united to undertake a renewed foray into the export market, winning orders for small products tankers from the USSR and medium-sized crude carriers from Norway. Affirming their determination to master the intricacies of specialised ship construction, these yards were also indulging in the building of catamaran crane barges, passenger ferries and container vessels at the tail end of the 1980s.

Division of labour consistent with horizontal integration has reached its ultimate stage in other parts of Eastern Europe, not least owing to its transformation into something of an institution at the hands of COMECON. In the late 1940s the USSR gave precedence to warshipbuilding. Rather than consecrating mercantile building yards, it preferred to invest, for example, in a massive undercover submarine-building hall at Severodvinsk where the boats were virtually mass-produced and to indulge in a concerted massing of resources at Nikolayev where the series production of large surface combatants was put into effect. Ironically, it was fully alive to the benefits of horizontal integration, imposing a distinctive division of labour upon its new naval construction assets. Kaliningrad (the ex-Schichau yard) and Kerch, for instance, were devoted to frigates; Zelenodolsk, Petrovskiy and Khabarovsk were dedicated to patrol craft; Leningrad/Zhdanov was given over to destroyers, Leningrad/Baltic to cruisers and Leningrad/Admiralty joined Komsomolsk and Gorkiy in the manufacture of submarines.[42] Of necessity, the USSR was obliged to extend the horizontal integration outwards to its satellites, with Poland and East Germany expected to furnish the bulk of the mercantile tonnage of the USSR as well as meet their own needs. As part of that grand design, the Soviet Union procured its more sophisticated tonnage from Finland: initially through reparations but, after affirmation of the Agreement on Friendship and Co-operation in 1948, on a regular basis in conjunction with the imperatives laid down in the national five-year plans. This tie was especially valued because it allowed the USSR to acquire Western process technology through the Finnish intermediary. In fact, Finnish and Soviet yards often swapped work between each other in order to capitalise on differing degrees of expertise. In return for completing complex jack-up rigs in 1989, for example, the Rauma yard of Rauma-Repola Oy subcontracted the bow and hold sections of a bulker on its books for a Finnish owner to the Vyborg yard in the USSR.[43] Horizontal integration was given a fillip in 1959 when the USSR, Poland and East Germany officially sanctioned the reduction in the number of ship classes from 30 to 11.[44] Quantity production of a limited variety of standard ships was viewed as being favourable to the achieving of scale and learning economies. In this vein, the state organisation charged with controlling the East German yards – Kombinat Schiffbau – categorically refused to countenance 'one-off' ships, and to press home the point, rejected outright the building of any ship class whose size breached its self-imposed cap of 35,000 grt. Within these limits, however, the yards were allowed to specialise: Warnowwerft in Warnemünde concentrated on container and multipurpose vessels, Mathias-Thesen Werft in Wismar stuck to small bulkers, reefers and Ro-Ro ships, while the Neptun yard in Rostock built bucket dredgers to complement its multipurpose and Ro-Ro vessels. Along with the Polish Gdansk yard, the Volkswerft Stralsund provided most of the units of the Soviet deep-sea fishing fleet.

Still nourishing some hopes of realising significant production economies, the East German and Polish yards were steadily expanded through to the 1970s, although their dimensions never matched the gargantuan dock developments occurring elsewhere in the world. Poland enjoyed much the bigger expansion of the two, with its major yards at Gdansk, Gdynia and Szczecin tackling mounting order-books. The first shipbuilding complex dealt with medium-sized vessels and, to that end, the Lenin Shipyard was arrayed with five building berths, a works to erect MAN/B&W engines under licence and a plant to fabricate ships' boilers. The Paris Commune Shipyard in Gdynia was earmarked for larger vessels and uniquely equipped for Poland with docks capable of taking large tankers. Extending for 380m in length and 70m in breadth, the yard's main building dock could conceivably turn out a 400,000 dwt ULCC. Commissioned in 1977 after its intended market had vanished, the dock was inaugurated with orders for two 200,000 dwt VLCCs for domestic owners and four 116,000 dwt OBOs for the USSR. Substitute work, soon to overshadow the large ships, was sought in the form of considerably smaller, but much more sophisticated, LPG carriers. The Stocznia Szczecin, for its part, focused on ferries, offshore supply vessels and oceanographic research ships. The only apparent problem impinging on the Polish industry until well into the 1980s – albeit one hindering the completion of an impressive backlog of orders – was a severe labour shortage brought on, ominously, by poor wages and perceptions of disagreeable work conditions. This affliction grew to alarming proportions, however, fuelled by artificial pricing to grasp hard currency from the AICs on the one hand together with stagnating investment in new technology on the other.[45] By the late 1980s the government was openly conceding that the industry was uneconomic and, pausing only to lay the blame for the mess on labour unrest, admitted to its serious structural plight. Taking the bull by the horns, so to speak, it chose in 1989 to delete the most chronic loss-maker, the Lenin Shipyard. Evidently, as this Polish example so vividly endorses, shipyard operations within an umbrella of horizontal integration receive no privileged exemption from the troubles confounding the industry at large. Less ambitious both in size and scope, the shipbuilding industries of Romania and Bulgaria were set up along similar lines to their bigger COMECON brethren. On account of an official desire to utilise shipbuilding as an agent of modernisation, the Constanza Shipyard in Romania was modernised in the mid-1970s with Soviet assistance. As a symbol of the gravity of the exercise, it was equipped to construct tankers in the 150,000 dwt class. At nearby Mangalia, a new yard was laid out to produce a series of 55,000 dwt ore carriers. Nor were small ships overlooked, since the Galatz and Bräila yards were given over to the production of 4,700 dwt and 6,000 dwt cargo vessels. As for Bulgaria, its chief establishment, the Georgi Dimitrov Shipyard in Varna, excelled itself to the extent of completing a 98,000 dwt tanker in 1977. The complementary Burgas and Ruse yards, finished with Soviet assistance during the five-year plan beginning in 1976, concentrated, respectively, on 25,000 dwt bulkers and 2–5,000 dwt river and coastal tankers.[46] The two Black Sea states persisted in investing in shipbuilding throughout the 1980s, enabling Constanza, for example, to build vessels of 171,875 dwt by 1989 and Mangalia to tackle bulkers of 100,000 dwt. While Romania focused on orders for COMECON, China and Cuba, its neighbour was dabbling in hard-currency exports, leavening its domestic and Soviet orders with a sprinkling of contracts for Norwegian shipowners. Whether these Balkan industries are more viable than their Baltic counterparts is questionable, but nothing unequivocal can be concluded about them in the absence of verifiable information on their economic standing. One must be content with the thought that they are regarded by their governments as fulfilling the vital aim of modernisation, a goal which they attempt to meet by operating as horizontally integrated state enterprises.

SUMMARY

In the years following the shipping disruptions of the 1970s all shipbuilders were forced to come to terms with drastically altered circumstances. Some abandoned any pretense of being able to cope with the harsher environment and shut down. Others that had not recoiled before the body-blows delivered in the 1970s were obliged to give ground in the following decade. A spate of mergers, take-overs and scrapping of capacity ensued, much of it inspired by the Japanese anti-recession cartels and European wholesale nationalisations. The banner year of 1977 witnessed state bail-outs of industries in Sweden and the UK which just credibly could be imputed to the dictates of co-ordinated rationalisation and the imposition of a working form of horizontal integration (division of labour) among production units deemed worthy of retention (a justification voiced by the defenders of Eastern European shipbuilding organisation). As was made abundantly clear, however, rationalisation in these instances eventually courted disaster, reducing the consolidated enterprises to bare relics that could hardly proclaim to inspire the trumpeted economies arising out of horizontal integration. Following the path trod by the Swedes and the British, the lion's share of the industry in Finland – incontestably technically excellent, of high business probity and seemingly imbued with optimism – succumbed to partial rationalisation, evident horizontal integration and, at length, bankruptcy. In so doing, the Wärtsilä case again appears to give the lie to the presumed beneficial effects inherent in merger of shipbuilding firms. Yet, the grouping together of firms into larger corporate entities continues to be justified on the grounds of the theoretical benefits supposed to issue from horizontal integration. These focus on the advantages associated with size; advantages that turn on technical and pecuniary economies, to say nothing of the greater market presence enjoyed by the enlarged organisation. Much of what has been said above has reflected on the actions of firms convinced of the merits of horizontal integration. A few other examples, generally anodyne in their effects on the actors, warrant mention here. Blohm & Voss (B&V) effected a combined rational-isation and horizontal integration scheme in the late 1980s, seemingly with encouraging results. It decided to close down the Ross Industries subsidiary in Hamburg, recently acquired from HDW, and concentrate its repair functions on the main B&V Steinwerder complex in the same city. Ship construction was run down in Hamburg when B&V officially merged with the shipbuilding subsidiary of its 60 per cent owner, the Thyssen steel combine. Nominating the Emden yard of Thyssen Nordseewerke as the prime new-building hub for the group, Hamburg would specialise in ship repair. Also in West Germany, Bremer Vulkan simultaneously re-emerged as a consolidated group accounting for most of the shipyard business undertaken in the Bremen area. Shipbuilding became the preserve of Bremer Vulkan itself and the united Schichau–Seebeckwerft enterprise whereas ship repair became the province of Lloyd Werft Bremerhaven and Neue Jadewerft.[47] In neighbouring Denmark, a bevy of shipbuilders implemented a merger at the beginning of 1987 which turned the three formerly autonomous firms of Aalborg Vaerft, Frederikshavn Vaerft and Elsinore Shipbuilding into a new organisation, Danyards AS. Under the aegis of Danyards, the parent companies stripped the Frederikshavn and Elsinore sites of their new-building functions while reducing the number of building berths at Aalborg from two to one. All three yards were retained, however, with an eye to bolstering the group's presence in the ship-repair market.

Nevertheless, so long as mergers of the horizontal kind occasion outcomes which are decidedly unrewarding for the enterprises involved, their application compels the sounding of a cautionary note. In a nut-shell, one is bound to say that the reactions of managements tend to defray the potential advantages accruing from horizontal integration. Merger and the seeming assurance of enhanced importance stemming from corporate enlargement might work against the urge to strive for efficiency, substituting a sense of security which could deteriorate into complacency. Besides, the desire for growth and the apparent protection arising out of bolstered size could help foster a distorted corporate strategy in which market control and the ability to stifle competition are stressed at the expense of profitability. These negative repercussions have made the more astute managers pause and ponder the wisdom of embarking on defensive horizontal integration when all too often it promotes structural rigidities in the public sector and degraded profitability in the private sector.[48] The current difficulties rocking the foundations of Polish shipbuilding, an industry designed around horizontal integration, testify to the dangers attendant on structural rigidities. Horizontal integration, judging by these reservations, may be safely rejected in favour of other means of enterprise reinforcement. The whole question of diversification away from the activity giving rise to the problem might repay more attention from the enterprise, as shall be made explicit in the next chapter.

4 Diversification within the marine industries

From time immemorial, shipbuilders constrained to find alternatives for the vanishing merchant new-building orders accompanying cyclical downswings in trade conditions have resorted to warshipbuilding or, failing that, have temporarily revoked shipbuilding in order to concentrate on ship repair. The first has the obvious merit of utilising to the full plant and labour accustomed to new building whereas the second, while dispensing with the need for building berths, is a profligate user of manpower and, in these latter days, steel-fabrication plant, fitting-out facilities and graving docks: all surplus to new building and conveniently available for instant reuse. In the event, these expedients frequently fail to offset the decline in merchant new-building activity, in large part because they, too, are often concurrently undergoing the throes of recession. Tempted to transgress into businesses liberated from the cycle simultaneously dampening the operations of all marine industries, the shipbuilder could begin to undertake activities divorced from new building and increasingly remote from the marine sector to boot. Moderating this temptation, however, is the sobering thought that taking on businesses progressively removed from the competence of the shipbuilder's core business is akin to stirring up a hornet's nest in that it is inclined to foster perils aplenty. For a start, unfamiliarity with the novel operations is likely to breed managerial discord and multiply the difficulties preventing profitability. New-entry strategies are liable to fall back against the entrenched advantages of incumbents while entry via acquisition is apt to draw resources from the core activity, perhaps to its detriment. In all likelihood, such heightened riskiness will blunt any atavistic desire to plunge into diversification outside the marine sector; at any rate, until dire conditions in the core business drive shipbuilders into the perilous game that requires their penetration of unrelated and, all too often, unknown activities. This is not to say that involvement in related marine industries is devoid of risk and uncertainty for the shipbuilders. The verdict of history soon quashes any illusions that may be held on that score. Diversification into allied operations has repeatedly been shown to be troublesome to shipbuilders. It has led, in short, to episodic patterns of diversification, with active acquisition of related activities occurring mainly during prosperous periods in shipbuilding and, in acknowledgement of a kind of symmetry, with divestment of such industries following as a virtual corollary of downturns in ship production.

The generic name 'diversification' embraces and partly masks a variety of strategies available to the firm. Shipbuilders partaking of naval construction or ship repair are scarcely diversifying at all, but merely applying the bulk of their stock of production factors, marshalled in the main for merchant new building, to operations that strongly resemble the prime function of the firm. By the same token, enterprises constituted with the aim of pursuing naval construction or ship repair as the mainspring of their business should, in theory, experience little disruption when diverted into merchant new building. On the whole, there are few technical barriers to entry for these ventures.[1] For example, not a few Japanese shipbuilders owe their presence in the sector to the intrepid actions of their ship-repair forebears who were eager to try the seemingly more rewarding building option. Three cases speak for them all. First, the Uraga Dock Company began ship repair in 1900, enticed into the industry by the shipping boom consequent upon the Sino-Japanese War. By 1911 it had projected its activities into new building, an occupation it kept up until 1961 when, as Uraga Heavy Industries, it was absorbed into SHI (who subsequently maintained a new-building element at Uraga until 1979). Secondly, the Yokohama Dock Company crystallised in 1897 to discharge the repair needs of Mitsubishi's NYK shipping line. Enjoined to enter shipbuilding in 1917 as a result of the First World War boom, it proceeded to add such complementary activities as boiler, steel frame and machinery manufacture. By 1935 it was recast as the MHI Yokohama complex. Thirdly, the Kasado Dockyard Company persisted in ship repair from its founding in 1918 (as Kasodoshima Dockyard) until 1956 when it chanced to embark on new building.

However, once shipbuilders trespass into areas beyond their immediate knowledge and for which their plant is not particularly suited, a significant 'conversion' cost is unavoidable and firms must expect to incur 'learning' penalties. Shipbuilders persuaded to enter offshore oil-platform fabrication or diesel engine manufacture would be confronted with such costs. They are, nevertheless, still firmly rooted in their own sector, that of marine industries. In fact, one of the examples cited is embedded within the vertical-linkage chain of shipbuilding: as vital ingredients in ships, diesel engines comprise a backward linkage from shipbuilding itself. In order to safeguard the supply of all key ingredients, the shipbuilder might decide to 'internalise' some or the entire span of the backward-linkage chain, becoming involved in marine engineering, production of steel plate, steel smelting and the mining of the ores used in the furnaces. Under the same rubric, it could determine to regulate its market through gaining control, via forward integration, of the customers for its product; in a word, shipowners.[2] The other example proffered is less easily categorised. Platform fabrication makes use of steel inputs that would otherwise have been deployed for new building and, therefore, acts as an alternative to ship construction. Neither enmeshed in the vertical-linkage chain nor a candidate for horizontal integration as would be another shipyard duplicating the plant of a predatory firm, platform fabrication is a substitute for, or parallel activity to, the main new-building business. Of course, it is broadly similar to the prime activity of new building and is best envisaged as a related non-vertically-linked alternative to ship construction. Platform building can be undertaken using existing production assets and, therefore, answers for 'new entry' diversification on the part of the shipbuilder. As a general rule, though, shipbuilders find it inexpedient to meddle in new entry with its risky trial-and-error gestation and prefer, instead, to purchase existing enterprises and effect entry through acquisition strategies (although, as in all things, the Japanese tend to defy this generalisation).

Conglomerates accumulate businesses which are not only devoid of any semblance of functional connection with the original group core, but which persist in bearing little correspondence with each other. They are truly diversified enterprises revolving round a corporate hub which maintains them for purely financial reasons and not because of any technical or production ties between the motley assortment of activities. Captivated by the conglomerate model which incorporates an enormous counter-cyclical capability, some shipbuilders have been drawn into entering unrelated activities, believing that such a strategy guarantees the survival of the group in the long run and bolsters the firm's profitability in the short term. Profitability, in turn, will ultimately set limits on the degree of diversification tolerable to the shipbuilder. Highly profitable ventures can not only accommodate forays into related businesses of the vertical-linkage kind, but they allow their managements to discount the risks involved in taking on unrelated businesses. In other words, firms must be successful shipbuilders before they can amass a range of diversified enterprises. Short of wholesale acquisition, firms can settle for partial vertical integration so long as they enjoy the freedom of action commensurate with a stable market and assured prosperity. Unfortunately, stability and reasonable returns are the exception rather than the rule in shipbuilding, and the tendency to follow strategies of diversification, whether of the vertical or unrelated mode, is just as much hostage to fluctuating economic environments as is the main new-building occupation of the shipbuilders.

Diversification, then, comes in spasms, with the active bout and passive indifference alike depending on the firm's sensitivity to the existing economic environment and its appraisal of near-term changes in those conditions. However, superimposed on the interaction between managers and the outside environment is an endogenous influence of overriding significance; that is to say, a set of constraints imposed on corporate behaviour arising from the firm's willy-nilly entanglement in the life-cycle obtaining for its core activity. An industry just embarking on maturity and populated with firms spared the rigours of excessive competition would be more likely to throw up enterprises capable of exhibiting the disposition and demeanour consistent with risk-taking behaviour. Some of that behaviour could be reflected in a bent for diversification. Conversely, an industry fully embroiled in the strictures of deep and all-embracing maturity presents a totally different context for its participants. The longstanding firms are resigned to depredations of their markets at the hands of low-cost producers in the NICs, have steeled themselves to the possibility of eroding profitability and, more to the point, have little in the way of a surplus for lavishing on activities falling outside their core business. In short, they will be chary of ambitious diversification plans. This ingrained prudence may be over-turned, presumably after an upheaval in managerial practices, if the firm foresees steadily poorer returns from sticking to its core business and musters the energy, acumen and resources necessary to effect a tangential turn away from the familiar activity towards something new. Such a course would be fully in keeping with the behaviour predicted by the life-cycle theory of firms poised to enter senescence. Since ship-building in the 1980s finds itself on the threshold of senescence, outcomes tantamount to diversifying the firm away from shipbuilding should not catch the observer unawares. Equally in consonance with this line of reasoning, an older-established firm may choose to diversify entirely out of shipbuilding in the search for a new lease on life as a 'start-up' in a different sector. When current aspects of the economic environment are bracketed together with the internal dynamic of the industry life-cycle, firms are left with four choices. In the first place, they can eschew diversification, both in the name of specialisation and the minimising of risk, and check any impetuosity which would shatter their resolve to refrain from anything smacking of the unfamiliar. Secondly, they can settle on narrow-spectrum diversification; that is, deliberately restrict their involvement to ancillary industries, those closely linked in an input-output sense with the core activity. Thirdly, they can choose broad-spectrum diversification; an option which removes the fetters on outside involvement and allows the firm to indulge in activities far removed from the original kernel. Finally, they can be perspicacious enough to anticipate their own demise and forestall it by shifting, lock, stock and barrel into a wholly different business.[3] At that point, they must be redefined around another core activity and no longer subscribe to the original kernel which served as the reference point for diversification.

This last option is easier said than done. Mindful of the behavioural implications of maturity, some observers see vertical integration as being detrimental to mature firms precisely because it tends to frustrate this last choice. Paradoxically, the advantages stemming from vertical integration – those working to strengthen co-ordination of the production process at less risk to the firm – lead to charges being levelled against it for encouraging static, as opposed to dynamic, efficiency.[4] Apparently, the achievement of substantial risk reduction turns the firm into an organisation singularly ill-equipped to deal with environmental uncertainties and consigns it to a behavioural lassitude from which its managers cannot wrench themselves. Since vertical integration is undertaken for defensive reasons by mature firms, they retreat into an economic fortress of their own making. This strategy serves to erect exit barriers, preserving the firms from extinction for awhile longer and rendering them immune to easy dismemberment, but at the cost of obstructing their disengagement from declining businesses. Some would argue that the integrated marine enterprises forged round the Japanese zaibatsu subscribe to this category, although, as we shall remark on later, these firms have substantially downgraded their reliance on shipbuilding in recent years. To be sure, the presence of excess capacity and vicious price-cutting, intertwined phenomena so characteristic of global shipbuilding, can upset the cosy security of vertical integration and force firms to focus all their energies on their core activities.[5] Consequently, the firms rapidly reverse the process of integration, dispensing with all but their chief preoccupation. Two British shipbuilding groups effectively suffered this fate. One, the Lithgow Group, functioned in the 1950s as a shipbuilder running the Fairfield, Ayrshire Dockyard and William Hamilton yards as well as its own Port Glasgow establishments. It also exercised backward links to marine engine makers (British Polar

Engines, Rankin and Blackmore and David Rowan), manufacturers of marine equipment (Stockes Castings, Security Patent Anchor and Lancefield Foundry) and a steelworks (Glasgow Iron and Steel), not to mention the forward links executed through the Dornoch Shipping Company. The other, established in 1954 as Sunderland Shipbuilders, eventually amalgamated a number of yards (J. L. Thompson, Laing and Doxford), ship repairers (T. W. Greenwell), engine builders (Doxford) and suppliers of marine equipment (John Lynn, Sunderland Forge, Wear Winch and Foundry and Wolsingham Steel). Lithgows eventually merged with Scott's, later losing all its linked activities as a result of its absorption into BS, and later still, forfeiting its new-building capability shortly after privatisation. Sunderland Shipbuilders succumbed to a take-over bid from a shipping company, Court Line, in 1972; was summarily nationalised soon afterwards on the failure of its owner; lost its linked subsidiaries in the larger state take-over spawning BS; and ultimately came to grief in the late 1980s as part of NESL.[6]

In a nutshell, firms inured to maturity should behave in a fashion which corresponds exactly to that of firms facing market downturns and, moreover, their tendency to 'dis-integrate' and disown their former core activity should prevail regardless of the state of the business cycle. Given these conflicting properties and outcomes of diversification in general, and vertical integration in particular, a measured view of their relevance to shipbuilders is clearly called for. This chapter attempts to fulfil that objective, beginning with an appraisal of the legacies of diversification strategies of the past before grappling with the conditions impinging upon programmes of diversification of the present. Owing to the vastness of the topic, only strategies of vertical integration and parallel diversification initiated by the marine industries are contemplated here: those touching on the shipbuilding interests of conglomerates with roots outside the marine sector are more fittingly dealt with in the succeeding chapter.

PRECEDENTS

The first major episode of merger and acquisitions for industries as a whole, that occupying the stage between 1895 and 1905, was essentially motivated by considerations of horizontal integration. The next upsurge of such behaviour, straddling the 1920s, occurred partly to consolidate market share and partly to transform enterprises into vertically linked organisations.[7] That period seems especially germane to our purposes, since shipbuilders faithfully reflected the ethos of the times. In the last chapter, examples were drawn from the historical record to show how firms mingled their new-building operations so as to greet upcoming market prospects from the strengthened position that horizontal integration permits. Building on that precedent, we can do no better than to initiate this chapter with a review – presented here in a most abbreviated fashion – of enterprise responses to the opportunities for vertical integration. To stress the episodic flavour of those reactions, however, we will extend the time frame to delve into an era when a rising market gave way to a recession which drove most of the builders to the brink of calamity; that is to say, the half-decade or so following 1922. The advent of a postwar boom in shipping promised fat returns for British builders, the lead firms of the age, and the more prophetic of them were already taking steps to leaven their new-building activities with other maritime pursuits. Indeed, many of them were pre-empted in their expansion plans by the designs of other branches of the marine fraternity, in particular shipowning companies. Several of these, replete with profits but denuded of cargo-carrying bottoms, jumped the gun by purchasing shipyards in order to cement backward integration and, thereby, procure a 'captive' supplier to safeguard the provision of much needed new tonnage.[8] A leading Liverpool shipowner, Lamport and Holt, acquired both the Archibald McMillan yard in Dumbarton and the Ardrossan Dockyard for this purpose; whereupon the floodgates were opened for a spate of such acquisitions. The Tees yard of Harkess submitted to a bid from Cardiff shipping interests, Blyth Shipbuilding was bought by Newcastle shipowners, the three Port Glasgow firms of Clyde Shipbuilding, Murdoch and Murray and Ferguson Brothers fell under the sway of the London shipping firm of John Slater, while perhaps most peculiar of all, Ross and Duncan, marine engineers of Govan, were snapped up by Murray McVinnie, ship chandlers of Glasgow. Some shipowners, in contrast, preferred to enter shipbuilding by way of 'greenfield' shipyards. For example, Hansen Shipping spent £50,000 operationalising a site at Northam in Devon; a partnership of Liverpool and Glasgow shipowners laid out the Hawthorn's yard in Leith; whereas the Newcastle shipowner, R. S. Dalgliesh (subsequently to own two Blyth yards), set about erecting a new shipyard at Hebburn. Shipbuilders were also intent on affirming backward linkages. To this end, H&W took over the Clyde diesel engine works of the Danish B&W concern and, thereafter, penetrated even further back along its linkage chain to absorb the Motherwell steelmaker, David Colville. Acting in parallel, fellow Belfast shipbuilder, Workman Clark, took control of the Lanarkshire Steel Company. Keen to internalise engine supply, Lithgows of Port Glasgow took under its wing the large engine building firm of David Rowan, leaving Swan Hunter – a major Tyneside shipbuilder – to garner two other leading Clyde engine makers: Kincaid and the North British Diesel Engine Works. Convinced of the desirability of gaining a captive supply of ship plate during an interlude of steel shortages and high prices, shipbuilders united to purchase enterprises in that sector. One consortium, consisting of Beardmore, Swan Hunter and its affiliate, Barclay Curle, secured control of the Glasgow Iron and Steel Company; another, made up of Stephen, Yarrow, Greenock Dockyard, Ardrossan Dockyard and the Blythswood, Campbeltown and Lloyd Royal Belge yards, instituted a take-over of the Steel Company of Scotland. These grander integrations were pregnant with implications for shipbuilding but, being by and large fleeting constructions, failed to live up to expectations: at any rate, they offered shipbuilders no long-term safeguards or cross-subsidies of the kind emanating from the Japanese zaibatsu.

By the early 1920s, shipbuilders existed in groups which were veritable coalitions of vertically related activities. The group revolving round Lord Pirrie's Royal Mail shipping empire was the most eminent. Pirrie, the flamboyant director of a host of shipping lines, forged links with H&W and John Brown (a giant of the steel industry besides being a shipbuilder) in order to facilitate ship supply. The onset of recession forced the dismemberment of Pirrie's empire, but as late as 1929 – and just prior to its spectacular crash – the Royal Mail Group under his successor, Lord Kylsant, owned H&W and Ardrossan Dockyard in the shipbuilding, repair and engine building spheres, David Colville in the steel sector and at least two-score firms in its core activity of shipping. Yet Kylsant's group had already been overtaken by events. Presaging things to come, the Belgian shipowner, Brys and Gilsen, axed its Glasgow new-building branch of Lloyd Royal Belge as early as 1921, declaiming at the excessively high production costs then prevailing. Other shipping ties with shipbuilding were to be severed in the harrowing years that followed: for example, J. C. Gould, a Cardiff shipowner, pulled out of his recently acquired Tees yard of Richardson Duck in 1927 while, in 1928, the Hebburn yard of Renwick and Dalgliesh, Newcastle shipowners, was put up for sale without ever having built a ship (a fate also befalling their Ritson's yard in Blyth). Vertical linkages endorsing manufacturing synergies quickly evaporated, too. Workman Clark, for instance, dissolved its steel connections in 1927, retreating into shipbuilding for a brief interlude before disappearing altogether. Its downfall was part and parcel of the demise of the Northumberland Shipbuilding group, that embodiment of horizontal integration which attracted our attention in the last chapter. The appalling shipbuilding slump which finished the Northumberland empire conspired to force all surviving shipbuilders to draw in their horns at the same time as the shipowners were regretting their incursions into new building. When the veil of depression was lifted a decade later, surviving builders and shipping firms were generally bereft of vertical ties. By a twist of fate, conditions conducive to a renewal of links between shipbuilders and shipowners reappeared at the end of the Second World War and led, for example, to the purchase outright of Greenock Dockyard by Clan Line Steamers and the take-over of Blyth Dry Docks by a group representing Stanhope Steam Ship and the Moller Line.

The disarray of the 1920s and 1930s was especially unnerving to shipbuilders because not only were they forced to come to terms with a severe and extended downturn in the business cycle – with its concomitant impact on merchant new buildings – but they had to face a world in which the traditional countercyclical alternative of warshipbuilding was almost eradicated. Alas, the shipbuilders were trapped in a downward spiral of defence cuts! Savage pruning of navies and a prolonged drought in warship ordering through to the mid-1930s coincided with a virulent trade depression. During previous trade recessions, successful recourse had usually been made to the state, which responded – as was its wont – by providing assistance cloaked in the rhetoric of national security. While cynical manipulation of policies to profit from warship orders may be imputed to some firms short of work to occupy their yards, statesmen for the most part were willing accomplices in the political manoeuvring which led to the practice of topping up yard order-books with government contracts.[9] They were sympathetic, in short, to the argument proffered by the firms that commercial shipyards constituted strategic assets worth preserving through the periodic injection of naval orders. In this light, even primarily merchant new-building yards substituted as 'reserve' or 'surge' capacity for times of war and were deserving of special consideration in consequence. The emergence of dedicated private-sector naval shipyards, geared to fulfilling the voracious appetites for warships engendered by arms races, has been dealt with elsewhere and thus needs no repeating here; but the fact remains that the naval alternative was, and continues to be, of overwhelming importance to shipbuilding in general: so much so, indeed, as to command some elaboration.[10]

Attention to the historical record is again instructive. Just as the forward integration schemes joining armour manufacturers with shipyards were implemented with half an eye of the steelmakers on the useful property of defence contracting to serve as a counter to the downswings in the steel and coal trades, so too did some shipbuilders positively welcome the opportunities offered by periodic bursts of naval expansion. That milestone in British strategic thinking, the Naval Defence Act of 1889, not only triggered the process which was to bring the private-sector armaments complexes into existence, but it furnished a plenitude of orders sufficient to entice several merchant shipbuilders into the fold of defence contractors. That temptation became more compelling by the time of the follow-on Spencer programme in 1893 because the trade boom preoccupying the industry in 1889 had been replaced by a downturn and a dearth of merchant bookings. Yards hitherto resistant to the seduction of naval work saw fit to change their tune and bid for warship contracts. The Clydebank yard, for example, had become heavily reliant on defence contracts when its inability to win liner orders had prompted a reorientation in the direction of warship work: a resort which sufficed to tide it over several difficult years until new merchant orders could be gained.[11] What is more, the general profitability of naval work – at least in times of defence build-ups entailing an escalation in warshipbuilding – served to defray losses accrued in periods of trade downturns when merchant ship orders were taken at low prices.[12] In the years between the two world wars, a similar contingency arose; albeit of more alarming proportions for the shipbuilders. A period of malaise occasioned by the confluence of defence cutbacks and sliding trade ruined many shipbuilders and was only brought to a close by a renewed naval programme of the later 1930s. This rearmament programme, therefore, echoed the Spencer programme of the 1890s in that it provided relief to work-starved yards and restored a semblance of viability to the industry. The spate of Admiralty orders was doubly welcomed by the desperate builders on account of the labour-intensity of warshipbuilding.[13] For example, a cruiser absorbed the same labour input as 20 cargo vessels of equivalent dimensions, whereas warship fitting-out work exercised a disproportionate call on the services of yard manpower. By one estimate, a typical warship required at least five times the manpower of a cargo vessel during this terminal stage and, thereby, acted as a godsend to yards accustomed to building passenger liners – equally profligate in outfitting requirements – but denuded of orders for them during the depression.

Unhappily, dependence on naval shipbuilding as a countercyclical strategy brought with it two debilitating repercussions for the yards, both of which fed on each other. In the first place, some yards in pursuance of warship contracts managed to underestimate costs and incurred losses. Secondly, in order to overcome their competitive disadvantages in relation to dedicated warship suppliers, some yards transformed themselves into defence contractors and lost the ability to remain competitive in merchant new building: an outcome which became uncomfortably apparent when restrictions on merchant demand lifted, the commercial market beckoned, and the firms responded to realise less-than-impressive results. It has been observed, for example, that even during the massive pre-1914 naval expansion, Clyde yards – with the exception of the Yarrow establishment, an innovator of destroyers – contrived to create numerous problems for themselves when engaged in naval construction. Being basically merchant builders prompted into entering defence contracting, they could not marshal the resources and expertise necessary to render them equal to specialist warship producers and, perforce, were obliged to play second fiddle to the likes of Vickers and Armstrong Whitworth.[14] Paradoxically, however, the very fact of their persistence with warshipbuilding drove them into the dangerous condition of over-dependence on a tiny core of clients. In the words of Peebles:[15]

> Warshipbuilding may not have been undertaken at the expense of merchant shipbuilding but, by 1914, what remained of the warship-builders' merchant businesses was largely domestic in origin, and the most profitable part of it depended on the loyalty of a few customers with whom yards had longstanding connections. When these cus-tomers switched their allegiance or went out of business, the warship-builders were unable to replace them.

The erosion of international competitiveness in the mainstream business of merchant new building, the issue at the heart of the matter, was to return to haunt these builders after the Second World War at a time when much reduced naval programmes could not even pretend to take up the slack left by the elimination of merchant order-books. These matters, under the guise of contemporary conglomerate interest in US warshipbuilding, will be brought back into focus in the next chapter.

Unlike warshipbuilding, ship repair could be embraced by the average shipbuilder at a moment's notice. Since the demand for ship repair rises in concert with upswings in the ship-supply cycle, some builders espouse repair in a big way, collecting ship-repair facilities in a fashion analogous to their simultaneous indulgence in horizontal integration on the new-building front.[16] During the expansionist 1960s, for instance, Japanese builders were expeditious in staking claims in the burgeoning field of tanker repair, seeing it as a useful sideline to their growing tanker-building operations. MHI went so far as to commission two dedicated ship-repair docks at its Nagasaki and Yokohama yards (the Koyagi and Honmoku Works), specifically designed to overhaul VLCCs. These plants gave it 2 million gt of annual repair capacity. On its side, NKK rebuilt its Asano Dockyard in Yokohama, a facility expressly geared to ship repair.[17] Another serious intruder, Sasebo Heavy Industries, settled for the conversion of a 66,000 dwt-capacity dock into one able to overhaul 300,000 dwt VLCCs. Smaller builders were also eager to gain advantages from ship repair as is evidenced by the decision of Niigata Engineering to establish a yard at Misaki exclusively for this purpose. Vindication of these investments was not long delayed. For example, the profit margins on ship-repair contracts won by the ten major shipbuilders during 1967–9 averaged 17.3 per cent in contrast to the average profit of 5 per cent earned on shipbuilding contracts (and notwithstanding the fact that the magnitude of sales associated with the latter was more than six times the scale of repair sales).[18] However, ship repair can remain buoyant even in periods of shipbuilding recession owing to the requirement of regular ship overhauls imposed on shipowners by insurers (i.e. 'stemming'). It thus offers a degree of immunity from the shipbuilding cycle, although it falls short of vouchsafing a true countercyclical alternative. At all events, builders bereft of new-building jobs during cyclical downturns in shipbuilding often attempt to shift the burden of maintaining adequate plant and labour utilisation rates onto ship repair. Their hope is that ship repair will offer a sanctuary sufficiently robust to ensure survival of the enterprise until it can be galvanised into action as a new-building entity upon an upturn in demand for new construction. The interwar period can be mined once more to illustrate this basic truism. Irvine's Shipbuilding in Hartlepool, for instance, was recapitalised in 1930 so as to concentrate on repair in the belief that such activity would enable the firm to rebuild its fortunes – it had failed to construct a vessel in six years – before returning to the new-building market (in the event, an unfulfilled hope). As the depression deepened, other enterprises followed suit: Ayrshire Dockyard, for example, abandoned new building for ship repair in September 1933 whereas the Ellesmere Port yard of Manchester Dry Docks endured a twelve-year spell extending from 1925 during which building was forsaken for repair. In obedience to the same evidently immutable law in which repair acts as a countervailing occupation to new building, Japanese yards turned in mass to ship repair in the late 1970s, suppressing building docks only to have them reappear in the guise of repair docks (recollect Chapter 2). Indeed, they had good cause to put their faith in ship repair. After the Second World War, many yards in Japan looked to repair for salvation simply because new building had been disallowed at Allied insistence. Table 4.1 intimates that in 1950, despite the resumption of new construction, most of the leading yards were oriented more to repair than building. Between

Table 4.1 Japanese shipyard capacities, 1950

Firm	Main yard	Annual new-building capacity (gt)	Annual ship-repair capacity (gt)
W. Japan HI	Nagasaki	80,000	427,000
C. Japan HI	Kobe	30,000	565,000
E. Japan HI	Yokohama	40,000	397,000
KHI	Kobe	80,000	99,000
Mitsui	Tamano	60,000	499,000
Harima	Aioi	50,000	462,000
Harima	Sakurajima	20,000	150,000
Ishikawajima	Tokyo	30,000	232,000
Hitachi Zosen	Innoshima	25,000	509,000
Kawaminami	Koyakijima	60,000	39,000
NKK	Tsurumi	40,000	–
Uraga Dock	Uraga	18,000	139,000
	Total (12)	533,000	3,518,000
All-Japan	Total (91)	802,000	7,246,000

Source: Far Eastern Economic Review, 18 May 1950, p.657

them, the Western, Central and Eastern Japan Heavy Industries (later coalesced into MHI) deployed 150,000 gt of annual new-building capacity as opposed to 1,389,000 gt of annual repair capacity; in other words, a ratio of more than nine-to-one in favour of repair.[19] The three principal yards of Harima and Ishikawajima Heavy Industries (later combined into IHI) mustered 100,000 gt for shipbuilding and 844,000 gt for ship repair, or a ratio of more than eight-to-one in favour of the latter. An average ratio of 6.6:1 obtained for the twelve main yards whereas, on taking all 91 shipyards into account, the ratio stabilised at nine-to-one on the side of ship repair. The difference between the two ratios is tantamount to an admission that larger yards enjoyed more of a new-building bent than their smaller counterparts: testimony, if such be needed, of the overwhelming importance of repair to the average builder.

In a foretaste of the recession of the 1970s, several British shipbuilders were caught unprepared for the new-building downturn of 1962 and turned to ship repair for solace (e.g. Inglis, Ardrossan Dockyard and Blythswood). Unfortunately for these firms, as for many others, hopes of riding out shipbuilding recessions by means of recourse to repair work turned out to be no more than a Pyrrhic victory; in effect, providing the yards with a short-term palliative before inevitable closure. On other occasions, though, new building has been permanently abandoned and the firm has taken on the trappings of a dedicated ship repairer. The successor to the famous Palmer shipbuilding establishment is a case in point. A casualty of the 1930s shipbuilding depression, Palmer's Hebburn yard was revived in 1935 under the tutelage of Vickers–Armstrong to function solely in ship repair, and continued to serve in that capacity until closure in the 1970s. Its sister yard at Jarrow was acquired by a company specialising in shipbreaking. Indeed, the government of the day was keen on encouraging ship demolition partly to eliminate the excess of redundant ships and provide some work for the yards in replacing old tonnage, but also to employ surplus shipyard manpower in the acknowledged labour-intensive occupation of ship scrapping. The contemporary UK scrap-and-build scheme, for example, surmised that the removal of 3 million gt of old tonnage would require 15,000 man-years of work.[20] Certainly, the demolition of a large passenger liner at Jarrow sufficed to engage the attention of 200 workers for two years; and not a few shipbuilders tried scrapping for want of other work. The Sunderland yards of Bartram's and Swan Hunter Southwick have been mentioned in this regard.[21] Of course, a scrap-and-build scheme was an integral part of the comprehensive shipbuilding rationalisation plan concocted by Japan's MoT in the late 1970s. Echoing British antecedents, a few Japanese shipbuilders hesitantly took up shipbreaking with the aim of employing redundant shipyard workers.[22] In view of Japan's high labour costs relative to Taiwan, Pakistan and South Korea, however, the builders in question encountered problems of profitability and, loath to persist with an unpromising venture, abandoned it for new building at the earliest opportunity.

JAPANESE INTEGRATED FIRMS

These examples underscore the episodic flavour of diversification, affirming a pattern highly dependent on conditions applying in the main new-building market. Essentially, builders pursued diversification in good times and bad. The former is exemplified by deviations into naval work during arms races or digressions into ship repair as an auxiliary to horizontal integration. The latter is reflected, on the one hand, in the headlong rush by the builders to countermand declining returns at the beginning of a shipbuilding recession through indulgence in ship repair and, on the other, in the sight of the same firms entreating governments to bolster naval programmes and distribute contracts to the yards without delay as the recession begins to be felt. Government faith in shipbreaking as a valuable provider of work in severe downturns also may come to the fore and be taken up by some of the yards. Prolonged recession, however, strangles the diversification urge. Difficulties with shipbuilding, combined with a relative inability of the diversified activity to replace the stream of earnings deriving from this core activity, impels the firm to cut its losses by dispensing with the non-core activity. These reactions are symptomatic of an industry at an earlier stage of its life-cycle, one broaching maturity. It is now opportune to peruse modern-day shipbuilding, an industry deeply immersed in maturity and hardened by years of constraints, and infer the extent to which diversification comes to bear on its operations. The vertically integrated marine enterprise offers the perfect point of departure on this quest. The lure of vertical integration remains strong because it holds out a means of controlling the economic environment: an inducement for any firm, mature or otherwise, during trade recessions, but doubly attractive for firms such as latter-day shipbuilders on the verge of senescence.

To confuse the issue, vertical integration in the marine industries takes on an implicit guise as well as the conventional explicit mode. Nowhere is this more apparent than in Japan. Not only do the zaibatsu retain a vast superstructure of industrial activities, of which many are susceptible to supplying on attractive terms components and parts used in shipbuilding, but their shipbuilders are also accorded privileged access to the latent forward linkages invested in the shipping lines and trading houses (Sogo Shosha) affiliated with the groups. Some of the material benefits of linkages cemented between builder and shipping line were exposed in the last chapter. For their part, the trading houses are not merely useful in drumming up cargoes for ships which, ideally, will emanate from the groups' building docks, they are also involved in smoothing the path of the backward linkages maintained by the shipbuilders. In short, the trading houses play a leading role in sustaining shipyard subcontractors, furnishing these small enterprises with the contacts, materials, equipment and finance vital to their existence (and, of course, critical to the competitive standing of their shipyard clients).[23] These vertical linkages, more implied than stated in formal parent/subsidiary ties, are overshadowed by the explicit connections between the subordinate branches of the shipbuilding enterprises themselves. Consider KHI for instance. Known initially as Kawasaki Dockyard, the firm traces its origins to 1886 when one Shozo Kawasaki bought the government-owned Hyogo Dockyard in Kobe; a facility dating back to 1870. By 1896 the enterprise had branched out into the production of boilers and iron products as complements to its staple business of shipbuilding; but, additionally, had entered into the manufacture of land machinery in a gesture aimed more at making full use of plant and equipment than with any premeditated view to entertaining admission into a countercyclical business. Once commenced, the process gained its own momentum, however. By 1906, the firm was committed to the manufacture of railway locomotives and rolling stock: a logical extension of its existing devotion to boilers, metal products and machinery. Though unrelated in a vertical integration sense, these diversifications retained a technological likeness to the fabrication of ship items. No such ambiguity surrounded the next stage of expansion; for the opening of a steel mill in 1915 endorsed a backward linkage from the shipyard whereas the establishment of the 'K' Line in 1918 confirmed the ultimate forward linkage for a shipyard: the securing of an outlet for its products. At this juncture, the awkwardness of organising numerous activities within a monolithic shipyard management structure was beginning to tell and, consequently, the rolling-stock section was hived off to constitute a separate division in 1928. Separate status, too, was granted to the aircraft manufacturing section in 1937; an operation which had begun in the immediate aftermath of the First World War. However, entry into production of electrical machinery, signalled through the 1943 opening of the Okadaura Works, was not accompanied by distinct divisional status, presumably on the understanding that such machinery was best visualised as an adjunct of ship production. Postwar growth both in the shipbuilding mainstay and the secondary activities led to a renewal of the fragmentation process, with steel manufacturing emerging as a separate entity in 1950 and electrical machinery achieving comparable status nine years' later. Kawasaki Steel was deemed worthy of autonomy because, by then, it had become patently obvious that the labour relations prevalent in steelmaking were strikingly different from those predominating in shipbuilding and, consequently, it was accepted that the required contrasting management styles were best catered for through distinct organisational bodies.[24] In the event, the integrated steel mills established by the new corporation at Chiba and Mizushima continued to provide a secure source of material supply for the shipbuilding arm of the Kawasaki empire even though they had been conceived with the totally different object of reaping dividends from Japan's exploding demand for general steel goods. Such privileges did not deter Kawasaki Dockyard from attempting other forays smacking of vertical integration. As recounted in Chapter 2, it descended on the metals industry to snap up smaller firms and therein ensure supplies of pipes, frames and propellers for direct application to ship construction.

The desire of shipbuilders of the likes of KHI to broaden their portfolio of manufacturing interests was no mere caprice, nor for that matter was it spurred strictly by economic considerations. In fact, the government strongly encouraged the builders to take up as wide a range of activities as possible. By its reckoning, the yards were the principal repositories of engineering expertise in the land and the only organisations having the scale, stature and verve to manage industrial development: both factors colluding to make shipbuilders ideally suited for marshalling into existence a host of other sectors. The government, in short, enlisted the aid of shipbuilding managements in furthering its own dreams of national industrialisation. Besides inciting the creation of ancillary industries, they were charged in the 1920s and 1930s with overseeing the spawning of car-, truck-, and aircraft-making enterprises.[25] In respect of the last, KHI was joined by MHI and Ishikawajima Jukogyo in prosecuting an industrial strategy geared to setting up warplane production capacity. The upshot was that, at the time of their revival after the Second World War, the yards were habituated to the running of diverse activities, both those inextricably bound up with shipbuilding and those exhibiting nothing but the most tenuous links to it. Each of the larger yards was an adept at turning its hand to new entry, and saw little that could be construed as reprehensible in instituting the novel activity from its own resources rather than accomplishing the same end through the apparently easier course of entry via acquisition. This predilection obviously harked back to the time when candidates for take-over were notable solely for their absence and, equally, it was incontestably a legacy of the extended period when the yards had been bestowed with the pathbreaking task of introducing innovative activities to the country's stock of industrial assets. Having such responsibility conferred on them by the authorities, the shipbuilders naturally accumulated a plethora of businesses, many carried on under the umbrella of the main shipbuilding organisation, but some achieving distinct status as autonomous enterprises. One of the latter, Nippon Strick, represented MES in the nascent business of container manufacturing. A joint venture of MES, Mitsui and Company, Fuji Heavy Industries and the US Strick Corporation (the technology donor), the enterprise's foundation was sparked by the container revolution of the 1960s.[26] As an indispensable ingredient in container shipping, the manufacture of these boxes represented a convoluted backward linkage into MES, a shipbuilder which aspired to furnish the container vessels that were needed to accommodate them.

A firm of the standing of MHI is the outcome of such past practices; that is to say, while masquerading as a shipbuilder, it is at one and the same time an integrated marine enterprise and a centre of operations for a diverse set of other activities. From the perspective of the former, no fewer than four of the firm's shipyards also doubled as sites for marine-engine production; namely, Kobe, Hiroshima, Shimonoseki and Nagasaki. Indeed, MHI belonged to a select group of enterprises equipped to produce main diesel engines for ship propulsion, the majority of which were also shipbuilders. Hence while Akasaka Diesels and Fuji Diesel were specialist engine makers, MHI along with Hitachi Zosen, IHI, KHI, MES, Niigata Engineering, NKK and SHI were drawn from the ranks of shipbuilding enterprises. Together with KHI, IHI and SHI, the Mitsubishi enterprise also maintained a manufacturing presence in steam-turbine propelling machinery. For MHI, as for the other shipbuilders, the fundamental backward linkage between ships and marine engines is thus assured through the 'internalising' of production within the single enterprise. While the manufacture of ships' engines is generally construed as the cornerstone of the marine-industrial complex supporting shipbuilding, MHI also admits to in-house production of an array of deck machinery including winches, windlasses, steel hatch covers, cranes and heavy derricks, to say nothing of electronic components vital to ship automation. In the wider marine field, it tackles marine structures of the likes of drilling and production platforms, gathering stations, caissons, offshore plants and storage facilities, tanker terminals, single-buoy moorings and floating cranes. Bordering on the bizarre, it has spun out its offshore initiative to build what it terms prototypes of floating cities: the Aquapolis built in connection with the 1975 International Ocean Exposition in Okinawa is held up as proof of the firm's all-round capability in marine undertakings. As if this versatility was not enough, MHI remains the chief aircraft manufacturer in Japan and since 1970, when its car division was spun off to form Mitsubishi Motors in conjunction with Chrysler, has penetrated the world automobile market as well as the domestic one. Among its other assorted products are construction equipment and tractors, forklift vehicles, food-packaging equipment, nuclear power plant, heating equipment and 'turnkey' industrial plants.[27] In point of fact, this leavening of shipbuilding with other businesses is a practice hallowed by tradition. While Mitsubishi had entered the new-building arena in the 1880s consequent upon its purchase of the Nagasaki yard, shipbuilding had only risen to account for 12.1 per cent of the firm's aggregate assets in 1894; a relatively poor showing in comparison with mining (37.6 per cent) and property development (38.8 per cent). Even as late as 1914, after the firm had opened a second yard at Kobe, shipbuilding constituted just over one-fifth (22.8 per cent) of the company's assets: only slightly more than the shares taken up by metal mining (19.9 per cent) and coal mining (18.7 per cent).[28] It is revealing to record that in 1963, on the eve of consolidation, MHI dominated

Japanese shipbuilding with 27 per cent of the industry's capacity: a share bettered only by IHI with 30 per cent. More to the point, however, it controlled one-half of the country's boiler-making plant, 40 per cent of its aircraft-manufacturing plant, 30 per cent of both papermaking equipment and turbine-production capacity and 7 per cent of automobile-manufacturing capacity.[29] Therefore, while ostensibly a shipbuilding enterprise, Mitsubishi was much else besides. In reality a composite company holding assets both in and out of the marine sector, its involvement in the latter centred on a vertical linkage chain extending from energy and raw materials supplies through to end products. The proclivity for internalising production has never deserted the firm. If anything, it has strengthened its grip in recent years as the repercussions of maturity in the shipbuilding industry life-cycle have begun to bite.

A handy means of grasping the degree of diversification embodied within ostensible shipbuilders such as MHI, KHI and MES is forthcoming upon application of the Herfindahl Index. It is defined as:

$$D = 1 - \sum_{i=1}^{n} P_i^2$$

where 'D' is the diversification benchmark for the firm and 'P' stands for the amount of sales in any one activity ('i') set against the total sales of the firm (i.e. the sum of all 'i'). In a nutshell, the Herfindahl Index provides a summary measure of diversification for a firm at any given time, since the closer the 'D' approaches zero the more the firm concentrates on a single activity and, conversely, the more the 'D' draws near to unity the more likely is the firm to spread its business equally among a multiplicity of activities. Comparison of 'D' indices over a run of years serves to discern trends either towards or away from diversification. Table 4.2 enables us to divine, for instance, that MHI was well diversified even on the brink of the zenith of shipbuilding. In other words, this putative shipbuilder registered a 'D' of 0.773 for the 1973 fiscal year (ending March 1974): a value fully in harmony with its constant attention to related and unrelated industrial investments. The collapse of the tanker markets, which pitched MHI into the turmoil plaguing the shipbuilding industry throughout the second half of the 1970s, was instrumental in fostering a measured policy of yet further diversification at the expense of shipbuilding. Thus, while this mainstream activity comprised 37 per cent of the total sales of MHI in the

Table 4.2 'D' indices for leading Japanese builders

Builder	Fiscal year						
	1973	1975	1976	1977	1978	1979	1980
MHI	.773	.775	.782	.805	.868	.860	.854
KHI	.773	.753	.756	.811	.825	.813	.761
IHI	.484	.466	.495	.394	.295	.320	.375
Hitachi Zosen	.515	.692	.689	.666	.791	.818	.832
MES	.513	.586	.572	.683	.841	.863	.875
Sasebo HI	.556	.517	.559	.516	.700	.777	.662
Hakodate Dock	.392	.426	.391	.442	.578	–	–

Source: Computed from data contained in *Japan Economic Yearbooks*

1973 fiscal year, its share had retreated to 18 per cent by 1978 and 19 per cent by 1980. In direct correspondence, the 'D' indices shifted upwards to 0.868 by 1978 and to 0.854 by 1980. That other evident stalwart of shipbuilding, KHI, is also revealed in the table to be a thoroughly diversified enterprise: indeed, it appeared to have reached a plateau in its level of diversity, for its 1973 'D' value – exactly equal to that gracing MHI – underwent a marginal diminution by 1980. This was so even though the proportion of total sales imputed to shipbuilding had suffered a decline from 28 per cent to 15 per cent between those two years. Clearly, other activities that had been relatively insignificant in the early 1970s had grown to rival and, perhaps, supersede elements of shipbuilding in the interim. The manufacture of industrial plants is especially noteworthy in this respect, accounting for 19 per cent of the KHI corporate sales in 1978 but 37 per cent in 1980. Other business lines, though, diminished in significance at the same time, thus restoring the Herfindahl Index to its level of the early 1970s. The third shipbuilding Goliath, IHI, was noticeably more specialised than its contestants in the shipyard sector. To some extent, this may be the result of a statistical quirk (the company preferring to lump all its non-shipbuilding activities into the 'machinery' category), but, that aside, IHI still defied the overall trend by diminishing its degree of diversification through the 1970s. For their part, Hitachi Zosen, MES and Sasebo Heavy Industries were decidedly more diversified in 1980 than they were in 1973; although the Sasebo enterprise, befitting its standing as a long-time specialist shipbuilder, conspired to trail the others. While data on the second-tier builders are elusive, the example offered by Hakodate Dock suggests that they too were intent on embracing the diversification trend in the late 1970s, albeit at a more leisurely pace than the main builders.

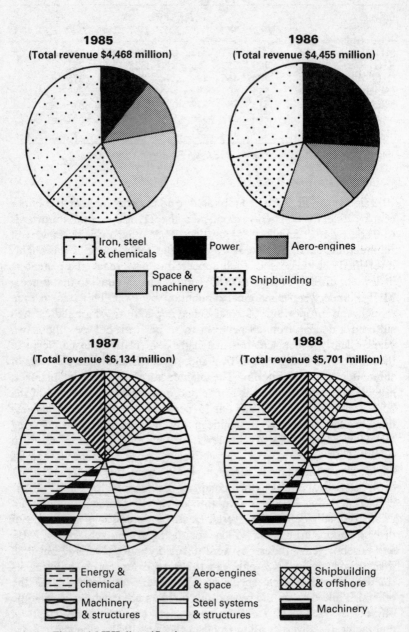

1985
(Total revenue $4,468 million)

1986
(Total revenue $4,455 million)

- Iron, steel & chemicals
- Power
- Aero-engines
- Space & machinery
- Shipbuilding

1987
(Total revenue $6,134 million)

1988
(Total revenue $5,701 million)

- Energy & chemical
- Aero-engines & space
- Shipbuilding & offshore
- Machinery & structures
- Steel systems & structures
- Machinery

Figure 4.1 IHI diversification

The tendency whereby shipbuilders have assumed a greater involvement in more lines of business has continued by and large throughout the 1980s. To be sure, there is no denying the fact that the share of total sales credited to shipbuilding has fluctuated widely – accounting, for example, for 17.6 per cent and 10.4 per cent, respectively, of KHI's sales in the fiscal years 1984 and 1985 – but the declining importance of shipbuilding is beyond dispute. In the case of MHI, the reversal in shipbuilding fortunes is strikingly told in a comparison of the employment and sales appertaining to 1975 with those obtaining for 1985. At the earlier date, shipbuilding accounted for one-third of the firm's 85,000 workers and 40 per cent of its sales; a decade later the equivalent numbers were 17 per cent of 53,000 workers and 15 per cent of sales.[30] Figure 4.1 throws some light on IHI, the firm that apparently resisted the trend away from shipbuilding in the late 1970s. Although data disclosure practices do not admit of time-series comparisons, they do allow for a limited evaluation of diversification tendencies in the second half of the 1980s, and that insight is sufficient to dismiss any suggestion of a persistence in the specialisation stamping the firm in the 1970s. A breakdown of sales for the 1985 fiscal year elicits the interesting finding that shipbuilding sales, while amounting to one-fifth of corporate revenues, were greatly overshadowed by sales of iron, steel and chemical products (accounting for 38 per cent of the total) and equalled by sales of space equipment and machinery. The proportion of aggregate sales attributable to shipbuilding eroded to 17 per cent in the next fiscal year. Despite sector rearranging, sales deriving from shipbuilding and offshore activities slipped to 14 per cent of the total in the 1987 fiscal year and a mere 9 per cent in the year following. Since the absolute value of shipbuilding contracts declined in line with the weakening relative shares, this erosion represented real cuts in IHI's stature as a force to be reckoned with in maritime affairs. The significance of this change is underscored by the recollection that IHI spearheaded Japan's assault on the global shipbuilding market throughout the 1960s and 1970s. Be that as it may, by the late 1980s fully one-third of all the enterprise's sales were put down to machinery and structures, 27 per cent to energy and chemicals and 14 per cent to steel systems and structures. Even aero-engines (to power the warplanes made by MHI and KHI) and space equipment had exceeded shipbuilding as a source of revenue for the firm. This last finding hints at the emergence of defence contracting as a significant income earner for the marine-industrial groups.

The naval option

In reality, the growth of defence business in the Japan of the 1980s is more of a reassertion of an old occupation which was long in abeyance or, more properly, long eclipsed by other, more rewarding endeavours, than a new-entry activity. A combination of restored Japanese great power status and doubtful profitability in an uncertain merchant shipping world has prompted the major builders into reappraising the defence market, especially as it comes to bear on shipbuilding. Having the capability to furnish the best part of the array of components from their own resources, the builders were naturally drawn to the construction of naval vessels. A memory of the stirring times when the zaibatsu functioned as Japan's integrated arms complexes undoubtedly played a part in encouraging this inclination. For example, from the turn of the century through to the Second World War, MHI and Kawasaki Dockyard had borne the main burden (along with the state dockyards) of building the combatants of the Imperial Japanese Navy. Denied the use of government shipyards, the restored navy (oddly styled the Maritime Self-Defence Force) was compelled to obtain its vessels from the private yards, and in the 1950s began to foster ties with the new zaibatsu. Its procurement body qualified a group of builders in 1953 for destroyer construction and they were to form a core of defence contractors which thereafter controlled the warshipbuilding market. This select group consisted of two Mitsubishi companies (later combined into MHI), IHI, Mitsui Zosen (later MES), Uraga Dock (later amalgamated into SHI) and Iino Shipbuilding (a former naval dockyard, later reconstituted as Maizuru Shipbuilding and eventually taken over by Hitachi Zosen). From the outset these companies acted in concert, established a kind of clearing house and apportioned naval orders among their yards on a roughly equal basis. For many years they were less than enthusiastic about naval work, partly because of its limited incidence, but mostly because the fixed-price contracts attached to naval orders did not permit the profit margins then generally available on merchant orders. Nevertheless, berths were found for defence work and the builders enforced a form of division of labour. The lion's share of naval contracts (one-third of all ship purchases by value) over the years 1962–6 fell to MHI, and it allocated destroyers to Nagasaki and Kobe, submarines to Kobe, auxiliaries to Yokohama and small craft to Shimonoseki.[31] Runner-up KHI (with 12.9 per cent of ship purchases), concentrated its destroyer, submarine and patrol craft orders on the Kobe yard. For its part, IHI placed its destroyer work in Tokyo, MES assigned its destroyers to Tamano, SHI was content to give its contracts to Kanagawa, while Hitachi Zosen made use of Maizuru (Kyoto). Significantly, while MHI's large slice of naval contracts only represented 0.87 per cent of its total sales during the period in question, the contracts awarded to KHI comprised 12.9 per cent of its total sales. Nevertheless, MHI was a defence contractor of the first order. Besides producing warships, it was building F-104 fighters under licence from Lockheed, manufacturing Sikorsky helicopters and their Allison engines, assembling Nike and Hawk surface-to-air missiles, turning out the Model 61 tank and supplying military trucks and jeeps.[32]

Along with the other marine-industrial enterprises, MHI went from strength to strength in the defence field. Quite simply, these firms needed a countercyclical market to occupy some of their vacant shipyard assets, and the rediscovery of a military posture by the Japanese Government thus appeared most timely to them. Other allurements were not lacking, either. While little can be said of the profits accruing from warshipbuilding in view of the secrecy surrounding contract content, the firms could take advantage of generous depreciation allowances granted to them in return for setting aside capacity for defence work. Since that plant was largely surplus to merchant new-building requirements in any case, its allocation to the navy as 'reserve' capacity presented the firms with no opportunity costs and gave them some tangible benefits besides. Therefore, MHI and the other builders were not averse to participating whole-heartedly in the revitalised warshipbuilding programmes of the 1980s. For example, MHI was receiving in 1988 more than one-fifth by value of all the defence contracts disbursed by the Japanese Defence Agency, and these contracts answered for 15 per cent of the firm's sales. With the current of public opinion running in favour of defence expansion, the firm was hoping to boost defence sales to a level amounting to at least one-quarter of overall sales. KHI, the second largest defence contractor, already counted on defence contracts for almost 30 per cent of its corporate sales.[33] Rising from 14.3 per cent of aggregate revenues in the 1982 fiscal year to 29.6 per cent in the 1987 fiscal year, defence contracting had become the single most important business for the company and was credited with accounting for 55 per cent of recurring profits. Significantly, however, the value of the firm's production of military aircraft surpassed that of its warship work as the biggest contributor to defence revenues.

An indication of the scale of naval awards can be gained through perusal of Table 4.3. With three destroyers and a replenishment tanker to occupy its attention in 1988–9, the Tokyo yard of IHI materialises as the major beneficiary of naval largesse. However, the Nagasaki yard of

Table 4.3 Japanese naval building, 1988–9

Builder	Yard	Nature of work
Hitachi Zosen	Kanagawa	2 x 440 disp minehunters[1]
	Maizuru	1 x 8,300 disp replenishment tanker[1]
		1 x 3,450 disp destroyer[2]
		1 x 1,900 disp frigate[2]
IHI	Tokyo	1 x 8,300 disp replenishment tanker[1]
		3 x 3,450 disp destroyers[2]
KHI	Kobe	2 x 2,400 disp submarines[3]
MHI	Kobe	2 x 2,400 disp submarines[3]
	Nagasaki	1 x 7,200 disp cruiser[4]
		1 x 4,450 disp destroyer[5]
		1 x 3,450 disp destroyer[2]
MES	Tamano	1 x 3,450 disp destroyer[2]
		1 x 1,900 disp frigate[2]
NKK	Tsurumi	1 x 2,200 disp support ship
		2 x 440 disp minehunters[1]
SHI	Uraga	2 x 3,450 disp destroyers[2]
		1 x 1,900 disp frigate[2]

Notes: 1. Diesel engines contracted to MHI
2. Rolls-Royce SM-1A gas turbines contracted to KHI
3. MAN/B&W diesels contracted to KHI
4. GE LM-2500 gas turbines contracted to IHI
5. Rolls-Royce Olympus gas turbines contracted to KHI

MHI, accommodating a cruiser and two destroyers, is not far behind. IHI, MHI and KHI, all integrated marine firms, receive additional benefits as the suppliers of the propulsion machinery for every warship on the stocks, including those adorning the premises of Hitachi Zosen, MES, NKK and SHI. On first appearances, the workload of the seven contract recipients may seem puny in comparison with the weight of commercial tonnage turned out by their yards. Such evident insignificance, however, is belied by two offsetting factors: the higher value of naval work (usually carrying higher profit margins and always requiring more intensive use of labour) in the first place, and the healthy quantity of work relative to the naval programmes of other nations in the second. Table 4.4 displays the domestic naval contracts under way in commercial shipyards (i.e. excluding the new-building load of the French naval dockyards) of the five principal European naval powers during 1988–9. If destroyer and frigate building is singled out as the current epitome of warship work, then Japan, with five participants, is seen to support more suppliers than any of the European powers. France assigns its orders to

Table 4.4 European naval building, 1988–9

Country and builder	Contracts
France	
Chantiers de l'Atlantique	6 x 2,600 disp frigates
CMN	1 x 423 disp patrol vessel
Dubigeon[1]	1 x 4,880 disp landing ship
NORMED[1]	1 x 17,800 disp replenishment tanker
Italy	
Fincantieri (Monfalcone)	4 x 1,660 disp submarines
(Riva Trigoso)	2 x 5,000 disp landing ships
	2 x 4,500 disp destroyers
	3 x 1,285 disp corvettes
(La Spezia)	3 x 1,285 disp corvettes
	4 x 360 disp patrol vessels
Intermarine	6 x 520 disp minehunters
Netherlands	
KMS	8 x 3,320 disp frigates
RDM	4 x 2,450 disp submarines
Van der Giessen-de Noord	2 x 510 disp minehunters
UK	
Cammell Laird	1 x 4,200 disp frigate
	3 x 2,400 disp submarines
H&W	1 x 31,500 disp replenishment ship
Swan Hunter	1 x 31,500 disp replenishment ship
	3 x 4,100 disp frigates
	1 x 3,500 disp frigate
VSEL	2 x 15,000 disp nuclear submarines
	3 x 4,200 disp nuclear submarines
	1 x 2,400 disp submarine
Vosper Thornycroft	1 x 615 disp minehunter
	5 x 450 disp minehunters
Yarrow	2 x 4,200 disp frigates
	6 x 3,500 disp frigates
West Germany	
Abeking & Rasmussen	7 x 400 disp mine warfare vessels
B&V[2]	4 x 4,490 disp frigates
Bremer Vulkan	2 x 3,600 disp frigates
Kröger	6 x 400 disp mine warfare vessels
Lürssen	7 x 400 disp mine warfare vessels
Neue Flensburger	3 x 2,400 disp surveillance vessels

Notes: 1. Yard now closed
2. B&V is lead yard, but construction shared with Bremer Vulkan, HDW and Thyssen Nordseewerke

Chantiers de l'Atlantique (as well as the navy's own Brest and Lorient Dockyards), Italy has its orders fulfilled by the Riva Trigoso yard of Fincantieri, the Netherlands places all its frigate contracts with de Schelde (KMS), while the UK consigns the bulk of its orders to Yarrow and allots the remainder to Swan Hunter and the Cammell Laird subsidiary of VSEL.[34] West Germany, which for political (unemployment alleviation) reasons apportions its frigate orders to B&V, Bremer Vulkan, HDW and Thyssen Nordseewerke in approximately equal shares, appears to come closest to the Japanese practice of dispersing this kind of work to all yards qualified to handle it. Indeed, Japan goes so far as to support two submarine builders, the same number as the UK (although both British yards belong to VSEL) which also carries the burden of sustaining a submarine-based nuclear deterrent.

The offshore adventure

The uneven order of business consonant with merchant new building, and by no means eradicated by resorting to warshipbuilding, made Japanese shipbuilders receptive to the beckoning prospects of offshore activities. These prospects were especially inviting because the integrated firms were already conversant with the fabrication of steel structures. Rig building – the main practical expression of the new industry – was envisaged by the shipbuilders as merely an extension of their steel operations. The two common rig types, semisubmersible and jack-up, seemed tailor-made to utilise much of the shipyard infrastructure. The former are drilling platforms which achieve stability by means of submerged pontoons attached to their nether parts whereas the latter, as their name implies, are platforms held in position by protruding 'legs' which extend to the seabed. In consequence, semisubmersible rigs are conditioned to deeper water operations than the jack-up variety. Apart from a spell when it was fashionable to build in concrete, the platforms have been prodigious consumers of steel. A platform, irrespective of type, consists of a steel deck, 'jacket' (the tubular steel uprights) and modules containing the equipment, machinery and accommodation facilities. As well as the large labour forces accustomed to steel fabrication, the shipbuilders possessed the range of plant and the large site lay-outs appropriate to rig assembly and outfitting. Best of all, the demand for offshore energy arose at exactly the same time as the demand for giant tankers began to expire (the two, of course, being interrelated) and promised an immediate use for facilities which would otherwise be embarrassingly denuded of a purpose (as borne out by the example cited in Chapter 2 of MHI switching its redundant Hiroshima yard to this new use).

To smooth their passage into the new, 'parallel' business, Japanese shipbuilders could learn from the experiences of others in the USA and Europe. In the light of their early postwar incursions into offshore energy extraction in the Gulf of Mexico, a number of American firms had innovated the chief rig types and excelled in the design and production of drilling equipment. Some had become giants in the province of rig fabrication (Marathon le Tourneau, Brown and Root and McDermott) while others had built up envious reputations as suppliers of equipment for the platforms (e.g. Baker Tools, Combustion Engineering and National Supply). Tentative exploration of the North Sea undertaken in the late 1950s and early 1960s was highly reliant on American know-how, but much of the actual rig fabrication and assembly work was done in Europe. In the decade following 1958, for example, British shipyards turned out a dozen rigs, including three of the semisubmersible type; but the 'conversion' costs incurred by the yards were so prohibitive as to register net losses on the contracts. This salutary lesson acted to discourage them from persevering with offshore activities and they were content to relinquish the field to consortia of civil engineers which for the most part established purpose-built rig-production sites outside the shipbuilding communities.[35] Only one shipyard, the failed Clydebank yard of Upper Clyde Shipbuilders, successfully transformed itself into a facility exclusively devoted to rig building; and its checkered course was blighted with a litany of woes ranging from intermittent want of orders and initial dependence on government subsidies, to instability occasioned by the exchanging of American ownership for that of the French (i.e. from 1972 to 1980 it was under the sway of Marathon and thereafter was controlled by UIE Shipbuilding). A belated attempt at re-entry into rig building in the late 1970s under the auspices of BS proved less than encouraging; for, to put it no more strongly, in the interim the UK yards had lost to interlopers – including some from Japan – any competitive edge that they may once have enjoyed in offshore activities. The dedicated BS offshore yard of Scott Lithgow, a remodelled VLCC yard, was sold to Trafalgar House in 1984 for £12 million after suffering huge cost overruns on rig-building contracts. The change in ownership proved unavailing, however, and after fruitlessly spending £186 million on recapitalising the Clyde site, the new owner gave up the struggle and placed it in 'mothballs'.[36] The other BS front runner in the field, Cammell Laird, quietly reverted to ship construction as a unit of VSEL when privatised shortly afterwards. To set the record straight, it must be stated that the offshore experiences of other European shipyards, while unsettling, were not so traumatic as their British peers. The Norwegians, in particular, refused to withdraw from the activity despite early reverses comparable to those undergone by the British. Several shipbuilders turned enthusiastically to rig building. One specialist constructor of fishing vessels, Ulstein, took up the business with gusto and switched to the design and production of offshore supply vessels. Two others, the Aker Group and the Trosvik Group, opted to specialise in rig building. In due course, they became leaders in platform technology, with the first formulating the Aker H–3 rig and the second innovating the Big Buoy 6000 and Bingo rig designs. Yet, technical mastery was no substitute for cost competitiveness, and by the late 1970s Norwegian yards were hard-pressed to win orders handicapped as they were with costs estimated at 30 per cent higher than world prices. Only preferential procurement policies instituted by the government saved the industry from eventual ruin.[37]

Denied easily accessible offshore resources, the Japanese ship-builders had viewed these preliminary efforts from the standpoint of onlookers from afar. They were not entirely uninterested, however, and contrived to learn from the obstacles unearthed by the pioneers. MHI was the first of the Japanese builders to venture into the business, delivering a semisubmersible rig in 1965 and proceeding thereafter to acquire the know-how to produce jack-up rigs.[38] Success attended its efforts, and the other integrated firms and specialist builders at length followed suit. MES had jumped into the fray by the early 1970s, constructing a drilling barge and a clutch of rigs before rededicating its Tamano Works to offshore pursuits. Infused by the all-pervasive enthusiasm for the new business engendered by the energy crisis, MES decided to take this yard in hand. The previous lay-out accommodating three docks for ship repair was rendered suitable for offshore work after being reshaped into one huge dock which was designed expressly to erect the semisubmersible and jack-up rigs that the firm aspired to build under licence from Levingston of the USA and Aker of Norway. At about the same time, Sasebo Heavy Industries embarked on the production of semisubmersible rigs. Hitachi Zosen chose instead to specialise in jack-up rigs and put its Innoshima yard and its Naikai Zosen affiliate at the disposal of the new business. SHI also plumped for jack-up rigs, signing them over to its Toyo Works. For its part, NKK began hesitantly with pipe-laying barges but soon took the plunge, so to speak, by announcing its intention to participate in rig construction. The Shimizu yard was set aside for this purpose. Similarly erring on the side of caution, KHI started on self-elevating platforms before declaring its plan to reserve the Kakogawa Works for rig fabrication and the greater part of the Sakaide yard for rig assembly. Even sceptics repudiated their doubts and entered offshore construction in earnest. IHI fell into this class. It had turned out a solitary jack-up rig as early as 1960 and, in a manner resembling its British counterparts, had then refrained from further involvement. Caught up in the fever of the mid-1970s, however, and avid to regain lost ground, it re-entered the field by pledging its Nagoya yard to rig-building activities. From that time onwards, offshore business began to creep into the workloads of yards not officially designated for rig building. The Tsu yard of NKK, for instance, had been opened in 1969 to produce VLCCs in series and by the mid-1970s was consuming 30,000 tons of steel every month to that end. Ten years' later, only 5,000 tons per month were being worked into ships, and the yard was allotting 30 per cent of its efforts to rig fabrication and another 30 per cent to the manufacture of bridges and pressure vessels.[39]

Yet more exotic activities were to preoccupy the yards, in large part offshoots of steel fabrication and rig building. We have already alluded to the 'floating city' projects of MHI. At a more mundane level, specialist offshore yards could take a leaf out of the book of Götaverken Arendal, the dedicated Swedish rig builder which, when faced with non-existent platform orders, would find useful employment fabricating floating docks. For example, in rejoicing in the ability to lift 600,000 dwt vessels, the one it supplied to Murmansk in the USSR was reckoned to be the largest floating dock ever built.[40] Familiarity with all aspects of steel fabrication confers on the yards a capability not unlike that enjoyed by civil engineering concerns which are able and willing to tackle jobs covering the spectrum from port construction to power-station erection. Desirous of attaining equivalent comprehensive capability, the big shipbuilders have not shrank from taking on ambitious all-embracing projects. Inspired by MHI's Aquapolis, they lobbied long and hard – but ultimately unsuccessfully – for government approval to undertake the construction of a string of floating airports around Japan's coast: a solution to the problem of shortage of national airport capacity which, they claimed, possessed the merits not only of overcoming space restraints on shore, but of mitigating aircraft noise and of finding work for large numbers of 'blue-collar' workers. In a similar vein, MHI unveiled a plan to establish floating storage facilities.[41] Again, the idea was promoted on the supposition that limited land for development required use of offshore 'artificial islands' to contain the more disagreeable and polluting aspects of economic advancement. On the export front, meanwhile, a consortium of Mitsui Ocean Development and Engineering, MES, Mitsui and Company, Nippon Steel, Niigata Engineering and the Abu Dhabi Oil Company conceived and established the Arab Heavy Industries complex at Al Zora Creek in Ajman. Centred on a ship-repair yard, this project also came endowed with plant for steel fabrication, barge building and offshore repair services. Since the integrated firms had long been involved in producing 'turnkey' factories and processing plants and, on occasion, even had them towed to their destinations, these 'radical' projects were nothing more than extensions to their offshore platform operations and land machinery diversions. Their attractions are such as to ensnare the non-integrated firms as well. Tsuneishi Shipbuilding, for example, set aside any qualms it may have entertained and established a leisure resort on the Inland Sea complete with hotels complex, cruise-ship port, helicopter base and marinas. The firm was repaid for its trouble by instant public acclaim and patronage. Indeed, it would appear that any endeavour replete with mass-market appeal is grist to the mill of Japanese shipbuilders these days. For example, to exercise some measure of control over the growing market for higher-value foodstuffs, NKK set up a Bio Project Team to explore the benefits issuing forth from investment in fish-farming and asparagus cultivation.[42] These ventures, however evocative of marine pursuits, are far removed from ship repair, that basic palliative of diminished new building; but it is to this alternative that most shipbuilders still turn, and therefore so must we.

THE SHIP-REPAIR PILLAR

As a rule, shipbuilders have not attained profitability since the collapse of the tanker markets in the 1970s and, in consequence, those denied the security provided by larger, corporate ownership have found themselves decidedly poorly prepared to undertake wide-ranging diversification strategies. The great exception to this indifference to diversification concerns ship repair. Many shipbuilders have sought respite through it owing to the virtual absence of barriers to entry. From the mid-1970s, then, a large contingent of builders have stressed their repair offerings. They have done so in spite of the existence of a multitude of established and aspirant repairers on the one hand, and in the face of a market replete with its own drawbacks on the other. Not least of the latter is the uneven nature of demand. This tendency to emphasise ship repair occurred at the same time as many builders determined to cut loose their ties with engine building, that centrepiece of integrated marine-industrial complexes. British shipbuilders, in conforming to the injunctions of Geddes, were already severing their links with engine building, and such ruptures were to become commonplace in all the AICs except Japan. To be blunt, indifferent results in new building deriving from an inability to keep the berths fully occupied were not conducive to the upkeep of 'captive' engine works which were left destitute of work in hand. Forced to tout for subcontracts from other firms, the engine building affiliates of these struggling shipbuilders found themselves hampered by their ties to competitor shipyards. The corporate ties, now something of a liability to the engine builders, also served to drain the flagging resources of their shipbuilder parents. Thus the severing of relations was seen to be of mutual benefit.[43] The most publicised rift occurred during the crisis afflicting B&W, the erstwhile integrated Copenhagen shipbuilder, engine builder and shipowner.[44] Reconstituted as distinct shipbuilding and engine building entities, the latter, B&W Diesel, was absorbed by the large German MAN organisation in 1980. In an uncanny replay, the bail-out of the Finnish Wärtsilä Marine concern in 1989 necessitated the separation of the successful engine division, Wärtsilä Diesel, from the bankrupt new-building division.[45] Given such inauspicious outcomes, shipbuilders have shown little inclination to return to engine building. Only Japanese shipbuilders and, as we shall see, a band of NIC newcomers have remained faithful to the link, and this, to all intents and purposes, is made possible through their ability to keep their 'captive' works gainfully employed. Bulging new-building order books, quite simply, are absolutely critical to the wresting of any benefits from the housing of yard and engine works in the same corporate home.

By way of contrast, those shipbuilders encumbered with the impediment of vastly underutilised capacity as a result of their inability to garner anything but spasmodic new-building work have been left with little choice but to set their sights on ship repair. They have been inspired in this course by the aggressive moves of upstart repair organisations which, seemingly, have managed to squeeze satisfactory returns out of their efforts. The examples of A&P Appledore and South-west Marine bulk large in the calculations of incipient repairers. The first, once a subsidiary of the group containing the Austin and Pickersgill shipyards and Appledore Shipbuilders, was established in 1971 to manage marine undertakings in various parts of the world. While noted for its advisory role in establishing South Korean shipbuilding, the firm built up an especially strong forte in ship repair. At various times it managed yards in Gibraltar, Greece, Singapore and Dubai. Receiving a new lease of life in the 1980s as a member of the Highlands Participants diversified holding company, it soon came to dominate a revitalised British ship-repair industry. Expanding from a base in Falmouth, A&P Appledore acquired repair yards in Milford Haven, Dover, North Shields and Chatham (in the former naval dockyard), and had the nerve to rescue the troubled Hall Russell new-building yard in Aberdeen. The second was founded in San Diego in 1976 and began on a course of expansion in 1981 with the purchase of the former Bethlehem San Pedro yard. Two years' later, a small government yard in American Samoa was secured; the San Francisco premises of Todd Shipyards were bought in 1987; and the process of growth through acquisition culminated in 1989 with the addition of the Northwest Marine Iron Works (a ship repairer despite its name) in Portland, Oregon.[46] Already, some shipbuilders have taken heart from such examples. The former Amsterdamsche Droogdok, for example, which had retired bankrupt from shipbuilding at the beginning of the 1980s, was revived in 1987 as Shipdock Amsterdam under a management resolved to seek redemption exclusively in ship repair. Similarly, Lisnave in Portugal owed its survival to ship repair after forsaking new building. Lisnave emerged from obscurity in the late 1960s with the help of the Dutch RSV Group and Swedish shipbuilders Kockums and Eriksberg. A small repair yard dating from 1937, the enterprise was taken in hand and converted into a yard of major proportions with the inauguration of a new site on the south side of the Tagus in 1967. Yet, the disarray arising out of the 1974 Revolution, together with the imposition of labour laws prohibiting work-force reductions, effectively undermined the yard's competitiveness in new building. Shipping recession accompanied by strikes and labour unrest threatened to accomplish the same end with ship repair. Fortunately, a resurgence in the repair market, combined with currency devaluation and a drastic overhaul of manning practices, saved the day and, in the late 1980s, the Lisbon yard looked set to experience a period of stability as a dedicated VLCC repair centre. Convinced of its regained confidence and competence, the owners of the ASRY ship-repair yard in Bahrain selected Lisnave to furnish their managerial needs. If further justification for partaking seriously in ship repair was sought by hesitant and undecided shipbuilders, then the entire Greek shipyard experience offered both a salutary example of its advantages and a measure of reassurance for would-be practitioners. A digression into the circumstances enveloping the Greek industry is essential in order to distil the particular lesson for shipbuilders.

Greece

With a view to fostering economic development, the Greek Government requested the country's large shipowning community to institute backward linkages into a latent indigenous shipbuilding sector.

A transition period was envisaged during which the new yards would function as repair operations. Once they had proved themselves equal to the task, the yards would progressively switch their main efforts to new building. In accord with such thinking, Eleusis Shipyards – an offshoot of the Andreadis shipping business – first established itself in repair and then, in 1970, commenced shipbuilding on the basis of the series production of a standard design of 5,900 dwt minibulker.[47] At the outset, the deep-laid scheme of the government appeared to be conforming to expectations. Indeed, a clutch of yards, mostly of recent foundation, announced grand shipbuilding projects. In 1971, for example, Hellenic Shipyards in Skaramanga, part of the Niarchos shipping group, disclosed that it had won an order for six 300,000 dwt VLCCs even though it had yet to construct the building dock needed to accommodate them.[48] Hard on the heels of this divulgence, United Shipyards in Perama launched a 4,000 gt luxury liner while Hellenic started to turn out a batch of SD14 cargo vessels built under a licence acquired from Austin and Pickersgill of Sunderland. At the same time, this latter yard declared an interest in marine-engine building, striking an agreement with GMT whereby the Italian firm granted it a licence to manufacture diesels. Preparatory to its entry into the supertanker market, Hellenic further stated that it would build a 500,000 dwt-capacity dock to supplement its recently commissioned 250,000 dwt-capacity facility. Yet, even these capacity additions fell short of the anticipated new-building boom, and the government called for more virgin yards. Argo Shipyards on the island of Salamis was initiated on the strength of an order for nine 3,066 dwt minibulkers from its ship-owning parent, the Polemis Group. More dramatic by far, the Karageorgis shipping group revealed a plan to build a 500,000 dwt-capacity repair dock on the island of Pylos together with a cluster of building berths for producing 60,000 dwt vessels. These newly hatched schemes were thrown into disarray, however, by the shipping slump of the mid-1970s and, to the consternation of their proponents, were nipped in the bud. The yards that had actually progressed to the operational stage also encountered great difficulties. In 1976 United Shipyards went into receivership scarcely five years after its founding. The Eleusis Shipyards, suddenly deprived of viability, lapsed into government ownership with debts in excess of $100 million. To unsettle matters further, the flimsy bedrock of the industry was exposed with the announced withdrawal of the Goulandris shipping group from the Neorion Shipyard on the island of Syros. In explaining the inevitability of closure, the Neorion management claimed that Greek production costs were totally uncompetitive by virtue of the fact that all materials and equipment installed in ships had to be imported and, consequently, bestowed excessive overhead expenses on the yards. In truth, Greek shipbuilders did not make much of a dent in global markets, relying instead on order books inflated, by and large, with contracts awarded by their shipping owners. The situation obtaining at Hellenic was typical. There, 15 of the 19 standard BC35 type of 37,000 dwt bulkers had been built for the Niarchos account. Despite such a damning indictment, Neorion was not allowed to close: rather than face the embarrassment of further job losses the government preferred to spare it through the expedient of state ownership. Its rescue was executed by the Hellenic Industrial Development Bank which secured an 85 per cent shareholding, leaving Goulandris with the residual stake. Its future activities were to be confined to repair, however, and management of the yard was handed over to A&P Appledore.

The paltry new-building market remaining for the yards could not answer the purpose for which all the extra capacity was intended. Only ship repair was equal to the emergency. It allowed the only profitable yard, Hellenic, to register earnings of $13 million in 1977. Recognising this reality, Hellenic quickly redirected its brand-new 500,000 dwt-capacity dock into ship repair to augment its smaller dock already mustered in that role. By this point, the earlier official hopes for shipbuilding had abruptly evaporated and fears for the survival of any vestige of the industry were not without foundation. Yet ship repair held disaster at bay, even serving to bolster yard revenues in the late 1970s and early 1980s. Unfortunately, the subsequent shipping recession, in combination with excessive price-cutting by the yards so as to attract COMECON repair contracts, conspired to reaffirm the fragility of the Greek industry.[49] To make matters worse, government employment policy imposed an additional burden on the yards, compelling them to retain large work-forces and countermanding any attempts on the part of management to boost labour productivity. It was the impossibility of containing labour costs which effectively scotched plans to set up a shipbreaking sector. This last was a rather drastic ploy to offset the scarcity of repair work then prevailing (although, in all fairness, the absence of a Greek smelting capacity constituted another major obstacle). The lingering bastion of new building, Hellenic, floundered in enormous debts by 1985, obliging the Niarchos management to bow to the inevitable and pass control of the enterprise into the hands of the state. Along with Eleusis, it looked for salvation to land machinery (manufacturing railway locomotives) or to naval contracts conjured up by the government. The Khalkis Shipyard, unable to ride out the crisis and passed over for state-orchestrated rescue, was forced to shut down in 1986. This was the nadir of the recession, however, and the repair market began to pick up in that year. Buoyed by timely government orders and a stirring in the market, the fortunes of the yards took a turn for the better. On an optimistic note, state-owned Hellenic reported an eight-year guarantee of work for its 3,800 labour force as a result of a navy frigate new-building contract and an order for four reefers from the USSR; but, in a gloomy reminder of past adversities, was unable to shrug off the encumbrance of debt, recording deficits of $21 million in 1987 and $33 million in 1988. More promising, state-owned Eleusis hoisted its ship-repair revenues from $18.2 million in 1987 to $34.5 million in the next year and, most promising of all, the defunct Khalkis yard was reopened in early 1989 by the Lelakis shipping group. Styled the Alvis Shipyard, it was resurrected in hopes of benefiting from the rising demand for repair. In sum, Greek initiatives in new building and repair had been reduced through force of circumstance into a strategy tolerating a residual amount of the former strictly for defence purposes while harbouring measured ambitions for the latter based on its real prospect of viability. In certain respects, this experience echoes the saga of the Hong Kong industry, although yards in that territory have a far longer history of involvement in ship repair. Some amplification of the Hong Kong situation will not go amiss at this juncture.

Hong Kong

One of the ancestors of Hong Kong's present leading shipyard traces its origins to the Hong Kong and Whampoa Dock Company which was founded as the colony's first limited-liability enterprise in 1863. To be sure, the first vessel listed as being built in the colony dates from 1843 while the Lamont Dock opened for ship repair in 1860, but by 1880 the Hong Kong and Whampoa had emerged as both the monopoly provider of repair services and the principal supplier of new tonnage. That commanding position was only challenged in 1906 with the opening of the Taikoo Dockyard. Thereafter the two contestants dabbled in new building – achieving the distinction of launching vessels of a respectable size (10,000 gt) in the First World War – but relied on repair for the lion's share of their earnings. During the interwar period, vessels of 10,000 tons again were tackled, although after 1945 the yards settled for new buildings of about half that size. Even in the expansive days of the late 1940s, they were constrained by 'high costs and difficulty in obtaining steel' which 'prevented any large-scale shipbuilding'.[50] Still, they were employing 7,000 men in rebuilt premises which, in the case of Taikoo, also contained boiler-making plant and engine works for the licensed production of Sulzer and Doxford diesels as well as Brown Curtis and Parsons turbines. By paying attention to best practices such as block prefabrication and electric welding, Taikoo was able to snap up orders from Norwegian owners for small cargo vessels in the early 1950s; but, ominously, the yard was compelled to devote some of its plant to the production of household furniture even during this spell of swelling shipping demand.[51] With the onset of the 1960s, new building became less and less viable and was kept up basically to sustain the pool of permanent workers and not for any lingering belief in its long-term profitability. In the main, the yards were now dependent on local shipowners for any orders: Taikoo, for example, gained an order in 1964 for a 10,700 gt cargo vessel from China Navigation, a member of the Swire Group as was Taikoo itself. Throughout this period ship repair constituted the backbone of the yards' business and, in order to benefit fully from it, the two of them merged in 1973 to form Hong Kong United Dockyards (HUD). As a unified enterprise, HUD could summon the resources needed to establish repair facilities for vessels as large as 150,000 dwt: a marked step up on its existing 36,000 dwt capacity. To that end, it progressively transferred its assets to a new yard on Tsing Yi Island, abandoning the old yards in Kowloon and Hong Kong Island – and new building with them – to the voracious appetites of urban redevelopers. Its example stimulated other marine investments. The Yiu Lian Machinery Repair Works, a venture controlled by the Chinese Government, also relocated to Tsing Yi; while a start-up company, Euroasia, was sited on the island in 1980. This last and Chung Wah Shipbuilding, a constructor of vessels up to 5,000 gt, were the only local firms remaining faithful to new building. Euroasia was even more intent, however, on balancing ship-repair opportunities with those expected to flow from the exploitation of offshore energy reserves in the region. While including representation from Chung Wah and A&P Appledore, it was formed round a core consisting of Overseas Shipyard, the in-house repair organisation of the Tung shipping empire. In fact, the Tung interest was merely the latest example of a longstanding local tradition of shipping integrating with ship repair. Some of the more eminent of Hong Kong's shipping firms were trading houses which, like their Japanese counterparts, accumulated shipowning functions. The founders of Taikoo, the Swire Group, were of this mould, actively participating in airlines (Cathay Pacific), aircraft engineering (Haeco), hotels, insurance, manufacturing, property, trading, shipping (including Swire Shipping and China Navigation), port operations (Modern Terminals) and marine engineering. Its partner in HUD, Hutchison International, was almost equally diverse. Hutchison had acquired the

Hong Kong and Whampoa company in 1969, but its part owner, Wheelock Marden, had once ran White's Shipyard in Southampton, England. Wheelock Marden, a major shipowner, subsequently merged its shipping interests into World-Wide Shipping, the organisation conceived and controlled by Sir Yue Kong Pao. Along with the Tung Group, Pao's World-Wide became one of the world's largest shipping companies in the 1970s. Continuing this theme, another local ship-owner, International Maritime Carriers, declared in 1989 that it wanted to create its own repair yard, possibly under a joint venture arrangement with a Japanese shipbuilder. For its part, HUD thrived in the 1980s, benefiting from the surging growth of Hong Kong as the global leader in container shipping.[52] It retained a core of 1,000 permanent shipyard workers, supplementing them with contracted labour as the need arose. Specialisation in repair – and the unsentimental extinction of new building – had ensured the profitability of the territory's main player in marine industries. Its principal rival was the repair industry of Singapore, and that case, too, is worthy of consideration.

Singapore

Bequeathed like Malta with an unwanted British naval dockyard, Singapore began in earnest to establish a ship-repair sector in the late 1960s. Hitherto, it had dabbled in shipbreaking and toyed with setting up a shipbuilding capability. In 1963, for example, the government's Economic Development Board (EDB) had struck an agreement with IHI to create the Jurong Shipyard on Semulun Island adjacent to the Jurong industrial estate. Accorded 'pioneer' status and thus eligible to receive preferential tax concessions, the joint venture with the Japanese firm (49 per cent EDB and 51 per cent IHI) was planned with a 44,000 dwt-capacity repair dock in mind. A small building dock capable of handling 1,500 dwt vessels (later to be extended to 15,000 dwt) was also envisaged; added to which the enterprise was intended to manufacture IHI-designed cranes, winches and derricks.[53] By 1965 the yard was turning out barges for Pakistan, had cut its teeth on small-scale repair using a floating dock and was on the verge of commissioning its repair dock, now expanded to 90,000 dwt capacity. The abrupt decision of the British to withdraw from the island prompted the EDB to designate ship repair as a key development activity. The former naval base was reconstituted as Sembawang Shipyard under EDB ownership but managed, at least initially, by Swan Hunter of the UK. These managers also discharged the EDB's obligations to the Keppel Shipyard, a government-owned facility previously operated by the Port of Singapore

Authority for routine ship repairing but now directed to the task of complementing that activity with the construction of small vessels. At this time – 1967 – ship repair in Singapore was worth S$73 million a year whereas shipbuilding grossed S$18 million. The former was in process of expansion thanks to a 400,000 dwt-capacity dock under construction at Sembawang Shipyard while the latter was being supplemented with Jurong Shipbuilders, a spin-off of the joint EDB:IHI enterprise founded for the express purpose of constructing the Japanese company's 'Freedom' class of standard cargo vessels. All told, marine industries employed 10,000 shipyard workers plus 3,000 subcontract and casual workers. A booming repair market, owing largely to the island's ability to accommodate VLCCs, effected an explosion in the industry's employment over the next few years. By 1971 the work-force had climbed to 18,000 and turnover had reached S$300 million, a full one-third greater than the amount recorded just the year before. Three large yards preponderated: Jurong, Sembawang and Keppel. Plans for several others were on the drawing boards. As the shipping boom entered its final uplifting phase, so too did Singapore's industry rise to the occasion. Start-up enterprises vied with established firms in proclaiming ambitious plans. The original Jurong Shipyard completed a 300,000 dwt-capacity repair dock in 1972 while its subsidiary, Jurong Shipbuilders, produced a brace of 11,000 grt Freedom vessels and was busy working on four more. The specialist repairer Sembawang Shipyard, tackling tankers of up to 120,000 dwt, was confidently expecting to have remodelled premises ready for 400,000 dwt ULCCs by 1974. Waiting in the wings was Robin Shipbuilders, a brainchild of local entrepreneur, Robin Loh, who wanted to build 100,000 dwt tankers by 1978. Loh had been instrumental in founding Hitachi Zosen Robin Dockyard, a joint venture with the well-known Japanese shipbuilders. This enterprise had been constructing barges since 1970 and was about to finish a 300,000 dwt-capacity repair dock. Also in process of formation was yet another joint venture with the Japanese: in this case an alliance between the EDB and MHI. Styled Mitsubishi Singapore Heavy Industries, this project centred on an embryonic 400,000 dwt-capacity repair dock in Jurong. Amidst this flurry of activity, the EDB had not neglected to sponsor ancillary businesses. The Keppel yard had co-operated with the government's Development Bank (DBS) to provide an engineering services company (known as Western Eagle) whereas the Jurong Shipyard had set up Jurong Engineering for general engineering and had already despatched a team to Kuwait to help install generating plant. Best of all, the industry was establishing a foothold in the exciting new offshore business. Sembawang Shipyard, for instance, had begun to fabricate offshore platforms. Conditions were so propitious that two of the yards were forced to look to India in order to overcome local labour shortages, and a contingent of 200 workers was initially recruited. At its peak in 1974 the industry employed 30,000 or 10 per cent of the island's manufacturing labour and recorded gross revenues of S\$720 million, half of which amounted to export earnings.

The energy crisis intervened to prejudice all of this success and for a time in the second-half of the 1970s the fortunes of the marine industries in Singapore were at a very low ebb. Rig building had stepped into the breach, accounting for half of the industry's turnover by 1975. Offshore activities at first were in the hands of American interests which had descended on Singapore at government behest. Bethlehem Singapore (70 per cent owned by Bethlehem Steel and 30 per cent by DBS), Far-East Levingston or FELS (51 per cent owned by Keppel and the balance by Levingston) and Marathon le Tourneau inducted Singapore into this business. Low labour costs in rig building rendered the island a production cost edge of 5–8 per cent over the average prevailing in the AICs. Most production revolved round the relatively simple jack-up rigs, although the Americans also introduced semisubmersible technology to the island. Official encouragement of offshore activities served in addition to diffuse technology to local yards lacking in other work. To Robin Shipyard it acted as something of a lifeline, while Sembawang Engineering was specially commissioned to fabricate platforms, jackets and modules. Periodic repair of rigs, requiring about 10,000 man-hours of work (as opposed to the half million required in rig construction), provided useful supplementary tasks to yards bereft of building jobs to occupy their facilities.[54] Unfortunately, the shipping recession had induced the Japanese to take up offshore activities, and their encroachment into tug, barge and auxiliary vessel supply – once the preserve of Singapore's small new-building yards – did little to allay the gloomy demeanour of the remaining shipbuilders. An ingrained cost advantage in ship plate (30 per cent cheaper in Japan) conferred on the main Japanese builders the ability to undercut the prices of their Singapore rivals by as much as 60 per cent. In desperation, the government offered inducements to Singapore shipowners so as to persuade them to purchase their small vessels from home yards: in this vein, the DBS was empowered to offer loans to cover up to half the contract value of new ships of below 5,000 dwt. The DBS was prepared to extend loans to the yards into the bargain. However, the overcoming of a temporary dearth in rig orders combined with a spurt in shipbuilding soon presented the yards with an alternative to dependence on a highly unreliable repair market. In 1976, for instance, repair accounted for only 37 per cent of the S$1.25 billion gross revenues of the industry. Compounding the problems for this sector, the impending completion of Mitsubishi Singapore Heavy Industries' 400,000 dwt-capacity repair dock and Keppel's 150,000 dwt-capacity Tuas dock promised to exacerbate an already excessive supply situation. From 1978 the rig builders scored a series of successes which not only assured Bethlehem, Marathon and FELS of adequate work, but also bolstered the ebbing fortunes of Robin and Promet.[55] This well-being attracted to Singapore a number of equipment suppliers, as evidenced by the appearance of Hughes Tools to manufacture drill bits, and they formed the nucleus of a marine-industrial complex. These ancillary businesses invested more than S$250 million in plant and equipment, and employed 1,900 workers. On the eve of the second energy crisis, the industry's revenues fell to S$1.045 billion, with repair pushing its share upwards to 52 per cent. Offshore work tended to defy the downward trend, however, rising from S$140 million in 1974 to S$281 million in 1979 and reaching S$350 million in 1981. Attempts were made to broaden the marine-industrial base further. Assembly of diesel engines had begun in 1978 when Sweden's Hedemora forged a joint venture with Sembawang. Three years' later, Wärtsilä Diesel licensed its Vasa medium-speed engine to Keppel, and actual manufacture of marine propelling machinery started in Singapore.[56] In pursuance of vertical integration, Keppel bought Straits Steamship from Ocean Transport and Trading of London in 1983 and, at one fell swoop, entered oilfield servicing, data processing, food manufacturing and property development besides coastal shipping. Horizontal integration was also espoused by Keppel since it boosted its holding in rig builder FELS to 62 per cent. A range of unrelated acquisitions – financial services in particular – rounded out the company's expansion strategy, but these actions drove the firm seriously into debt and led to criticisms being levelled at it for managerial errors and miscalculations.[57] Part of the debt burden had been occasioned by the disastrous fall in the industry's turnover following the temporary apex achieved in 1981. That year's gross sales of S$2.4 billion dropped steadily to the S$1.1 billion obtaining for 1984, with rig building alone collapsing by 53 per cent between 1983 and 1984 to register S$183 million for the latter year. Over the same year new-building sales slumped by 36 per cent to register S$277 million. Only repair avoided taking a drubbing, recording revenues of S$668 million in 1984: a mere one percentage point down on the 1983 receipts. At the same time, the industry began to announce cutbacks. Robin Shipyard first contracted its work-force from 1,000 to 300 and then quit new building altogether. It also pulled out of its joint repair venture with Hitachi Zosen. Weng Chan Engineering went into liquidation; Mitsubishi Singapore Heavy Industries, pleading losses of S$53 million, closed its huge repair dock to focus on plant engineering; and Keppel disclosed losses of S$174 million (although much of those were written down to the operations of its Straits and Kepmount shipping lines). Worse was to follow: in 1985 industry sales plummeted to S$651 million.

Thoroughly alarmed, the government commissioned a US consulting firm (McKinsey and Company) to ponder the industry's future. This august body advocated the amalgamation of Keppel and Sembawang preparatory to the elimination of Keppel's Main and Tuas yards (the latter just three years old). Since the government had deliberately championed shipyard expansion and owned the lion's share of the island's 2.3 million dwt of repair capacity, it was directly accountable for the oversupply situation and, in the end, responsible for rationalising the industry.[58] For political reasons, however, it was reluctant to drastically prune the collection of state yards which, apart from Keppel (68 per cent owned) and Sembawang (74 per cent), also embraced Jurong Shipyard (43 per cent), Singapore Shipbuilding and Engineering or SSE (86.8 per cent), the expiring MHI joint venture (49 per cent) and Bethlehem Singapore (30 per cent). Despairing of ever attaining profitability, the Mitsubishi Singapore venture was wound up in 1985. While averse to outright closure of more yards, the government abetted a slimming programme for Keppel which excised 45 per cent of the repair capacity, concentrated all activity on the Tuas yard and enforced a wage freeze among the labour force. These measures began to take effect and, fortuitously or by design, the industry's total revenues started to revive, climbing to S$724 million in 1986. Ominously, though, the revival was confined to repair. In stark contrast, new-building revenues fell 26 per cent to S$113 million in that year and rig building crumbled to S$20 million from the S$52 million of the previous year. To drive home the point, ship repair was reckoned to account for a massive 82 per cent of the industry's total revenues in 1986, almost double the 43 per cent share it had enjoyed in 1981. Accordingly, steps were taken to enlist the aid of other markets. Reminiscent of similar moves afoot in Japan, the Bethlehem rig-building yard turned its attention to the construction of a large floating hotel. Occupying 450 workers for 16 months, the hotel job compensated for the firm's failure to book any rig orders after 1981. Equally imaginative, Hitachi Zosen Singapore, the wholly Japanese-owned survivor of the Robin joint venture, busied itself making the wall linings and overhead viaducts for the island's mass-transit railway. Additionally, it manufactured containers, heat exchangers, building frames and, on spare land in the yard premises, undertook prawn cultivation and despatched the shellfish by air to Japanese markets. Not to be outdone, FELS aggressively affirmed its faith in new building by acquiring the huge repair dock abandoned by Mitsubishi Singapore; a facility it put to immediate use building ocean-going barges. With a view to making it eligible for shipbuilding, a 600 ton lift-capacity Goliath gantry crane dispensed with by Celsius Industries was procured for the dock.

The accent of the industry remained firmly on ship repair, however. Turnover increased to S$1.109 billion in 1987, a 53 per cent improvement over 1986, and 62 per cent of the total was attributable to repair (i.e. a 16 per cent rise to S$688 million). As 1988 advanced, the island was credited with being the cheapest repair centre in the world. Prices were so competitive, indeed, as to induce a West German ship-owner, Egon Oldendorff, to bring a pair of newly completed Warnowwerft-built standard cargo vessels to Jurong Shipyard. There, the vessels were subject to rebuilding, receiving 16m mid-body insertions, and having their weight augmented from 18,230 dwt to 20,500 dwt. The combination of cheap East German construction and cheap Singapore conversion was judged by the shipowner to be unbeatable, and certainly more economical than ordering new buildings of the requisite size. Nevertheless, there were factors detracting from this bullish outlook. In short, growth was beginning to bring a fresh set of problems in its wake: a reality encapsulated in the statement that 'because Singapore's shipyards have only one another as real competition, their biggest problems will be how to raise closely guarded repair rates amicably and deal with an increasingly pressing labor shortage'.[59] Moreover, while a depreciating currency had allowed Singapore repairers to offer prices fully one-quarter less than those quoted by their South Korean adversaries, the same factor was preventing them from pushing earnings higher than 60 per cent of the peak levels attained at the beginning of the decade. These price-cost pressures prompted a reorganisation of the state yards. The Sembawang Group took over the government interest in Jurong Shipyard and Jurong Shipbuilders from Temasek Holdings before going on to acquire the Bethlehem yard. Determined to address the labour problem, Sembawang was openly deliberating a geographical split in its activities which would entail the relocation of tanker repairing to cheaper labour sites in Sri Lanka, Thailand, Indonesia, the Philippines or China, while preserving the Singapore yards for higher value-added vessel conversion operations. The firm was anxious, none the less, to retain a 'captive' market by virtue of its Sembawang Maritime subsidiary, an operator of tugs and salvage vessels. From the other side of the coin, a 'captive' ship-repair yard was valued by Singapore's premier shipping line, Neptune Orient Lines. NOL's preliminary inroad into repair occurred in March 1989 when it gained control of Atlantis Engineering, a local firm specialising in shipboard repairs. The shipowner revealed plans to set up its own repair yard as an upshot of this action. In fact, the linkage between yard and ship operation has been a hallmark of marine industries, persisting through good times and bad. Its modern variant is deserving of some elucidation.

THE SHIPPING UMBILICAL CORD

In truth, the persistence of the shipyard–shipping link has been qualified by periodic fits of enthusiastic adherence counterbalanced by episodes of disgruntled severance; a fact made crystal clear in the earlier part of this chapter. As with other integration strategies, the cementing of ties between the two sectors was painted in the most glowing colours during upturns in the trade cycle while falling prey to rationalisation during the inevitable downturns. Of course, a few resolute enterprises maintained a steadfast commitment to integration regardless of the state of the market: the zaibatsu offer a cogent reminder of organisations exhibiting a longstanding allegiance to it. The merits of permanent integration have also been recognised by Danish firms. Since the First World War, shipowners in Denmark have done their level best to safeguard ship supply by ensuring that they controlled a segment of the shipbuilding industry. A. P. Moller, the owners of the large Maersk Line, set up a shipyard from scratch at Odense which launched its first ship in 1918. Refashioned in the guise of the Lindö yard in the 1960s, this example of integration was actually pre-empted by the East Asiatic Company's ownership of Nakskov Skibsvaerft (dating from 1916). For its part, the Lauritzen Group owned Aalborg Vaerft (bought in 1937), Frederiks-havn Vaerft and Elsinore Shipbuilding (the last two inherited from DFDS which acquired them in 1913).[60] Latterly, rationalisation of Danish shipbuilding has blurred these organisational linkages, but a modicum of vertical integration remains intact. Other enterprises – as the aforementioned Singapore examples duly attest – are recent creations, cobbled together to allow the yard to unload some of its new-found wealth while, at the same time, affording it a semblance of diversification. The customary reason for formalising the connection between the two parties rests on the merits supposedly ensuing from either a 'captive' market, if the instigator is a shipyard, or a 'captive' source of new-buildings and repair services should the driving force originate in the shipowning camp. We could do worse than to maintain this distinction in delving further into the fundamental linkage between two sectors of the marine industry. Straddling both, however, is a peculiarity thrown up by the Japanese called the 'shikumisen' system. This system, which has fallen into disrepute in recent years, enabled arm's length participation of Japanese shipbuilders in shipping markets. A few comments in explication are in order.

To all intents and purposes, the 'shikumisen' system was an alternative to the government's official JDB-controlled merchant fleet build-up programme, that survivor of state-orchestrated revival dating from the early postwar years. Under the formal mechanism, shipowners could receive up to 65 per cent of building costs advanced in the form of loans from the JDB and a much smaller portion from the commercial banks, leaving them to find as little as 5 per cent of the costs in up-front capital. Despite its apparent generosity, the government scheme fell short of meeting all the country's demand for shipping. Anxious to capture an increasing share of the demand, heretofore consigned reluctantly to foreign vessels, Japanese trading houses, shippers and builders concocted a substitute ploy which offered definite advantages over the official programme. The substitute hinged on the long-term chartering by Japanese principals of new ships built in Japanese yards for foreign – usually Hong Kong – ownership.[61] This extra tonnage would not only permit Japanese charterers to steal a greater share of the market but, since it was flagged under open registry (Liberia especially), would enable them to compete very effectively with Japanese-flagged merchant vessels (and not least in the manner of restraining Japanese crews when they were moved to agitate for wage increases). Besides presenting operating-cost advantages for the shippers, this alternative scheme was equally beneficial in the matter of ship procurement. Owing to their status as foreigners, the Hong Kong owners were eligible for financing made available on very favourable terms by Japan's Export–Import Bank. When the scheme was widely adopted in 1971, these terms comprised a package of loans covering 70 per cent of ship cost (the balance being secured by the charterer and builder through Japanese commercial banks) which was repayable over seven years at an 8.5 per cent interest rate. The alternative scheme, therefore, conspired to kill two birds with one stone: it added market share to Japanese shippers and trading houses (incidentally, boosting the importance of Hong Kong shipping magnates) and it enlarged the order-books of Japanese shipbuilders. Unsurprisingly, its inception was condoned by shipper and builder alike, and enthusiastically espoused by them in the 1970s. At the beginning of that decade, 399 ships totalling 11,062,000 dwt were tied up in Japanese charters; three years later the tally stood at 734 ships aggregating 27,700,000 dwt; and, at its pinnacle in 1976, no fewer than 1,199 ships of 50,609,000 dwt subscribed to this category. Thereafter, the 'shikumisen' system declined; in large part on account of a change in banking law. After 1975 Japanese banks were authorised to establish overseas branches, and these offices were soon put to use financing the offshore subsidiaries of Japanese shipping companies. Once enabled to run flag-of-convenience ships of their own, crewed with cheap foreign seamen, the Japanese companies were no longer obliged to use Hong Kong shipowners as intermediaries. The government abetted this stratagem to wean Japanese shipping companies off the substitute scheme, notwithstanding the fact that its replacement – Japanese owned open-registry shipping – was not greeted with rapture by the seamen's trade union. Without doubt, though, the 'shikumisen' and its replacement system showered benefits on Japanese shipbuilders. In short, they were the suppliers of all the tonnage in question and, while officially unconnected with the owners, they were actively involved in financing the ships through the Japanese trading houses and shipping firms that chartered them. This veiled participation of a builder in the financing and subsequent operation of ships is hardly new in the annals of shipbuilding, but its scale hitherto had never approached that engendered by the 'shikumisen' system.[62]

The steps taken by builders to control a segment of the shipping market are usually plain for all to see. Sometimes builders who would not generally be disposed to interfere in ship operations are left with no option but to work their own newly-built vessels. This contingency arises either because a shipowner has reneged on its contract to take a vessel or is the consequence of yard policy to keep the workers occupied during order famines with own-account contracts. Swedyards and Hyundai were exponents of the first course while any number of builders have practised the second.[63] CNR, now one of the constituents of Fincantieri, favoured own-account construction: in 1980, for example, its Palermo yard completed a 63,000 dwt OBO for Navigazione Arenella, the builder's shipping subsidiary. BS, for its part, went so far as to create a joint Anglo-Polish company, 51 per cent owned by the builder, to charter all 24 ships ordered from Poland in 1977: in effect, the firm was guaranteeing employment of its own new buildings while acquiescing in foreign ownership of them. The last builder in Belgium of any consequence, Boelwerf of Temse, has consistently resorted to own-account shipbuilding when no other orders were in the offing. In 1988, for example, it completed the sixth in a series of product tankers for its own shipping offshoot. On the other hand, some builders are actuated to buy into shipping firms in a fashion comparable to the Japanese practice highlighted both earlier in this chapter and in Chapter 3. New-building contracts as a result of such minority stakes do not always materialise, but Bremer Vulkan's involvement in the Senator and Conti container lines are reckoned to have rewarded the builder with new business in the late 1980s.[64] If all else fails, shipbuilders can take the momentous decision of allowing themselves to be taken over by shipping companies.

While, in truth, this usage fell out of favour during the Great Depression when most shipowners found to their cost that they could no longer afford the trappings of vertical integration, the practice underwent a measure of rehabilitation in the era of trade and shipping expansion following the Second World War. Possibly, some shipowners were too rash in embarking on vertical integration. Certainly, the experience of Seatrain Lines lends itself to this conclusion. Having built up a presence in the rapidly growing Pacific container trades, this US shipping company set out on a broad-based expansion programme. In 1976 it bought Pride Refining and entered the field of petroleum refining and distribution. Banking on an internally generated market for both container vessels and tankers, the firm had earlier acquired the redundant Brooklyn Navy Yard and reopened it as the Seatrain Shipbuilding Corporation. The yard was immediately pressed into service constructing a string of four VLCCs. Despite the provision of government subsidies, building costs were dismayingly high: so much so, in fact, as to deter the booking of follow-on orders. Notwithstanding contracts for Ro-Ro pusher barges and a floating power station, losses of $13.5 million incurred in 1978 were deemed just cause for slating the yard for closure in 1979.[65] Ironically, the retreat from shipbuilding did not restore Seatrain's fortunes, and it was compelled to abandon its shipping interests over the next few years. Seemingly indifferent to such woeful experiences, some shipowners have repeatedly elected to involve themselves in various shipbuilders. The Swire Group, for instance, has not only played a leading role in Hong Kong shipyards, but once owned 16 per cent of Scott Lithgow on the Clyde. Also, as recounted elsewhere, Ludwig's infatuation with tanker construction for his National Bulk Carriers took him from Virginia to Kure. By the same token, some yards have been especially prone to incursions from shipowners. H&W is a case in point. At the time of full nationalisation in 1975 the Belfast yard was 26 per cent owned by the Greek shipping magnate, Aristotle Onassis.[66] After its stint in government hands, H&W was privatised in 1989 with control reverting to a coalition of the yard's management and employees along with Norwegian shipowner, Fred Olsen. In return for the state shouldering debts of £400 million and furnishing assistance worth £98 million, Fred Olsen placed an £87 million order for three 135,000 dwt tankers to tide the yard over its transition period.[67] Remarkably, Norwegian shipowners have also bulked large in revamping a debt-ridden state yard in Portugal. Long overshadowed by its Lisnave peer, Setenave was established 40 kms south of Lisbon at Setubal as a symbol of the government's resolve to foster industrial development. As related elsewhere, its genesis owed much to the actions of Eriksberg: a Swedish yard in search of a spare ULCC facility for sub-contract work. Inaugurated in the heady days of the shipping boom of the late 1960s, it came fully equipped with a 700,000 dwt-capacity building dock and a 500 ton (as pp. 188, 222) lift-capacity Goliath crane. Clobbered in the subsequent tanker recession, Setenave escaped dissolution by a hair's breadth. After all, as just another surplus ULCC construction facility, it did not have very much to recommend it, especially as the country – like Greece – was deficient in industrial infrastructure and therefore vulnerable to expensive materials imports. Ship repair offered the only respite for Setenave, although the yard was scarcely able to scrape a living from it. By 1989 the yard's debt load had ascended to $400 million and, previous attempts to revive it having come to nothing, the government's hand was forced. Conceding defeat, it rented the yard to Solisnor, a consortium composed of local tanker owner Soponata (with a 40 per cent share), Lisnave (35 per cent) and three Norwegian companies: Wilh Wilhelmsen and its subsidiary, Barber International (together taking 15 per cent), and R.S. Platou (10 per cent). Reportedly, Barber was particularly eager to utilise Setenave as a repair base for its large fleet of owned and managed vessels.[68] Scandinavian firms, in fact, have shown a strong propensity to extend their shipping interests into shipyard operations. The Danes, as mentioned, are noteworthy in this respect, while Swedish shipowners also delved into shipbuilding prior to its wholesale nationalisation as Swedyards (recall Chapter 2). In a strange contemporary manifestation of this theme, Finnish shipowners have been dragged into active involvement in shipbuilding much against their better judgement. The rescue of Wärtsilä Marine at the end of 1989 was partly incumbent on clients – including EFFOA Finland Steamship Company – procuring a stake in the successor, Masa Yards.[69]

SUMMARY

The futures of many shipbuilders have hung in the balance in the last few years as a result of the alarming reversal in shipping demand first provoked by the energy crises of the 1970s and then perpetuated by the erratic and fitful recovery of the 1980s. Most enterprises found that they could do little about it short of summoning the assistance of the government, countenancing diversification, or both. Short-term palliatives in the form of contrived shipping contracts and outright socialisation of risk proved woefully inadequate in enabling the yards to prosper signally, and they were compelled to look searchingly at diversification for deliverance. In fact, the recourse to activities other than merchant new building to provide relief from its cyclical short-comings is an age-old strategy of shipbuilders and is generally implemented either through resort to warshipbuilding or through resignation from new construction altogether in favour of ship repair. Preferably, these options are undertaken in tandem with merchant new building rather than in place of it: in so doing, the enterprises avoid depending on a single market or, worse still, a solitary client. All yards of any stature readily espouse repair, while many attempt to balance defence contracts with at least a vestigial amount of merchant new building. The Japanese majors comply with this approach, as do such European firms as Chantiers de l'Atlantique, Fincantieri, Van der Giessen-de Noord, H&W, Bremer Vulkan, HDW and Thyssen Nordseewerke. The larger enterprises split the responsibility of merchant new building, warshipbuilding and repair between different yards. For example, Fincantieri instituted a division of labour whereby the first was delegated to five yards (Ancona, Castellammare di Stabia, Genova Sestri, Livorno and Venezia Marghera), warshipbuilding devolved to Muggiano and Riva Trigoso (with Monfalcone dabbling in both merchant and naval work) and repair was allocated to a half- dozen others (in Trieste, Venice, Genoa, Palermo, Naples and Taranto).

Of course, some shipbuilders – more obdurate than the rest – can spurn diversification, both in the name of specialisation and on the grounds that it diverts management, labour and plant from their prime purpose of shipbuilding. Yet in averting the perils roused when trespassing into less familiar lines of business, these firms compound the risk of reliance on a fragile market which may frequently fail to sustain them. A number of yards – most notably Wärtsilä Marine – attempted to ride out the fickle new-building market of the 1980s by redoubling efforts to bolster competitiveness in their shipbuilding mainstay. Vaunted specialisation notwithstanding, these yards had a hard time of it. Better by far, most builders reckoned, to acquire a substitute source of income. Moreover, recognising that broad-spectrum diversification was liable to exhaust their capabilities, most yards confined themselves to narrow-spectrum diversification; that is to say, they indulged in activities such as naval work, repair, rig building and shipping which bore a distinct resemblance to their previous mainstream business of merchant new building. Actuated by this ambition, they engaged in a variety of strategies which involved acquisition, new entry and new-firm formation, to say nothing of shipbuilders acquiescing in take-over gambits executed by other marine enterprises. This chapter has proffered a wealth of examples of narrow-spectrum diversification. Not invariably efficacious, this brand of diversification was marred by its inability to break out of the straitjacket imposed by its own limits: unhappily, the cross-subsidies expected to ensue from it are not always forthcoming because the diversified activities are insufficiently dissimilar to diverge from the business cycle that afflicts shipbuilding. A true countercyclical capability can only be achieved by deliberately courting the risks entailed in broad-spectrum diversification, a course of action antagonistic to the basic instinct of minimising uncertainty. Sensible of their place in the industry life-cycle and hemmed in by cost squeezes and emerging contestants, a not inconsequential number of firms were willing to pay the price exacted by this more demanding variant of diversification. The conversion of shipbuilders into conglomerates, or in what amounts to the same thing, the ingestion of shipbuilders by conglomerates, is the theme of the next chapter.

5 Conglomerates and shipbuilding

Resort to business lines not directly connected with shipbuilding has long been a strategy of great importance to shipyards, not least because it may offer the last chance for enterprise survival. At the mundane level, absence of ship orders has frequently compelled yards to volunteer their services as general engineers. For example, a clutch of Japanese yards endured a temporary dearth of new-building work in 1979–80 by stooping to the manufacture of steel structures (IHI Chita), environmental equipment (MHI Yokohama), chemical plant (MHI Hiroshima), atomic power equipment (IHI Yokohama), containers (MES Fujinagata) and process plants (Hitachi Zosen Ariake).[1] Desirous of evading the insecurity of such short-term expedients, other yards have sought a permanently available alternative in businesses divorced from shipbuilding: in a word, they have espoused the conglomerate option. In recent years the view has taken hold that American-style conglomerates have outlived their usefulness. Condemned as unwieldy and blundering leviathans, they are castigated for their inability to focus on cogent and dynamic activities, their obsession with short-term profit-making at the expense of systematic long-term sectoral nourishment and their presumed tendency to extinguish innovation and entrepreneurship as they go about their business of snapping up vibrant small enterprises.[2] Yet some aspects of conglomerate operations work to annul the carping directed against them and will ensure that, despite periodic set-backs, this form of industrial organisation will outlast the current predilection to disparage holding companies and the unrelated diversification that they stand for. The very size of conglomerates affords them the means to underpin sectors deemed worthy of support by their managements: as a result, cross-subsidies can sustain a favourite budding subsidiary through thick and thin (and, paradoxically, this capability summons nothing but approbation from Western observers of the Japanese version of conglomerates). Their ability to choose among a set of industries injects a sound screening process into the investment decision; that is to say, since conglomerates are granted privileged knowledge about a number of alternative firms and in view of the fact that they are given to subscribing to the profit-maximising motive, their managements will respond by selecting only the truly deserving for growth funds while, simultaneously, allowing the undeserving to wither on the vine. In line with this thinking, the tendency of vertically integrated firms to withstand the dictates of the industrial life-cycle and delay the needed rationalisation of units bordering on senescence – a force rightly judged to be inimical to effective structural change – is overcome by conglomerate manage- ments, imbued as they are with goals of market dominance and profit maximisation.[3]

Truth to say, those goals may work at cross-purposes with the needs of infant and adolescent businesses struggling to create effective markets and not yet granted the security of profitability. Yet, it does not stretch the bounds of credibility too much to believe that Western conglomerate managements can be taught, like their Japanese peers, to value the nurturing of unprepossessing activities should these latter have the makings of future greatness. Above all, however, conglomer-ates are the only corporate medium really capable of effecting and benefiting from a countercyclical property. By virtue of its ability to assume responsibility for a number of firms in different businesses, the conglomerate is neither hostage to the repercussions of a single business cycle nor, indeed, is it constrained by the particular pattern of impacts revealed by a single industry life-cycle. Acknowledgement of a nucleus of benefits adhering to the conglomerate form of organisation, then, promises to perpetuate it and, more to the point, invokes a response from its management aimed specifically at realising such gains. In other words, badly run conglomerates will disappear, leaving the field open to better-managed survivors and successors. Critically, however, the advent of efficiently run conglomerates, conducted with the object of realising profitability across the board and over an extended time horizon, offers mixed prospects for their shipbuilding subsidiaries. As loss-making mature enterprises, shipyards are likely to be clinically removed; but as profit centres (actual or potential), they can expect nothing less than the backing of parent organisations blessed with prodigious resources. We have already perused the approach of the zaibatsu to shipbuilding and marvelled at their determination to retain a presence in the industry at virtually any cost. Their example of fortitude in the face of adversity has offered a salutary and awe-inspiring lesson to the rest of the world's shipbuilders. That example is predicated on a distinct genesis and evolution, not to say nourishment, under the benign eye of the state. Since it has been analysed elsewhere in this book, it serves no useful purpose to repeat that record in this chapter: instead, our attention will be restricted to the actions of non-Japanese conglomerates, albeit some – the chaebōl – heavily influenced by the zaibatsu.

SOME PRELIMINARIES

Historically, non-Japanese conglomerates have not displayed much reluctance in dispensing with shipbuilding, especially when the yards have cut but a poor figure in comparison with other corporate interests. The defence and heavy engineers, persuaded of the superfluity of shipyards during phases of disarmament, have been in the vanguard of corporate actions of this tenor. After the First World War, for instance, Armstrong Whitworth phased out its Elswick yard while, a little later, Beardmore shrugged off its Dalmuir facility. Similar measures were implemented in the aftermath of the Second World War with, for example, John Brown acquiescing in the transfer of its Clydebank yard to a doomed merchant-oriented successor. In the 1980s, US defence contractors have also seen fit to renounce shipbuilding as an inevitable concomitant of cutbacks in naval programmes. Lockheed serves as a handy illustration. This aerospace giant entered shipbuilding in 1959 convinced that it could reap benefits from the synergy presumed to exist between warshipbuilding and other branches of defence contracting. Two yards were acquired in Seattle which, by 1982, were employing 2,500 workers almost exclusively on naval new building, along with an additional 500 devoted to ship repair. In that same year, Lockheed as a whole employed 70,200 workers and relied on the US Government for in excess of three-quarters of its total sales. Some 95 per cent of those sales derived from aerospace (47 per cent alone attributable to its missiles and space subsidiary), leaving shipbuilding to account for the tiny remainder.[4] The viability of Lockheed Shipbuilding underwent steady erosion throughout the 1980s as the backlog of landing ships – its speciality – was worked off without replacement. To the detriment of Lockheed, the US Navy was electing to procure its ships from fewer suppliers. In 1979 five yards amassed 70 per cent of all Navy new-building contracts by value; ten years later the proportion had risen to 93 per cent. Squeezed out of a market which was beginning to contract anyway, Lockheed axed its Seattle yards and, for good measure, sold its small landing-craft building yard in Thunderbolt, Georgia, to Trinity Industries.[5] Its focus had unequivocally returned to aerospace matters. All the same, conglomerates are just as likely to plunge into shipbuilding should circumstances appear propitious. The British electrical and electronics engineering giant, GEC, eagerly snapped up Yarrow in 1985 when BS put its warshipbuilding division up for sale. Bestowed with a full order-book for frigates, Yarrow was bought for £34 million and deemed cheap at the price. It was regarded as a perfect complement to GEC's other defence interests, in particular its large defence electronics portfolio. Of course, alluring conditions need not be confined to defence markets. Commercial shipbuilding has coaxed investment out of conglomerates when its star appeared to be in the ascendant. One of the more salient instances concerned the incursion of the American International Corporation into the industry. Founded in 1915 as a branch of the National City Bank of New York, this organisation proceeded to gain control of the Pacific Mail shipping company, began to make and export steel, grasped the selling rights for US machine tools, started manufacturing sugar and construction machinery, made inroads into railway and canal building in China and, generally, adopted the trappings of a multinational trading house.[6] In conjunction with a group of other US companies it entered shipbuilding via acquisition, buying the New York Shipbuilding Corporation of Camden, New Jersey. Reacting to the insatiable demand for cargo bottoms occasioned by hostilities, it brought its marine involvement to a climax in 1917 with the opening of the Hog Island yard, then the largest new-building facility in the world.

Contemporary hints of a shipping revival have again induced non-marine firms to actively seek involvement in shipbuilding. Although owing much to the invitation of government, the rise of the South Korean shipbuilding industry is emblematic of this phenomenon and will receive its due in the pages which follow. However, one case drawn from the Western AICs cries out for immediate notice; namely, the record of Kvaerner Industrier of Norway. Of late, Norwegian participation in shipping and shipbuilding has become a byword for a reawakening of the maritime instincts of the AICs and the activity of Kvaerner is no exception in this regard.[7] Unlike other Norwegian firms with their shipping origins (recall the last chapter), Kvaerner boasts an engineering background. A diversified group, it spread its interests over offshore, mining and hydro-electric power activities. Its first exposure to shipbuilding came via control of Moss Rosenberg Verft; a company which simultaneously granted it an entrance into shipping. Bent on applying energy engineering expertise to the marine industries, Kvaerner adapted its shipyard into a specialist supplier of gas and chemical tankers while electing, at the same time, to acquire Dido A/S as a nucleus for operating a large fleet of LPG carriers (which, upon take-over of the P&O fleet of gas ships, exceeded 1 million dwt by 1988). In 1981 it had bolstered its shipbuilding holdings through adroitly releasing the government from the politically important obligation of sustaining the rescued Fredriksstad yard. Global circumstances intruded to impose a change in direction, however. Wholesale collapse of competitiveness in Norwegian shipbuilding forced Kvaerner to expunge its larger new-building assets at home and look further afield for in-house capacity. In 1988 it paid £6 million to obtain Govan Shipbuilders in Glasgow where unit labour costs were barely one-quarter the Norwegian level, and a year later was making overtures to the Polish Government with the object of procuring the Gdynia yard complete with its 400,000 dwt-capacity building dock. Govan was turned to fulfilling Kvaerner's gas carrier production and Gdynia, already licensed to build the Norwegian firm's LPG carrier design, was envisaged as functioning along similar lines. As matters stood at the end of the 1980s, shipping accounted for three-quarters of the group's profits of NKr286 million (on a 1988 turnover of NKr8.470 billion). Besides Govan, the group could call on the services of yards in Omastrand (Fjellstrand A/S) and Bergen (Solheimsviken and Mjellem & Karlsen) and was the principal shareholder of HLD, the operators of Ferguson Shipbuilders in Port Glasgow and Clark Kincaid marine engine builders in Greenock. Essentially, Kvaerner owes its transformation into a shipbuilder of major proportions to its facility for switching resources from losing propositions (e.g. Moss Rosenberg) to ones bearing latent potential (e.g. Govan): an aptitude made possible on the strength of earnings transferred from the energy or shipping sectors.[8] Like the South Korean chaebŏl, it demonstrates the positive role of conglomerates in fostering shipbuilding. More ambivalent outcomes have attended conglomerate participation in US shipbuilding, however, and it is to that venue that we first address our comments before reverting to an appraisal of the chaebŏl.

AMERICAN AMBIVALENCE

Defence contracting is the bedrock upon which conglomerate interest in contemporary US shipbuilding rests. Without the need to continually feed a large navy with replacement vessels, American shipbuilding would simply fade away. Periodically, yards benefit from a surge of work as governments stoke up defence demand: the Reagan fleet build-up of the early 1980s – worth a minimum of $17 billion to the yards in the five years terminating in 1988 – is exemplary in this respect.[9] Shipbuilders hitherto quiescent, producing the odd merchant vessel for the cabotage trades or the subsidised liner routes, were suddenly inundated with a cornucopia of naval orders. By the same token, however, completion of the build-up deprived the yards of the fructifying factor and forced many of them either to revert to a regimen of ship repair interspersed with the rare commercial new building or to cease operations altogether. By their very nature conglomerates are intrinsically better equipped than shipbuilding-only enterprises to outlast the violent swings in business generated by such periodic defence programmes. They rejoice in a broad and diverse business base promising a steady stream of earnings; enough, at any rate, to subsidise shipyards in times of waning defence contracting if the corporate management is so minded. But, in truth, there is another side to the coin: if the returns from the yards are unimpressive even during episodes of waxing defence budgets, the parent organisation might see little virtue in retaining the facilities. Certainly, declining order books can incite drastic restructuring, as is evident from the Lockheed closures. Moreover, the Ogden Corporation released its Avondale yard in New Orleans to an employee-owned successor in 1985 believing that the chances of follow-on naval orders were slight. Paradoxically, reputable warshipbuilders with secure order books may be deleted from the conglomerate assemblage because the parents no longer feel able to support them in view of their other commitments. Bath Iron Works fell into this category. A veteran defence supplier dating from the 1880s, Bath Iron was absorbed into the Congoleum Corporation in 1975. The parent, preoccupied with its main activities in the house construction and mass-consumer fields, acceded to a $500 million offer from the yard's management in 1986. At that time Bath Iron revelled in a $1.46 billion backlog of orders from the Navy and, as lead yard for the new 'Arleigh Burke' destroyer class, was destined to receive regular naval contracts for years to come.[10] As with any owner of facilities adjudged strategic assets, the government might urge a conglomerate shipyard owner to reconsider its intention to sever ties with shipbuilding. Judicious granting of contracts generally suffices to retain their interest. For example, a sum of $173 million was appropriated in the 1985 defence budget to enable the Navy to order two surveying ships from Bethlehem Steel and thereby keep this firm's Sparrows Point yard active in new building. A number of other yards were the beneficiaries of Navy largesse in ship repair, receiving contracts to convert commercial vessels into naval auxiliaries. NASSCO of San Diego is a case in point. Long a unit of Morrison Knudsen, an engineering company and major player in public works projects, NASSCO was contracted in 1983 to convert a pair of tankers into

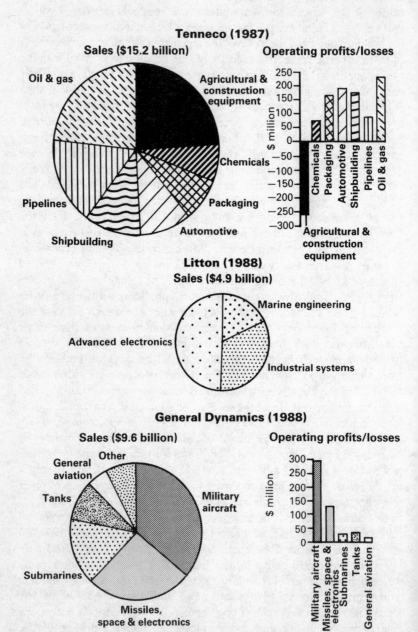

Figure 5.1 US conglomerates

hospital ships in a \$524 million programme.[11] Bereft of equivalent commercial work at the time, the naval business conspired to sustain activity levels in the yard.

The three principal conglomerate participants in US shipbuilding have long enjoyed privileged standing as prized suppliers to the Navy. Newport News Shipbuilding, owned by Tenneco of Houston, serves as the Navy's only source of aircraft carriers and as a supplementary supplier of nuclear patrol submarines. Employing 30,000 workers, it registered its sixth consecutive year of record profits in 1986 and boasted a backlog of Navy work worth in excess of \$5 billion. Newport News had turned its back on merchant new building following losses of more than \$200 million in the mid-1970s. There is more than a touch of irony in the fact that Tenneco's 1968 purchase of the yard had been inspired solely by the desire to build tankers for the transport of North Slope oil from Alaska and not by any wish to succeed as a large defence contractor. Motivation notwithstanding, Newport News accounted for about one-fifth of Tenneco's work-force, and about 11 per cent of the parent's 1987 sales. Overall, Tenneco was hampered by problems afflicting its Case International Harvester division, a maker of agricultural implements and tractors. This Achilles' heel drove the whole group some \$218 million into the red in 1986.[12] In contra- distinction, shipbuilding was a decidedly worthwhile activity for Tenneco: its operating profits of \$175 million in 1987 were bettered only by the automotive division and the much larger oil and gas division (Figure 5.1). Thus, while it was prepared to sell its oil and gas division to defray system-wide difficulties, Tenneco would not countenance the sale of Newport News.

The other two conglomerates, Litton Industries and General Dynamics, are incontestably defence firms through and through. The former traces its origins to Electro Dynamics Corporation, a small electronics firm revamped by two ex-Hughes Aircraft executives in 1953. Its labour force three decades later stood at 75,000, with advanced electronics systems accounting for 15,900 and marine engineering for 13,000. As can be elicited from Figure 5.1, advanced electronics is the largest constituent of Litton, responsible for sales amounting to almost half of the conglomerate's total. Consisting of inertial guidance and navigation systems, such electronics are, by and large, geared to aerospace markets but frequently find their way into warships as well. This fact helps explain Litton's penetration into shipbuilding (incidentally, setting a precedent that was used by GEC to justify the acquisition of Yarrow). Its marine engineering division was established in the 1960s and centred on Ingalls Shipbuilding of Pascagoula, a firm equipped with a new yard design to reflect those modular construction and assembly-line techniques usually associated with aerospace production. By 1988 marine engineering held a backlog of orders worth $3.5 billion, mostly for the Navy, and answered for 18 per cent of corporate sales. Ingalls was the chief source of cruisers of the 'Ticonderoga' class, besides being earmarked as a second source for the impending 'Arleigh Burke' destroyer class.[13]

General Dynamics, for its part, is primarily a supplier of military aircraft, missiles and defence electronics, although it deigns to leaven these offerings with main battle tanks and submarines. Its founder, John Hopkins, took over Electric Boat in 1947 as a prelude to incursions into warplane manufacture with the ultimate objective of forging his disparate interests into a general defence contractor. Electric Boat was the paramount submarine supplier to the US Navy and had been founded early in the century to specialise in that area. The former Fore River shipyard in Quincy, purchased from Bethlehem in 1964, added to General Dynamics' naval presence and gave it a footing in commercial new building to boot. By 1977 submarine building at Electric Boat engaged the attention of nearly 30,000 workers divided between the main yard in Groton and a secondary site in Quonset Point. Yet, while Electric Boat went from strength to strength in concert with naval expansion, the Quincy facility discovered that profit-making was beyond its capabilities. Its merchant backlog vanished in the early 1980s, leaving the yard entirely dependent on defence work. Failure to land Navy contracts worth $454 million condemned it to closure in 1985 with a loss of 4,200 jobs.[14] Electric Boat's charmed life came to an abrupt end in 1987, however, when earnings fell by 40 per cent. Labour unrest in the following year exacerbated the yard's problems. Therefore, while it accounted for 16 per cent of the corporation's total sales, the yard could only lay claim to 6 per cent of General Dynamics' operating profits (Figure 5.1).[15] Still, as the repository of the Navy's Trident-missile submarine expertise and the lead yard for its upcoming 'Seawolf' class of attack submarines, Electric Boat is an asset which General Dynamics holds dear. However, since it is devoid of any pretensions to commercial new building and therefore extremely sensitive to defence budgets, the yard's future is unmistakably held hostage by the Pentagon. While undoubtedly impressive in the naval arena, the performances of the likes of General Dynamics, Litton and Tenneco pale in comparison with the explosive growth of Korean shipbuilding conglomerates. The story attached to that growth is well worth relating, as we do forthwith.

KOREAN SINGLE-MINDEDNESS

South Korea owes its NIC status in large part to the synchronising of the corporate planning of its conglomerates with the interventionist approach of its governments. While conglomerate aspirations predate the military revolt of 1961 which brought onto the scene Park Chung Hee, national five-year economic plans and the supervisory Economic Planning Board, the real push for growth dates from the implementation of the first economic development plan in 1962. That plan was largely a trial balloon, leading to two follow-on plans and a decade of effort which stressed the provision of basic and light industries, the whole climaxed by the fourth plan of 1977–81 centred on the heavy and chemical industries, not least of which was shipbuilding. At first, emphasis was placed on an import-substitution form of industrialisation, whereupon home producers of cement, fertilisers and refinery products would spring up to replace reliance on imports of these goods. In short order, though, the onus of industrial development switched outwards, initially depending on the export of textiles, clothing and electronics before the climactic fourth plan ear-marked to heavy machinery – and prominently, ships – the task of shouldering the export burden. Erecting the industrial fabric was thus fundamental to all plans. In designating machinery, steel and petro-chemicals as target industries, for instance, the second plan laid the foundations of the Pohang integrated steel mill and thereby ensured the future self-sufficiency of many downstream activities, including shipbuilding. The Masan Free Export Zone, established in 1970, acknowledged the importance of foreign investment and know-how, and its administrators actively courted their presence through joint ventures and subsidiary operations. Among its occupants was Korea Tacoma, a shipyard established to utilise technology furnished by Tacoma Boatbuilding of the USA and later destined to earn laurels as an exporter of small naval vessels. Indeed, government plans set store by the ability of Korean enterprises to build on technology bought from abroad, and this aspect of industrialisation was to infuse shipbuilding as much as any other branch of manufacturing.[16] Of note in the third plan was the Industrial Site Development Promotion Law, a measure dedicated to setting aside land for industrial parks. One of its offspring was the Changwon Machine Industry Base, later an industrial complex critical to the formation of a marine engineering sector. At the end of the fourth plan, after 21 years of frenetic growth, South Korea's GNP had expanded from $12.7 billion (in 1980 prices) to $63 billion, a remarkable five-fold increase.[17]

The groundwork

By the onset of the fourth plan, however, the conglomerates had already began to earn their spurs as shipbuilders, implementing far-reaching projects aimed at propelling them to the forefront of world ship-building. Breath-taking in scope, these projects were also inherently risky. The story is told of Chung Ju Yung, the founder of the Hyundai chaebōl, who at the urging of President Park set about creating the world's largest shipyard in spite of the fact that the country had never built a vessel larger than 10,000 gt. An order from a Greek shipowner for two VLCCs in April 1972 gave the scheme credibility even though the outright cancellation of the yard's first new buildings in 1975 led to its virtual demise: a fate narrowly averted through the personal intercession of Park.[18] This example of the ultimate guarantee of unstinting government support for the shipyard projects was of immeasurable benefit to the chaebōl, sufficing to make palatable projects which would otherwise have appeared to bear unjustifiably high risk. In the light of such government sanction for extravagant program-mes in the 1970s, it is not surprising that conglomerates rose to the challenge by formulating increasingly grandiose schemes. These plans of the early 1970s contrasted dramatically with the substance of the industry of the day. To be blunt, South Korean shipbuilding barely warranted notice among the global shipping fraternity (recall Figure 3.1). Small beer it may have been, but inconsequential it was not to remain for long. Yet, strangely by later standards, the core of the industry, KSEC, had originally been a state enterprise singularly unremarkable in any way. Located on Yong-do Island near Busan, this yard had been founded in 1937 as the Chosun Heavy Industrial Company. Confiscated by the government after the ejection of the Japanese, it had come to life during the Korean War as a ship repairer. In 1952, for instance, it had worked on 230,000 gt of shipping. Its new-building facilities were sorely deficient, however, allowing it to tackle no vessel greater than 300 gt. A moderate expansion put into effect by the Ministry of Commerce and Industry (MCI) over the next 15 years enabled the yard to turn out a brace of 6,000 dwt freighters in 1968 and commence delivery, in the following year, of South Korea's first ship exports; that is, a series of tuna fishing boats for Taiwan worth $6.1 million. Rigidly enforced protectionism helped conjure up business for the yard. The government insisted, for example, that all domestic ships below 4,000 gt (13,000 gt from 1969) must be built at home and, in order to encourage orders, went on to offer subsidised loans to shipowners which bore interest rates of 7.5 per cent as opposed to the normal bank rate of 25 per cent. It also agitated for maximum indigenous content in the locally built ships (reckoned in 1969 at 70 per cent in coasters and fishing vessels but only half that in the larger freighters). To that end, it incited diesel engine companies to build small marine diesels under Japanese licences: a practice taken up by Hankook Machine Industry with Kubota technology, Daedong Industrial using MHI designs and Chinil Machines adopting Yanmar Diesel types. As the 1970s dawned, bold ambitions were already stirring at KSEC. A 25,000 dwt-capacity building dock was finished in 1969, enough to give the enterprise a potential annual output of 66,000 dwt; but this facility was to be steadily augmented, first to accommodate 100,000 dwt ships by 1972 and, secondly, to handle vessels of 300,000 dwt by 1976. Since 1968 KSEC had functioned as a private company, with 51 per cent of its shares appropriated by Namyoong Ryon, president of the Far Eastern Shipping Corporation. True to most state undertakings, KSEC had run up debts during its sojourn as a unit of the MCI (amounting to Won 5.7 billion) and the successor firm only agreed to inherit it on condition that the state put up the Won 3 billion ($9.67 million) needed to implement the capacity-boosting scheme.[19] As noted in Chapter 1, the first fruits of expansion for KSEC occurred in 1972 when Gulf Oil lodged an export contract for six tankers. In the meantime, output remained pitifully small despite the plans, registering only 18,500 gt for all South Korea in 1969.

Feverish expansion and setbacks

From this point onwards KSEC's role in national shipbuilding was to be overshadowed by the big conglomerates. The nature of Hyundai's induction into the industry's ranks has just been outlined. The instrument of that initiative, HHI, was built by Hyundai Construction Company using Norwegian design expertise. Conceived with the object of building five 259,000 dwt VLCCs each year, HHI's estimated cost was put at $60 million; some $5 million of which originated with Hyundai, $10 million derived from a government loan and the balance was mustered from loans forwarded by European banks.[20] When completed in 1976 this Ulsan yard would combine with KSEC and other incipient ventures to drive up the country's new-building capacity to the planned level of 1.9 million grt, a far cry from the 190,000 grt available at the beginning of the decade. Affirming its taste for the gargantuan, Hyundai plunged into ship repair. A subsidiary, Hyundai Mipo Dockyard Company, was also established at Ulsan and aspired to the title of the world's largest individual repair yard. Its facilities embraced four docks varying in size from 280,000 dwt capacity to 400,000 dwt capacity and

2.6 kms of alongside berths: together, these assets were designed to handle up to 25 vessels at any one time.[21] Yet, these plans had scarcely been formulated before the government, succumbing to second thoughts, proffered revised targets. It was soon voicing a goal of 4.25 million grt as the national shipbuilding capacity for 1981 and, as the cornerstone of that development, was advocating a gigantic agglomeration of nine yards located cheek-by-jowl on Koje Island, 40 kms south of Busan. One of the island's would-be occupants was to be a branch of KSEC specially equipped to produce eight 300,000 dwt VLCCs each year. This proposed yard was to be the upshot of combining Japanese technical acumen with Korean enterprise: the $33 million venture associated Hakodate Dock and trading house Marubeni from the Japanese side (holding 45 per cent of the equity) with the Korea Deep Sea Company, KSEC and the Hanjin Group from the native side. As it was, HHI had already forged technology transfer agreements with the British which were to repay the builder in very practical currency; namely, by confirming its credibility and standing as a reputable member of the global shipbuilding fraternity. Symbolic of that accomplishment, Govan Shipbuilders hit upon the cost-saving expedient of subcontracting to the Ulsan yard 10 of its 23 'Clyde' class of 23,000 dwt cargo vessels building for the Kuwait Shipping Company.[22] Recognition of this calibre merely fuelled HHI's ambitions, and its facilities grew by leaps and bounds. Its massive 700,000 dwt-capacity building dock was brought into service and plans were put in hand to give the yard a 1977 throughput of a dozen each of 300,000 dwt and 60,000 dwt vessels. It booked export contracts for 12 VLCCs in the heady days of 1972–3 and assumed that this was but an augury of better things to come. Of course, the shipping crisis of the mid-1970s tempered these plans and, along with them, those of the MCI which had grown correspondingly to envisage a 9 million grt capacity by 1985. Immediately shelved was a joint venture of Samsung Heavy Industries and IHI which had been conceived with the idea of erecting a 1 million ton-capacity yard at Chungmu on the south coast. Also disrupted was the KSEC venture with the Japanese on Koje Island. Gone was the huge tanker-building facility and in its place there was talk of substituting two smaller yards of 80,000 dwt capacity. The country still had 2.39 million grt of new-building capacity on its hands at the end of 1975 and was at a loss to find a use for it all. The government, however, would brook no opposition to its vision of shipbuilding as a pillar of national economic development. Consequently, it applied all its powers to sustaining the industry and, in so doing, the conglomerates which actually operated the establishments. Survival was sought in the dry cargo and Ro-Ro markets rather than in tankers, and the MCI made available additional export credits to entice overseas shipowners into ordering in South Korea. In a similar vein, the government dipped into the newly established National Investment Fund in order to finance new-building contracts initiated by domestic shipowners. Under the new rules, local shipowners were required to find as little as 8 per cent of ship contract prices, the rest was furnished in the form of loans from the fund. The government estimated that 1.1 million grt could be funded in this manner, enough to bolster the merchant fleet to 3.8 million grt by 1981 and, not incidentally, sufficient to keep the new yards moderately busy until that year.[23]

Furthermore, as we have noticed, the state was prepared to execute yard bail-outs. Stuck with VLCCs rejected by both Livanos and the Tung Group, HHI was effectively rescued by the government when the latter found gainful employment for these vessels. Moreover, the yard was given the opportunity of a new start, diversifying away from tankers through a contract to build six container vessels under the rubric of the domestic fleet expansion programme. Beset by a 1978 capacity utilisation rate of only 44 per cent, HHI was fortunate in being able to transfer one-third of its underemployed work-force to other firms in the Hyundai chaebŏl on the one hand, while exercising many of the remainder in the lucrative ship-repair sector on the other. In an interesting aside, HHI bought the state-owned Inchon Iron and Steel Company in 1978 both to obtain its plant for making rolled steel and to extend its Inchon site into shipbuilding. Along with Ssangyong and Dongkuk Steel, this firm was responsible for the budding South Korean shipbreaking industry. Under HHI tutelage, the Inchon scrapping berths were enlarged and new ones opened at Ulsan. The figure of 50,000 light disp tons of shipping demolished under the aegis of Inchon Iron and Steel in 1978 was to be boosted to 1.4 million by 1983, whereupon HHI would control 90 per cent of the industry. Similarly circumstanced, KSEC created its own shipping subsidiary (Far Eastern Marine Transport) and contrived to build a string of chemical and product tankers for it. The veteran shipbuilder's Koje Island project, materialising as the Okpo yard, was finished with a view to building barge-mounted floating industrial plants in a fashion reminiscent of the Japanese majors. Helpful as ever, the government raised in 'soft' loans half of the $200 million initially estimated as necessary for yard completion. Significantly, however, at the time of commissioning Okpo was no longer a KSEC venture, and the government loans bordered on a bail-out incentive to prevent the yard from foundering. Appalled at the heavier than anticipated start-up costs and troubled by the ramifications of market recession, KSEC had willingly turned over Okpo to a syndicate representing Daewoo and the Korea Development Bank. On hand-over to its new owners in 1978 the Okpo yard, a brainchild of the design skills of A&P Appledore, was nothing less than a masterpiece of shipbuilding ingenuity. Blessed with a spacious lay-out expressly modelled to accommodate optimum flow-line principles, it abounded in superlatives: employing 8,100 men on a site containing a 530m-long building dock equipped with a Krupp crane capable of lifting 900 tons (one of the two largest shipyard cranes in the world) and enjoying, besides, fabrication plant fully attuned to the demanding needs of such complex ships as chemical and gas carriers. On the debit side, however, its protracted construction eventually cost $500 million, enough to require Daewoo to pay $146,000 per day in interest charges (and this despite the fact that the government had assumed more than 60 per cent of the costs burden).[24] As we shall see, the liabilities accompanying this consecration were never completely eradicated by Daewoo: on the contrary, they were progressively to worsen as the 1980s unfolded.

The neighbouring Koje Island yard, opened by the Samsung chaebŏl, was undergoing initiation rites and, resolved to avoid excessive reliance on tankers, was about to begin production of bulkers, general cargo vessels and container ships. What was to become SSHI had begun life as a provisional enterprise known as Woojin Shipbuilding. Samsung's original intention to co-operate with IHI in setting up a shipyard had been overtaken by events, a casualty of the gloom engendered by the shipping recession, and the Korean firm appeared to absolve itself of shipbuilding altogether. In an evident about-face, however, it re-entered the lists, persuaded by the government of the future viability of the industry. The stillborn Woojin, already floundering, was relieved to be taken over by Samsung. Hedging its bets, as it were, the SSHI management terminated the yard's expansion plan at the end of the first phase, preferring to make do with a 100,000 dwt-capacity building dock rather than the 500,000 dwt monster envisaged for the second phase. Fellow conglomerate, Daewoo, had also capitulated to the fervour for shipbuilding, committing itself to what was to become the DSHM yard at Okpo on the withdrawal of KSEC. Its interest in marine activities did not end there, however. In pursuance of a desire to cut a commanding figure in the industry, Daewoo took over the Hankook Machine Industry in 1976, an enterprise poised to expand as a supplier of diesel engines. Since the government was intent on enlarging the domestic content of all the materials and components used in shipbuilding, this acquisition – revamped as part of DHI – was likely to have a promising future. Calculated at 46 per cent in 1976 and 60 per cent in 1978, the indigenous share of ship values was set to rise to 80 per cent by 1981.

Already the Pohang steelworks was being called upon to furnish a wide range of steel products and, in a complementary move, DHI, Ssangyong and Hyundai were designated by the government as prime sources of marine engines. As Hankook, DHI traced its beginnings to the Chosun Machine Works of 1937. An industrial machinery manufacturer, this Inchon establishment was nationalised in 1945 and subjected to 23 years of government ownership before being judged sufficiently robust to qualify for release to the private sector. It merged with the Bugok railway rolling stock works in 1973 and two years later began making MAN diesel engines under licence. Originally tailored to truck and bus markets, the mandate of the new diesel plant was extended under Daewoo management to deal with marine applications and a crash programme of import substitution was instituted. For example, the MAN type D0846M engine, used in road vehicles, power generating plant and ships, witnessed a rise in domestic sourcing of parts from 40 per cent in 1975 to 59 per cent in 1978. By the 1981 target date, 77 per cent of the engine was made in South Korea, a proportion that climaxed at 90 per cent in 1984.[25]

Policies compatible with shipbuilding expansion were conducted with a vengeance by the government in the second half of the 1970s. Set on providing a 'captive' market for the builders, the recently formed Korea Maritime and Ports Administration (KMPA) declared its intention of ensuring that the country not merely adhered to the UNCTAD liner code on shipping, but bettered it. The international body, acceding to the demands of Third World nations for more control over global shipping, had stipulated the so-called 40:40:20 rule for the liner (as opposed to the tramp) trades. In other words, two-fifths of the cargo entering and leaving a country's ports in liner shipping should be carried aboard domestic-flag ships, an equal proportion should be reserved for the ships of the trading partner, while the balance could be given over to cross-traders; that is, to ships belonging to neither the importing country nor the exporting nation.[26] The KMPA, unimpressed by the proposed share for domestic vessels, wanted half of all cargo involved in the liner trades touching the country to be transported in Korean ships by 1981. To that end, it disbursed loans to shipowners, notably to those in sympathy with its aim of subjecting 65 per cent of cargo movements to containerisation. Local yards were the recipients of contracts associated with this fleet expansion, valuing in particular the receipt of orders for relatively sophisticated container ships. Not overlooked for one moment, though, was the fact that yards had been nominated to lead economic development as export earners. Determined to endorse their export function, the government attracted orders to the builders from foreign shipowners by bolstering the export credit level to 85 per cent (with repayment terms of up to ten years at 7–8 per cent), raised the price competitiveness of the yards through effectively waiving import taxes on shipbuilding materials and, to cap it all, managed to find $175 million to invest in shipyard expansion. Between them, the MCI and the Economic Planning Board were asking the yards to export ships worth $438 million in 1980, some $2.5 billion by 1986 and no less than $5 billion by 1991. By way of comparison, motor vehicles were expected to earn $255 million in 1980, $2.9 billion by 1986 and $8.8 billion by 1991. The champion of light industry, electronics, was given the objective of achieving exports worth $780 million in 1980, $2.1 billion by 1986 and $3.5 billion by 1991.[27] Clearly, shipbuilding was visualised as constituting a major plank in the government's industrialisation plan for years to come. Consistent with this long-term vision, the MCI enforced a number of changes in the heavy industries which affected the division of labour between the chaebŏl. Ssangyong, for instance, was instructed to fold its power transformer business into that of Hyosung Heavy Industries but, in compensation, was accorded the honour of becoming the country's main supplier of marine diesel engines, taking over the responsibilities of DHI and HHI (although the first was designated as the national supplier to the automotive industry while the second was appointed to the position of monopoly supplier of large marine diesels beyond 6,000 bhp).[28] As part of the same reorganisation, HHI was deprived of its power generating equipment business and was forced to concur with its transfer to DHI. Some solace could be taken from the fact that HHI was permitted to retain a stake in that aspect of power generation having a direct bearing on shipbuilding. While noteworthy, these attempts to establish a solid foundation of marine engineering were greatly overshadowed by raw ship production facilities. Thus, by 1980, South Korea could boast a new-building capacity of 4 million grt, of which 1.2 million had come on stream in the previous 12 months with the inauguration of the Okpo yard. At that juncture, HHI held title to 2 million grt of the national total and KSEC owned 350,000 grt. The four chief builders exported 1.2 million grt of shipping in 1979 worth a tidy $1 billion and, thereby, achieved export earnings well in advance of the targets set them.

Heightened competitiveness

The fifth five-year plan, initiated in 1982, was as attentive to the needs of shipbuilding as had been its illustrious predecessor. Revised targets were laid down, with output ordained to reach 2.8 million grt in 1987:

an amount worth a hefty $5 billion in export earnings. The state set aside Won 648 billion for the industry's expansion, the highlights of which included the extension of Okpo to 2 million grt capacity and the upgrading of SSHI from 100,000 grt to 600,000 grt capacity. Of equal if not greater significance, however, was the attention given to ancillary activities, especially those capable of substituting for the engines, navigation equipment and special steels which had to be imported from Japan and, alarmingly, constituted up to 60 per cent of ship values. To remedy that failing, the government asserted that local content must be raised to account for 90 per cent of ship values by 1987. Marine diesel engines, in particular, were targeted for domestic production, and the aim was to eliminate imports altogether once the new plant had been erected. Another thrust of great import was directed at diversifying the offerings of the yards, turning them, in effect, away from a vulnerable reliance on cheap, unsophisticated bulkers and tankers to a situation in which they could rival Japan in the provision of sophisticated vessels and offshore structures. As a unique installation, the Okpo yard set the pace on the last score. Upon commencing operations, it basked in an order-book which included two chemical tankers, six semisubmersible and two jack-up drilling rigs and a seawater treatment plant.

Yet, the vast weight of orders built up by the four leading builders in the early 1980s (revealed in Figure 1.6), and perpetuated throughout the decade (illustrated in Figure 1.7), stubbornly kept them wedded to the production of bulkers and tankships. Confounding expectations, South Korea gravitated away from diversification (Figure 1.4), registering a shift in its index of concentration from 0.36 to 0.74 between 1984 and 1988. Comparable indicators of diversification, or the lack of it, have been calculated for the individual builders, using for the raw data work in hand for each October of 1983, 1985, 1987 and 1989. As far as the South Korean benchmark is concerned, the indices have moved marginally towards specialisation from an already high level, although with a value of 0.91 the banner year for this leaning was evidently 1987 and not 1989.[29] Table 5.1 goes on to evince the finding that DSHM and Inchon Engineering, a medium-sized builder belonging to the Halla chaebŏl, are consistently more specialised in their ship output profiles than the nation as a whole. Excepting for 1983, HHI also conformed to this tendency. Conversely, SSHI and KSEC tended to display the opposite proclivity, grasping for greater diversity in ship offerings.[30] In recording an index of 0.90 for 1989, though, the Samsung enterprise had dramatically reversed its previous predilection, becoming in fact one of the more specialised Korean builders. A better feel for the instability in shipbuilding that obtrudes to prevent a smooth transition into product

Table 5.1 Indices of concentration, South Korea

Firm	As of October of			
	1983	1985	1987	1989
DSHM	0.79	0.84	0.93	0.87
HHI	0.74	0.82	0.95	0.84
Inchon Engineering	1.00	0.99	1.00	0.95
SSHI	0.70	0.80	0.82	0.90
KSEC	0.70	0.84	0.87	0.79
South Korea	0.74	0.79	0.91	0.79

Table 5.2 Indices of dissimilarity, South Korea

Firm	Change period		
	1983–5	1985–7	1987–9
DSHM	14.45	59.05	12.50
HHI	20.73	65.69	51.30
Inchon Engineering	3.68	100.0	16.25
SSHI	49.14	20.31	51.67
KSEC	44.79	33.08	27.32

diversification can be got from a perusal of Table 5.2. A matrix of indices of dissimilarity, this table admits of a comparison of changes in output content between, first, 1983 and 1985, then 1985 and 1987 and, finally, 1987 and 1989. Like the index of concentration, this index is a Gini coefficient; but its value ranges on a scale from 0 to 100, with the lower limit representing no substantive change in content and the upper limit intimating a totally upended product composition.[31] From the magnitudes of the indices, it is clear that DSHM, HHI and Inchon Engineering experienced relatively modest changes in product differentiation between 1983 and 1985 whereas SSHI and KSEC underwent appreciable restructuring. The inverse situation marked the 1985–7 period as the first three firms sprang to catch up with the changes previously enacted by the Koje Island and Busan enterprises.[32] At the tail end of the 1980s, HHI and SSHI together were undergoing the throes of a considerable change-over in output composition while the other three had departed only moderately from their 1987 profiles.

The dubious success of the diversification strategy was unsurprising in the light of South Korea's unbeatable competitiveness in the bulker and OBO markets. By one measure, a typical chaebōl could turn out a 30,000 dwt ore carrier for $16.365 million in comparison with the $46.55 million that an equivalent vessel floated out by NORMED would cost.

Labour costs of $3.54 per hour obtaining for the former in contrast to the $23.40 per hour applying to the latter were largely to blame for the French builder's disadvantage.[33] A price for forced diversification was also being exacted; a price which, in no uncertain terms, tended to dissuade yards from lightly surrendering their bulker and tanker specialities. SSHI, for instance, was barely profitable in 1982 despite a healthy 90 per cent capacity utilisation rate and a willingness to undertake varied new-building jobs. HHI's Ulsan yard could turn its hand to chemical and product tankers, reefers, semisubmersible and jack-up rigs, offshore jacket systems, modules and floating industrial plants while its Mipo yard was a dedicated ship repairer and its engine works fabricated MAN/B&W and Sulzer slow-speed diesels under licence, to say nothing of medium-speed SEMT-Pielstick diesels and Kobe Steel crankshafts and propellers.[34] Nevertheless, it could only attain a 2.5 per cent profit margin on a turnover of more than $1 billion in 1983. DSHM's fortunes were more parlous still, losing $10 million in 1982 and scraping profits of $6.3 million (or a 1.3 per cent margin) from a turnover of $500 million in 1983.[35] This occurred in spite of the Daewoo yard selling seven semisubmersible drilling rigs, as against a mere one by HHI, and netting a $571 million order for a dozen container vessels from US Lines; at the time, the largest single commercial new-building order ever placed anywhere. Evidently, yard versatility consistent with diversification was responsible for heightened overheads which, in turn, degraded profit margins. By mid-decade, in fact, all the builders were suffering. The Hyundai chaebōl was moved to acquire Korea Merchant Transport to secure a 'captive' market for unwanted container vessels building at Ulsan. DSHM, for its part, stood to lose at least $15.7 million – and more likely multiples of that – on its acclaimed US Lines contract when that American operator of container ships inconveniently collapsed. Its announcement of a $50 million contract to construct a barge-mounted power station for the coastal city of Khanom in Thailand seemed paltry compensation by comparison. All told, the MTI estimated that the country's shipbuilders had lost $55.7 million on sales of $3.28 billion in 1985 and that employment growth in the industry had not merely halted but had gone into reverse. DSHM alone was said to have relinquished 4,000 workers.[36] Nor was there any relief in sight in the first quarter of 1986 and the industry refused to relent on its retrenchment. Some 3,500 of its remaining 72,000 shipyard workers received their dismissal notices at this time.

Worse still, the plan to broaden the industrial base was encountering problems. A key link in the chain connecting the state Pohang steelworks to the chaebōl yards, machinery supplier Korea Heavy

Industries and Construction (KHIC), was faltering. Formerly an offshoot of Hyundai and a victim of poor management, this Changwon enterprise had been nationalised in 1980 to prevent its dissolution. Yet it persisted in being a severe trial to its new owners. Its construction equipment division was handed over to SSHI in an attempt to restore efficiency, but the very future of the machinery sector in the country appeared doubtful. Local content targets for the value of ships and their ingredients became unattainable in consequence. On one account, the 50 per cent average indigenous content by value of ships produced in 1984 declined to 30 per cent in 1987 as boilers, pumps, purifiers and navigation equipment continued to be imported. To make matters worse, the boost in ship demand after the first quarter of 1986 caught the local engine builders unawares and ship propulsion plant had to be bought abroad. Determined to make amends, the engine builders embarked on a programme of expansion. Valiant efforts were made by Ssangyong Heavy Industries, the part of the Ssangyong chaebōl discharging the group's responsibility for diesel engines, to meet rising demands. By December 1988 its cumulative sales of diesels surpassed the 4 million bhp mark, and the company was confidently casting around for foreign shipyard customers for its engines. Hyundai, concentrating on bigger engines, actually began to export licence-built MAN/B&W engines to West Germany for incorporation into container ships building at the HDW yard, while the once sluggish KHIC managed to have its Sulzer engines installed in container vessels building at Bremer Vulkan.[37]

Good times, bad times

Occasioning more immediate disquiet to the government and the chaebōl was the unprofitability of shipbuilding in the light of harsh price competition with the Japanese (as related in Chapters 2 and 4). In truth, the chaebōl builders accumulated market share at the cost of substantial, albeit undisclosed, cross-subsidies from other corporate businesses in conjunction with massive government subventions, again veiled in a cloak of obfuscation. The cost spilled over to unleash distress and confusion among the work-force as well. Ulsan, for instance, retired one-quarter of its labour force in the middle years of the 1980s. Drawing attention to these drawbacks do the industry no more than justice and offset the tendency to limit appraisal to its glowing production record. Ostensibly, the industry was riding on the crest of a wave, wreaking havoc among Japanese and European shipbuilders alike. In reality, the lion's share of the orders wrested from these competitors were garnered at below-cost prices. At the end of 1986, HHI's order-book had accumulated to 1,629,400 gt, DSHM's equalled 1,033,300 gt, KSEC's totalled 254,400 gt while SSHI brought up the rear with 206,650 gt. Fully 89 per cent of the HHI backlog was destined for overseas customers while 88 per cent of Daewoo's order-book was for export.[38] The two laggards were not so export dependent (79 per cent in the case of KSEC and 54 per cent for SSHI), but the difference was one of degree rather than substance. On the one hand, excessive reliance on unstable world markets – bought, in any event, at such a cost – was pregnant with dire implications but, on the other, it may have acted as an unmitigated blessing in view of the perilous state of the domestic shipping sector. In 1987 the Economic Planning Board was forced to intervene in the affairs of the Korea Shipping Corporation, Won 700 billion in debt, and institute a programme of restructuring. In order to forge a viable unit, the firm was transferred to the Hanjin chaebōl and merged into Hanjin Container Lines.[39] However, these efforts were too late to afford an enriched domestic market for the builders. In April of that year KSEC requested the Seoul Civil District Court to step in and grant it protection from its creditors. The refusal of two Norwegian shipowners to take delivery of a half-dozen vessels, judged inadequately built, proved to be the last straw for KSEC. It reported debts of $675 million as against assets of only $475 million. Ironically, this period witnessed South Korea overtake Japan in the new-building order league. More to the point, the market at length had condescended to allow prices to rise and they had dutifully responded by increasing some 30 per cent between the beginning of 1986 and late 1987. Such macro-level changes, promising better times for the beleaguered industry, did not on that account make matters more palatable for the individual yards. By mid-1988 HHI, DSHM, KSEC and SSHI had reputedly run up debts of $4.5 billion; added to which the first pair were plagued with labour unrest. Indeed, worker disputes and disruptions were to become a hallmark of the late 1980s for the chaebōl. The major cliffhanger of the period swirled round the question of whether the besieged builders would survive. Cassandras were prophesying the extinction of at least one major yard at the hands of its workers, and with good cause. The industry had shredded its work-force from 75,000 in 1984 to 51,000 by the end of 1988 and the workers were disillusioned, not to say downright militant, in consequence. HHI transferred many workers to its automotive affiliate, effectually cutting its employment base from 30,000 in 1985 to 23,000 three years later. Drastic measures of this nature enabled it to record a scarcely discernible profit of Won 32 million on a 1987 turnover of Won 963 billion.[40]

In even worse shape, DSHM reported debts of $1.42 billion and Kim Woo-Choong, founder of the Daewoo chaebŏl, was begging the government to provide a $1.15 billion (Won 800 billion) loan. Pay increases in the order of 40 per cent in 1986 and 1987 for the yard's 14,000 workers had been conceded in a forlorn attempt to avert disarray, but they had also acted to boost DSHM's losses in the latter year to Won 88.4 billion on sales of Won 513.9 billion. Wage concessions of 24 per cent for two years running, granted in June 1989 so as to terminate a bitter strike, simply served to accelerate the waning validity of the yard's business plan. Desperate assurances from Kim that DSHM would regain profitability within three years sounded hollow, but he was already diversifying the firm into the manufacture of helicopters and other defence equipment (including submarines) as well as planning to make Suzuki minicars on part of the yard site. Eventually, after the state steel and electricity enterprises had rebuffed attempts to have them acquire DSHM, the government consented to bail-out Kim provided he met certain conditions. In return for Kim selling off prime property interests so as to raise Won 400 billion ($593 million) as his contribution to the rescue plan, the government agreed to recapitalise DSHM (which, after all, was still 33 per cent owned by the state's Korea Development Bank) and safeguard its future. An attenuated shipbuilder, earmarked for merger with DHI by 1992 and set to lose half its work-force to other Daewoo affiliates, the surviving organisation would be relieved for seven years from its obligation to pay interest on the Won 250 billion that it owed to the Korea Development Bank and, additionally, would receive an injection of Won 150 billion from the bank. Stern stuff, no doubt, but perhaps more than could be expected for a yard which lost Won 213 billion on sales of Won 460 billion in 1988 and which had amassed debts of Won 1.2 trillion.

Soaring labour costs also subverted the viability of the other yards, compounding the problems brought on through their intense price competition with the Japanese. HHI reported its first loss in 1988 (Won 29 billion or $88 million), the results from SSHI suggested a loss of Won 19 billion, whereas KSEC was in limbo, continuing under the bankruptcy protection accorded it by the Bank of Seoul to work through a declining merchant order-book and find solace in naval contracts for a handful of frigates. In 1987–8 losses realised by the four main builders mounted to Won 635 billion ($1.01 billion) and looked set to worsen since labour costs had more than doubled during this two year span (Table 5.3). A strike at Ulsan in 1989 paralysed HHI for more than three months and resulted in $760 million of lost production.[41] The threat to their very existence from this quarter compelled the chaebŏl, at the

Table 5.3 Shipyard returns, South Korea

	Fiscal year profits and losses in Won billion				
Firm	1984	1985	1986	1987	1988
DSHM	5.9	9.8	44.6	88.4	212.8
HHI	3.6	2.8	0.2	0.03	28.9
KSEC	2.8	7.6	9.4	244.5	51.1
SSHI	15.9	13.6	28.3	9.2	19.2

Source: Far Eastern Economic Review, 25 May 1989, p.71

behest of the South Korean Government, to first sink their differences and suppress their inherent yard rivalry before relaxing their intransigence towards the Japanese on the subject of ship pricing. Compounding the gravity of the crisis evoked by labour unrest were difficulties generated by supply bottlenecks and currency appreciation. In spite of its ability to produce steel one-fifth cheaper than imported supplies, the Pohang steel mill could only provide 70 per cent of the builders' needs. Reliance on foreign producers of expensive special equipment further exacerbated the problems of supply.[42] This, together with a rising Won (appreciating by 15 per cent in the two years following January 1988) and a bruised management licking its wounds after confronting the work-force, sufficed in the first place to break the deadlock in intercorporate relations and, in the second, led to a relenting in the hard-line attitudes all too common previously. Early indications of a shift in the rules which hitherto had governed rivalry between the chaebōl emerged in April 1989 when HHI and DSHM jointly agreed to fulfil a Swedish order for a series of OBOs. Signs of a rapprochement with the Japanese were more circumspect. At any rate, by late 1989 a shadowy accord had been struck between Japanese and Korean builders which allowed both groups to refrain from crippling competition and even meditate co-operation. A dark suspicion began to surface in the rest of the world that an invidious oligopoly was in the making; a supplier cartel evident, some would suppose, in Japanese builders acquiescing in the amassing of bulker orders by the chaebōl in return for the Koreans giving them a free-hand in the VLCC market.[43] In a kindred move designed to restore shipyard viability, the government sought to relieve KSEC both of its financial burdens and organisational uncertainty. A solution was found in its sale to Hanjin in May 1989. The government gave credence to the merits of vertical integration, believing that Hanjin would use the yard not only as an in-house means of vessel replacement but also as a 'captive' ship-repair base. In deference to this conviction, it was prepared to contribute an unspecified amount towards retiring the old company's Won 600 billion ($900 million) debt. As a result, Hanjin could press ahead with its plans to restructure the Busan yard, integrating it into the conglomerate's shipping operations; these last, one might recall, having already been bolstered through government intervention.[44] There is wry justice in the KSEC outcome, for this cornerstone of South Korean shipbuilding which had pioneered the industry's expansion at the bidding of the government was, in the end, forced to submit to a bail-out imposed by the alliance of state and conglomerate interests in order to persist in the business as a barely tolerated mature enterprise.

SUMMARY

As one commonly held view has it, conglomerates are dinosaurs constrained to follow organisational grooves inimical to innovation and obsessed with short-term profitability. By another estimation, conglomerates are organisations charged with a mission to succeed and fully alive to the value of new technology in fulfilling that object. Either view is acceptable, depending on the circumstances informing the observer's opinions. The former prevails in the West where conglomerate operations have increasingly become associated with large, inflexible bureaucracies and misguided business planning. The latter is more germane to East Asia. At any rate, it pervades the Western view of zaibatsu, the Japanese approximations of conglomerates which are credited with masterminding much of that country's economic resurgence. The relative merits and demerits of the conglomerate form of organisation come to a head in shipbuilding. Theoretically, shipyards can suffer under the conglomerate yoke, consigned to oblivion as a punishment for failing to keep up with the more profitable business lines maintained by the holding group. Conversely, they can prosper under the watchful and benign eye of a conglomerate management willing to overlook temporary shortfalls in returns on the understanding that continual support will pay dividends in the long run. The first outcome, centred on the accusation of opportunism, appears to be well founded in the Western context. In recent decades, American conglomerates have displayed little interest in shipbuilding, a mature industry assailed on all sides by better-placed competitors, except where they can anticipate profits through pandering to the government and its naval ambitions. Unable to appreciably improve the competitiveness of US shipbuilding, they have settled for warshipbuilding complete with its institutionalised protectionism. However, their staying power in this arena is often ephemeral, contingent on the swings in defence spending. Only the entrenched producers, enjoying commanding or monopoly control of niche markets (e.g. Tenneco with aircraft carriers and General Dynamics with ballistic-missile submarines), have persisted with the industry over an extended period, investing heavily in facilities and reconstructing yards to make them fully compatible with their intended roles.

Unmarked by the overpowering weight of defence considerations, the South Korean chaebōl have preferred to devote their energies to merchant new building. Like the zaibatsu they extol the virtues of international competitiveness, but like them, too, they have government contrived and stimulated domestic markets to fall back on. Thanks to various state industrialisation programmes, the chaebōl have emerged as key players in global shipbuilding, outdoing all their competitors apart from the zaibatsu. This supreme feat exacted a heavy price, however, and brought some of the chaebōl to the brink of catastrophe. Only a last minute accommodation with the Japanese prevented wholesale bankruptcy of their shipbuilding divisions. Serious labour disruptions at home revealed another, graver handicap; one threatening to overturn their vaunted international competitiveness. Indeed, this state of affairs has moved some to question the wisdom of their leaders.[45] Allegedly overdiversified and undermanaged, the chaebōl have traditionally had recourse to a sympathetic government when problems became too pressing. In return for seizing a sizeable share of the world market and executing a rapid expansion of capacity, the government always saw fit to excuse their blunders through implicit or explicit socialisation of risk. Ironically, that policy has sufficed to endow South Korea with a massive shipbuilding industry, but one which can scarcely be described as profitable. To be blunt, the policy enforced by the government, if not a recipe for financial disaster, is certainly not a model of fiscal rectitude. Far too frequently, it seems to precipitate its actors into crisis. In any event, its day is probably over, for the government has found other obsessions. The contemporary concern of state planners with realigning the chaebōl in the direction of high-technology growth industries has ominous overtones for South Korean shipbuilders, although the revival in world shipping expected to characterise the 1990s may go some way towards restoring their fragile viability.

6   Inchoate marine industries: the seeming paradox

Developing countries have entertained the belief that industrialisation is critical to their ideals of advancement. They have pursued two routes aimed at accomplishing it. The first pivoted on import substitution while the second focused on export promotion. In actuality, these strategies need not be mutually exclusive and the more hopeful of the developing nations adhere to the view that, in the fullness of time, the first will naturally shade into the second. After all, as we have just noted in the last chapter, South Korea was effectual in weaning its economy from reliance on import substitution to one guided by the lights of export promotion and, not coincidentally, attached much weight to shipbuilding in the process. In fact, shipbuilding became something of an object of veneration among the proponents of Third World industrialisation. It was celebrated for its ability to furnish domestic tonnage along the lines advocated by the United Nations Conference on Trade and Development (UNCTAD) (i.e. through a variety of import substitution) while simultaneously offering the promise of export earnings. Other would-be benefits were also evident. In view of its status as a mature industry, entry barriers are relatively low; insufficient, at any rate, to obstruct the emergence of a determined interloper. Equally alluring, the neophyte producer can quickly aspire to international competitiveness once it brings its labour-cost advantages to bear and that prospect opens up enormous possibilities for the penetration of export markets. By dint of concerted effort, mobilisation of a latent labour force and an element of protectionism, planned shipbuilding has the potential – like few others in the manufacturing sector – to propel the late-entry producer to the forefront of the global pack within a comparatively short period of time. Again, South Korea stands as the supreme example, but a host of others, ranging from Brazil to Yugoslavia, stand as only slightly less illustrious exponents of this creed.

Seeing the opening presented by this industry, many developing countries have been bent upon establishing a new-building sector complete with the size and range of facilities judged necessary to compete with long-established producers. Some of these contenders performed admirably despite blemishes on their records and the ever-present instability and dubious profitability that afflicted their newfound shipyards. Brazil, Taiwan and China are particularly noteworthy in this regard. While none matched the South Korean performance, their grasp of the essentials of shipbuilding and ability to bolster capacity bore comparison with the leaders. Others committed errors of judgement, gambling away resources on this sector which could have been better invested elsewhere. Nevertheless, they succeeded in endowing their countries with a sizeable industrial sector. India and Argentina are cases in point. In the final analysis, they could console themselves with the thought that domestic shipping could be provided from local sources (albeit usually at an inflated cost). What is more, the boon of a strategic asset could always be invoked should a government feel bound to justify its penetration into the industry. This rubric was perfectly amenable to allowing states to declare the shipyards sacrosanct as important defence installations. The greater number of aspirant producers, disappointed in the fruits of their half-hearted dabbling, settled for an infant industry which was unable to rival the handful of serious NIC contenders and survived, if it survived at all, only on government sufferance. These last will not take up much of our attention in this chapter and will only distract us as and when they have some bearing on the actions of the major players. Mitigating circumstances apply to these unfortunate participants, however (as indeed they do to all countries bequeathed with an incipient shipbuilding industry), and those stem from the blow dealt to shipping by the energy crises of the 1970s and the resultant disarray wreaked on global shipbuilding. The upshot, as well we know, was accentuated competition and the virtual impossibility of deriving profits from the industry for any sustained period. Denied profitability, developing countries had to be content with a shipbuilding industry that provided foreign-exchange earnings (or savings, if substituting for imported vessels) on the one hand and the fundamentals of a mechanical engineering fabric on the other.[1]

Crucial both to the unfolding of the industry life-cycle and the creation of plant in NICs is the competent implementation of a programme of technology transfer. In other words, the aspirant producer must strike an accord with an extant producer so as to acquire state-of-the-art process and product technologies. Short of cost-effective means of undertaking production, the neophyte would be handicapped from the outset: a prospect condemning it either to speedy oblivion or to permanent receivership as a protected sector marred by a serious want of international competitiveness. Similarly, inability to present the market with a product capable of meeting its specifications will not serve the aspirant well. As a result, the mechanisms governing technology transfer cannot be taken lightly. In this respect, as in many others, the NICs have resort to the example set by Japan. As the most cogent case of an ex-developing country, belatedly adopting industrialisation to grasp AIC status, Japan also adds the compelling example of a shipbuilding industry which, by courtesy of technology transfer from the West, transformed itself into the global leader and a highly successful export earner at one and the same time. The latter-day emulators rightly conclude, therefore, that the Japanese approach to technology adoption (and adaptation) repays close scrutiny. A brief commentary on that historical phenomenon serves us equally as an apt point of departure for considering NIC initiatives in shipbuilding.

Prior to the Meiji Restoration in 1867, Japanese shipbuilding practice was inauspicious and the scale of its operations was negligible. The ancestors of the Mitsubishi yard in Nagasaki and the Kawasaki yard in Kobe were transferred, along with the establishments of Ishikawajima and Uraga, to the Departments of Military Affairs and Industry at the Restoration (although they were privatised again in 1884). The climate of opinion was very much in favour of taking these yards – only eligible to build sea-going ships since 1853 – under the wing of the state. Managed shipbuilding, rooted in naval work, was to be the means of their modernisation. Already, the government had set about acquiring Dutch-built warships and provisions were made to build Western-style naval vessels at home. The Ishikawajima establishment in Tokyo actually succeeded in building, over an extended period from 1862 to 1866, a steam-powered combatant which used an engine manufactured at the Nagasaki Iron Foundry (a plant completed in 1861 and equipped with Dutch machinery). The Ishikawajima yard, founded in 1853, was the forerunner of the giant contemporary shipbuilding group bearing its name while the Nagasaki foundry was to be the centrepiece of the future MHI. Presaging dramatic change, though, was the appearance of a technical mission despatched from France. It was responsible for establishing the barebones of a naval dockyard system. In particular, the Japanese owe a great deal to the French engineer, Francis Verny. Discharging his duty as master of the Yokosuka Iron Foundry, he built a replica of the Toulon naval arsenal and founded what became the Yokohama Dock Company and the Yokosuka naval shipyard. A host of expatriates from France, Britain, Germany and America staffed these and similar establishments.[2] For example, the precursor to the Kure naval shipyard – Onohama Dockyard – was created by an Englishman named Kirby in 1883 whereas another of his countrymen, E. H. Hunter, founded Osaka Iron Works, the forebear of Hitachi Zosen, in 1881.

Despite the stamp of foreign influence, control of the new industry remained firmly in the hands of the natives (and the same cannot be said of all NIC emulators of the Japanese). Warshipbuilding spearheaded the process in which foreign technology was amalgamated with domestic capital and control. Japan pioneered the practice of purchasing first-of-class warships from overseas builders and having follow-on vessels built at home: a process brought to a climax with the pre-First World War battlecruiser programme whereby the fleet's largest vessel, the 'Kongo', was built at Barrow by Vickers and the subsequent three sister ships were constructed at home by Yokosuka naval shipyard, Kawasaki and Mitsubishi.[3] The idea was to tempt a foreign lead yard to participate in technology transfer in return for a building contract. As an alternative, the Japanese Government pressed its new plant into production of vessels designed overseas without benefit of foreign production of class leaders. In this instance, the Japanese yard would develop production standards (systems integration skills) and acquire the expertise vital to conceiving product innovations of its own. The first locally built major combatant, the protected cruiser 'Akitsushima', was assembled at the Yokosuka naval yard between 1890 and 1894 using parts furnished by Armstrong in the UK. Subsequently, and in concert with the laying down of an indigenous heavy-industrial base, Japan eschewed warship imports in favour either of building copies of foreign designs or going a step further and building vessels of local design. More and more of Japan's warship classes were formulated at home as well as built there. Indeed, an astonishing indication of the speed in which the Japanese were able to master ship design is presented by the 'Suma' class of cruisers. Barring the British-supplied guns, these domestically designed vessels of the 1890s were also built entirely of indigenous materials. After the First World War, import substitution was virtually complete and the country could lay claim to a warshipbuilding industry rivalling in scale and scope the best that existed in the West. Spill-overs from warship work infused merchant new building, allowing for both technical cross-fertilisation and an assortment of business benefits revolving round countercyclical issues and cross-subsidies.

In recent years, a significant number of aspirant shipbuilders have attempted to follow suit. Reasoning that naval construction can force the pace, they have faithfully copied the practice of procuring first-of-class vessels from lead yards in the AICs while formulating technology transfer agreements that expressly cater to the need to supply additional vessels from the NICs themselves. This usage of defence programmes for technology acquisition frequently entails the erection of plant, indeed often complete shipyards, and answers to the purpose of introducing a new industry into the economy. Argentina, Brazil, India, the Koreas and Thailand have all pursued naval expansion programmes which doubled for shipbuilding industrialisation policies.[4] In South Korea's case, the impact was admittedly small (focused on Korea Tacoma), while Thailand's ambitions remained very modest. An impending ship-repair complex at Laem Chabang should be able to accommodate merchant vessels of up to 13,000 gt, but new construction in Thailand is confined to small naval ships and constitutes a duopoly of Italthai Marine and the navy-run Bangkok dockyard.[5] On an altogether grander scale, India's shipbuilding efforts have been managed in part by the country's defence ministry. The naval aspect intrudes in much of Latin American shipbuilding too. In Argentina, the state AFNE enterprise constructs B&V-designed MEKO 140 frigates while the state Astilleros Domecq Garcia (one-quarter owned by Thyssen, the parent of B&V) builds TR1700 submarines under licence from Thyssen Nordseewerke. Early MEKO vessels (Type 360) were built in Hamburg whereas the first pair of TR1700 submarines originated in Emden, with that German source also producing parts for the boats assembled at Tandanor by Domecq Garcia. For its part, Brazil signed a contract (worth about £100 million) with Vosper Thornycroft of the UK in 1970. Under its terms, four Mark 10 frigates were built in Southampton and the last pair were built in Rio de Janeiro by the state's Arsenal de Marinha.[6] Equipping the Brazilians with the know-how to design and produce future classes of warship was an integral part of the contract: a capability since demonstrated in the V28 frigate class (although some assistance from the German Marine Technik design firm was solicited by the Brazilian Naval Design Office for this project). To round out their shipbuilding competence, the Brazilians signed a contract with HDW in 1984. This made provision for the Kiel yard to supply a Type 1400 submarine before readying the Arsenal de Marinha not only to build subsequent boats of the same class, but also to help it cultivate the proficiency to develop follow-on classes, including nuclear-powered vessels.[7] Indeed, Brazil offers a rich vein both for technology transfer and for foreign involvement in shipyard operations. It is opportune, therefore, that we begin our discussion of NIC forays into marine industries with a review of the evolution of its shipbuilding industry.[8]

FOREIGN INVESTMENT: THE BRAZILIAN MODEL

While the naval imperative played its part in buttressing a native shipbuilding industry, and not least in terms of inspiring an autonomous capability in naval architecture, the principal impetus for Brazil's ship construction efforts originated with the commercial side. Thanks to a receptive government, foreign direct investment was the main catalyst for transforming a few small yards with a smattering of shipbuilding know-how into a new-building sector of some international consequence. In effect, a bargain was struck between the government and foreign shipbuilders whereby the former would provide the latter with a base replete with low labour costs, not to mention a protected domestic market, while, for their part, the foreign investors would inject capital and technology: providing, in short, a shot in the arm for Brazil's drive to industrialisation. Revival of the 'law of similars' in the 1950s, a piece of legislation dating from the 1890s which had been designed to prohibit imports of products that could be made domestically, afforded the would-be shipyard investors a copperbottom guarantee of protectionism. Similarly, an injunction of 1955 allowed foreign companies to import plant and equipment without let or hindrance so long as an equity stake was set aside for Brazilian investors. Rather than tolerate local interference, foreign firms could opt for full ownership of the new ventures: a course especially likely to be condoned if indigenous interest proved lacking or local capital was found wanting. This last option was taken up by Japanese and Dutch investors in shipbuilding. At first, Brazil's paucity of skilled labour served as an impediment to foreign investment and only IHI and Verolme were prepared to absorb the risks that this obstacle presented. In the case of the Japanese, investment in Brazil was partly a ploy undertaken to counter the prospective drop in competitiveness at home brought about by yen revaluation in the late 1950s and partly the seizing of a chance to secure markets for the diversified conglomerates. As one commentator puts it: since 'Japanese shipbuilding firms began to emphasise the export activity of their heavy-machinery divisions (in which they had scarcely developed their own technologies to a point that would compare with their reputed shipbuilding technologies), they realised that helping other countries to build shipyards was an effective way of generating demands for plant exports'.[9]

Brazil acted as a prototype overseas production platform for Japanese builders, and the successful outcome of the IHI venture, Ishibras, prompted this firm and others to invest with celerity in Singapore when the opportunity subsequently arose. Indeed, from their

Table 6.1 Planned shipbuilding, Brazil

| Firm | Five-year building plan (late 1970s) | | | |
	Number of vessels (dwt)	Aggregate tonnage	Highlights	
Verolme Brazil	17	1,630,000	6 x	135,000	ore/oil
			3 x	116,000	tanker
CCN–Maua	64	1,233,200	24 x	26,500	bulker
			12 x	15,000	bulker
			28 x	14,900	dry cargo
Ishibras	10	1,185,000	4 x	276,000	VLCC
Caneco	37	1,164,000	15 x	37,000	bulker
EMAQ	25	683,800	3 x	38,000	bulker
			15 x	37,000	bulker
Estaleiros Ebin So	26	84,080	4 x	8,100	dry cargo
Inconav	14	79,000	4 x	6,000	dry cargo
Total	193	6,059,080			

inception in the late 1950s, Ishibras and its Dutch counterpart, Verolme Brazil, constituted the core of the Rio de Janeiro shipbuilding complex. More to the point, they induced local capitalists to invest in what was to become by the end of the 1960s a burgeoning industry ripe for take off. The catalyst for explosive growth came from the Federal Superintendency of Merchant Marine which, thereafter, fed the yards with orders for domestic tonnage. It accomplished this object through Brazilian-flag shipping expansion programmes which not only brought business to the yards but counteracted the disadvantages stemming from their higher-cost operations. A directive of 1971, for example, established the groundwork which enabled CCN–Maua to sign contracts with seven shipping companies. The upshot of those arrangements, orders for 45 vessels worth $500 million, was only possible because of the financing made available by the Superintendency. A formula was devised, similar in conception to US construction differential subsidies, which defrayed the burden of ship costs. Using European ship prices as a benchmark, the government allowed domestic shipowners to charge to tax credits the difference between this standard and the more costly Brazilian price, and paid them a rebate rather than a direct subsidy. Overseas ship buyers were not neglected either: they could count on fixed-price dollar contracts (thus evading the vexatious inflation issue) and attractive repayment terms. In next to no time, CCN–Maua had progressed from building

SD14 dry cargo ships under licence from Austin and Pickersgill, to modifying that UK company's SD15 design (the Prinasa 121) and pressing it into production, before climaxing with its own design, a 26,500 dwt bulker known as the Prinasa 26/15.[10] Symbolic of the government's wish to usher Brazilian yards into the big league, a five-year plan initiated in 1975 called for 5.3 (later amended to 6.1) million dwt of new shipping worth $3.95 billion.[11] It capped a ship promotion scheme began in 1967 which would bolster investment in the shipyards to $1.6 billion and keep them working to capacity until 1980. Table 6.1 outlines the beneficiaries of the later, enlarged programme. By this stage, Verolme Brazil boasted three building areas, respectively capable of handling vessels of 45,000 dwt, 150,000 dwt and 600,000 dwt (this last verging on completion). Ishibras, meanwhile, had grown from a facility comprising, on opening in 1959, a building dock for 10,000 dwt vessels, another for 5,000 dwt vessels and a third, repair-only dock for 35,000 dwt ships, to a yard fielding two building docks, the largest of which could supply 400,000 dwt ULCCs.[12] This firm had also jumped into engine building, tackling Sulzer, SEMT–Pielstick and Daihatsu diesels (and later Wärtsilä designs too). Almost as impressive were the resources of the locally owned yards. EMAQ, for instance, possessed two berths and could accommodate 80,000 dwt vessels whereas CCN–Maua operated one berth with a 120,000 dwt capacity and one dock for vessels in the 20,000 dwt class. This last builder was leading the others in ship diversity, having made arrangements with Chantiers de France-Dunkerque to acquire technology suitable for producing container vessels, gas carriers and Ro-Ro ships.

A subsidiary plan, conceived with the object of creating a sizeable ship-repair sector, united Ishibras, CCN–Maua and three state shipping companies behind Renave, a venture that would use IHI expertise to remodel an old Rio de Janeiro yard into a modern repair centre. To complement it, and shipbuilding at large, the government encouraged the formation of an agglomeration of ancillary industries at Ilha do Caju in the neighbourhood of the Rio de Janeiro yards (and home to the Ishibras engine works). An area of 75,000m^2 was appropriated for equipment suppliers, and foreign firms were actively solicited to establish branch plants in the zone. Despite some misgivings on their part (centred on doubts about the eventual competitiveness of Brazilian shipbuilding which laboured under a 30 per cent cost penalty relative to EEC shipyards), the foreigners obliged and introduced local factories for the manufacture of boilers, davits, gears and shafting systems, hatch covers, winches and windlasses. In addition, the celebrated propeller-maker, Stone Manganese Marine of the UK, founded a branch in Rio de

Janeiro so as conveniently to supply propellers to Brazilian yards. Known as Helistone, it was a joint venture with shipbuilders CCN–Maua, EMAQ and Caneco. As a fillip to these organisations and their yard clients, the government promised to make the country self-sufficient in steel-plate supply.[13] Of course, the crisis in global shipping markets had blighted Brazilian marine industries prior to the termination of the expansion plan (recollect Figure 3.1). Anxious to restore order to shipping and shipbuilding both, the government attempted remedial action. In early 1979 it converted shipowners' credits to terms which effectively covered the entire cost of domestic new buildings.[14] Aid measures were at length extended to shipbuilders when a 25 per cent subsidy was granted for new buildings. Moreover, the government pushed the yards into diversification. For example, it offered material support to Verolme's plan to convert a new 600,000 dwt-capacity building complex from ULCC construction to offshore activities by persuading the state oil company, Petrobras, to order an exploration platform from the yard. Last but not least, the authorities could also rely on the foreign shipyard owners to enforce a global division of labour of ultimate benefit to their Brazilian holdings. As Verolme had passed into local hands in 1983 with the expiry of the RSV Group, the onus fell on IHI. In 1989, for instance, it booked an order for four 150,000 dwt tankers from Chevron of the USA. While the lead vessel is earmarked for construction in Japan, the rest of the class is allocated to Ishibras. In a similar vein, infusion of foreign capital was also sought by the government. In response, a Luxemburg shipping and banking concern put up $45 million during 1988 so as to gain a 45 per cent stake in Verolme Brazil.

The Brazilian experience heralded imitation by a limited number of developing countries, most notably Singapore. As we have intimated, most NICs were antipathetic towards foreign control of their new industrial assets and this sensitivity was especially acute in shipbuilding where, in view of its status as a strategic asset and its standing as a mature sector, the feeling prevailed that the industry's reigns of power should remain firmly in the hands of indigenous parties. Consequently, foreign shipyard investments in Singapore and elsewhere subscribed to the joint venture pattern whereby the native government or its proxy enterprise retained organisational control and exercised ultimate authority over the evolutionary path mapped out for shipbuilding. We have already remarked on the Singapore situation which drew a trio of Japanese builders (IHI, MHI and Hitachi Zosen) into joint ventures, and we have also noticed the veiled Japanese involvement in the Koje Island schemes in South Korea. It remains to comment on the important – if masked –

partnership role of Japanese and other overseas interests in the formative shipbuilding industries of Malaysia and the Philippines.[15] By most standards, the former has outstripped the latter in size and scope, but both industries pale in comparison with that of their Singapore neighbour: indeed, some would argue that the very success of this last has encroached upon their growth prospects. Since they must compete against seasoned yards elsewhere in the region, the futures of the Malaysian and Philippine industries stand, and may possibly fall, together. Interestingly, as well as calling on Japanese shipyard expertise, they have had recourse to other outside assistance; namely, West German in the case of Malaysia and Singaporean in the case of the Philippines. To begin with, we shall dwell on the Japanese imprint and, in the second place, we shall acknowledge alternative sources of capital and technology. The main exponent of Japanese involvement is Malaysia Shipyard and Engineering (MSE): an undertaking which on inception was owned by the Malaysian Government (51 per cent), SHI (24.5 per cent), International Maritime Carriers of Hong Kong (12.25 per cent) and the Kuok Brothers (12.25 per cent). Built on swamp at Pasir Gudang, some 30 kms from Johor Baru, MSE was a M$183 million ($83 million) project equipped with a 400,000 dwt-capacity drydock, the largest between Suez and Japan, together with a second dock of 140,000 dwt capacity and three outfitting quays. Designed simultaneously to handle six VLCCs, the shoreside workshops had a basic fabrication and engine-repair facility bestowed on them by SHI. While the plan for MSE germinated in the shipbuilding boom, the venture did not commence operations until 1976, scarcely a banner year for VLCC construction. Forced to fall back on tanker repair, the yard was hard pressed to find work for its 1,200 employees. Subcontracts for steel storage tanks and accommodation modules for offshore platforms enabled it to eke out a moderate income, but an annual turnover of M$50 million by 1980 still fell short of break-even levels. It was, for all its impressive plant, lacking in profitability: to such an extent, indeed, that the government was obliged to assume a larger share (78 per cent) of its ownership relative to SHI (diminished to 10 per cent). In fact, MSE was encumbered with a singular inability to make money, realising profits only in 1988 when a paltry $2.8 million was earned. By one estimate, Malaysian shipbuilding costs exceed those of Japan by as much as 30 per cent notwithstanding the cheaper labour obtaining in South East Asia. This outcome is just another expression of the handicap borne by neophyte builders left with little option but to import significant amounts of their material and component requirements. Unsurprisingly, then, MSE tended to disparage new building in favour of repair. A loyal customer for its repair services is MISC, the Malaysian state shipping line. Rumours abounded in the late 1980s that this firm, along with Sembawang Holdings of Singapore, would welcome usurping the government's interests in the yard.[16]

Overshadowed by MSE in the 4,000 worker-strong Malaysian marine industry is Sabah Shipyard. Erected in 1982, this Labuan builder absorbed more than M$100 million in start-up capital. Concentrating on modest cargo vessels of under 20,000 dwt in size, it was plagued with losses from the outset (reaching M$28 million in 1987 and M$18 million in 1988) and was compelled to find solace constructing offshore platform modules. The Japanese connection is made manifest in product technology. Determined to stay in shipbuilding, Sabah Shipyard persists in producing loss-making cement and log carriers as well as various kinds of tankers. Most recently, it won an order from MISC for a brace of 16,900 dwt palm oil and chemical tankers. Besides supplying the materials and components worked into these vessels, Kurushima Dockyard furnishes the designs. Over in the Philippines, Japanese involvement is confined to the Philippine Shipyard and Engineering Corporation in Subic Bay. A joint undertaking of KHI (40 per cent) and the National Investment and Development Corporation (60 per cent), this yard is primarily a ship-repair entity complete with a 300,000 dwt-capacity graving dock and three repair berths. Sustained by protectionist laws mandating that Philippine ships must be drydocked at home, the Subic Bay yard nevertheless has performed badly, accumulating debts of $114 million by the beginning of 1990. The government was looking to privatisation for relief and, reportedly, was deliberating rival bids made by Sembawang and Keppel for the purpose of acquiring the yard. The second of these Singapore organisations already controls, via its Keppel Philippines Shipyard subsidiary, smaller yards in Batangas province and Cebu.[17] The flag-bearer for European involvement, meanwhile, is Hong Leong-Lürssen in Butterworth, a suburb of Penang. Distinguished as Malaysia's first major shipyard, this M$20 million venture of 1972 combined local firms Hong Leong and Pernas with Lürssen Werft of West Germany (the latter holding a 42 per cent stake).[18] Weaned on patrol craft and other small naval ships, the project deliberately set out to transfer the German firm's vaunted expertise in these areas to Malaysia. In return for a string of government contracts and a cheap export-production site, the German company was willing to comply with this aim and, recognising the disquiet occasioned by foreign dominance of a defence asset, was not disposed to quibble over its minority shareholding in the yard.

INDIA AND STATE SHIPBUILDING

Outside of communist states, India is in many ways the apotheosis of state instigated and controlled industrialisation. That interventionist approach gave the tone to the country's shipbuilding industry. While the advent of the industry precedes independence and imperative planning, the precocious private yards were all gathered up and placed under the aegis of the state. In fact, the infant industry existing at the time of independence owed much of its development to the stimulus of war orders lodged by the British. The Royal Navy had actively sought Indian-built vessels in the early 1800s, glorying in their cheapness and the soundness of their construction. The naval authorities had even established a dockyard in Bombay capable of constructing steam warships (although its evident uncompetitiveness in the age of iron and steam doomed it to closure in 1877). For India, the First World War had culminated in 1917–18 with an output of 142 vessels of 11,808 gt, but activity had faded fast thereafter. Seldom larger than 100 gt, the country was producing just 55 vessels of 2,418 gt by 1936–7. The onset of hostilities in 1939 prompted Scindia Steam Navigation, the foremost Indian shipowner, to lay out a yard at Visakhapatnam for the construction of vessels of up to 8,000 dwt. A spate of orders for corvettes, minesweepers, armed trawlers and patrol craft transformed smaller yards in Bombay and Calcutta overnight. In addition, a number of mechanical engineering concerns, railway workshops for the most part, were induced to begin manufacture of parts and components.[19] Restored to full capability in 1948 the Scindia yard was soon overtaken by events. Under a 1949 statement of intent the government reserved shipbuilding for state enterprises and conceded a ten-year period of grace to allow private firms to disengage from the industry. Consequently, Scindia relinquished control of its yard to the state in 1952, although it retained a minority shareholding for several years afterwards. Even at this juncture, the Hindustan Shipyard as it was termed, was highly reliant on government orders for cargo vessels to keep its berths occupied.[20] More alarming, it was dogged with problems preventing it from producing ships at competitive prices: a handicap which was to be inflicted upon the entire industry in due course. Undismayed, the government resolved both greatly to expand new-building capacity at the Hindustan yard and elsewhere, and to incorporate all extant yards into a state-orchestrated development plan. The first goal was partly achieved by allocating Rs 24 million to Hindustan for the first five-year plan, Rs 47 million for the second (beginning in 1956) and Rs 90 million for the third. Formation of a monolithic state shipping firm, SCI, in 1961 served to conjure up an organisation committed to channelling orders to Hindustan and its younger associates. The second goal was met by invoking the security card and sweeping up all remaining yards for revamping as defence facilities. Mazagon Dock in Bombay, a unit of the British P&O shipping company, escaped the government's clutches until 1960; by which time the Calcutta yard of Garden Reach (owned by British India, another branch of P&O) had also been appropriated by the Ministry of Defence. While these yards were to be dedicated to naval work, the government permitted them a residual commercial new-building function. In the meantime, expansion schemes were in full flood at the Ministry of Heavy Engineering (although jurisdiction for the non-defence yards was later shifted to the Ministry of Surface Transport). The Cochin Shipyard was founded in order to complement Visakhapatnam. By dint of a Rs 320 million allocation from the third five-year plan, the original yard would have its annual output raised from 20,000 grt to 50,000 grt while the new yard would cap that with an initial throughput of 60,000 grt per annum.[21] MHI was solicited to render assistance both in erecting the Cochin establishment and in presenting Hindustan with ship designs. The Indian seizure of Goa in 1961 brought with it a bonus in the shape of Estaleiros Navais de Goa, a repair yard. Placed by the Ministry of Defence under the wing of its Mazagon Dock subsidiary, this yard was earmarked for reconstruction as a new-building facility. Towards the end of the 1960s the Ranchi plant of the state's Garden Reach yard was turned over to marine propulsion machinery and its first licensed-built MAN marine diesel emerged in 1971.

With the dawning of that decade, irritants had begun to surface. Overruns had driven the investment cost of the Cochin yard to Rs 455 million, more than double the 1963 estimate of Rs 200 million. Moreover, it was taking an inordinate amount of time to reach completion and that tardiness was playing havoc with the government's plans to replace ship imports with domestic tonnage. Prior to the yard opening, government-directed ordering had presented Cochin Shipyard with a backlog of 20 Scott Lithgow-designed 75,000 dwt Panamax bulkers. In the event, the first bulker (ordered by SCI) was not launched until the beginning of 1980, some four years after its construction had started. For its part, Hindustan Shipyard was dilatory in producing its new series of West German-designed 21,800 dwt Pioneer cargo vessels, requiring no less than 649 days from keel-laying to launching for the first of class (although learning economies brought the time span down to 381 days for the fifth ship). Poor quality control and structural deficiencies were becoming pronounced. Constrained from the outset with plate-supply problems, state import restrictions compounded the builders' woes.[22] Besides, inferior quality steel from local sources conferred on the yards an egregious reputation for shoddy products. To make matters worse, the process of replacing imported components with domestic altern- atives had not progressed very far. True, India could manufacture engines and fabricate materials together accounting for 60 per cent of a locally built ship, but each Pioneer-class vessel required imported parts which added Rs 27 million (£1.7 million) to their costs. Given this situation, the official profit picture for the yards appeared contrived and unconvincing. Moderate earnings figures released by Hindustan, for example, disguised the fact that, denied substantial subsidies, the builder would have operated throughout at a loss. Even more worrisome, private domestic shipowners purchased from Indian yards only because the government instituted a practice of artificially lowering ship prices to levels comparable with competitors overseas and absorbed the difference as a charge on the exchequer. The hesitant steps into export markets could only be contemplated after the government had agreed to a 15 per cent subsidy on overseas sales.

The government reckoned on boosted investment as the answer to the troubles marring the industry. In the quinquennium stretching beyond 1978 Hindustan was granted permission to construct a Rs 550 million covered building dock in order to handle vessels of up to 45,000 dwt and, in conjunction with a Polish team, innovated a family of standard designs embracing cargo, semi-container and bulker functions and the size spectrum from 14,000 dwt to 27,000 dwt. At the same time, it and the other yards were encouraged to entertain diversification. Hindustan forged a technical collaboration agreement with Ulstein of Norway with a view to entering offshore platform production while, in an attempt to invigorate the ship-repair sector, Keppel of Singapore formed a joint venture with Chokhani International aimed at setting up a major complex in Madras.[23] Additionally, plans were drawn up to establish brand-new yards at Paradip in Orissa and Hajira in Gujarat, and an allocation of Rs 3,500 million (£186 million) was requested for them. The former would tackle ships below 30,000 dwt leaving the latter to accommodate vessels of greater size. Yet, severe financial difficulties afflicting Indian shipping, to say nothing of the reluctance on the part of the few healthy operators to purchase at home, constrained the government in its industrial policy; effectively intervening to make it pause in its new shipyard plans. A government committee concluded that the indigenisation process was hemmed in by practical restraints. Relatively low levels of demand, the specialised nature of the articles, difficulties in obtaining scarce raw materials and a shortage of expertise all united to frustrate complete self-sufficiency in the marine industries.[24] Rather than press ahead with the plan for autarky, the committee concluded that the government would be better advised to address the want of competitiveness in the existing ship products. A construction time of three to five years was usual for cargo vessels built in India: a far cry from the 18 to 30 months usual elsewhere. Furthermore, SCI estimated that locally built vessels cost up to half as much again as those procured on the international market despite subsidised pricing. On one account, the real cost of a Panamax bulker emanating from Hindustan Shipyard was Rs 630 million ($47 million) compared with an enforced selling price of Rs 230 million. In the light of these revelations, the lack of viability attaching to yards dealing with commercial new buildings became a stark fact of life. Together, Hindustan and Cochin recorded losses of Rs 1,230 million in the year ending in March 1986 and their liabilities continued to mount thereafter. Fortunately, the defence undertakings could take pride in their role as providers of ships for India's enlarged navy and could point to such prized products as the Type 16A frigate, tank landing ships, fleet tankers and, provisionally, even aircraft carriers.[25]

CHINA: CAUGHT AT THE CROSSROADS

While India might offer an object lesson in the perils of import-substitution shipbuilding, China illustrates the uncertainties attendant on penetration into export markets. This new force in ship production, long in gestation, boasts a profusion of facilities built up over the years for the purpose of attaining self-sufficiency in naval and mercantile tonnage (Figure 6.1). Never successful in achieving autarky in merchant shipping on account of the more complex ship types being beyond the country's capabilities, China latterly turned to export markets as a way to galvanise its shipbuilding industry and earn valuable hard currency. Pre-empted by the other NICs in this course, its latent strength centred on cheap labour. For example, average monthly wages in China in 1988 equalled $40, a mite below the $55–80 obtaining in Indonesia, Malaysia, the Philippines and Thailand; and considerably less than the $544 reported for Hong Kong, the $547 applying in Singapore, the $598 obtaining in Taiwan and the $633 prevalent in South Korea.[26] The obvious advantages of a competitive wage environment, coupled with the lowered technical barriers to entry associated with a mature industry, highlighted shipbuilding as a prime target for export promotion. Circumstantial evidence validated this generous factor-cost advantage. In the late 1970s, for instance, Chinese ship prices occupied

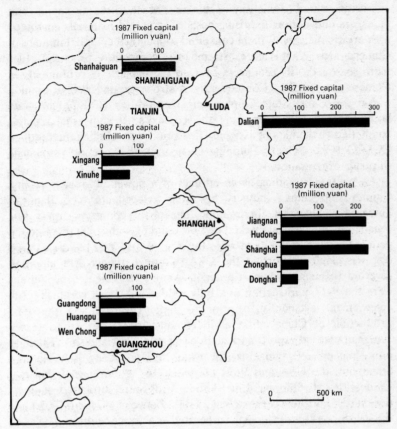

Figure 6.1 China's shipyards

a range 85–90 per cent of the standard pertaining to the more precocious NICs. Despite reliance on European designs and foreign-sourced components, the price of a coastal container vessel built at Zhonghua Shipyard in Shanghai was put at \$4.6 million in 1988: significantly less than the \$7.7 million quoted for an equivalent vessel built in a north European venue.[27] At about the same time, Hapag–Lloyd of West Germany ordered a larger container ship from China on the grounds that the vessel could be bought for a sum one-fifth cheaper than elsewhere. The fact remains, though, that China has come late to export shipbuilding and is not thoroughly convinced of its usefulness, suspecting it of meretricious rather than substantive benefits. Shipbuilding has been rocked by setbacks which have contrived to bring the Chinese authorities round to this way of thinking. Much to the dismay of their managers and customers, rising costs of imported materials combined with erratic delivery of them conspired to lengthen completion times at Chinese yards. What is more, extreme price competition practised by the more seasoned NIC producers ravaged the promise of profitability in Chinese shipbuilding. Consequently, a strong groundswell of opinion within the China State Shipbuilding Corporation (CSSC), the state body charged with overseeing the country's 89 shipyards, remains committed to the idea of assigning first priority to fulfilling the needs of COSCO (China Ocean Shipping Company), the monopoly domestic shipping organisation.

As befits its standing as an adjunct of a power of great longevity, China's shipbuilding industry has long antecedents. The Jiangnan Shipyard in Shanghai, for example, one of the country's largest, was founded in 1865 and embarked on new building with a 600 dwt wooden paddle vessel. It made its mark in the First World War building 14,700 disp vessels for export to the USA, although thenceforth attention reverted to meeting domestic needs. Among its salient contributions were the 1947 construction of a fully welded 3,000 dwt cargo ship (an achievement accomplished prior to Japan's yards) and the 1965 production of China's first all-indigenous 10,000 dwt cargo vessel. Jiangnan entered export markets in earnest in 1980, and since then has built ships up to Panamax size for owners in Hong Kong, Italy, Norway, Singapore, the USA and West Germany, to say nothing of the joint Chinese–Polish Shipping Line. Other yards were instigated as naval dockyards: Foochow constructing 24 ships between 1874 and 1907 while the Whampoa Dock in Shanghai operated as a repair centre. A few more owed their genesis to foreign interests providing repair facilities for visiting steamers. 'Liberation' in 1949 effected a major transformation, however. Gathered under the auspices of the First Ministry of Machine Building and the Ministry of Communication (for ship repair), these yards were presented with a central ship design department which evolved into the Shanghai Institute of Shipbuilding, a facility patterned after the Leningrad Institute of Shipbuilding. Utilising Soviet assistance, provision was made in the second five-year plan (beginning in 1958) to boost both naval and merchant tonnage. The Hudong Shipyard in Shanghai was extended to accommodate destroyer construction while Dalian Shipyard was also pressed into service as a supplier of larger naval combatants. Soviet designed diesel submarines, for their part, were built in series at the Jiangnan, Jiangzhou, Wuchang, Huangpu and Bohai (i.e. Huludao) yards. On the merchant side, a 16,000 ton cargo vessel was attempted, although all other vessels remained smaller than 10,000 grt. Jiangnan, for example, rejoiced in its ability to build 5,000 dwt coasters in as little as 76 days.[28] Unhappily, the severing of relations with the USSR crippled the country's shipbuilding effort. Naval work was restricted to incremental improvements of existing Soviet designs. However, withdrawal of Soviet assistance dealt a maiming blow to merchant production, cutting output to only two ships in 1961, one in 1962 and none at all in 1963. Valiant attempts were made by the Chinese to overcome this action of the Soviet Union which entailed not only a peremptory denial of design assistance, but a refusal to supply key components as well. In 1963 a special agency for shipbuilding (the Sixth Ministry of Machine Building, later styled the Ministry of Shipbuilding) was conjured up and authorised to push for self-sufficiency. Within a brief interlude it was claiming that 85 per cent of machinery and 90 per cent of steel plate used in the yards derived from local sources. Concomitantly, production of merchant vessels picked up, and by 1970 had almost broached the half-million ton mark (Table 6.2). One measure of the scale of the effort was the extraordinary feat of the Shanghai Shipyard in building a 20,000 ton cargo vessel in premises equipped to build only 3,000 ton vessels. In default of a suitably sized berth, the vessel was positioned with its stern looming over the river. Fit for working on only at low tide, the ship's rear 'section was assembled upside down. There was no crane in Shanghai big enough to turn it right-side up. The workers sealed it, pushed it into the river, and there with the water taking most of the weight, used a borrowed crane to turn it over'.[29]

All this was but preparation for the export offensive. In 1975 export orders were booked for small vessels in the 5,000 dwt class and within two years contracts were taken for larger vessels. Stumbling blocks

Table 6.2 Chinese shipbuilding output

Year	Output ('000 gt)	Year	Output ('000 gt)
1951	173.1	1980	817.8
1957	24.0	1981	916.3
1960	286.4	1982	1,024.5
1965	355.0	1983	1,293.7
1970	484.3	1984	1,654.2
1975	702.6	1985	2,219.4
1977	815.5	1986	1,756.7
1978	860.7	1987	1,979.1
1979	809.3		

remained, however. Attractive prices were offset by obsolescent technology, want of standardisation between supposed sister ships and bottlenecks in supply. These hurdles were gradually surmounted as international certification societies (e.g. Lloyd's Register of Shipping) were prevailed upon to supervise construction and foreign shipbuilders were commissioned to overhaul China's yard lay-outs and process technologies. The former made good the void left by the departure of Soviet advisers in the early 1960s. Supplementing them was an expanded domestic design and engineering base, much of it justified in the name of national defence. To this end, the China Ship Scientific Research Centre was established at Wuxi and endowed with test facilities which included a towing tank, cavitation tunnel and seakeeping basin.[30] In respect of the latter foreign involvement, MHI was contracted to revamp the Jiangnan Shipyard, BS agreed to modernise the Dalian Shipyard while A&P Appledore was brought in to upgrade the Guangdong site. Furthermore, engine technology was procured from the main European diesel firms. Under a 1978 pact, Sulzer allowed its slow-speed diesels to be manufactured by the Shanghai and Dalian yards as well as the Zheng Guang Machine Plant. Shortly afterwards, B&W Diesel granted licences for its medium-speed engines to the Zhen Jiang plant and licences for its slow-speed diesels to the Hudong Shipyard. Its impending partner, MAN, permitted the Xinzhong Power Machine Plant in Shanghai to make four-stroke marine diesels. With a view to entering the offshore sector, the Dalian Shipyard had fabricated jack-up rigs, outfitting them with Japanese-supplied equipment. The more complex semisubmersible field was tackled by virtue of a technology-transfer agreement cemented with Aker of Norway. These initiatives soon began to bear fruit. Export orders for commercial ships rose by leaps and bounds, reaching 900,000 dwt by 1982. A legion of ship types were embraced in the ordering spree, including offshore support vessels, general cargo vessels, bulkers and tankers (although capacity restraints limited the largest size of the last to 115,000 dwt). In addition, the Shanghai and Dalian yards were accepting foreign orders for drilling rigs. As can be elicited from Table 6.2, output was hovering round the million ton mark by this time: a figure virtually double the level prevalent in the early 1970s. Moreover, as the 1980s advanced, output was set to climb to about 2 million grt; a weight of production more than sufficient to place China among the ranking shipbuilding nations. Not all of this growth stemmed from export orders, for production to meet the needs of domestic shipping was also lifted to new highs. Under the sixth five-year plan, for example, COSCO was empowered to boost its fleet with 2.5 million dwt of home-built tonnage; that is, to present the yards with a supplementary 400,000 dwt or more of business each year. This sudden emergence of the country as a major producer of merchant tonnage was mirrored by a resurgence in China's warshipbuilding capabilities. Symptomatic of this second thrust in the marine industries was China's participation in the select nuclear-submarine club (with boats built at the Huludao Shipyard) on the one hand and, on the other, its transfer of process technology to North Korea and Romania to assist these countries in building diesel submarines and fast attack craft respectively.[31] Not to be overlooked either is the sale of warships to non-Communist countries. For example, Hudong Shipyard pulled off something of a coup during 1989 in selling four Jianghu V-class missile frigates to Thailand.

Greatly bolstered ship production necessitated extensive investment in yard facilities throughout the 1970s and 1980s. The upshot of this programme is summarised in Table 6.3. Representative of the restructured industry is Dalian Shipbuilding Industry Corporation. In truth, this entity is no mere shipyard but a combination of plants and installations with the Dalian Shipyard at its core. Embracing the Bohai Shipyard, Dalian Marine Diesel Engine Works, Liao-Hai Machinery Factory and the Dalian Marine Valve Plant besides the Dalian Shipyard, the complex is a subsidiary organisation of CSSC assuming responsibility for its own accounts, outlays and returns. The Soviet Union was largely instrumental in delimiting the complex, first during its spell of occupation after the Second World War and later as a token of its

Table 6.3 Main Chinese yards

Yard	1985 output ('000 gt)	Employment ('000)	Largest berth ('000 gt capacity)
Jiangnan	122.1	14.7	40.0
Hudong	117.5	11.7	42.0
Dalian	71.9	15.1	100.0
Shanghai	67.5	9.5	25.0
Guangdong	55.3	8.0	15.0
Xingang	47.4	6.4	30.0
Wuchang	37.1	–	5.0
Zhonghua	31.8	5.9	15.0
Qiuxin	21.8	9.5	5.0
Chuangdong	18.6	–	1.8
Chongqing	18.1	–	4.0
Huangpu	14.0	–	3.0
Jiangzhou	12.1	–	10.0
Bohai	10.9	–	7.0
Donghai	10.3	3.3	3.0
Wuhu	10.2	–	10.0

fraternal interest in China prior to the rupturing of relations in the early 1960s. Expansion of the complex has continued apace ever since. Currently employing in excess of 30,000 workers, the industry corporation also engages in land machinery production as a foil to discontinuities in ship production. Among its range of products are rolling machines, steam turbines, industrial boilers, pressure vessels, die-casting machines, oil storage cars and metal furniture. Its regular ship offerings include 115,000 dwt shuttle tankers, 69,000 dwt chemical and product tankers, 35,000 dwt bulkers and 11,000 dwt coal carriers; added to which are missile destroyers, offshore rigs and production modules.[32] Alive to the opportunities inherent in the tanker market, Dalian had extended its building berths and boasted the largest such in China. In this spirit, it was authorised to begin work on a 200,000 dwt-capacity building dock in 1988. Nevertheless, these facilities leave much to be desired in comparison with the mammoth docks existing elsewhere and Dalian – and China along with it – have been effectively excluded from the VLCC market. As a result, the yard has pinned its export hopes on bulkers and medium-sized tankers, conferring on Hitachi Zosen the role of technical adviser. However, Dalian does not spurn technical help from other quarters: its largest vessel – a 125,000 dwt shuttle tanker for Norwegian owners – duplicated a vessel built by DSHM in South Korea from Norwegian blueprints. Aiming to become as self-reliant as possible, it makes B&W diesels using its Japanese partner as a source for the more complicated engine parts (crankshafts, high-pressure pumps and cylinder heads).

The relative strengths and weaknesses of China's shipbuilding industry became evident as the 1980s progressed. On the positive side, CSSC – the organisation set up at the beginning of the decade to co-ordinate the yards and foster exports – was sufficiently flexible to admit of uniformity in direction without stifling local autonomy. It acceded, for example, to the plan of the Guangdong Shipbuilding Corporation (the operator of Guangdong Shipyard) to enter the rig-building business by virtue of a joint venture with Hong Kong interests in the first place and a licence to build Bethlehem Steel designs in the second.[33] By the same token, it is prepared to concede that domestic design skills continue to fall short of the best international standards and is not averse, in consequence, to the import of foreign designs. The pattern for the chemical and product tankers emanating from Dalian, for instance, was conceived by the Libaek firm of naval architects in Norway whereas the design for a series of container vessels issuing from the same yard for COSCO is an adaptation of the Maierform model formulated in West Germany. Turning to the negative side, doubts about the quality control enforced in Chinese yards may linger. To be sure, the problem of structural defects that arose on some of the early export vessels appears to have been overcome and embarrassing episodes in which clients publicly repudiated their new buildings are not likely to recur (although reports of late deliveries and lack of proper management control cropped up in the aftermath of the 1989 disturbances in the country).[34] Yet, a tarnished reputation is not easily subdued and, in any event, irritants persist in ship financing. In the first flush of export promotion, a woefully inadequate export financing arrangement, basically rejecting credit for cash on the nail, deterred much foreign buying: to be blunt, ships priced some 5–10 per cent lower than those of other producers seemed much less attractive to potential buyers when deprived of an accompanying credit package. Only in 1982 did this omission begin to be remedied, for at that time the Shanghai Shipbuilding Industry Corporation (the supervisory body for all the yards in the city) was forced to advance credit to Norwegian principals in order to clinch orders for two offshore support vessels. In the following year the Bank of China entered the fray, disbursing credit for export orders on a basis roughly comparable with international standards. A grave caveat remains, however. Questionable ability to finance large contracts, together with the drain on hard currency imposed by the need to pay for the 50–60 per cent of equipment that still must be imported for the more sophisticated vessels, continues to place severe limits on the competitive position of China's yards in relation to shipbuilding industries in either the more affluent AICs or bountiful NICs. This caveat alone would suffice to give Chinese shipyard planners pause to consider the supposedly unalloyed merits of export shipbuilding.

TAIWAN: CAPITALIST STATE SHIPBUILDING

Notwithstanding its obscure origins, the shipbuilding industry of Taiwan has grown to major proportions in recent years. Strikingly anomalous in an entrepreneurial society imbued with freewheeling capitalism, the industry – like other commanding heights of the economy – was cultivated by the state and remains a ward of it. A perpetual loss-maker, the government has persevered with shipbuilding because of its pivotal role in industrialisation. The state has shouldered the burden of promoting a heavy industrial complex and has impressed upon its planners the need to sustain key elements – steel, shipbuilding and heavy machinery – despite their propensity to impose heavy demands on public coffers. Currently, two large state enterprises constitute the bulk of the industry; namely, CSBC and the Taiwan

Machinery Manufacturing Corporation (TMMC). The former operates sites at Keelung and Kaohsiung, with the second being by far the larger. The Keelung yard, the nub of CSBC, deploys three docks – two of 130,000 dwt capacity and the third of 30,000 dwt – plus a 32,000 dwt-capacity building berth. It employs 4,000 workers and is equipped to turn out 300,000 dwt of new buildings every year along with 200,000 dwt of repaired vessels. For its part, the Kaohsiung yard revels in a dock of 1 million dwt capacity (on completion, second in size only to MHI Nagasaki) that is served by two Goliath cranes each capable of lifting 350 tons. Manned by 5,000 workers, this yard can build up to 1.5 million dwt of vessels in any given year as well as repair up to 2.5 million dwt. Various other activities are entertained by CSBC. It countenances manufacture of offshore exploration equipment and indulges in the fabrication of heavy steel structures, among which are power station tanks and smokestacks, petrochemical plant, rolling mills, container cranes and an assortment of deck machinery. Best known for its engine production in support of the neighbouring CSBC Kaohsiung yard, TMMC offers much else besides. For a start, it maintains a shipyard for vessels too small during normal conditions to be contemplated by its much bigger neighbour; that is to say, cargo vessels under 7,000 dwt, fishing boats, tugs, dredgers, barges and harbour ferries. This yard has the potential to produce about 20,000 dwt of new construction a year. TMMC also runs heavy machinery and foundry works for making diesel engines, sugar and cement machinery, conveying and hoisting equipment and boilers; a steel products works for electrolytic tinplate and railway rolling stock; and an alloy steel works for forging, heat treatment, hot-rolled steel and cold-finished steel. As far as marine engineering is concerned, TMMC boasts a plethora of licences for the manufacture of diesel engines (from the likes of Niigata Engineering, MAN/B&W, Mirrlees Blackstone and Sulzer), ships' generators (Daihatsu Diesel) and steam boilers (MHI). All told, it employs 4,000 at its four Kaohsiung sites.[35] Between them, these two state under- takings have overseen the rise of Taiwan from a producer of little consequence in the early 1970s to a producer of the first rank in the 1980s which has overtaken most of the traditional shipbuilding nations (recall Figures 1.1 and 1.4). Remarkably, the government is fully accountable for this occurrence, having single-mindedly pursued a course which from the very outset was bent on making the Taiwanese industry a force to be reckoned with. Yet, as implied above, a proviso is in order: this achievement was not consummated without heavy cost, the repercussions of which plague the industry to this day. However, that it was achieved at all is a singular event, fully deserving of elaboration.

Responsibility for the marine sector was initially thrust upon the government. The precursor to CSBC, the Taiwan Shipbuilding Corporation, had begun in 1919 in Keelung as a repair shop for mining machines. Falling into Chinese hands in 1945 on the abrupt termination of the Japanese occupation of the island, this company – by now a confirmed shipbuilder – struggled through the next few years, relying for the most part on ship repair. Government interference in its affairs was inevitable since it was obliged to seek a succession of bail-outs which called for state-regulated orders. By the mid-1950s the yard had become a state enterprise and was employing 1,600 people operating a pair of drydocks, a machine shop, a forging shop and a foundry. TMMC, meanwhile, began in 1946 as an assemblage of state units bequeathed to the Chinese administration by the Japanese. The original Taiwan Machinery and Shipbuilding Corporation (renamed TMMC in 1948) melded the Taiwan Iron Works with Taiwan Dock, and was to expand over the succeeding years with the addition of the Taiwan Steel Mills (in 1958), the Taiwan Factory of the Central Standards Bureau (1964) and the Chung Hsin Alloy Steel Works and Military Vehicle Plant (1978).[36] The turmoil attendant on the affairs of 1949 and the consolidation of the Nationalist Government on the island blighted the industry's prospects in the early 1950s. Indeed, ship output registered a derisory 565 gt in 1952 and by and large remained at this low ebb until 1958 when it leapt to 23,178 gt.[37] The escalation in production was in response to provisional planning efforts started by the government. Approval was granted in 1957 under the terms of the second four-year national economic plan to augment shipping output to 102,000 gt by 1960. Moreover, US assistance in the form of Ingalls Shipbuilding Corporation was invoked and the Keelung yard was reorganised as the Ingalls Taiwan Shipbuilding and Dry Dock Corporation. Unfortunately, as Figure 6.2 reveals, the early take-off soon encountered obstacles and production spluttered in the early 1960s. In large measure, these originated in the Keelung yard where the new American managers complained of being hamstrung by the practices of their Chinese partners in the joint venture.[38] Threatening to withdraw from the venture on account of heavy losses incurred during the protracted take-over of the yard, Ingalls was eventually mollified by a conciliatory move on the part of the government which resulted in the award of an order for a pair of 12,500 ton freighters. Overruling the wishes of the Taiwan Navigation Company, a shipowner anxious to order in Japan at Iino Shipbuilding owing to the better prices obtaining there (quoted at $2.249 million for the materials and engines, along with $0.84 million in labour costs), the government ensured that Keelung was awarded the contract (despite

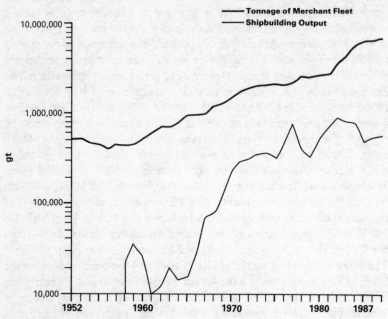

Figure 6.2 Taiwanese growth trends

materials and engines costs of $2.716 million and labour costs of $0.728 million).[39] In the end, however, the rift between Ingalls and its Taiwanese partners was never fully healed and the ten-year contract with the US firm was curtailed in 1962 with the yard reverting to indigenous state control.

Wanting to dispel the cloud hanging over the yard, the government increasingly tied its merchant fleet enhancement programme to domestic shipbuilding capacity. Figure 6.2 elicits the correspondence between the two as they rose in tandem from the mid-1960s until the late 1970s when shipbuilding, wallowing in the doldrums triggered by global recession in shipping, was summarily uncoupled from the secular growth trend of the Taiwanese merchant fleet. Several criticisms had been volunteered about the Keelung yard by the previous American management and, in an attempt to overturn them, the state enterprise forged an agreement with IHI. Not only would the Japanese firm endeavour to bring overhead staffing at Taiwan Shipbuilding down from the appalling 40 per cent of the work-force to the more usual 4 per cent of Japan, but it would supply the Keelung yard with materials and engines at prices comparable to those it charged Japanese customers. IHI formulated ship designs for Keelung and was responsible for ensuring that the imported materials – fully 90 per cent of all materials, including steel plate, worked into the ships building there – were consistent with international standards. At the same time, TMMC was permitted to enter the marine diesel field, new plant was installed and licensing agreements with foreign firms were sanctioned. Enlightened management at Taiwan Shipbuilding was combined with yard rebuilding, resulting in the erection by 1968 of a 100,000 dwt-capacity building dock (and two 70,000 dwt tankers for the state's Chinese Petroleum Corporation were earmarked as its first occupants). Mindful of the need to provide ever-larger vessels for state shipowning firms such as Chinese Petroleum, to say nothing of the craving to engage in export shipbuilding, the government began to encourage start-up initiatives in the late 1960s. The CSBC was mooted as early as 1968 and in its first manifestation was to be a $6 million project initially devoted to ship repair which would unite the backing of the local government, MHI and the local subsidiary of Hong Kong's Tung shipping interests.[40] That venture faded into oblivion, however, and in 1970 a successor organisation centred on technology donor Cammell Laird of the UK was proposing to erect a Kaohsiung complex complete with one 350,000 dwt-capacity dock, one 150,000 dwt-capacity dock and two docks each of 30,000 dwt capacity; all equal to the task of turning out 1.8 million dwt of new buildings a year. Eager to play a supporting role, the government outlined plans for an integrated steel mill (the future China Steel Corporation) on a site adjoining that set aside for the new yard and went about canvassing foreign interests to provide technical assistance. The mill would not only provide all the plate requirements of the new yard, but it would eradicate the need of the Keelung yard to import vast quantities of materials from Japan. Incidentally, the booming ship-breaking sector in Kaohsiung, already the world's largest, would play a major part in affirming the viability of the mill by supplying it with attractively priced scrap. By this juncture, the shipyard project had congealed into a mixed public and privately owned CSBC which planned to deploy 1.4 million dwt of new-building capacity and 2 million dwt of ship-repair capacity a year. Steered by the private consortium led by Gatx Oswego Corporation of the USA, the start-up firm commissioned Kajima Construction of Japan to construct the world's second largest building dock, instructing it to have the installation ready before the end of 1975 so as to accommodate the first of four 445,000 dwt ULCCs ordered by Gatx. Of course, the new yard came on stream at a most inopportune moment: tanker markets had collapsed; Burmah Oil, the charterer of the Gatx vessels, faced bankruptcy and refused to take up more than two of the vessels; while, worst of all, the contracts had been booked at a concessionary fixed price which rendered them serious loss-makers for the infant CSBC. The proportion of Taiwanese new-building capacity in operation dropped from 65.4 per cent in 1973 to 25.6 per cent in 1975 and 26.3 per cent in 1976 as the massive Kaohsiung yard entered production concurrently with the erosion of global shipping markets. Given the dire prospects, the government had no choice but to intervene, bolstering its minority stake into virtually a complete shareholding of CSBC and doubling the yard's capital base to NT$4.4 billion.

While the Kaohsiung yard was in gestation, all efforts were focused on Taiwan Shipbuilding and the Keelung enterprise was expanded with alacrity. Annual new-building capacity was raised from 160,000 dwt to 300,000 dwt. Repair capacity jumped commensurately when a 100,000 dwt dock was opened for that purpose. More daringly, the yard turned its hand to container vessels as well as bulkers and tankers in order to play a leading role in the government's new brainchild of making Taiwan a major force in container shipping. Vindicating these efforts, Taiwan Shipbuilding constructed vessels aggregating 220,000 gt in 1971: a sevenfold increase on the 1966 level (embracing, for instance, the island's first 100,000 dwt tanker). Learning economies began to take effect too. A 28,000 dwt bulker required 12 months to build in 1966, but only half that time in 1973 and 5.5 months in 1975; similarly, a tanker required 14 months in the late 1960s as against nine months in 1975.[41] Caught in the shipbuilding slump like its young peer at Kaohsiung, the Keelung facility could take solace from the fact that the shipping promotion scheme launched by the government in 1977 envisaged home yards providing 43 ships of 1.6 million tons by 1981. As part and parcel of the plan to co-ordinate domestic production, CSBC and Taiwan Shipbuilding merged at the beginning of 1978 under the banner of the former. To prevent the industry from unduly flagging as a result of the international shipping downturn triggered by the second oil crisis of the late 1970s, the government – by now a past master in the art of demand stimulation – conceived a plan in 1980 to order 1.98 million dwt from CSBC on behalf of state enterprises. This entailed Chinese Petroleum reserving a trio of 200,000 dwt VLCCs, China Steel contracting for three 125,000 dwt ore carriers and three coal carriers of comparable dimensions and Taiwan Power adding its weight with orders for a brace of 120,000 dwt bulkers and a half-dozen Panamax (65,000 dwt) bulkers. Adhering in spirit to the UNCTAD liner code, the government subsequently initiated a large programme of container-ship new buildings for the state's Yangming shipping line and persisted with CSBC as the supplier despite that builder's higher prices and occasional late deliveries. Notwithstanding this very useful fillip, CSBC was constrained to disclose a deficit of NT$1.8 billion in 1979. It was sufficiently competitive, however, to win orders for export tankers from the likes of Exxon and the Kuwait National Petroleum Company. Hai-po Yen, the president of the builder, was moved to confess that, while CSBC prices were 3–5 per cent lower than those applying in Japan, they remained 5–20 per cent higher than those charged by South Korean builders. Indigenisation, it was hoped, would close the gap with the latter, and in 1980 TMMC was able to claim that some 30 per cent of its licence-built Sulzer engines was made locally; a proportion which was expected to rise to 60 per cent as the dependence on IHI was gradually lessened.[42] Even more significant progress towards self-sufficiency could be demonstrated by CSBC: its ships now enjoyed a local content of 72.2 per cent of the total of materials worked into them, while a local design office – the state's United Ship Design and Development Centre – had usurped foreign designs for all but the novel areas of drilling rigs and gas carriers.[43]

Desperate attempts to garner export orders exacted a heavy toll on the shipbuilder, however. For example, in a misguided ploy to match Japanese prices, it agreed to build five 8,500 ton container vessels for West German owners for $5 million each, about half the real cost of production. Reputedly, $5 million was lost on each of the four Exxon tankers and $3 million on each of the six Kuwaiti tankers as well.[44] Ominous signs of pent-up problems were beginning to surface. In early 1981 it was revealed that the firm's debt-to-equity ratio stood at 10.8:1, with its net worth of NT$3.3 billion totally outweighed by its debts of NT$36 billion: evidently, the Kaohsiung operation had never recovered from the 200 per cent cost overrun incurred at the time of its inception (i.e. start-up costs of NT$8.4 billion or $221.1 million). As ever, the government was prepared to lend a hand. Under the terms of the third four-year shipbuilding plan, a veritable fleet of new construction was programmed to emanate from CSBC by the end of 1986; namely, 20 bulkers of 25,000 dwt, a dozen container vessels of 8,000 dwt and 14 coal carriers varying in size from 13,000 dwt to 63,000 dwt. In order to encourage the likes of Evergreen, Taiwan's vibrant new container line, to buy at home, the government was ready to advance loans to finance 80 per cent of ship prices; loans which were repayable over 10 years at 10 per cent interest rates. These initiatives afforded CSBC some satisfaction, and it reported a NT$1 billion profit for the fiscal year ending in June 1984. That relief was decidedly temporary, though, and in June 1985 profits had dissipated to a mere NT$17 million. On cue, the government conceded a new export promotion scheme which envisaged loans repayable over 12–15 years at 8 per cent interest rates. It was accepted by the authorities that, as domestic demand for tonnage was almost sated, CSBC must increasingly rely on foreign orders (such as the couple of 305,000 dwt OBOs it was awarded by Wah Kwong Shipping of Hong Kong).[45] Already economies were being enforced: in 1984 some 400 workers were released and 1,500 subcontractors' jobs were eliminated while, in the following year, the 8,500 work-force was depleted by an additional 1,000 from Keelung and 400 from Kaohsiung. Yet piecemeal reforms were scarcely adequate in the light of the alarming revelations which were coming to the fore. It was estimated at the end of 1985, for instance, that the builder was losing NT$200 million ($5 million) a month simply in consequence of its obligation to pay off accumulated debts. The injection of NT$62 billion ($1.55 billion) by the government into a long-term low-interest (7.5 per cent) ship loan scheme was mandated by the parlous state of the shipbuilding firm's finances. To add to its woes, CSBC was confronted with the prospect of an upstart competitor in 1987. The extraordinarily successful Chang Yung-fa, founder of what was soon to become the world's premier container line (the combined Evergreen International, Evergreen Marine and Uniglory Marine concern), announced plans to create a shipyard at Taichung under the guise of the Evergreen Heavy Industrial Corporation. Long a patron of Japanese yards (Onomichi Dockyard in particular), Chang had grudgingly conceded the merits of CSBC and ordered a sizeable number of his new buildings there. Now, the proposed Taichung yard would create a vertically integrated organisation capable not only of repairing the Evergreen fleet, but also of annually building three or four container ships in the 50,000 dwt class. The stated intent of Chang to use three-quarters of Taichung's output for his own line and, in any case, to abstain from undercutting CSBC in global markets, was of little comfort to the state builder if only because the rival yard would deprive it of the custom of one of the world's top shipping enterprises.[46] A crushing run of losses – NT$1.16 billion on revenues of NT$9.2 billion in 1986 and NT$2.98 billion on lowered revenues of NT$7.79 billion in 1987 – was ample testimony to CSBC's existing difficulties. Symptomatic of the builder's hunger for work was its decision to enter the market for fishing vessels in 1987 (an arena from which it soon secured orders) notwithstanding the bitter opposition of TMMC which claimed that, in violating its agreement to avoid the small-ship market, CSBC had jeopardised the future of TMMC's shipyard.[47]

Fortunately, conditions changed for the better in 1988. In the first place, Evergreen retreated from its shipyard project, citing the appreciation of Taiwan's currency and the concomitant erosion of the island's competitive production costs as the main culprits for this about-face.[48] What is more, it transferred eight of its container vessels to CSBC's Kaohsiung yard for enlargement, a contract fully in keeping with the builder's new emphasis on repair and conversion work. Secondly, the provision of low-interest loans began to bear fruit. While accumulated losses had reached NT$5.9 billion by mid-1988, the signing of contracts for 23 vessels in the preceding eight months offered the builder the chance to break even by 1990 or 1991. Thanks to government loans expected to mount to NT$10 billion in the succeeding three years, the president of CSBC, Yeh Man-sheng, was able to describe the builder's financing packages as aligned, at long last, with those of the chaebōl.[49] The fact that the government obtained the funding for buttressing the faltering CSBC from proceeds realised from the partial sale of China Steel attests to its deep commitment to Taiwanese shipbuilding. Thirdly, the government pronounced the strategic importance of CSBC, articulating that it was an indispensable element in future defence plans. A smaller branch of the firm at Tsoying was already devoted to the construction of fast attack craft, and the government was inclining to the view that the main merchant yards could be partly switched to quantity production of frigates. While it was prepared to consider a relaxation of state ownership at CSBC on the understanding that private management might boost efficiency and contain losses, the government adamantly refused to countenance the dissolution of the shipbuilder. At the same time, it endorsed the legitimacy of TMMC in a different manner: despite losses of over NT$2 billion, it averred that the engineering firm was too important either to undergo privatisation or to be allowed to fall into disarray. In other words, TMMC would persist as a state enterprise come what may. Brave statements aside, the viability of CSBC remained very much in question. Losses of NT$1.9 billion in 1988 were ascribed, on the one hand, to the continuing need to import expensive parts from Japan and, on the other, to the drain imposed by annual interest repayments in the range of NT$800 million (as the yard had accrued foreign loans of NT$28.8 billion). Thus after two decades of effort – a period seldom punctuated with economic rebuffs for Taiwan as a whole – the chief shipyards have yet to throw off their burden of severe financial liabilities. In spite of prodigious investment in plant and an undeniably impressive penetration of export markets, the outlook for CSBC and TMMC appears bleak and they continue to survive only by dint of government bail-outs. The rub lies in this contingent survival. Deemed pivotal to industrialisation and economic growth, the yards fall short of emulating the success of other branches of the marine sector, most vividly exemplified by Evergreen and container shipping. Paradoxically, a government dedicated to promoting competitive private export activities is equally wedded to a loss-making state heavy machinery sector. A revision in this political stance, liable to occur at any moment, could quickly remove the lifeline that the yards have come to rely on.

SUMMARY

Industrialisation and the mature industries go hand in hand. They are prized by the NICs both for their ability to confer basic engineering skills on the work-force and for their aptness as an underlying structure of essential supplier industries for downstream sectors. Apart from bestowing a bedrock of manufacturing on the country, vital for building a myriad of spin-off activities, mature industries such as shipbuilding and marine engineering also offer a useful bridge between strategies rooted in import-substitution industrialisation and those focused on export promotion. By their very nature massive absorbers of capital and labour, the marine industries are nothing if not difficult to arouse and develop without systematic planning. It is hardly surprising, then, that governments and state enterprises have loomed disproportionately large in the emergence of these industries in the developing countries. Indeed, the government imprint is customary everywhere in the Third World, and is often validated in the name of national defence. From Communist China to interventionist India and capitalist Taiwan, the government-owned shipyard has shouldered the burden of leading the advance of shipbuilding. Moreover, state-orchestrated planning occurs even in countries not disposed to favour state enterprises in ship-building and disinclined to tolerate unproductive activities in this or any other sector. The Brazilian Government, for example, actively sought foreign investment in the shipbuilding industry and paved the way for home-grown yards to germinate and flourish in the shadow of the multinational enterprises. The South Korean Government, too, deliberately steered the country's set of private conglomerates into the industry and energetically laboured to ensure that conditions were sufficiently propitious to enable them to thrive. In this respect, South Korea was merely aping the Japanese experience; and the progeny of those pioneer efforts to invoke an industry and render it productive – the present-day major Japanese shipbuilders – are still at work conjuring up incipient industries throughout the Third World.

Numerous references to their role as technology donors have been made in the body of the chapter, and yet other examples could be summoned. We will settle for just one more: that dealing with Indonesia. Long committed to establishing a native shipbuilding industry, Indonesia's efforts have not been an unqualified success. As recently as 1989 the government, exasperated at the slow rate of development, attempted to provoke the country's limited stock of yards into action by having the state oil company, Pertamina, announce plans to order 31 coastal tankers from them.[50] PT Pal, the principal builder which employs 6,000 workers in Surabaya, relies on MES for design assistance and the supply of key components, including marine engines. For its alternative occupation of steel-structure fabrication, it relies on technology furnished by MHI.[51] This is not to say, of course, that the NICs do not look to other donors for their technology. The Europeans have been prominent contributors to the shipbuilding industries of Brazil, India and – especially through their Soviet manifestation – China, whereas the USA has left its mark on the Taiwanese industry. The European influence continues to wax in other venues. In Chile, for instance, the state's Asmar Shipping and Docking Company operates a facility in Valparaiso in conjunction with Bazan of Spain.[52] Evidently, ship-building and the technology transfer which makes it possible, continues to be regarded with approbation by many countries that are convinced of the virtues of industrialisation: perhaps a remarkable state of affairs in view not only of the fact that planned shipbuilding, in whatever guise, is immensely costly, but that the verdict is still open as to whether it can ever aspire to sustained profitability.

7 Conclusions

It is not going too far to say that at the beginning of the 1970s the likes of the NICs were beneath the notice of Japan in the shipbuilding field. In fact, Japan's ascendancy was so overwhelming that Western Europe, the traditional heartland of the industry, was struggling to retain both its composure and its substance as a producer of major proportions. It was being trounced, indeed, by a competitor which not only had grown remorselessly since the early 1950s, but which had contrived to capture the lion's share of a market that had expanded by leaps and bounds and had yet to reach its climax. Of course, that agreeable state in which orders abounded for Japan, and were even plentiful for those European producers astute enough to grasp them, was soon to be truncated, rudely overturned after 1973 when the actions of the oil suppliers of the Third World dealt a shattering blow to shipping markets in general and the tanker trades in particular. Overtaken by events and cushioned only by the hasty application of government bail-out measures, the established shipbuilding producers underwent a straitened period of retrenchment, rationalisation and restructuring during which many succumbed to outright closure. Adverse conditions, tantamount to wholesale depression, usurped growth for the succeeding 15 years. In constituting the normal environment for engaging in shipbuilding, these conditions succeeded in circumscribing the surviving firms in the AICs, dashing the hopes of their managements and instilling in them attitudes detrimental to the long-term revival of the industry. More alarming still, this uncongenial environment gradually sobered Western governments to the futility of sustaining activities for which the writing seemed to be on the wall. By the early 1980s the inauspicious outcomes of state support were becoming readily apparent everywhere in the West and governments, resigned to the inevitability of cutbacks, were finding cause for retreating from the industry. Nor was Japan spared. The solid foundation of past achievement which had hitherto accounted for its mastery was unable to detach shipbuilding from the global downturn, and the results of a major reorganisation and rationalisation of the industry appeared less than promising. Desperate to salvage a significant shipbuilding industry, the Europeans bandied together and claimed the assistance first of the OECD and then of the EEC in their endeavours to impose order on their own vulnerable establishments and the chaotic market at large. With a view to stabilising global competition, they leagued with the Japanese and tried, fruitlessly in the event, to manage ship supply. Much to their dismay (and latterly, to the discomfort of the Japanese as well), the NIC producers demurred at these machinations, refusing to adhere to globally managed production. Only as the 1980s came to a close was there the first appearance of harmony between Japan and the NIC champion, South Korea, and this tentative understanding was regarded with something approaching suspicion by the European producers (although both Japan and South Korea have sought to quell any disquiet felt on this score).

It is fair to say, though, that Europeans and Japanese alike had looked askance at the entire phenomenon of new-entry shipbuilding throughout the 1970s and 1980s. Led by South Korea, the most strikingly successful of the upstart producers which had butted their way onto the world scene, the NICs had persisted – perversely in the eyes of many of the established producers – in consolidating their entry into the industry. Admittedly, several had taken the irrevocable step of committing sizeable resources to the industry in the heady days of the early 1970s and, like everyone else, had been caught unawares by the subsequent crash. Left with little option but to persevere, they had doggedly built up their yard assets throughout the latter part of the 1970s and across the full span of the 1980s at exactly the same time as the older producers were reducing theirs. The more thoughtful advocates of NIC shipbuilding could argue that history favoured them, however. The history in question alluded to the industry life-cycle obtaining for shipbuilding. As a longstanding mature industry bordering on senescence, shipbuilding and its associated marine engineering was unequivocally mired in the phase of standard process and product technologies; a phase in which innovation, while not entirely dormant, was characterised by modest incremental improvements at best. Consequently, prominent among the denizens of shipbuilding were yards that had endured from the industry's youth and which were, in consequence, constrained by site lay-outs notwithstanding belated attempts at modernisation. These yards peppered the shipbuilding districts of the traditional producers and their evident disarray inevitably occasioned instances of severe localised unemployment.

Despite a thorough overhauling, for example, H&W – and Northern Ireland shipbuilding as a whole – witnessed its work-force shrink from 24,100 in 1960 to 9,800 in 1970 and to 7,400 in 1980.[1] In more recent years, the total has diminished further, to a figure, in fact, barely one-sixth of the 1960 level. What is worse, too many of them were invested with managements immune to the technological dynamism of other, less mature industries and generally resigned to stagnant business prospects: both properties inimical to economic revival. Therefore, they were poorly equipped to profit from government relief measures when the helping hand was extended to them. In the USA, for example, many yards lingered in the building sphere at the whim of conglomerate parents solely interested in that branch of the industry which offered reasonable profits consistent with a protected market; namely, warshipbuilding. Similar tendencies were discernible in Europe too, although a substantial number of builders elected to specialise in products other than warships (e.g. cruise liners, Ro-Ro ferries, container vessels, gas carriers and offshore support vessels). Newer, acutely conscious of productivity gains and enjoying the blessing of corporate owners inclined to the belief that marine activities were worthwhile and ready, as a result, to tolerate the misfortunes plaguing shipbuilding, the Japanese yards were able to spring up from the wrenching process of rationalisation in a much healthier state than was general in the West. It was they, then, that bore the brunt of the competition with the NICs. Stripped of the cheap labour advantage inspiring NIC shipbuilders, the Japanese yards were obliged to compete on the grounds of higher productivity, superior quality and attractive pricing: the last realised in part through corporate ability to sustain loss-making contracts and partly through government manipulation of domestic shipping markets in order to conjure up demand. The upshot of a decade of intense competition is that Japan and South Korea enter the 1990s as sparring partners, bruised and battered by circumstances but still vying with each other for the laurels of top producer notwithstanding perceptible moves towards marketing co-operation. To date, Japan clings to the first rank, having effectively countered the Korean challenge and blunted the ruinous price-cutting that became rampant in the 1980s. It knows, however, that other NICs are waiting in the wings and that a slimmer, more competitive European industry remains a force to be reckoned with in certain product areas and offers a comprehensive repository of expertise not to be dismissed lightly. The point of this, the concluding chapter, is to underscore the salient features, the milestones, as it were, which have given rise to the contemporary shipbuilding situation and, in the light of that backdrop, to speculate on what the immediate future holds for the major players.

INDUSTRIAL UPHEAVAL AND DISLOCATION

Explosive growth in capacity and sharp reduction in customer demand are unhappy bedfellows and yet they put their stamp on the global shipbuilding industry of the second half of the 1970s. Enforced capacity retirement in the AICs and incremental additions to capacity in the NICs marked the 1980s, although by this time the pattern of demand had taken on an air of stability, albeit languishing at a level far inferior to that typifying the feverish markets of the early 1970s. The onset of the 1990s tentatively appeared to bring down the curtain on an act of the shipbuilding saga which most producers were not sorry to see disappear; that is to say, a suggestion of revival was ushering in the new decade and the surviving producers were greedily topping up their order-books. One observer, Seiji Nagatsuka of the Japan Maritime Research Institute, was opining that the revival in demand evident in 1989 would likely persist well into the 1990s and that Japanese builders in particular would be major beneficiaries of the renewed interest in shipping.[2] Sadly, this respite in what had come to be regarded as an interminable period of gloom and despondency came too late for many shipbuilders, especially those resident in the traditional producer nations. The closure of NESL in 1989 and the extinction of Sunderland as a shipbuilding centre after the best part of a millennium is perhaps the most cogent single instance of this want in synchronism. It was merely the culmination of a parting of the ways between those, increasingly rare, advocates of shipbuilding support and the revisionists who saw little merit in sustaining an evidently disappearing industry. The faltering producers of Western Europe had espoused state intervention, believing that centralised co-ordination coupled with government largesse could counter the pitfalls of the market and preserve, virtually intact, the breadth and depth of the industry. Soon disabused of this notion, the policy-makers in the UK and Sweden expressed their disenchantment with shipbuilding by dismantling their monolithic nationalised industries. In the British case, several yards imitated the American model and fled to the niche market of defence whereas in the Swedish instance all the yards were extinguished with the exception of a residual defence sector (Karlskronavarvet and an attenuated Kockums Marine) and a dedicated offshore yard (Götaverken Arendal).[3] Enduring comparable discouraging experiences of state interference, the shipbuilding industries of the Netherlands and France partly withered away whilst under state tutelage. For their part, the government-controlled enterprises of Italy and Spain succeeded in upholding their organisational form and conserving the bulk of their industrial assets, but at a huge cost to their national treasuries. Fiscal probity and managerial competence go together, of course, and it manifestly was hardly inspirational in the COMECON countries either, as is evidenced most starkly by the virtual collapse of the Polish state shipbuilding organisation. Even Finland, the emblem of successful shipbuilding against all the odds, suffered a reverse in 1989 with the demise of Wärtsilä Marine, the linchpin of its marine-industrial base.

Japan did not escape the need for some painful contraction, a process which took its toll of both plant capacity and manpower. The baptism of fire for Japanese yards occurred in 1978 at government instigation. An intrusive government alone, however, could not overcome the serious imbalance between capacity and demand, and in the latter part of the 1980s Japanese officialdom was again compelled to intrude in the affairs of the country's builders. On this occasion it lent its support to the formation of industry coalitions – subsequently to coalesce into production groups – geared to the object of aligning capacity to perceived markets. Through matching supply with demand once and for all, the government reasoned that it would be bestowing on the surviving restructured industry the foundations for future unsurpassable international competitiveness. Only by the end of the decade was the production control and cartel arrangement waived, but by then eight large groups had crystallised to constitute Japan's front line in the continuing battle waged to dominate global ship supply markets. The eight in question – IHI, Hitachi Zosen, SHI, MES and the Kurushima Dockyard clutch, together with amalgamations of MHI and the Imabari yards, KHI and NKK, not to mention the combination of Tsuneishi Shipbuilding, Onomichi Dockyard and Minaminippon Zosen – represented the cream of Japan's corporate interests. Some stood as vast diversified corporations in their own right (MHI is the epitome) while others could draw on alliances with companies which spanned the spectrum of manufacturing, trade and service activities (with the IHI–Toshiba affiliation being a case in point). Most of the Japanese builders had undergone, with varying degrees of success, a spell dedicated to reducing their exposure to new building, but, by and large, they had gladly resumed their shipbuilding preoccupation at the first signs of a revival in the marine sector during 1989. MES, for example, decided early in 1990 to revive merchant new building at its Tamano yard after an interval of three years during which the facility had fallen back on its function as a supplier of naval vessels (frigates) and a purveyor of offshore activities.[4] A steady programme of naval expansion had played a notable, if unsung, part in sustaining Japan's shipbuilding pre-eminence. The naval option had provided the likes of MHI, KHI and IHI with a useful supplementary (or, indeed, for some yards, substitute) business during the darker days of the 1980s recession. In its capacity as a diversion for underused plant and labour, naval construction also found much favour elsewhere. In the USA it sustained the yards of Newport News, General Dynamics, Ingalls and Bath Iron Works; in Canada it ensured the well-being of Saint John Shipbuilding; in Britain several newly privatised yards came to rely on it (including VSEL, Yarrow, Swan Hunter and Vosper Thornycroft); in France it became the lifeblood of Chantiers de l'Atlantique; whereas in the Netherlands it acted to underpin KMS and RDM.[5]

Resort to warshipbuilding was only one (albeit, an important one) of the many diversification ploys taken up with gusto by the longer-established builders during the late 1970s and 1980s. Indeed, the popularity of diversification strategies fluctuated in inverse relation to the state of shipping markets, rising in concert with diminishing demand for merchant tonnage and fading in tune with rejuvenation of yard order-books. Almost all shipyards undertook to reduce the vulnerability caused by low ship prices and many of them made a stab at unrelated activities. Their attempts were many and varied. Fish farming, railway engineering, airport construction and the manufacture of a welter of process machinery were all grist to the mill of shipyards not fully occupied in their traditional functions. However, it was to related activities that most attention was directed. In this respect, the Japanese enjoyed something of an advantage. The zaibatsu fashioned the heavy industry, trade and shipping groupings which persist, despite organisational transformations, in the latter-day Japanese conglomerates. For example, not only does MHI encompass an integrated ship-production complex complete with engine works and accessories plants, but it maintains organisational links with some of its shipping customers. It is scarcely surprising, then, to learn that this firm has consistently displayed little or no reluctance in combining with its corporate affiliates in order to gain entry into new markets. Recently, for instance, MHI united with shipowner NYK and trader Mitsubishi Corporation (to say nothing of West Germany's Hapag–Lloyd shipping line and US interests) with the intention of forming a cruise line. As part and parcel of the joint venture arrangement, MHI's Kobe yard received the order for the line's first vessel.[6] For the most part bereft of the conglomerate linkages assumed by Japanese shipyards, the European builders were thrown back on their own resources. Applying management talents to related businesses became commonplace and a legion of yards struck out for repair and offshore pursuits as well as the cognate defence field. Some even went so far as to attempt to forge formal ties with independent manufacturers of marine engines and, in so doing, effect a reversal of a longstanding trend to sever this natural, but pragmatically problematic, form of vertical integration. The most contemporary instance of this phenomenon has West Germany as its provenance. With the failure of the grand horizontal integration scheme of MAN/B&W to absorb its Sulzer competitor, the way was left open for a pair of prominent shipbuilders, Bremer Vulkan and HDW, to join forces with the East German Rostock yard so as to mount a take-over bid for the Swiss marine diesel maker.[7] Persuaded of the need to compete vigorously with Japanese and NIC yards, the European builders were at last taking steps to fashion anew the internalised comprehensive marine-industrial capabilities so esteemed by their Asian protagonists. However, these attempts of the shipbuilders to fuse complete marine undertakings out of disparate yards and engine works paled in comparison with the initiatives got up by shipping firms eager to acquire a stake in shipyard operations. Presenting by far the most dramatic example of the incursion of shipping on shipbuilding was the 1989 absorption of KSEC, a large but troubled South Korean builder, by the Hanjin chaebŏl. An integrated transport organisation of the first order, Hanjin controlled a major container line as well as the principal airline of the country. Pending its revamping as a dedicated supplier of in-house tonnage, KSEC would earn its keep as the shipping group's very own repair and overhaul centre. Having hit upon a means both to guarantee ship supply and to make certain of the maintenance of existing fleets, the more assertive shipowners hastened to secure holdings in shipyards in the waning days of the 1980s. The Norwegians were especially notable in this respect, snapping up substantial shares in H&W, Govan Shipbuilders (and the neighbouring Clark Kincaid engine works) and Setenave, to say nothing of their penetration of COMECON shipbuilding by virtue of Kvaerner's involvement in the Paris Commune Shipyard in Poland. Yet, on at least one occasion – the collapse of Wärtsilä Marine in Finland – shipowners leapt into the shipbuilding void not for any calculated embracing of vertical integration but, rather, with a view to rescuing a shipyard about to founder. The Masa Yards successor was cobbled together by the government and a number of shipowners (including Carnival Cruise Lines with an 11 per cent stake) desirous of seeing their half-built tonnage brought to completion. These acts throw in bold relief the differential revival experienced by the two arms of the marine sector: on the one hand, shipping was sufficiently recharged to initiate a business offensive on the construction and repair side whereas, on the other, a sizeable element of construction and repair was ill-prepared to grasp the changing circumstances, at a loss how to make the best of reviving ship markets, and therefore liable to succumb to outside take-over bids.

In common, shipping and shipbuilding have long enjoyed the status of privileged industries in the NICs. The rise of South Korea has received great play in this book, but its growth trajectory merely overshadows the solid performances demonstrated by the likes of Brazil, Taiwan and Singapore. Thanks to a judicious mix of private enterprise and public participation – with the latter being much the more important – these countries have emerged as leading exponents of the marine industries. Their governments have not only rendered the economic environment propitious for maritime activities in a fashion analogous to that of South Korea, but, unlike the South Koreans, have actively entered into the running of shipyards (although, in the case of Brazil, state yards are restricted to naval work).[8] What is more, in interposing itself between the world market and local latent production bases, the government has lent its influence to the formation of yards of a stature beyond the critical mass necessary for survival. Besides, these yards have gained access to process and product technologies solely on account of government willingness to cultivate foreign partnership agreements. In short, governments in South Korea and the three aforementioned NICs have been bent on promoting shipbuilding as a major plank in their respective industrialisation platforms and not least as a vital earner of export income. No effort was spared to ensure that shipbuilding overcame the teething troubles incident to the development of any nascent industry. Their shipbuilding industries, by any measure, have aspired to significant size in consequence. Commanding stature has been bought at a heavy price, however. The yards have been dogged by losses and forced to trim their ambitions and make economies; indeed, their work-forces have often taken the brunt of these adjustments. A painful restructuring involving labour cutbacks, strikes and work disruptions afflicted the South Korean industry for much of the later 1980s and has not yet run its course. At the beginning of 1990, for example, both SSHI and DSHM announced plans to chop their labour forces: the former intends to cut 500 from its 2,500 complement at Koje Island while the latter wants to eliminate 3,000 jobs from its pool of 12,000 employed at Okpo. Inflated costs have arisen from these structural problems and may already be seriously undermining the competitive stance of the yards. By one account, British shipowner P&O baulked in early 1990 at the prices demanded by a consortium of SSHI and HHI for building a series of container vessels, proclaiming that they were almost one-fifth higher than prices prevailing a year earlier.[9]

Losses without the comfort of export earnings have branded many other NIC shipbuilding ventures, however. While mostly small-scale affairs, there are a few notable exceptions. India has sunk considerable investment into its marine sector without a commensurate return on the export front. China, too, has devoted prodigious energies to the exercise of expanding its marine industries and, much to its dismay, has discovered that export-oriented new building is plagued with problems of quality control, pressured deadlines and costly components imports which combine not only to undermine many of the presumed benefits but, to add insult to injury, subject the country to a barrage of criticism from independent-minded shipowners. Such difficulties notwithstanding, some NICs are determined to press ahead with expansion plans. In part this conviction is tolerated only because of the government's ability to insulate the national industry from the rigours of global competition. The Indian Planning Commission, for instance, advocated in 1990 that India should not delay in establishing a new yard with an annual capacity of 150,000 dwt even allowing that the proposed facility would require an investment of $130 million. The fact that the country's existing yards were neither profitable in aggregate, nor operated in a manner to recommend their products to the world's shipowners, can be conveniently disregarded when the prime objective of the state is to foster import-substitution industrialisation. In default of export successes, the shipyards of India can retire to the shelter of a protected market; an option which some managers of the shipbuilding industry in China are equally prone to find reassuring in the face of export difficulties. Truth to say, all shipbuilders are apt to find solace in alternative markets when escalating difficulties in export ship markets become pronounced, and many cases have been paraded through the pages of this book. Singapore's builders, however, stand as supreme examples of enterprises able and willing to execute strategies of masterful diversification. Blessed with a government which mediates between the interests of privately owned, largely Japanese shipyard subsidiaries on the one hand and publicly owned local shipyard entities on the other, the marine enterprises of the island republic have blossomed (admittedly, after a stint of misfortunes in common with builders elsewhere) as suppliers of offshore rigs and support craft, have earned for themselves a daunting reputation as repairers and specialists in ship conversion and have exercised the option of running shipping lines. Of late, they have even taken to presiding over multinational operations, wielding control or partnership ties with yards in the Philippines, India, the United Arab Emirates and Thailand.

OUTLOOK

After plumbing the depths of the shipping recession in the mid-1980s, shipbuilders began to experience a modest revival of activity; sufficient, at any rate, to warrant cautious optimism by the end of the decade. That bugbear, prices falling short of costs, appeared destined for oblivion (or, more realistically, could be jettisoned until the next demand downturn) and the market was promising profits on new buildings for the first time in many years. While hardly cause for rapturous celebration, the fact that the average price per cgrt for vessels booked in Japan at the end of 1989 stood fully one-fifth higher than average prices pertaining to Japanese new buildings of 1983 was taken as a token of solid progress and an omen of better things to come. One small but important indicator of the putative turnround in shipbuilding's fortunes emanated from South Africa, a developing country seemingly set on joining the band of embryo ship producers. A longstanding ship repairer by virtue of its geographical position as a hub on major trade routes, this country had produced a trickle of small ships over the years, mostly for local fishing or defence interests. At the beginning of 1990, though, Dorbyl Marine of Durban confirmed that it had won an order for four container ships from a Cyprus-based ship-management firm.[10] In itself, entry into shipbuilding is no momentous occurrence. After all, Australia – the country which almost casually watched its merchant shipbuilding industry expire in the 1970s – has spent the best part of the 1980s endeavouring to establish a domestic warshipbuilding industry.[11] What lends substance to the South African example, however, is the decision not just to undertake merchant new building, but to prosecute it in its most decidedly competitive guise; namely, export shipbuilding. The South Africans are wagering, of course, on all the signs and portents coming true and conforming to expectations of a healthy supplier's market in the 1990s. Available indicators guardedly substantiate their optimism, all combining to suggest an upsurge in activity, albeit highly skewed in its effects on producer countries.

On the surface, the year 1989 marked a discontinuity in that it displayed a sharp rise in shipbuilding activity relative to its predecessor. The total of 31,054,560 gt of merchant shipping on order around the world at the end of 1989 was a hefty 26.5 per cent increment on the 24,553,389 gt constituting the global order book at the end of 1988. Moreover, this sanguine indicator of uplifting activity in force at the termination of the 1980s was fully 45.4 per cent greater than the 21,364,165 gt recorded for the end of 1986; that is to say, almost half as much again as the level obtaining for the low point of activity for the decade. Looking further back, the total order book at the beginning of 1980 registered 28,301,858 gt; some 9.7 per cent less than the figure prevailing for the onset of the 1990s. Thus, by any yardstick, the reigning market has escaped from the doldrums and, much to the delight of the shipbuilders, has adopted an ascending track, fuelled by the increasingly pressing need to replace old tonnage dating from the heyday of the tanker boom of the early 1970s.[12] Japan, basking in rebounding activity levels, has been singled out by the pundits as an example of the rewards awaiting those producers prepared to stand fast behind a mature industry. Certainly, the evidence corroborates a significant rebirth of the marine industries that are located there. With 33.1 per cent of the world order book in December 1989, Japan accounted for almost exactly the same dominant share of the global market as it had held under its sway in December 1979 (33 per cent), but with the gratifying twist that its actual work in hand at the later date represented a 10.2 per cent increase in tonnage terms over the earlier date. Even more cheering, the December 1989 order book elicited the vast improvement in competitiveness staged by the industry. Japan's 30.7 per cent share of activity during the global nadir of December 1986, while only slightly out of line with past practice, was, at 6,568,035 gt, a good 56.5 per cent lower in tonnage terms than what it was to become three years later. More impressive still was the extent of the recovery which occurred between December 1988 and December 1989. Having slipped to a position where it was responsible for only 24.3 per cent of the world order book, Japan instituted a commendable about-turn in which the tonnage in question, amounting to 5,959,328 gt in December 1988, swelled by as much as 72.5 per cent over the succeeding twelve months. This last-minute spurt contrasts dramatically with South Korea's performance. In the year extending from December 1988 to December 1989, that country's order book grew by just 2.8 per cent, from 5,865,160 gt to 6,027,442 gt. To a great degree, this uninspiring record owes more to the labour strife paralysing the South Korean yards for much of the period than it does to any extraordinary upturn in productivity hit upon by the Japanese yards. Yet the fact that Japan's order book rose some 56.5 per cent between the end of 1986 and the end of 1989 whereas South Korea's only picked up by 42.7 per cent speaks volumes for the more far-reaching restructuring inspiring Japanese builders during these years. Over the longer horizon, though, the Japanese performance pales in comparison with that of South Korea. Reporting a December 1979 order book of 1,271,261 gt, or 4.5 per cent of the global total, the South Korean shipbuilding industry effected an astonishing 374.1 per cent gain in the absolute size of its order book by the end of 1989 and answered for 19.4

per cent of the world order-book (which, while impressive, admittedly was inferior in a relative sense to the 23.9 per cent which it had accounted for in December 1988). It almost goes without saying that this gloss of heightened activity is neither synonymous with enhanced long-term profitability nor is there any way, consistent with the vital principle of opportunity costs, in which it can be said to justify the investment of scarce resources in founding newborn shipbuilding enterprises in yet more developing countries. Despite repeated attempts undertaken since the late 1970s to expunge redundant shipyards, the sheer weight of available shipbuilding capacity is of such enormous proportions that, conceivably, some of it currently slumbering in gentle repose could be brought out of retirement and turned to full use with devastating effect: reimposing acute price cutting among shipbuilders and transforming overnight their buoyant returns into sharp losses.[13] Indeed, only the distinct chance of a labour-supply bottleneck brought about by years of work-force shrinkage in Japan may be standing in the way of the return to shipbuilding of yards long since turned over to repair or other purposes.

Nevertheless, those NICs with their own yards, especially those stubborn enough to have insisted on sizeable ventures from the outset and sufficiently doughty to have endured the years of discouragement, are now poised to reap the benefits promised by industry life-cycle theory. Their inherent advantage was starkly summed up in the words of Loh Wing Siew, managing director of Keppel Shipyard, when commenting on the exemplary performance of Singapore in the contemporary ship-repair context.[14]

> We are much more cost-effective and hence competitive than either Europe or North America – partly because the standard of living in the region is not quite as high and also because workers are prepared to work longer hours, harder and at odd times. This gives us a good edge on our competitors.

By extension, the same sweeping generalisation applies to shipbuilding (and for good measure, may have force in shipping where labour shortages and costs in the AICs are increasingly augmenting the value of NIC ships and crews). Further elaboration of the division of labour, and the geographical dispersal of production which ensues from it, bodes well for the future of mature industries in the NICs, promising to enlarge their capacity at the expense of the traditional producers.[15] To be sure, Japan's recent revival tends to belie both the optimism of managers such as Loh and the veracity of the predictions arising from life-cycle theory, but its achievement can be explained in terms of the advantages of size combined with a singular lack of complacency exhibited by the corporate executives and government officials charged with ensuring its survival. As others have pointed out, Japan's insistence on overall cost leadership – matching price cuts in the NICs with improved productivity at home – has typified its handling of the automobile and steel sectors, together comprising mature industries which it has no wish to see undermined.[16] When espoused by the shipbuilding industry, this strategy has been equally effective, sufficing to assure Japanese yards of a continuing hegemony. Denied the size advantages of Japan and lacking its coherent direction besides, the producers of Western Europe and North America have been enjoined to shift their efforts to serving niche markets. Control of niche markets will not only bring in its train the prospect of revitalised shipyards, rendered such by the economies consonant with specialisation, but, should those markets be carefully selected to emphasise technology-intensive ships, conspires to offer the promise of sustainable profitability as well. In eroding the relative importance of labour costs in the production process, technology-intensive products such as cruise liners, gas and chemical carriers and, above all, warships, endow these yards with a counter to the competitive edge possessed by NIC yards in the array of standard products.

The sight of European shipyards scrambling to find an alcove for their talents is a far cry from the situation of a generation ago when the continent's producers vied with Japan for dominance of the global industry. It is even more outlandish when contrasted with the situation obtaining during the years spanning the shipbuilding industry's adolescence and early maturity. Apart from the occasional rude interruption engineered by interlopers such as the USA in both world wars, the Western Europeans shouldered the burden of responsibility for shipbuilding progress in both qualitative and quantitative senses. Faithfully reflecting that central plank of life-cycle theory which avers that an industry will first prosper in proximity to the cradles of its inception, steel shipbuilding was for so long a largely Western European affair centred on a British heartland. The continent's strength lay not only in that it disposed of a formidable battery of designers, innovators and research facilities, but in that it enjoyed an unchallenged lead in cost competitiveness. The first real challenger, the USA, could not turn innovative flair to cost advantage whereas Japan, a producer whose strong suit turned on cheaper labour, could not match European productivity. The Second World War changed the situation for ever. Prescient observers were already voicing grave concern over Europe's chances of retaining the lead in shipbuilding when the American emergency shipbuilders had forcibly brought home to traditional practitioners of the shipbuilding art the errors of their ways. It would only require the amalgamation of the new methods with a locale fashioned round cheaper labour to upset the European position, and that eventuality was on the cards. Quick to grasp the standardised production processes so ably demonstrated by the Americans, the Japanese applied them to the supertanker product innovation and, in so doing, transformed themselves within the space of a decade into the world's foremost ship producer. While giving currency to the outcomes postulated by life-cycle theory, the stunning success of the Japanese also exposed the pivotal role that governments could exercise in fostering the industry through planned shipbuilding: a circumstance which tends to be downplayed by those proponents of the theory who argue the case for the inevitability of industrial relocation in search of factor-cost advantages. At any rate, the importance of government's enabling role was not lost on other states wishing to hit upon a vehicle suitable for effecting their industrialisation plans. Beginning with Poland after the Second World War, a long line of embryo ship producers entered the lists. It is not going too far to claim that the contemporary NIC upholders of the industry, and not least the South Korean champion, owe their genesis and flowering to that lesson of planned shipbuilding learned from the Japanese. Ironically, too, the rearguard action fought by Western European producers – before so many of them atrophied into the milk-and-water shadows of their past glories – rested on the moral, organisational and financial support mobilised by their governments: a strategy which only began to falter when the conviction gained ground in official quarters that subsidy was no substitute for competitiveness in an industry condemned to flee high-cost locations. All is not lost for the traditional producers, however. Life-cycle theory itself holds out the promise of redemption, foretelling industry rebirth for those enterprises perceptive enough to arouse a new product cycle through a fresh round of innovation. In pursuing programmes of niche specialisation in high-technology ships, a goodly proportion of Western European yards are clearly veering in that direction. For the heavyweight, Japan, a future which remains mired in uncertainty is an altogether different matter. Its fortunes never deteriorated to the very low ebb experienced by other AIC producers and, as a result, its shipyards were never marginalised to the same extent as those in Western Europe and North America. Furthermore, the provisional revival in the global shipping market was seized upon with great avidity by the Japanese yards as justification for renewed investment in the industry. Determined to remain major players and resolved to maintain a comprehensive capability embracing everything from standard bulkers to highly sophisticated cruise liners, the Japanese yards must calculate to a nicety the benefits of shipbuilding in the light of two daunting challenges. Failure to handle satisfactorily these two questions will likely plunge the industry back into contentious price-cutting detrimental to the interests of all producers. On the one hand, Japanese builders must push to break the technology impasse in the 'mass' market standard lines – VLCCs and bulkers in particular – in which they find themselves under remorseless pressure from builders in the likes of South Korea, Taiwan, Brazil, Poland, Romania, Yugoslavia and, of late, China. On the other hand, the Japanese builders must continue to keep pace with their counterparts in the Western AICs in the high value-added variant of shipbuilding, a prospect far from assured when the zaibatsu may come to feel themselves better served through investment in fields bearing higher profit margins. Undoubtedly, Japan's aptitude for applying flexible manufacturing systems and automated production processes, hints of which are already discernible in the shipyards, will tell in its favour as the 1990s unfold. Technical enhancement and con-comitant productivity rises are means fully consistent with the confronting of both challenges. Moreover, the Japanese conglomerate form of organisation has much to recommend it in this respect: cross-fertilisation of the shipyards by corporate affiliates in the high-technology areas is a definite likelihood. Provided the conglomerates address these issues squarely and in conjunction, one with the other, the Japanese builders are not likely to be easily upset from their position atop the world shipbuilding league. What cannot be taken for granted, though, is the persistence of a benign market, and the fact remains that no deep-laid scheme of boosting productivity on the part of Japanese shipbuilders is equal to the task of overcoming demand shortcomings. The precedent of 15 long hard years extending from 1973 has left such a searing impact on the shipbuilders, Japanese and others, as to caution against any unwarranted optimism concerning a permanent end to the industry's woes.

Notes

1 CLIMAX AND DEBACLE

1 Taken from *Fortune*, July 1954, p. 96. In truth, shipbuilding ceased at Bethlehem's San Francisco yard shortly afterwards; but its large Quincy yard, latterly in General Dynamics' hands, endured for another 30 years.

2 In 1988, for instance, Bethlehem was preoccupied with the construction of two oceanographic ships for the US Navy. See *Navy International*, May 1989, p. 229.

3 Reported by Seth Payne in *Business Week*, 12 January 1987, p. 70.

4 The early bail-out ploys are covered in B.W. Hogwood, *Government and Shipbuilding*, Saxon House, Farnborough, 1979.

5 Recounted in *The Economist*, 26 March 1988, p. 54 and 26 November 1988, p. 63. By one account, its 1988 losses of £20 million (compared with £50 million in the previous year) amounted to £5,000 per worker; that is, just one-third of the per worker losses ascribable to BS. See *The Engineer*, 14 July 1988, p. 8. Incidentally, the H&W work-force has shrunk further, registering 2,631 employees on the eve of privatisation.

6 The first real subsidy programme affecting UK shipbuilders was the Trade Facilities Act initiated in 1921, a measure aimed at facilitating capital investment through the provision of loan guarantees. The scheme had regional undertones. A plant renewal project of H&W, for example, was subject to a government rider stipulating that equipment orders must be distributed to the hard-pressed Northern manufacturing cities. Refer to M. Moss and J.R. Hume, *Shipbuilders to the World*, Blackstaff Press, Belfast, 1986, pp. 231–2.

7 Painful contraction was not restricted to the UK in the 1960s, however. Even the resurgent West German industry was exposed to the pitfalls of shipbuilding: in 1961, for instance, Schlickler Werft encountered difficulties which led to pleas for government aid. While Schlickler abandoned shipbuilding, government aid became a permanent feature of the industry. Refer to K-D. Schmidt, 'West Germany: another industrial policy victim' in T.E. Petri, *et al.*, (eds), *National Industrial Policy*, Westview, Boulder, 1984, pp. 63–9.

8 The first vessel to emerge, a product of the Gdansk shipyard, was a 2,500 dwt bulker in 1948. Refer to I. Chrzanowski, *et al.*, *Shipping Economics and Policy*, Fairplay Publications, London, 1983, p. 174.

9 Details are furnished in B. Stråth, *The Politics of De-industrialisation*, Croom Helm, London, 1987, pp. 55–6. For example, the government engineered the formation of Chantiers de l'Atlantique out of the merger of Chantiers de Penhoët–Saint Nazaire with Les Ateliers et Chantiers de la Loire's Saint Nazaire yard, besides forming Dubigeon Normandie as a successor to the two companies of Chantiers Dubigeon at Nantes and the Nantes division of Ateliers et Chantiers de la Loire. These early interventions led to yard closures, imposed 12,000 lay-offs and, under the same 1959 plan, set limits on output (a ceiling of 400,000 grt).

10 Like France, the government could not refrain from enforced mergers. The Howaldtswerke–Deutsche Werft (HDW) complex, a joint federal and state (Land) government undertaking, dates from this epoch. See Stråth, *Politics of De-industrialisation*, pp. 26–7.

11 The quotation is taken from M. Ratcliffe, *Liquid Gold Ships*, Lloyd's of London Press, Colchester, 1985, p. 152.

12 Estimates derived by Fearnleys and presented in *The Economist*, 28 January 1989, p. 101.

13 Stråth, *Politics of De-industrialisation*, p. 23.

14 Reported in *Far Eastern Economic Review*, 28 February 1975, pp. 9–10.

15 Striking testimony to the inversion of the tanker market comes from the knowledge that a shipowner purchasing a tanker in 1972 could expect to profit from that vessel to the tune of 3.5 times the building cost eight years later, but that same shipowner purchasing a vessel in 1974 and disposing of it in 1982 would incur losses amounting to nearly twice the building cost of the vessel. Refer to *Far Eastern Economic Review*, 16 February 1984, p. 37. The American Petroleum Institute reckoned that 126 tankers of 240,000 dwt and up were built between 1976 and 1980, but only six were built in the following three years. As much as $10 billion in loans outstanding on tankers burdened the banking system, with perhaps 40 per cent having to be written off.

16 OECD estimates cited in *Far Eastern Economic Review*, 20 November 1986, p. 89.

17 Recounted in *Shipping and Transportation*, November 1988, p. 45.

18 See *Far Eastern Economic Review*, 12 May 1988, pp. 59–61.

19 Reported in *Shipping and Transportation*, July 1986, p. 34.

20 A saviour in the shape of US businesswoman Barbara Piasecka Johnson emerged in 1989. Her Gdansk Shipyard Company promised to take over the Lenin Shipyard on the first day of 1990 and inject up to $100 million in it for the purpose of restoring profitability. The story is related in *Lloyd's List*, 3 June 1989, p. 1.

21 See *Fairplay*, 17 August 1989, p. 5.

22 Recounted in *The Economist*, 7 February 1987, p. 64.

23 The speech is reproduced in *Far Eastern Economic Review*, 29 October 1987, p. 51 and p. 53.

24 Signalling such a restoration, expansion in the world fleet during 1989 reversed a downward trend which had begun in 1982. Between 1988 and 1989 it grew by 7.1 million grt to reach a total of 410.5 million grt.

25 Only C.Y. Tung's 'Seawise Giant', at 564,764 dwt, exceeded this size, although this vessel (a joint effort of Sumitomo and NKK) only took on these enlarged dimensions after rebuilding.

26 See *Japan Shipping and Shipbuilding*, September 1962, p. 24. Kure Zosen had been founded in 1946 as an affiliate of Harima, but gained its independence in 1954. It had operated four building berths alongside Ludwig's dock. Later, it became the IHI Kure Shipyard.
27 Discussed in A. Albu, 'Merchant shipbuilding and marine engineering' in K. Pavitt (ed.), *Technical Innovation and British Economic Performance*, Macmillan, London, 1980, pp. 168–83 and W. Al-Timimi, 'Innovation led expansion', *Research Policy*, vol.4, 1975, pp. 160–71.
28 Reported in *Japan Shipping and Shipbuilding*, special supplement, November 1966, p. 14.
29 Detailed in *Far Eastern Economic Review*, 10 November 1955, p. 598.
30 Mentioned in *Zosen*, January 1968, p. 24.
31 Described in various issues of *Zosen*, especially October and December 1972.
32 Quoted in *Far Eastern Economic Review*, 31 October 1968, p. 248.
33 See *Far Eastern Economic Review*, 26 February 1973, p. 10.
34 Noted in *Fairplay*, 7 January 1971, p. 135.
35 Reported in Lloyd's Register of Shipping, *Annual Report 1970*, p. 83.
36 Related in *Shipping and Transportation*, October 1971, p. 16.
37 The data are drawn from tabular material contained in Lloyd's Register of Shipping, *Merchant Shipbuilding Return*, issues of December 1978 and December 1988.
38 Descriptions of which are available in D. Greenman, *Jane's Merchant Ships 1985–86*, Jane's Publishing, London, 1985.
39 The index for a given country is defined as a ratio. Its numerator is the difference between the cumulative percentage of individual ship type contributions to the total workload of that country and the equivalent sum for Poland. Its denominator is arrived at from the difference between the maximum cumulative percentage (assuming 100 for each of the eight ship types) and the sum for Poland again.
40 For an explication, see W. Isard, *Methods of Regional Analysis*, MIT Press, Cambridge, Mass., 1960.
41 Its use in the shipbuilding context is first explored in D. Todd, 'Technological change, industrial evolution, and regional repercussions', *Canadian Geographer*, vol.27, 1983, pp. 345–60.
42 Information on workloads is culled from *Fairplay*, issues of 19 January 1984 and 26 January 1989.
43 In gt terms, the world order-book slipped from 32.6 million in December 1983 to 24.6 million in December 1988. See Lloyd's Register of Shipping, *Merchant Shipbuilding Return: December 1988*, Table 12.
44 Quotations taken from *The Economist*, 23 November 1985, p. 80.

2 SHIPBUILDING AS A STRICKEN INDUSTRY

1 Output data utilised in Figure 2.1 derive from various Lloyd's Register of Shipping sources.
2 See OECD, *The Crisis in the Shipbuilding Industry and International Cooperation Efforts Geared Towards Positive Adjustment in the Industry*, CPE/PAP (80) 29, Paris, 1980.

3 Discussed in D. Todd, *The World Electronics Industry*, Routledge, London, 1990.

4 A point proffered by R. Vernon on p. 204 of his article, 'International investment and international trade in the product cycle', *Quarterly Journal of Economics*, vol.80, 1966, pp. 190–207.

5 For a review of the role of technological change in shipbuilding competitiveness, see D. Todd, *The World Shipbuilding Industry*, Croom Helm, London, 1985, ch. 4. As a matter of fact, innovators of marine engines on the Clyde who extended their budding enterprises into shipbuilding included Robert Napier and Sons (1841), Thomson (1851), Randolph, Elder and Company (1860) and Inglis (1862). The first three became large builders, respectively celebrated as Beardmore of Dalmuir, Fairfield (now Kvaerner Govan) of Govan and John Brown of Clydebank. For their history, see F.M. Walker, *Song of the Clyde*, Patrick Stephens, Cambridge, 1984.

6 Quotation taken from p. 113 of E. Lorenz and F. Wilkinson, 'The shipbuilding industry 1880–1965' in B. Elbaum and W. Lazonick (eds), *The Decline of the British Economy*, Clarendon Press, Oxford, 1986, pp. 109–34.

7 Noted in *Fairplay*, 28 June 1979, p. 62.

8 The yards were the American International Corporation's 50-way Hog Island (then the biggest in the world) and Merchant Shipbuilding's 12-way Bristol, both in the vicinity of Philadelphia, and the Submarine Boat Corporation's Newark site boasting 28 ways. See K.J. Bauer, *A Maritime History of the United States*, University of South Carolina Press, Columbia, 1988, pp. 295–9.

9 Some enlightened UK enterprises followed the American lead. As early as 1918, for example, the Burntisland shipyard set up on a greenfield site by the Firth of Forth was constructing standard designs with prefabrication techniques. It was able to use untrained labour to erect subassemblies which were then moved to the berths for final assembly. A contemporary, Liberty Shipbuilding of Warrenpoint, Northern Ireland, indulged in semi-welded construction and was rewarded with 25 per cent savings in building times over riveting methods, not to mention 10–20 per cent savings in steel-plate requirements.

10 Analysed in L. Rapping, 'Learning and World War II production functions', *Review of Economics and Statistics*, vol.47, 1965, pp. 81–6.

11 Even some of the 'novel' postwar features were less innovative than is often presumed. The enclosed shipbuilding hall, for instance, while generally shunned by shipbuilders prior to the war, could trace its ancestry back to Glasgow in 1850 when the Tod and McGregor firm erected glass-roofed iron sheds over its berths. The neighbouring Stephen's yard at Kelvinhaugh quickly followed suit, while for a spell in the 1860s and 1870s Duncan's Port Glasgow establishment was so equipped. Outside the Clyde district, Swan Hunter built covered berths at its Tyneside premises in 1894. Refer to *Fairplay*, issue of 13 April 1894. By the same token, straight-line yard lay-outs were hardly new, as this quotation – referring to a new Tyneside shipyard of 1914 – makes clear. 'The whole of the shipyard machinery, as well as the plate and frame furnace, is placed between the plate racks and the building berths, in such a manner that no material passes twice over the same ground, but has an uninterrupted course from the time it enters the yard to the moment it is worked into the ship on the building berth.' See *The Shipbuilder*, March 1914, p. 167.

12 Refer to S. Pollard, 'The decline of shipbuilding on the Thames', *Economic History Review*, vol.3, 1950, pp. 1–23 and P. Banbury, *Shipbuilders of the Thames and Medway*, David and Charles, Newton Abbot, 1971.

13 An interesting addition to this list is the now-defunct Dutch Verolme (later RSV) concern which operated yards in Brazil and Ireland as well as a considerable number in the Netherlands itself. Bankruptcy of the parent concern, together with difficulties incurred in repatriating profits, forced the sale of the lucrative Verolme Estaleiros Reunidos do Brasil (i.e. Verolme Brazil) subsidiary in Rio de Janeiro to local interests in 1983. The Irish project proved to be a liability, however. Expanded out of a small ship-repair undertaking after 1958, the Verolme Cork Dockyard was equipped with new-building facilities capable of accommodating vessels of 72,000 dwt. It received strong backing from the Irish Government (including investment grants and preferential treatment in the allocation of state contracts), but even this was not sufficient to offset operating losses occasioned in part by the need to import many components. Sequestered by the government on the demise of RSV, the yard was effectively closed in 1985. An echo of the Dutch penchant for multinational operations survives thanks to Damen Shipyards. This company, producing coasters in four yards in the Netherlands, secured an interest in the UK's Richard Dunston (Hessle) Limited, another specialist in small ships, during 1987.

14 Features identified for mature firms in general but, in the event, particularly applicable to shipbuilding. See H.W. De Jong, 'Sectoral development and sectoral policies in the EEC' in A. Jacquemin (ed.), *European Industry: Public Policy and Corporate Strategy*, Clarendon Press, Oxford, 1984, pp. 147–71.

15 Soon after the Meiji restoration, the state sequestered private yards to revamp them as modern dockyards. Subsequently privatised, these yards benefited from the 1896 Laws for the Protection of Shipbuilding and Shipping which, in conjunction, provided new-building subsidies for shipbuilders and incentives for owners to purchase domestically built ships. It has been calculated that three-quarters of all government subsidies expended between 1897 and 1913 were aimed at the maritime industries. By 1911 tariffs on imported vessels had reached such punitive levels as effectively to eliminate importation as a practicable option for Japanese shipowners. Refer to T. Blumenthal, 'The Japanese shipbuilding industry' in H. Patrick (ed.), *Japanese Industrialization and its Social Consequences*, University of California Press, Berkeley, 1976, pp. 129–60.

16 Note T. Nakamura, *Economic Growth in Prewar Japan*, Yale University Press, New Haven, Conn., 1983, p. 178 and Mitsubishi Economic Research Bureau, *Japanese Trade and Industry*, Macmillan, London, 1936, pp. 300–2. The wage data, incidentally, are reworked from their original form which appeared in *The Shipbuilder*, August 1918, p. 52.

17 Cited on p. 795 of P. Trezise and Y. Suzuki, 'Politics, government, and economic growth' in H. Patrick and H. Rosovsky (eds), *Asia's New Giant*, The Brookings Institution, Washington, DC, 1976, pp. 753–811.

18 Refer to *Far Eastern Economic Review*, 10 November 1955, p. 597. Other government assistance included the maintenance of a very favourable exchange rate and the provision of extensive credit facilities through the offices of the Japan Export–Import Bank.

19 Refer to *Far Eastern Economic Review*, 16 April 1964, p. 173. Even in 1976,

Japanese builders were seeking to circumvent OECD guidelines. James Sherwood, president of Sea Containers, divulged that a Japanese yard was prepared to offer credit terms of 95 per cent (then 25 per cent above the OECD limit) over an eight-year repayment period (one year longer than the OECD period) when he put out two Ro-Ro vessels for tender. Related in *Shipping and Transportation*, August 1976, p. 15.

20 Taken from *Far Eastern Economic Review*, 7 September 1950, p. 280.

21 See Blumenthal, 'Japanese shipbuilding industry', pp. 145–50.

22 Note K. Imai, 'Iron and steel' in K. Sato (ed.), *Industry and Business in Japan*, M.E. Sharpe, White Plains, NY, 1980, pp. 191–244.

23 Reported in *Far Eastern Economic Review*, 13 September 1962, p. 497 and 28 January 1965, p. 147. The European cost data were compiled by the UK Shipbuilders and Repairers National Association and contained in their File S20, memorandum of 26 May 1959.

24 See G.C. Allen, 'Industrial policy and innovation in Japan' in C. Carter (ed.), *Industrial Policy and Innovation*, Heinemann, London, 1981, pp. 68–87. It was said of ship financing, for example, that 'Japan would be placed at a disadvantage in international competition because of a higher cost of vessels if the shipping companies rely on commercial bank loans even for a part of their shipbuilding funds'. The solution to the impasse: 'under the Interest Supplementation Law, the interest is fixed at 5 per cent per annum for shipping companies, the government contributing the difference between the same and the money rate of commercial banks', and with the cheap finance the companies were enabled to take up their quota of the annual domestic shipbuilding programmes. Note *Far Eastern Economic Review*, 26 July 1956, p. 109.

25 In spite of its name, Usuki Iron Works had entered shipbuilding soon after its founding as marine engineers in 1919. Its early concentration on fishing vessels gave way to larger merchant vessels after the Saiki shipyard was completed in 1955. The tie with IHI brought abundant business to Usuki, with the 1965 output of 32,800 dwt virtually trebling to 93,200 dwt by 1972. Refer to *Zosen*, March 1974, p. 22.

26 Mentioned in *Japan Shipping and Shipbuilding*, April 1965, pp. 20–1 and *Zosen*, August 1972, p. 16. Fujinagata of Osaka was formally incorporated into Mitsui in 1967.

27 In short, Japanese firms tend persistently to display low profit levels in comparison with their international counterparts. This is not a fair reflection of their profitability; rather it is a revelation of their response to a taxation regime which compels them 'to do almost anything to avoid declaring unnecessary profits'. The outcome is a predilection for investment in plant and an attempt to capture greater market share in order to keep that extra plant gainfully occupied. Alas, overcapacity frequently ensues. This has been the lot of the petrochemicals, colour TV and camera industries as well as shipbuilding. See *The Economist*, 27 May 1989, p. 15.

28 These data are extracted from *Zosen*, October 1980, p. 47 and December 1981, p. 47.

29 SHI had earmarked a site at Annan City for a 1 million dwt building dock, KHI had picked out a site for another to the south of Nagoya at Suzuka, while Sasebo Heavy Industries, Mitsui and NKK also had plans in hand. At that juncture, Hitachi Zosen, IHI and MHI all had recently established facilities

of this size (in turn, at Ariake, Chita and Koyagi). See *Shipping and Transportation*, August 1975, p. 25.

30 Reported on p. 197 of JSEA, *Shipbuilding and Marine Engineering in Japan 1980*, JSEA/SAJ, Tokyo, March 1980.

31 Mentioned in *Shipping and Transportation*, March 1974, p. 17.

32 Variously discussed in *Zosen*, April 1977, p. 5 and January 1978, p. 5; as well as *Far Eastern Economic Review*, 16 December 1977, p. 73 and *Fairplay*, 20 April 1978, p. 21 and 21 June 1979, p. 10. Note, Mie Shipbuilding re-emerged in 1979 under the government's rehabilitation policy.

33 In fact, two shipbuilders – Kurushima Dockyard and NKK – were principal shareholders in Sasebo Heavy Industries, holding respectively 25 per cent and 24.19 per cent of the stock. Refer to *Far Eastern Economic Review*, 8 September 1978, pp. 53–7.

34 Described in *Fairplay*, 25 January 1979, p. 26.

35 Refer to JSEA, *Shipbuilding and Marine Engineering in Japan 1985*, JSEA/SAJ, Tokyo, 1985, p. 15, R.M. Uriu, 'The declining industries of Japan', *Journal of International Affairs*, vol.38, 1984, pp. 99–111 and *Zosen*, August 1978, p. 5.

36 Cited in R. Dore, *Flexible Rigidities*, Stanford University Press, Stanford, 1986, p. 147.

37 Identified in *Zosen*, May 1980, p. 11. Another small builder, Kanrei Zosen, fell below the 5,000 gt threshold.

38 The calculations are performed on material which originally appeared in *Zosen*, April 1981, pp. 66–71.

39 See commentary of Martin Stopford in *Fairplay*, 15 December 1988, p. 22.

40 See *Far Eastern Economic Review*, 10 October 1985, p. 118.

41 Described in *Asian Wall Street Journal*, 1 June 1987, p. 13, 2 December 1987, p. 11 and 5 January 1988, p. 3; together with *Fairplay*, 21 April 1988, p. ii and 27 April 1989, p. xxiv; and *Lloyd's List*, 26 July 1988, pp. 5–7.

42 Mentioned in *Far Eastern Economic Review*, 14 February 1985, p. 44 and 22 June 1989, pp. 57–8; to say nothing of *Fairplay*, 9 July 1987, p. 8 and 15 October 1987, p. 5, and *Lloyd's List*, 5 July 1989, p. 2.

43 In fact, this builder had been vulnerable to closure since 1982 when, after accumulating losses of Y20 billion, shutting down its Shimizu yard and concentrating all activity on the Toyohashi shipyard, it came under the wing of Kurushima Dockyard. Note *Zosen*, December 1982, p. 9.

44 Refer to *Lloyd's List*, 23 June 1989, p. 2; *Fairplay*, 22 June 1989, p. 6 and 6 July 1989, p. 9; and *Asian Wall Street Journal*, 27 March 1989, p. 7.

45 Even Hitachi Zosen was able to contain its losses to Y17.1 billion, a sharp improvement on the deficit of Y44.6 billion recorded in 1987. The revival embraced MES, too. Its pre-tax profits reached Y11 billion, a marked turnabout on losses of Y1.3 billion in 1987. However, this uplifting trend was offset by MHI which saw its profits eroded from Y99.1 billion to Y87.1 billion. See *Lloyd's List*, 13 June 1989, p. 10.

46 Estimated in *Lloyd's List*, 18 July 1988, p. 2. In a similar vein, Yoshiyuki Abe, the general manager of ship sales at IHI, maintained that construction cost of a large tanker was of the order of $75 million in both Japan and South Korea; although market prices were hovering in the range of $35–40 million. His views are expressed in *Far Eastern Economic Review*, 20 October 1988, p. 72.

47 Reported in P. Mottershead, 'Shipbuilding: adjustment-led intervention or intervention-led adjustment?' in G. Shepherd, F. Duchême and C. Saunders (eds), *Europe's Industries*, Cornell University Press, Ithaca, NY, 1983, pp. 82–109. The countries that constitute his Western European group are France, Denmark, West Germany, Italy, the Netherlands, the UK, Norway, Sweden and Spain.

48 Drewry Shipping Consultants forecasts, reported in *Far Eastern Economic Review*, 10 October 1985, p. 118.

49 Notably, however, the OECD credit terms covering up to 80 per cent of the ship price, with minimum interest rates of 7.5 per cent and a repayment period of 8.5 years, were adopted by the EEC and used as a yardstick in its later shipbuilding directives.

50 Germane references are V. Lauber, 'The political economy of industrial policy in Western Europe' in S.A. Shull and J.E. Cohen (eds), *Economics and Politics of Industrial Policy*, Westview, Boulder, Col., 1986, pp. 27–46; V.C. Price, *Industrial Policies in the European Community*, St Martin's Press, New York, 1981, pp. 98–100; and D. Swann, *Competition and Industrial Policy in the European Community*, Methuen, London, 1983, pp. 159–61. Original sources for the Fourth and Fifth Directives, respectively, are L98/19, 11 April 1978 and L137/39 23 May 1981 of the Official Journal of the European Communities.

51 Note, these limits were less generous for small vessels costing less than ECU 6 million. For example, their 1988 level of 20 per cent was reset at 16 per cent in 1989. See *Fairplay*, 5 January 1989, p. 6. Early indications suggest that the EEC will compel all producers to abide by a 20 per cent subsidy maximum after 1990 regardless of ship size.

52 Summarised in table 4.4 of Mottershead, 'Shipbuilding', pp. 100–1.

53 Related in Stråth, *Politics of De-industrialisation*, pp. 191–2. For the discriminatory effects of British regional policy on the shipbuilders, see D. Todd, 'Area development or sectoral conflict?', *Environment and Planning C: Government and Policy*, vol.1, 1983, pp. 153–62.

54 Recounted in *Lloyd's List*, 22 July 1986, p. 2.

55 Note J. Savary, *French Multinationals*, St Martin's Press, New York, 1984, pp. 159–63.

56 See S. Faltas, *Arms Markets and Armament Policy*, Martinus Nijhoff, Dordrecht, 1986, p. 19 and Stråth, *Politics of De-industrialisation*, pp. 155–7.

57 B&W was temporarily taken over by the state's Export Credit Board. Affirming its relative success, B&W resurrected its line of Panamax bulkers in 1989. In truth, other Danish yards closed and the industry's work-force was cut by two-thirds between 1975 and 1988, leaving it at 6,300. See *Fairplay*, 20 July 1989, pp. 20–1 and *Lloyd's List*, 30 June 1989, p. 3.

58 Note *Fairplay*, 13 March 1986, p. 9.

59 See *The Engineer*, issues of 24 March 1983, pp. 12–13 and 14 July 1983, p. 15.

60 Note *Lloyd's List*, 23 July 1988, p. 1.

61 See *The Engineer*, 27 September 1984, pp. 27–8 and *Lloyd's List*, issues of 18 July 1988, p. 2 and 30 May 1989, p. 1.

62 Reported in *Lloyd's List*, 23 July 1988, p. 1.

63 The Industry Minister of the day, Tony Newton, claimed that EEC support for an Enterprise Zone in Sunderland would be jeopardised if shipbuilding was allowed to restart at NESL. See *Lloyd's List*, 14 July 1989, p. 1. By a quirk, marine activities have received a minor boost in Sunderland with the

decision of West German crane-maker, Liebherr, to use the razed Deptford shipyard site, closed by NESL in 1986, as a crane test area. The company is acclaimed for its ship and offshore lifting equipment. See *The Engineer*, 13 October 1988, p. 10.

64 The job losses were estimated by the Sunderland Shipyards Campaign group. Other figures bandied about included a shut-down cost to the government of £113 million by 1995 and a loss in local income circulation amounting to £53 million by the same year. In addition, some £100 million per year through to 1995 would be required simply to fund replacement jobs for those lost. See *The Engineer*, 20 October 1988, p. 6.

65 Although a large number of shipowners defaulted, forcing the government to repossess a veritable fleet of vessels in the late 1970s and early 1980s. Refer to *Fairplay*, 31 March 1988, p. 15.

66 Described in *Fairplay*, issues of of 4 June 1987, pp. 24–5; 24 November 1988, p. 9; 6 March 1989, pp. 15–16 and 13 July 1989, p. 5. Note also *Lloyd's List*, 10 July 1989, p. 1 and 11 July 1989, p. 6.

67 The discrete units merged into Fincantieri were Arsenale Triestino San Marco (ship repairers at Trieste), Cantiere Navale Luigi Orlando, Cantieri Navali e Officine Meccaniche di Venezia (ship repairers in Venice), CNR (builder and repairer with yards in and around Genoa, Ancona and Palermo), GMT (diesel engine builders), Italcantieri (with new-building yards in Monfalcone, Genoa and Castellammare di Stabia) and Societa Esercizio Bacini Meridionali. See *Fairplay*, 21 August 1986, p. 20.

68 Discussed in *Fairplay*, 7 July 1988, p. 34 and 8 June 1989, p. 28.

69 The views are those of Dr Friedrich Hennemann, quoted in *Fairplay*, 22 September 1988, p. 27.

70 Recorded in *Fairplay*, 12 October 1989, p. 5 and 19 October 1989, p. 5.

71 Noted in *Lloyd's List*, 20 July 1988, p. 7 and *Fairplay*, 4 August 1988, pp. 26–7.

72 See *Fairplay*, 8 June 1989, pp. 6–7. In truth, apart from its ship-repair operations, Wilton Fijenoord is now confined for the most part to naval work.

73 The firms are Haugesund Mekaniske Verksted in Haugesund, Kleven Mek Verksted in Ulsteinvik and Ulstein Hatloe (a member of Ulstein Holding AS) with its Laxenvaag yard in Bergen. Indeed, Kleven went so far as to purchase two defunct yards as a sign of its restored faith in the industry; namely, the former Anterlokken Group sites at Floro and Forde. Refer to *Lloyd's List*, 21 June 1989, p. 2 and 22 June 1989, p. 6.

74 See *Fairplay*, 23 March 1989, p. 6 and *Lloyd's List*, 12 June 1989, p. 9.

75 Reported in *Fairplay*, 18 May 1989, pp. 19–21.

3 INDUSTRIAL REORGANISATION AND THE ENTERPRISE

1 Originally set out in P.F. Drucker, *The Practice of Management*, Harper, New York, 1954.

2 For the Troon case, refer to *The Engineer*, 23 November 1978, p. 13, while for the Swedish example, note *The Economist*, 1 March 1986, p. 60. Reputedly, Volvo will employ 1,200 in Uddevalla and Saab–Scania will take up 2,700 in Malmö.

3 Note, innovators cannot be faulted for breadth of vision. Some of their envisaged future ship designs are represented in R. Schönknecht, *et al.*, *Ships and Shipping of Tomorrow*, MacGregor Publications, Hounslow, 1983.

4 A term given currency by W.E.G. Salter in his *Productivity and Technical Change*, 2nd edn, Cambridge University Press, Cambridge, 1966, p. 3.

5 The quotation is taken from W.J. Abernathy, *et al.*, *Industrial Renaissance*, Basic Books, New York, 1983, p. 24.

6 Discussed in *Fairplay*, issues of 12 November 1987, p. 35; 27 July 1989, pp. xxii–xxiv; and 3 August 1989, p. 20. Note, the M£40 million Marsa new-building facility suffered an extended gestation period, having been initiated in 1975.

7 Mentioned in *Fairplay*, 9 October 1986, pp. 22–5 and 12 October 1989, pp. 35–6, as well as *Lloyd's List*, 26 July 1989, p. 9. Echoing the Malta case, Sedef Gemi was obliged to import the main engines: in this instance the first dozen of the MAN/B&W type were contracted to Cegielski of Poland, a licensee of the designer, while the subsequent dozen were ordered from the designer's Alpha Diesel plant in Denmark.

8 Data are drawn from Lloyd's Register of Shipping, *Annual Report 1981*, p. 9 and p. 11.

9 Related in *The Economist*, 26 July 1986, pp. 64–5.

10 The most conspicuous direct subsidy to the shipyards, the Construction Differential Subsidy scheme, was dropped in 1981. See C.H. Whitehurst, *The US Shipbuilding Industry*, Naval Institute Press, Annapolis, 1986, p. 28.

11 Note *Jane's Defence Weekly*, 25 July 1987, p. 156.

12 Refer to *Business Week*, 31 August 1987, p. 38 and *Lloyd's List*, issues of 11 July 1989, p. 12 and 24 July 1989, p. 1. Note, while Todd Shipyards kept Seattle for ship repair, it had earlier quashed new building there.

13 See *Business Week*, 11 January 1988, p. 40 and *Fairplay*, 11 December 1986, p. 24.

14 The virtual extinction of merchant shipbuilding in Australia – an industry vastly uncompetitive by East Asian standards – occurred, in part, through the renouncing of new building by large industrial companies. BHP, the giant minerals to steel group, was prepared to forfeit its Whyalla yard (which had supplied it with ore carriers) on the grounds of reduced government subsidies, high overheads and high labour costs. Note *Far Eastern Economic Review*, 9 February 1979, p. 70.

15 Refer to *Lloyd's List*, 13 June 1989, p. 1. Krupp has not entirely severed its maritime connections, for it maintains an important electronic equipment subsidiary dedicated to shipboard systems (Krupp Atlas Elektronik of Bremen), a marine engine works (Krupp MaK in Kiel) and its own bulk shipping company (Krupp Handel of Hamburg) with a fleet of ore carriers. Note, the new-building arm of Seebeckwerft merged with Schichau Unterweser of Bremerhaven to form Schichau–Seebeckwerft AG.

16 See *Fairplay*, 24 August 1978, p. 63.

17 Reported in *Fairplay*, 24 July 1986, p. 21; 19 May 1988, p. 24; and 17 August 1989, p. 5.

18 Salter, *Productivity and Technical Change*, p. 83.

19 Dealt with in T. Yui, 'Introduction' in Committee for the International Conference on Business History, *Business History of Shipping*, University of Tokyo Press, Tokyo, 1985, pp. ix–xxix and R. Caves and M. Uekusa,

'Industrial organization' in H. Patrick and H. Rosovsky (eds), *Asia's New Giant*, The Brookings Institution, Washington, DC, 1976, pp. 459–523.

20 The Antimonopoly Law was further emasculated in 1978 when, as part of the Law Concerning Special Measures for the Stabilisation of Specific Industries, MITI obtained dispensation for the shipbuilders to allow them to unite in cancelling excess capacity. See C. Johnson, *MITI and the Japanese Miracle*, Stanford University Press, Stanford, 1982, p. 303.

21 Details of industrial affiliations derive from Dodwell Marketing Consultants, *Industrial Groupings in Japan*, Dodwell, Tokyo, 1978.

22 Listed in I. Nakatani, 'The economic role of financial corporate grouping' in M. Aoki (ed.), *The Economic Analysis of the Japanese Firm*, North-Holland, Amsterdam, 1984, pp. 227–58.

23 A shake up of group ties is also evident in marine engines. During 1989, for instance, IHI and SHI amalgamated their engine works into an entity termed Diesel United.

24 To be sure, tonnage shares conceivably could right the balance. Yet, SHI's share of the total tonnage commanded by MOL reached only 5.4 per cent; a shortfall on its share reckoned by number of units. Conversely, the tonnage attributable to MES is pushed upwards to 32.9 per cent, an outcome endorsing its privileged standing. Just to confuse the issue, the MHI position is degraded, falling in tonnage terms to just 11 per cent. These calculations are undertaken on data provided by Fairplay Information Systems Ltd, Coulsdon, Surrey.

25 Their origins are discussed in L.P. Jones and I. Sakong, *Government, Business, and Entrepreneurship in Economic Development*, Harvard University Press, Cambridge, Mass., 1980.

26 See *Far Eastern Economic Review*, 4 June 1982, p. 75.

27 The quotation is taken from p. 72 of G.C. Allen, 'Industrial policy and innovation in Japan' in C. Carter (ed.), *Industrial Policy and Innovation*, Heinemann, London, 1981, pp. 68–87.

28 As gleaned from a list of new buildings in progress at the end of September 1989. Refer to the Newbuildings Supplement in *Fairplay*, 26 October 1989.

29 K.J. Bauer, *A Maritime History of the United States*, University of South Carolina Press, Columbia, 1988, p. 294.

30 Recounted in D. Dougan, *The History of North East Shipbuilding*, George Allen & Unwin, London, 1968, pp. 137–40.

31 Details are to be found in D. Todd, *The World Shipbuilding Industry*, Croom Helm, London, 1985, pp. 117–22.

32 See Todd, *The World Shipbuilding Industry*, pp. 263–4. For the original recommendations, refer to R.M. Geddes, *Shipbuilding Inquiry Committee 1965–66 Report*, HMSO, Cmnd 2937, London, 1966.

33 Quotation is abstracted from p. 15 of C.R. Spruill, *Conglomerates and the Evolution of Capitalism*, Southern Illinois University Press, Carbondale, 1982.

34 The quotation is lifted from p. 389 of F.M. Scherer, *The Economics of Multi-plant Operation*, Harvard University Press, Cambridge, Mass., 1975.

35 Shipbuilding of that epoch confirmed an empirical observation pertaining to modern US industry in general; namely, that 'the acquisition route was chosen partly because a strong relative position could not be established via direct entry'. See G.S. Yip, *Barriers to Entry*, D.C. Heath, Lexington, 1982, p. 132.

36 A Shipbuilding Temporary Assistance Program, introducing a 14–17 per cent
   subsidy, had been instrumental in attracting C$1.3 billion of orders to the
   yards between 1970 and 1975. Its successor, the Shipbuilding Industry
   Assistance Program, initially reduced the subsidy progressively to 12 per cent,
   but in view of the dire situation obtaining in 1977, reversed its position and
   increased the subsidy to 20 per cent: reputedly, enough to clinch a C$100
   million order from Poland for four cargo vessels. Apparently dismayed at the
   bleak prospects of reviving the industry, the government reduced the subsidy
   to 9 per cent in 1980 and then cancelled it outright in 1985. See A.A.
   McArthur, *A Report by the Sector Task Force on the Canadian Shipbuilding
   and Repair Industry*, Department of Industry, Trade and Commerce, Ottawa,
   1978; CSSRA, '1983 annual statistical report', Ottawa, April 1984; and *The
   Financial Post*, 14 July 1984, p. 11.

37 One analyst argues that the subsidies leant heavily in support of the less
   competitive yards; that is, those most susceptible to closure on their removal.
   Note K.E.A. De Silva, *An Economic Analysis of the Shipbuilding Industry
   Assistance Program*, Economic Council of Canada, Discussion Paper 351,
   Ottawa, June 1988, p. 110.

38 See also *Fairplay*, 20 March 1986, p. 19; 27 November 1986, p. 25; and 7
   September 1989, p. 24.

39 Originating as Cornat Industries, the group had purchased the Burrard yards
   in North Vancouver and Victoria (the ex-Yarrow yard) in 1971. Canada
   Steamship Lines, for its part, shared with Upper Lakes Shipping the control
   of the Port Weller yard. It too is a member of Power Corporation. Also, note
   that while ostensibly an independent company, Saint John Shipbuilding is
   owned by the Irving family; a force to be reckoned with in Canadian shipping
   circles.

40 In truth, Versatile was experiencing grave difficulties with its non-marine
   activities, including a farm-machinery production unit in Winnipeg (see
   Winnipeg Free Press, 7 January 1987, p. 20). These larger problems
   prevented the resue of its shipbuilding operations through cross-subsidies.

41 Reported in *Fairplay*, 23 October 1986, pp. 41–3; 19 January 1989, pp. 21–3;
   and 15 June 1989, p. 27. Note, the low wage rates ($200 per month on
   average in 1989) are a mixed blessing: promoting competitiveness on the one
   hand, but encouraging skilled workers to emigrate and presenting the yards
   with problems of high labour turnover on the other.

42 Gleaned from B.W. Watson and P.M. Dunn (eds), *The Future of the Soviet
   Navy*, Westview, Boulder, Col., 1986.

43 Cited in *Lloyd's List*, 27 July 1989, p. 3.

44 Refer to D.M. Long, *The Soviet Merchant Fleet*, Lloyd's of London Press,
   London, 1986, p. 83.

45 See *Fairplay*, 25 August 1977, p. 27 and 25 April 1985, pp. 16–20.

46 Highlighted in *Fairplay*, 13 October 1977, p. 64.

47 The already extant Harmstorf Group, overseeing four yards outside these
   major centres (i.e. Büsumer Werft in Büsum; Deutsche Industrie Werke, a
   builder of river craft in Berlin; Flensburger Schiffsbau in Flensburg; and
   Schlichting Werft in Travemünde), fared relatively worse, losing its Büsum
   yard and only just staving off disaster with the help of the Land of
   Schleswig–Holstein. See *Fairplay*, 11 September 1986, p. 43. The ensuing
   restructuring threw up Neue Flensburger Schiffbau as the organisation

discharging the former group's new-building obligations. In late 1989 it was absorbed by HDW (itself one-quarter owned by Schleswig–Holstein) and reconstituted as HDW–Flensburger Schiffbau. See *Fairplay*, 23 November 1989, p. 9.

48 For the first outcome, recall the De Jong reference in Chapter 2; for the second, refer to G. Meeks, *Disappointing Marriage*, University of Cambridge, Department of Applied Economics, Occasional Paper 51, 1977. In respect of the first, one analyst calls into question the policies of forced merger of the horizontal integration kind, of which the formation of BS is symptomatic. He proclaims that they neither improved profitability nor advanced market penetration (as measured through export performance). See M.S. Kumar, *Growth, Acquisition and Investment*, Cambridge University Press, Cambridge, 1984, p. 149.

4   DIVERSIFICATION WITHIN THE MARINE INDUSTRIES

1 In reality, technical barriers often appear daunting to firms unaccustomed to the rigorous standards insisted on by defence ministries. Achieving certification of eligibility, in many cases, is so costly as to deter serious thoughts of entry by merchant shipbuilders.

2 There is an opportunity cost entailed in choosing vertical integration over horizontal integration. By pressing ahead with the former, the firm foregoes the chance of realising production economies through the greatly augmented output expected to arise from horizontal integration. In practice, as was made evident in the last chapter, these theoretical economies are notable more for their absence.

3 The distinction between the two diversification spectra was made in M.A. Utton, *Diversification and Competition*, Cambridge University Press, Cambridge, 1979, p. 25.

4 B.H. Klein, *Dynamic Economics*, Harvard University Press, Cambridge, Mass., 1977, p. 199.

5 K.R. Harrigan, *Strategies for Vertical Integration*, D.C. Heath, Lexington, 1983, p. 321.

6 Court Line had entered shipbuilding via Appledore Shipbuilders in 1963. Austin and Pickersgill, the other Sunderland shipbuilder which eventually coalesced with the ex-Court assets to form NESL, was also the subject of a raid from a shipping firm; namely, London and Overseas Freighters.

7 M.S. Salter and W.A. Weinhold, *Diversification Through Acquisition*, The Free Press, New York, 1979, p. 10.

8 Of course, shipowners had sometimes taken a fancy to running their own builders prior to the era in question. As well as the 1884 merger of Christopher Furness's shipping line with the Hartlepool builders Edward Withy, there were cases of shipowners directly activating their own yards: Sir John Priestman in Sunderland, for example, not to mention the Ropner enterprise on the Tees and the Anchor Line (D&W Henderson) and Charles Connell in Glasgow. On the other side, there are long precedents for shipbuilders seeking ownership slices of client shipping lines. To give but three examples: Scott's of Greenock was a major shareholder in China Navigation (Swire), Denny of Dumbarton maintained interests in Australian

United Steam Navigation and the Irrawaddy Flotilla Company, whereas H&W and the White Star Line exercised interlocking shareholdings.

9 The agitation by German shipbuilders for naval programmes at the turn of the century is ascribed to this cause. Krupp is regarded as the ringleader, clamouring for warship contracts to fill its Germania yard in Kiel. Note B. Menne, *Krupp or the Lords of Essen*, William Hodge, London, 1937, pp. 155–64.

10 The rationale for the formation of integrated naval armaments enterprises at the beginning of this century is presented in Chapter 4 of D. Todd, *Defence Industries*, Routledge, London, 1988.

11 H.B. Peebles, *Warshipbuilding on the Clyde*, John Donald, Edinburgh, 1987, pp. 36–7.

12 This is not to say that contract underbidding was not rife in naval work: Samuda, Hanna Donald and Wilson, and Earle's were all undone as a result of such practices, while Palmer's suffered grievous dents in its returns for several years as a fall-out from perpetrating it on a battleship contract.

13 G.A.H. Gordon, *British Seapower and Procurement Between the Wars*, Macmillan, Basingstoke, 1988, p. 188.

14 Note, specialist warshipbuilders were not spared the caprices of profitability. Beardmore, a chronic loss-maker in both naval and commercial new building in spite of its vertically integrated complexion, was a major Clyde builder whose defence specialisation proved troublesome. See J.R. Hume and M.S. Moss, *Beardmore*, Heinemann, London, 1979.

15 Peebles, *Warshipbuilding*, p. 157.

16 For example, H&W, Palmer's, Swan Hunter and Beardmore all initiated ship-repair expansion programmes at the end of the First World War, seizing the opportunity to establish widely scattered facilities in the chief ports.

17 Refer to *Far Eastern Economic Review*, 31 October 1963, p. 256 and 20 October 1966, p. 187. Also, see *Shipping and Transportation*, February 1972, p. 13 and *Zosen*, October 1967, p. 15 and July 1970, p. 32.

18 Reported in *Zosen*, November 1970, p. 13.

19 In truth, a bare tonnage-to-tonnage comparison of building and repair is slightly misleading, since the work content of the two functions may be markedly different. In other words, the labour and time required to build a 10,000 ton vessel could be much more demanding than the effort expended on 'stemming' a 10,000 ton ship. On the other hand, repair can entail conversion and rebuilding of ships; activities which in the event are more labour-intensive than ship construction in the first place (and which typified Japanese repair endeavours of the time). Suffice it to say, then, that the ratios are advanced simply to present an approximation of the balance between building and repair.

20 D.C.E. Burrell, *Scrap & Build*, World Ship Society, Kendal, 1983, p. 8.

21 J.W. Smith and T.S. Holden, *Where Ships are Born*, Thomas Reed, Sunderland, 1946, p. 65.

22 MHI, IHI and Tsuneishi Shipbuilding were the chief practitioners. See *Fairplay*, 14 December 1978, p. 8.

23 A.K. Young, *The Sogo Shosha*, Westview, Boulder, Col., 1979, pp. 140–1.

24 See *Japan Shipping and Shipbuilding*, April 1960, p. 14 and Y. Okamoto, 'The grand strategy of Japanese business' in K. Sato and Y. Hoshino (eds), *The Anatomy of Japanese Business*, M.E. Sharpe, Armonk, NY, 1984, pp. 277–318.

25 A. Gordon, *The Evolution of Labor Relations in Japan*, Harvard University Press, Cambridge, Mass., 1985, p. 10.

26 Reported in *Far Eastern Economic Review*, 6 July 1967, p. 33.

27 H. Okumura, 'Interfirm relations in an enterprise group' in K. Sato and Y. Hoshino (eds), *The Anatomy of Japanese Business*, M.E. Sharpe, Armonk, NY, 1984, pp. 164–93.

28 W.D. Wray, *Mitsubishi and the NYK, 1870–1914*, Harvard University Press, Cambridge, Mass., 1984, p. 254 and p. 459.

29 Mentioned in *Far Eastern Economic Review*, 26 September 1963, p. 775.

30 Cited in *The Economist*, 1 June 1985, pp. 70–1.

31 J.E. Auer, *The Postwar Rearmament of Japanese Maritime Forces, 1945–71*, Praeger, New York, 1973, pp. 232–5.

32 Noted in *Far Eastern Economic Review*, 31 July 1969, p. 288.

33 Recited in *Far Eastern Economic Review*, 13 October 1988, p. 67 and *Jane's Defence Weekly*, 10 December 1988, pp. 1479–81.

34 Moreover, the decision to award frigates to Saint Nazaire was political, impelled by the desire to give the work-starved yard 'a significant workload for the next few years'. See *Lloyd's List*, 23 July 1988, p. 3. Hitherto, French naval combatants had been reserved for the naval dockyards. Similar bail-out schemes for NORMED and Dubigeon (see Table 4.4) failed to prevent their demise.

35 The US specialists were prominent members of these consortia, but did not have the field entirely to themselves. Howard Doris, for example, was partly French owned while Heerema of the Netherlands operated the Lewis yard. See G. Arnold, *Britain's Oil*, Hamish Hamilton, London, 1978, pp. 211–14 and A. Hamilton, *North Sea Impact*, International Institute of Economic Research, London, 1978, pp. 123–30.

36 Trafalgar House engaged in a rancorous legal tussle with BS to extract compensation. See *Lloyd's List*, 5 May 1988, p. 7.

37 P.L. Cook, 'The offshore supplies industry' in M. Sharp (ed.), *Europe and the New Technologies*, Cornell University Press, Ithaca, NY, 1986, pp. 213–62.

38 See *Zosen*, January 1975, pp. 25–30 and April 1975, p. 22.

39 Reported in *Shipping and Transportation*, May 1984, p. 41.

40 Related in *Fairplay*, 15 January 1987, p. 6.

41 See *Fairplay*, 15 December 1977, p. 57, 12 May 1988, p. 27 and 29 June 1989, p. 7. Also *Zosen*, September 1976, p. 20 is germane to this theme.

42 See *Fairplay*, 9 July 1987, p. 8. Striking a similar chord, American Ship Building mooted the idea of harvesting Alaskan pollack for processing, via floating factories, into surumi fish paste for the Japanese market. Refer to *Asian Wall Street Journal*, 17 September 1986, p. 20.

43 Ironically, marine engineers have taken steps to restore 'captive' shipyard capacity following the dissolution of BS. Under new private management, the specialist ex-BS engine builder located in Greenock, Clark Kincaid (now restyled the HLD Group and controlled by Kvaerner), was set on securing a shipyard in 1989 and successfully bid for Ferguson Shipbuilders in Port Glasgow. The Appledore shipyard, meanwhile, was taken under the wing of Langham Industries, the owner of propeller manufacturer Stone Manganese Marine of Birkenhead. Refer to *Fairplay*, 2 February 1989, p. 5 and 12 October 1989, p. 6 as well as *The Engineer*, 18 May 1989, p. 7.

44 B&W had set up as shipowners in 1977 to operate vessels built in its own yard

but refused delivery by delinquent customers. The subsidiary, Rederiet Hamlet, was reinforced by the purchase of a UK ship management firm, W.A. Souter of Newcastle. These digressions are noted in *Fairplay*, 5 May 1977, p. 80.

45 Wärtsilä Diesel offers its own Vasa series and builds SEMT–Pielstick and Sulzer engines under licence. It also effectively controls Moteurs Duvant Crepelle in France, Wichmann in Norway, Lindholmen Motor in Sweden and Echevarria in Spain. Its purchase of Dutch engine builder Stork–Werkspoor Diesel in 1989 was enacted just prior to the filing for bankruptcy of Wärtsilä Marine.

46 See *Fairplay*, 16 November 1989, p. 27.

47 Lloyd's Register of Shipping, *Annual Report 1970*, p. 70.

48 Variously reported in *Shipping and Transportation*, October 1971, p. 9 and *Fairplay*, issues of 13 January 1972, p. 127; 10 January 1974, p. 103; 18 May 1978, pp. 61–5; and 22 June 1978, p. 23.

49 Note *Fairplay*, issues of 26 May 1983, p. 27; 31 May 1984, p. 33; and 11 February 1988, pp. 30–3; to say nothing of *Lloyd's List*, 1 June 1989, p. 6.

50 Quoted in *Far Eastern Economic Review*, 13 April 1950, p. 472.

51 See *Far Eastern Economic Review*, 29 October 1953, pp. 563–4; 19 September 1957, p. 375; 22 January 1959, pp. 109–12; 17 February 1966, p. 278; and 17 December 1976, pp. 38–9. Also, note *Fairplay*, 20–27 December 1979, p. 19.

52 See *Fairplay*, 16 June 1988, pp. 13–17 and 11 May 1989, p. 6.

53 The early Singapore ventures are covered in *Far Eastern Economic Review*, 21 February 1963, p. 397; 15 July 1965, p. 129; 24 July 1969, pp. 239–41; 17 June 1972, p. 64; and 26 February 1973, pp. 31–2. The EDB was set up in 1961 to oversee the First Development Plan through to 1964. Subsequently, it was responsible for furnishing industrial incentives, spinning off the Jurong Town Corporation in 1968 as the main vehicle for promoting manufacturing activities. In due course, much of its promotional mandate was assumed by the DBS. For a review, see E.F. Pang, 'Industrial policy and economic restructuring in Singapore' in R.E. Driscoll and J.N. Behrman (eds), *National Industrial Policies*, Oelgeschlager, Gunn & Hain, Cambridge, Mass., 1984, pp. 151–66.

54 See *Far Eastern Economic Review*, 12 September 1975, pp. 72–3; 19 December 1975, pp. 49–51; and 11 August 1978, pp. 67–8.

55 Promet was founded in 1971 as a Malaysian offshore service firm. It established a rig-building yard in Singapore and, in 1981, acquired the Asia-Pacific Shipyard there in order to build offshore supply vessels. A&P Appledore had assisted in the rig-building endeavours.

56 Refer to *Fairplay*, 30 July 1981, p. 33 and *Far Eastern Economic Review*, 30 June 1983, p. 64 and 6 December 1984, pp. 75–82.

57 The Sembawang Group also embraced shipowning (operating three reefers), property and construction, and financial services.

58 Described in *Far Eastern Economic Review*, 16 May 1985, pp. 86–7 and 26 September 1985, pp. 75–7; *Shipping and Transportation*, December 1986, p. 36; *Asian Wall Street Journal*, 21 September 1987, p. 1 and 23 September 1987, p. 1; *Fairplay*, 9 June 1988, p. 32 and 28 July 1988, p. 27; and *Lloyd's List*, 12 July 1989, p. 2.

59 Cited in *Asian Wall Street Journal*, 22 September 1988, p. 1.

60 O. Hornby, 'The Danish shipping industry, 1866–1939' in Committee for the International Conference on Business History, *Business History of Shipping*, University of Tokyo Press, Tokyo, 1985, pp. 157–81.

61 Reported in *Far Eastern Economic Review*, 24 March 1978, pp. 83–7 and 23 June 1978, p. 106.

62 Historically, family connections sometimes arranged unofficial 'captive' markets for shipbuilders. For example, the Elder Dempster Lines, later a member of the Royal Mail Group and then Ocean Transport and Trading, was founded in 1868 by Alexander Elder and John Dempster. Most of the company's tonnage was procured from the Fairfield yard (now Kvaerner Govan) of John Elder, Alexander's brother. See *Ships Monthly*, May 1989, p. 22.

63 Strangely, Uddevalla Shipping, a subsidiary of the Swedyards builder Uddevallavarvet, survived its parent. This firm owed its origins to the builder's need to utilise unwanted new buildings. Nowadays, it obtains its tonnage from non-Swedish sources (e.g. AESA). Note *Lloyd's List*, 16 June 1989, p. 1.

64 Note *Fairplay*, 18 May 1989, p. 22.

65 See *Shipping and Transportation*, January 1978, p. 33 and *Fairplay*, 12 July 1979, p. 3. Curiously, another ambitious shipowner later to disappear, the Salén Group, bought the Finnboda yard in Stockholm in 1970. For a brief period, Salén also controlled th Sölvesborg, Öresundsvarvet and Götaverken yards. See *The Dock and Harbour Authority*, March 1973, p. 454.

66 See *Shipping World*, January 1971, p. 117. Interestingly, Greek shipowners also expressed interest in taking over the moribund NESL during 1989. They, along with rival bidder, West German shipowner Egon Oldendorff, were to be frustrated in their plans. Note *Lloyd's List*, 8 June 1989, p. 1.

67 See *The Engineer*, 18 May 1989, p. 7 and *Fairplay*, 30 March 1989, p. 5. Fred Olsen obtained 47.5 per cent of the new H&W, leaving 47 per cent for management and employees, and the residual for other investors.

68 Reported in *Lloyd's List*, 7 June 1989, p. 5 and *Fairplay*, 27 July 1989, p. 6. Interestingly, Norwegian shipowner John Fredriksen declared an interest in 1989 in buying the AESA Juliana yard at Gijon.

69 Another major Finnish shipbuilder, Rauma-Repola Oy, has a 12.6 per cent interest in EFFOA Finland Steamship.

5   CONGLOMERATES AND SHIPBUILDING

1 Mentioned in *Fairplay*, 12 June 1980, pp. 35–7.

2 Some of the diseconomies associated with conglomerate operations are identified in F.M. Scherer, *Industrial Market Structure and Economic Performance*, Rand McNally, Chicago, 1970 and D.J. Ravenscraft and F.M. Scherer, *Mergers, Sell-offs, and Economic Efficiency*, The Brookings Institution, Washington, DC, 1987.

3 They are also enabled to pursue industrial concentration. The West German MAN conglomerate, for example, expanded from its engineering base to become the dominant force in marine diesel engines. After absorbing B&W Diesel in 1980, it acquired SEMT–Pielstick from the Alsthom group in 1988 and, soon afterwards, set about taking over Sulzer of Switzerland. In 1989 this

last move was thwarted by the West German anti-cartel office. If this 1989 strategy had not been proscribed, MAN would have enjoyed a virtual monopoly of the world's marine diesel technology applicable to merchant shipping.

4 Figures culled from K.A. Bertsch and L.S. Shaw, *The Nuclear Weapons Industry*, Investor Responsibility Research Center, Washington, DC, 1984, pp. 206–17.

5 See *Inside the Navy*, 8 May 1989, p. 5 and *Jane's Defence Weekly*, 21 January 1989, p. 112.

6 J.J. Safford, 'The United States merchant marine in foreign trade, 1800–1939' in Committee for the International Conference on Business History, *Business History of Shipping*, University of Tokyo Press, Tokyo, 1985, pp. 91–118. It virtually goes without saying that defence-oriented conglomerates also availed themselves of the opportunity to build cargo bottoms at the time. Schneider, for example, set up a yard at Harfleur near Le Havre to build standard cargo vessels; a facility merged in 1922 with the firm's main naval building outlet, the Bordeaux-based Forges et Chantiers de la Gironde. In turn, this last was merged into Chantiers de France, ultimately a constituent of NORMED.

7 Recorded in *Fairplay*, 22 November 1979, pp. 9–11; 5 February 1981, p. 8; 7 December 1989, p. 12; and *Financial Times*, 8 March 1989, p. 24.

8 Another conglomerate with significant energy and shipping interests had a less rewarding experience of shipbuilding. Trafalgar House, already active in rig building by virtue of its Cleveland Offshore, RGC Offshore and Redpath Dorman Long branches, succeeded in purchasing Scott Lithgow from BS in 1984. Unable to restore this specialist off-shore yard to profitability, the conglomerate closed it in 1988 after failing to secure compensatory naval orders. Ironically, in 1986 Trafalgar House bought John Brown, the former operator of the Clydebank yard and one-time builder of Cunard (also a Trafalgar House company) ships. As recounted elsewhere, Clydebank is now confined to rig building.

9 The values of Navy contracts to the yards are disputed. A total of $58 billion was set aside for warshipbuilding, but the shipbuilders claim that 70 per cent of that was expended on component purchases rather than yard services. See *Shipping and Transportation*, January 1988, p. 48.

10 Noted in *Business Week*, 23 June 1986, p. 47 and 17 April 1987, p. 282.

11 In the event, NASSCO was sold by Morrison Knudsen to the yard's own management and employees in 1989. Note *Fairplay*, 27 April 1989, p. 7.

12 See *Lloyd's List*, 17 July 1986, p. 7 and *Business Week*, 26 September 1988, pp. 130–2.

13 Refer to *Jane's Defence Weekly*, 4 July 1987, p. 1429 and 10 December 1988, p. 1505.

14 Considered in *The Economist*, 24 August 1985, pp. 68–9 and *Shipping and Transportation*, September 1985, p. 43. See also J. Goodwin, *Brotherhood of Arms*, Times Books, New York, 1985, p. 83.

15 See *Business Week*, 22 August 1988, pp. 70–1 and *The New York Times*, 17 December 1989, F8.

16 Y.W. Rhee, B. Ross-Larson and G. Pursell, *Korea's Competitive Edge*, Johns Hopkins University Press, Baltimore, 1984, pp. 39–49.

17 Y. Yoo, 'Industrial policy of South Korea' in R.E. Driscoll and J.N. Behrman

(eds), *National Industrial Policies*, Oelgeschlager, Gunn & Hain, Cambridge, Mass., 1984, pp. 167–76.

18 The three VLCCs at issue were taken over by the state's Korea Oil Corporation, effectively saving the yard from bankruptcy. See L.P. Jones and I. Sakong, *Government, Business, and Entrepreneurship in Economic Development*, Harvard University Press, Cambridge, Mass., 1980, pp. 357–8.

19 Refer to *Far Eastern Economic Review*, 27 August 1953, p. 274 and 19 February 1970, p. 52, and *Shipping and Transportation*, December 1970, p. 19.

20 See *Shipping and Transportation*, March 1971, p. 5 and *Far Eastern Economic Review*, 26 February 1972, p. 57.

21 Described in *Lloyd's List*, 4 July 1989, p. 1.

22 Note *Shipping and Transportation*, November 1973, p. 19 and *Shipping World*, January 1975, p. 80. Interestingly, A&P Appledore had helped design the Ulsan yard.

23 Note *Fairplay*, 14 July 1977, p. 29.

24 See *Far Eastern Economic Review*, 6 November 1981, pp. 87–8 and *Shipping and Transportation*, January 1982, p. 37.

25 J.L. Enos and W-H. Park, *The Adoption and Diffusion of Imported Technology*, Croom Helm, London, 1988, p. 169.

26 A discourse on the liner code and its implications for global (especially American) shipping is presented in A.W. Cafruny, *Ruling the Waves*, University of California Press, Berkeley, 1987.

27 See *Far Eastern Economic Review*, 18 May 1979, pp. 64–6 and 30 May 1980, pp. 53–4.

28 HHI obtained licences from Sulzer, MAN, MHI and SEMT–Pielstick for this purpose, while Ssangyong became a Wärtsilä Diesel licensee. The HHI engine works grew so large as to warrant separate status (as Hyundai Engine and Machinery Company) in 1978. With an annual output of 2 million bhp, it was reabsorbed by HHI in 1989. In that year, too, the restrictions placed on engine builders by the government were lifted, and HHI, KHIC and Ssangyong were allowed to manufacture diesels of any size.

29 The indices quoted in Chapter 1 differ from those enumerated here on account not only of different base periods but also of different class divisions (ship types) from which the relative shares are deduced and aggregate specialisations are arrived at. Moreover, allusion was made to a Polish yardstick in the first use of the concept, whereas the current focus of attention is restricted to South Korea.

30 One interesting aspect of this proclivity of KSEC was its involvement in the Jeddah Ship Repair Yard. Under a five-year contract signed in 1982, KSEC ran this new repair facility on behalf of the Saudi Ports Authority, progressively training local personnel in the arts of shipyard practice. Note *Fairplay*, 15 December 1983, p. 22. On the expiry of the contract, management was assumed by National Maintenance and Marine Services, a Singapore firm.

31 It is calculated from:

$$I = \tfrac{1}{2} \sum_{i=1}^{n} \left| X_i - Y_i \right|$$

where the Xs are the percentages of the total workload tonnage taken up by each ship type *i* at the earlier date and the Ys are percentages accounted for by the same types at the later date. For our purposes, there are eight ship types; namely, bulkers, container ships, dry cargo vessels, combination carriers, offshore supply vessels, reefers, tankers and Ro-Ro ships.

32 KSEC values include the tonnages accredited to its Ulsan subsidiary, Donghae Shipbuilding.

33 Cited in *Manchester Guardian Weekly*, 26 February 1984, p. 12.

34 It was subsequently to produce shipboard machinery under licence from the B&W shipyard of Denmark, besides making ship's automation systems under a permit obtained from Valmet Automation, the Norwegian subsidiary of the Valmet shipyard of Finland. From the product side, HHI introduced South Korean shipbuilders to LPG carriers in 1986, winning orders for ten in the next three years. Specialist plant for these vessels was procured from Liquid Gas Equipment, a branch of the Weir Group of Glasgow.

35 Reported in *Far Eastern Economic Review*, 19 July 1984, pp. 48–51 and *The Engineer*, 31 October 1985, pp. 23–4.

36 See *Asian Wall Street Journal*, 21 August 1986, p. 4; 16 December 1986, p. 13; and 17 December 1986, p. 3.

37 The restored viability of KHIC prompted the government to indicate its willingness to return the firm to the private sector in 1989.

38 Also recall Table 2.7.

39 See *Asian Wall Street Journal*, 25 March 1987, p. 1; 7 April 1987, p. 3; and 3 August 1987, p. 1. Also see *The Economist*, 19 September 1987, pp. 77–8. This bail-out was merely one manifestation of a larger phenomenon. All told, six shipping firms with liabilities totalling Won 3.2 trillion ($3.84 billion) were rescued through the government's willingness to reschedule their debts. Note, in undertaking enforced rationalisation South Korea was simply emulating the precedent established by the Japanese. In 1963 the MoT prosecuted a scheme whereby 95 shipping companies were virtually compelled to merge into six groups, together responsible for four-fifths of the national tonnage.

40 Variously referred to in *Far Eastern Economic Review*, 20 October 1988, p. 104; 8 December 1988, p. 52; *Asian Wall Street Journal*, 4–5 November 1988, p. 3; 9 November 1988, p. 1; *Business Week*, 28 November 1988, p. 51; and *Wall Street Journal*, 28 March 1989, A14.

41 Refer to *Business Week*, 10 April 1989, p. 45.

42 Reported in *Fairplay*, 27 October 1988, pp. 29–35 and 27 April 1989, p. 6.

43 To quote from *The Economist*, 9 December 1989, p. 79: 'One result of the new mood of co-operation is an informal arrangement that lets orders for new ships be parcelled out among not just Japanese yards but South Korean ones as well. This looks disturbingly like collusion.'

44 See *Fairplay*, 7 September 1989, p. 6.

45 A sentiment expressed in *The Economist*, 9 December 1989, p. 74.

6 INCHOATE MARINE INDUSTRIES: THE SEEMING PARADOX

1 In truth, the foreign exchange justification needs to be qualified. In many cases, and we have touched on examples in Greece and Portugal, the need to import expensive components offsets much of the savings from domestic production. Even South Korea, a successful producer on most counts, was troubled on this score.

2 Refer to S. Arima, 'The Western influence on Japanese military science, shipbuilding and navigation', *Monumenta Nipponica*, vol.19, 1964, pp. 118–45; U. Kobayashi, *Military Industries of Japan*, Oxford University Press, New York, 1922, pp. 185–6 and H. Jones, *Live Machines*, University of British Columbia Press, Vancouver, 1980.

3 See D. Todd, 'Technology transfer and naval construction: part 2', *Naval Forces*, vol.10, 1988, pp. 53–8.

4 See M.A. Morris, *Expansion of Third-World Navies*, Macmillan, London, 1987, pp. 79–81 and F. Hussein and R. van Tol, 'Naval construction in the Third World', *Naval Forces*, vol.8, 1987, pp. 70–83.

5 The latest intelligence suggests that Singapore's Sembawang and NOL will co-operate with local interests in setting up a combined repair and new-building yard at Laem Chabang. Refer to *Fairplay*, 25 January 1990, p. 6.

6 Vosper–QAF, a one-time subsidiary of Vosper Thornycroft based in Singapore (and now owned by Swan Hunter), concluded an agreement in 1988 with CCN–Maua devised with the object of enabling the Brazilian yard to licence-build its design of patrol boat. Deployment of personnel to the yard was part of the $20 million package.

7 DSHM in South Korea is also mining the expertise of HDW in order to acquire submarine production capability.

8 Oddly, some technology-transfer projects aimed at operationalising merchant yards proved unsound. Mexico set up a state enterprise, Astilleros Unidos SA, to transform the Veracruz repair yard into a fully-fledged building centre and called on A&P Appledore and AESA to furnish the appropriate know-how. The 1980 programme revolved round series production of 45,000 dwt product tankers: a scheme which, in the event, was overly ambitious. For example, an order for four vessels placed in 1983 by Pemex, the state oil company, was not fulfilled until 1989. A clutch of subsidiary yards – the most notable being Guaymas, one capable of building ships up to 25,000 tonnes – was added to the Veracruz organisation. Afflicted with second thoughts, the government unsuccessfully attempted to privatise Astilleros Unidos in 1988. See *Lloyd's List*, 28 June 1989, p. 5. Captivated by the tanker boom, SIMA of Peru declared in the early 1970s its intention to enter the VLCC market via a 300,000 dwt-capacity building dock designed by IHI in conjunction with A&P Appledore. As it happened, this venture was stillborn, but the Callao yard actually produced a string of 25,000 dwt bulkers under licence from Kaldnes Mekaniska Verksted of Norway. Note *Fairplay*, 10 January 1974, p. 108. Egypt, too, attempted to initiate a significant shipbuilding industry, using the Alexandria Shipyard as its core. Began with Soviet help in 1962, the yard commenced shipbuilding in 1969. From 1971 B&W assistance was requested and the Danish firm's 'Hamlet' class of

12,600 dwt cargo vessels were built into the 1980s. From 1976 IHI provided the yard with managerial assistance. Uncompetitive in part because of overmanning – the government refused the management the right to cut the 6,000 work-force – the yard survives on ship repair and the intermittent production of vessels for domestic account (currently to West German designs). See *Lloyd's List*, 10 August 1988, p. 13 and 5 July 1989, p. 2.

9 Quote taken from p. 132 of T. Ozawa, *Multinationalism, Japanese Style*, Princeton University Press, Princeton, 1979. See also C.H. Smith, *Japanese Technology Transfer to Brazil*, UMI Research Press, Ann Arbor, Michigan, 1981, p. 35.

10 Admittedly, Spanish marine consultants, Sener, had assisted the Brazilian yard in this design. See *Shipping and Transportation*, October 1973, p. 15.

11 Note *Fairplay*, 8 January 1976, p. 101; 20 January 1977, p. 88; and 31 March 1977, p. 10.

12 See *Japan Shipping and Shipbuilding*, March 1959, p. 6.

13 Reported in *Fairplay*, 19 May 1977, pp. 35–42.

14 See *Fairplay*, 17 January 1980, p. 55; 27 August 1981, p. 56; 15 December 1988, p. 5; 16 March 1989, p. 6; and 10 August 1989, p. 18.

15 Japanese shipbuilder, NKK, participated in a venture in Colombia. It was charged in the early 1970s with upgrading the Conastil yard in Cartagena to enable it to tackle 3,000 dwt vessels.

16 Refer to *Far Eastern Economic Review*, 9 February 1979, pp. 57–8; 14 February 1985, p. 59; 23 March 1989, pp. 76–7; and *Fairplay*, 16 November 1989, p. 8.

17 See *Fairplay*, 4 January 1990, p. 8. The flexing of Singapore's muscles is also reflected in the 1989 decision of Sembawang to open a ship-repair yard at Fujairah in the United Arab Emirates.

18 In fact, Straits Steamship had set up a small ferry-building yard at Sungei Nyok near Penang as early as 1924. Unable to compete with Hong Kong-built tonnage, it reverted to repair after the Second World War and was eventually phased out. See K.G. Tregonning, *Home Port Singapore*, Oxford University Press, Singapore, 1967, pp. 246–8.

19 Note N.C. Sinha and P.N. Khera, *Indian War Economy*, Orient Longman, New Delhi, 1962, pp. 242–50 and T.S. Sanjeeva Rao, *A Short History of Modern Indian Shipping*, Popular Prakashan, Bombay, 1965, pp. 34–7.

20 Refer to *Far Eastern Economic Review*, 26 July 1951, p. 119.

21 See *Far Eastern Economic Review*, 16 November 1961, p. 349; 18 October 1962, p. 135; and 9 July 1964, p. 91.

22 See *Far Eastern Economic Review*, 2 February 1961, p. 217; 25 October 1962, p. 261; 27 February 1971, p. 54; and 25 May 1978, pp. 23–4. Notably, a 1957 state venture in Pakistan, the Karachi Shipyard and Engineering Works, was constrained by similar problems. Uncompetitive new building (and it was equipped to build vessels up to 25,000 dwt) forced this yard to resort to repair for most of its revenues.

23 See *Asian Wall Street Journal*, 17 February 1987, p. 6 and *Fairplay*, issues of 4 December 1980, p. 11 and 30 April 1987, p. 47.

24 Note H.M. Trivedi, *Indian Shipping in Perspective*, Vikas Publishing House, New Delhi, 1980, pp. 419–21. Also see *Fairplay*, 4 February 1988, p. 6; 2 June 1988, p. 6; and 4 August 1988, p. 7.

25 See *International Defense Review*, April 1989, p. 505.

26 Revealed in *Business Week*, 26 June 1989, p. 78.

27 Cited in *Fairplay*, 30 June 1988, p. 6 and 8 June 1989, p. 20.

28 See D.E. Muller, *China as a Maritime Power*, Westview, Boulder, Col., 1983 and *Far Eastern Economic Review*, 26 November 1959, p. 885.

29 Quote taken from *Far Eastern Economic Review*, 18 September 1971, p. 65. Equally striking, a 5,000 dwt tanker was built on a beach at Tsingtao in the absence of a berth.

30 B. Hahn, 'China's submarine fleet', *Navy International*, vol.94, 1989, pp. 71–81.

31 Chinese 'Romeo' class submarines were built at Mayang-do in North Korea during the late 1970s. 'Shanghai' class and 'Huchuan' class fast attack craft were built at the Mangalia and Dobreta yards in Romania from 1973. See R. Sharpe, *Jane's Fighting Ships 1988–89*, Jane's Publishing, London, 1988.

32 Based on information supplied by CSSC and the Dalian Shipbuilding Industry Corporation.

33 See *Far Eastern Economic Review*, 3 April 1981, pp. 33–4; 1 September 1983, p. 108; and 14 February 1985, p. 50. Also note *Fairplay*, 30 June 1988, pp. 24–9.

34 Western shipowners also complained of tardy bureaucratic procedures intruding on ship contracting and expressed doubts at China's ability to meet future ship delivery deadlines. See *Fairplay*, 25 January 1990, p. 27.

35 I am indebted to CSBC and TMMC for this information.

36 See *Zosen*, February 1970, p. 20 and *Far Eastern Economic Review*, 18 February 1954, p. 210.

37 Information abstracted from Council for Economic Planning and Development, *Taiwan Statistical Data Book 1988*.

38 See *Far Eastern Economic Review*, 24 December 1959, p. 1010; 14 April 1960, p. 807; and 12 May 1960, p. 947. Ingalls Taiwan also expressed disquiet at having to borrow $9 million from the Bank of Taiwan at a high rate of interest in order to discharge its first contract: a $15 million project to build two 36,000 ton tankers.

39 Iino Shipbuilding was to become Maizuru Shipbuilding before falling prey to Hitachi Zosen (recall Chapter 4).

40 Note *Far Eastern Economic Review*, 31 October 1968, p. 265; 18 February 1974, p. 29; 23 May 1975, p. 40; *Shipping and Transportation*, May 1971, p. 10; December 1976, p. 24; and *Fairplay*, 22 June 1978, p. 45.

41 Note *Far Eastern Economic Review*, 28 February 1975, pp. 8–9; 11 February 1977, p. 60.

42 See *Shipping and Transportation*, April 1980, pp. 26–7; June 1980, p. 37; July 1981, p. 41; *Fairplay*, 3 July 1980, p. 41; and *Far Eastern Economic Review*, 5 February 1982, pp. 67–8.

43 Headed by Dr Y.S. Li, a naval architect trained in Britain, the United Ship Design and Development Centre had been established in Taipei in 1976 with its own CAD/CAM facilities.

44 Refer to *Far Eastern Economic Review*, 30 April 1982, pp. 55–6. By all accounts, it had profited on only five of the 68 ships built heretofore.

45 Refer to *Shipping and Transportation*, November 1983, p. 35; December 1985, p. 42; and *Far Eastern Economic Review*, 14 February 1985, pp. 66–7 and 13 February 1986, p. 61.

46 Formed in 1968, reputedly with the assistance of the Marubeni Corporation,

Evergreen earned $58 million on revenues of $1.39 billion in 1986. Separately, Evergreen Marine realised after-tax profits of $90 million on revenues of $942 million in 1988 while Uniglory's figures were $5.5 million and $115 million respectively. A pioneer of round-the-world container service, it had broken with its practice of buying in Japan when, lured by loans from government-controlled Taiwanese banks, it ordered 10 container ships from CSBC. See *Asian Wall Street Journal*, 17 July 1987, p. 5 and 16 February 1989, p. 3. Incidentally, Evergreen Superior Alloys, a group company, produces specialised steel which in part is destined for CSBC.

47 Reported in *Shipping and Transportation*, July 1987, p. 38.

48 Information communicated to the author by Evergreen.

49 See *Shipping and Transportation*, June 1988, p. 30; March 1989, p. 28; and *China Post*, 12 June 1988, p. 12; 9 March 1989, p. 12; and 23 March 1989, p. 6.

50 Noted in *Lloyd's List*, 7 June 1989, p. 3.

51 See *Far Eastern Economic Review*, 15 September 1988, pp. 84–6.

52 Asmar, in addition, recently completed a yard at Punta Arenas as part of a joint venture with Sandock Austral, a South African shipbuilding and engineering group. Refer to *Fairplay*, 14 September 1989, p. 39.

CONCLUSIONS

1 Related in R.T. Harrison, 'The labour market impact of industrial decline and restructuring', *Tijdschrift voor Economische en Sociale Geografie*, vol.76, 1985, pp. 332–44.

2 Nagatsuka noted that new-building tonnage booked in Japan in 1989 was of the order of twice the 1988 total whereas trends in South Korea and Europe displayed only moderate increases in 1989 relative to the previous year. His comments are cited in *Fairplay*, 1 February 1990, p. 7.

3 All three still belong to Celsius Industries. The two warship yards have been pared even further: their managements were merged and the combined work-force is being pruned from over 1,900 to 1,350. See *Jane's Defence Weekly*, 8 April 1989, p. 621.

4 Ironically, Mitsui had adopted the MES appellation in 1976 as a symbol of its commitment to land machinery in preference to shipbuilding; previously, the order in the title had stressed shipbuilding before engineering.

5 The reliance of Canadian yards on government contracts was made apparent in 1990 when, on the cancellation of a major icebreaker project, the future of 1,000 jobs and yards in North Vancouver and Victoria was threatened. See *Winnipeg Free Press*, 24 February 1990, p. 18. A generation earlier, the only other Victoria yard was compelled to close on the termination of government contracts. Note G.W. Taylor, *Shipyards of British Columbia*, Morriss Publishing, Victoria, 1986, p. 204. With frigate orders worth C$6.2 billion, Saint John Shipbuilding is thriving by comparison. See *Toronto Globe and Mail*, 10 October 1988, B18.

6 The vessel in question is a 6,700 grt exploration cruise ship. See *Fairplay*, 15 February 1990, p. 6.

7 Reported in *Fairplay*, 8 February 1990, p. 5.

8 The last point is touched on in R. Luria, 'The Brazilian defense industry: part 2', *International Defense Review*, vol.22, 1989, pp. 1675–8.

9 Reported in *Fairplay*, 22 February 1990, p. 7.

10 The vessels will be patterned on a design formulated by the Martin Jansen yard of Leer, West Germany. See *Fairplay*, 11 January 1990, p. 5.

11 Operating on two fronts, the Australian Government desired to establish one yard for surface combatants and another for submarines. The state-owned Williamstown Dockyard was privatised as the Australian Marine Engineering Corporation and eventually commissioned to build a series of B&V-designed frigates for Australia and New Zealand. A virgin yard, known as the Australian Submarine Corporation, was set up at Adelaide to construct a string of diesel-powered submarines to Kockums' design.

12 The order book totals are abstracted from Lloyd's Register of Shipping, *Merchant Shipbuilding Return, December 1989*, Table 12.

13 A scenario posed by the McKinsey consulting firm. See *Lloyd's List*, 19 June 1989, p. 1.

14 The quotation is taken from *Fairplay*, 15 February 1990, p. 41.

15 Note, for example, P. Dicken, *Global Shift*, Harper & Row, New York, 1986, and J. Grunwald and K. Flamm (eds), *The Global Factory*, The Brookings Institution, Washington, DC, 1985.

16 R. Ballance and S. Sinclair, *Collapse and Survival*, George Allen & Unwin, London, 1983, pp. 194–6.

References

Abernathy, W.J., Clark, K.B. and Kantrow, A.M. (1983) *Industrial Renaissance: Producing a Competitive Future for America*, Basic Books, New York.

Albu, A. (1980) 'Merchant shipbuilding and marine engineering' in K. Pavitt (ed.), *Technical Innovation and British Economic Performance*, Macmillan, London, pp. 168–83.

Allen, G.C. (1981) 'Industrial policy and innovation in Japan' in C. Carter (ed.), *Industrial Policy and Innovation*, Heinemann, London, pp. 68–87.

Al-Timimi, W. (1975) 'Innovation led expansion: the shipbuilding case', *Research Policy*, vol.4, pp. 160–71.

Arima, S. (1964) 'The Western influence on Japanese military science, shipbuilding and navigation', *Monumenta Nipponica*, vol.19, pp. 118–45.

Arnold, G. (1978) *Britain's Oil*, Hamish Hamilton, London.

Auer, J.E. (1973) *The Postwar Rearmament of Japanese Maritime Forces, 1945–71*, Praeger, New York.

Ballance, R. and Sinclair, S. (1983) *Collapse and Survival: Industry Strategies in a Changing World*, George Allen & Unwin, London.

Banbury, P. (1971) *Shipbuilders of the Thames and Medway*, David and Charles, Newton Abbot.

Bauer, K.J. (1988) *A Maritime History of the United States: the Role of America's Seas and Waterways*, University of South Carolina Press, Columbia.

Bertsch, K.A. and Shaw, L.S. (1984) *The Nuclear Weapons Industry*, Investor Responsibility Research Center, Washington, DC.

Blumenthal, T. (1976) 'The Japanese shipbuilding industry' in H. Patrick (ed.), *Japanese Industrialization and its Social Consequences*, University of California Press, Berkeley, pp. 129–60.

Burrell, D.C.E. (1983) *Scrap & Build*, World Ship Society, Kendal.

Cafruny, A.W. (1987) *Ruling the Waves: the Political Economy of International Shipping*, University of California Press, Berkeley.

Caves, R. and Uekusa, M. (1976) 'Industrial organization' in H. Patrick and H. Rosovsky (eds), *Asia's New Giant: How the Japanese Economy Works*, The Brookings Institution, Washington, DC, pp. 459–523.

Chrzanowski, I., Krzyzanowski, M. and Krzysztof, L. (1983) *Shipping Economics and Policy: a Socialist View*, Fairplay Publications, London.

Cook, P.L. (1986) 'The offshore supplies industry: fast, continuous and incremental change' in M. Sharp (ed.), *Europe and the New Technologies: Six*

Case Studies in Innovation Adjustment, Cornell University Press, Ithaca, NY, pp. 213–62.

De Jong, H.W. (1984) 'Sectoral development and sectoral policies in the EEC' in A. Jacquemin (ed.), *European Industry: Public Policy and Corporate Strategy*, Clarendon Press, Oxford, pp. 147–71.

De Silva, K.E.A. (1988) *An Economic Analysis of the Shipbuilding Industry Assistance Program*, Economic Council of Canada, Discussion Paper 351, Ottawa.

Dicken, P. (1986) *Global Shift: Industrial Change in a Turbulent World*, Harper & Row, New York.

Dodwell Marketing Consultants, (1978) *Industrial Groupings in Japan*, Dodwell, Tokyo.

Dore, R. (1986) *Flexible Rigidities: Industrial Policy and Structural Adjustment in the Japanese Economy 1970–80*, Stanford University Press, Stanford.

Dougan, D. (1968) *The History of North East Shipbuilding*, George Allen & Unwin, London.

Drucker, P.F. (1954) *The Practice of Management*, Harper, New York.

Enos, J.L. and Park, W-H. (1988) *The Adoption and Diffusion of Imported Technology: the Case of Korea*, Croom Helm, London.

Faltas, S. (1986) *Arms Markets and Armament Policy: the Changing Structure of Naval Industries in Western Europe*, Martinus Nijhoff, Dordrecht.

Geddes, R.M. (1966) *Shipbuilding Inquiry Committee 1965–66 Report*, HMSO, Cmnd 2937, London.

Goodwin, J. (1985) *Brotherhood of Arms: General Dynamics and the Business of Defending America*, Times Books, New York.

Gordon, A. (1985) *The Evolution of Labor Relations in Japan: Heavy Industry, 1853–1955*, Harvard University Press, Cambridge, Mass.

Gordon, G.A.H. (1988) *British Seapower and Procurement Between the Wars: a Reappraisal of Rearmament*, Macmillan, Basingstoke.

Greenman, D. (1985) *Jane's Merchant Ships 1985–86*, Jane's Publishing, London.

Grunwald, J. and Flamm, K. (eds) (1985) *The Global Factory: Foreign Assembly in International Trade*, The Brookings Institution, Washington, DC.

Hahn, B. (1989) 'China's submarine fleet', *Navy International*, vol.94, pp. 71–81.

Hamilton, A. (1978) *North Sea Impact: Offshore Oil and the British Economy*, International Institute for Economic Research, London.

Harrigan, K.R. (1983) *Strategies for Vertical Integration*, D.C. Heath, Lexington.

Harrison, R.T. (1985) 'The labour market impact of industrial decline and restructuring: the example of the Northern Ireland shipbuilding industry', *Tijdschrift voor Economische en Sociale Geografie*, vol.76, pp. 332–44.

Hogwood, B.W. (1979) *Government and Shipbuilding: the Politics of Industrial Change*, Saxon House, Farnborough.

Hornby, O. (1985) 'The Danish shipping industry, 1866–1939' in Committee for the International Conference on Business History, *Business History of Shipping: Strategy and Structure*, University of Tokyo Press, Tokyo, pp. 157–81.

Hume, J.R. and Moss, M.S. (1979) *Beardmore – the History of a Scottish Industrial Giant*, Heinemann, London.

Hussein, F. and van Tol, R. (1987) 'Naval construction in the Third World', *Naval Forces*, vol.8, pp. 70–83.

Imai, K. (1980) 'Iron and steel' in K. Sato (ed.), *Industry and Business in Japan*, M.E. Sharpe, White Plains, NY, pp. 191–244.

Isard, W. (1960) *Methods of Regional Analysis*, MIT Press, Cambridge, Mass.

Johnson, C. (1982) *MITI and the Japanese Miracle: the Growth of Industrial Policy, 1925–1975*, Stanford University Press, Stanford.

Jones, H. (1980) *Live Machines: Hired Foreigners and Meiji Japan*, University of British Columbia Press, Vancouver.

Jones, L.P. and Sakong, I. (1980) *Government, Business, and Entrepreneurship in Economic Development: the Korean Case*, Harvard University Press, Cambridge, Mass.

JSEA, (1980) *Shipbuilding and Marine Engineering in Japan 1980*, JSEA/SAJ, Tokyo.

—— (1985) *Shipbuilding and Marine Engineering in Japan 1985*, JSEA/SAJ, Tokyo.

Klein, B.H. (1977) *Dynamic Economics*, Harvard University Press, Cambridge, Mass.

Kobayashi, U. (1922) *Military Industries of Japan*, Oxford University Press, New York.

Kumar, M.S. (1984) *Growth, Acquisition and Investment: an Analysis of the Growth of Industrial Firms and their Overseas Activities*, Cambridge University Press, Cambridge.

Lauber, V. (1986) 'The political economy of industrial policy in Western Europe' in S.A. Shull and J.E. Cohen (eds), *Economics and Politics of Industrial Policy: the United States and Western Europe*, Westview, Boulder, Col., pp. 27–46.

Long, D.M. (1986) *The Soviet Merchant Fleet – its Growth, Strategy, Strength and Weakness 1920–1999*, Lloyd's of London Press, London.

Lorenz, E. and Wilkinson, F. (1986) 'The shipbuilding industry 1880–1965' in B. Elbaum and W. Lazonick (eds), *The Decline of the British Economy*, Clarendon Press, Oxford, pp. 109–34.

Luria, R. (1989) 'The Brazilian defense industry: part 2', *International Defense Review*, vol.22, pp. 1675–8.

McArthur, A.A. (1978) *A Report by the Sector Task Force on the Canadian Shipbuilding and Repair Industry*, Department of Industry, Trade and Commerce, Ottawa.

Meeks, G. (1977) *Disappointing Marriage: a Study of the Gains from Merger*, University of Cambridge, Department of Applied Economics, Occasional Paper 51.

Menne, B. (1937) *Krupp or the Lords Of Essen*, William Hodge, London.

Mitsubishi Economic Research Bureau, (1936) *Japanese Trade and Industry: Present and Future*, Macmillan, London.

Morris, M.A. (1987) *Expansion of Third-World Navies*, Macmillan, London.

Moss, M. and Hume, J.R. (1986) *Shipbuilders to the World: 125 Years of Harland and Wolff, Belfast, 1861–1986*, Blackstaff Press, Belfast.

Mottershead, P. (1983) 'Shipbuilding: adjustment-led intervention or intervention-led adjustment?' in G. Shepherd, F. Duchême and C. Saunders (eds), *Europe's Industries: Public and Private Strategies for Change*, Cornell University Press, Ithaca, NY, pp. 82–109.

Muller, D.E. (1983) *China as a Maritime Power*, Westview, Boulder, Col.

Nakamura, T. (1983) *Economic Growth in Prewar Japan*, Yale University Press, New Haven, Conn.

Nakatani, I. (1984) 'The economic role of financial corporate grouping' in M. Aoki (ed.), *The Economic Analysis of the Japanese Firm*, North-Holland, Amsterdam, pp. 227–58.

OECD, (1980) *The Crisis in the Shipbuilding Industry and International Cooperation Efforts Geared Towards Positive Adjustment in the Industry*, Special Group of the Economic Policy Committee on Positive Adjustment Policies, CPE/PAP (80) 29, Paris.

Okamoto, Y. (1984) 'The grand strategy of Japanese business' in K. Sato and Y. Hoshino (eds), *The Anatomy of Japanese Business*, M.E. Sharpe, Armonk, NY, pp. 277–318.

Okumura, H. (1984) 'Interfirm relations in an enterprise group: the case of Mitsubishi' in K. Sato and Y. Hoshino (eds), *The Anatomy of Japanese Business*, M.E. Sharpe, Armonk, NY, pp. 164–93.

Ozawa, T. (1979) *Multinationalism, Japanese Style: the Political Economy of Outward Dependency*, Princeton University Press, Princeton.

Pang, E.F. (1984) 'Industrial policy and economic restructuring in Singapore' in R.E. Driscoll and J.N. Behrman (eds), *National Industrial Policies*, Oelgeschlager, Gunn & Hain, Cambridge, Mass., pp. 151–66.

Peebles, H.B. (1987) *Warshipbuilding on the Clyde: Naval Orders and the Prosperity of the Clyde Shipbuilding Industry, 1889–1939*, John Donald, Edinburgh.

Pollard, S. (1950) 'The decline of shipbuilding on the Thames', *Economic History Review*, vol.3, pp. 1–23.

Price, V.C. (1981) *Industrial Policies in the European Community*, St Martin's Press, New York.

Rapping, L. (1965) 'Learning and World War II production functions', *Review of Economics and Statistics*, vol.47, pp. 81–6.

Ratcliffe, M. (1985) *Liquid Gold Ships: a History of the Tanker 1859–1984*, Lloyd's of London Press, Colchester.

Ravenscraft, D.J. and Scherer, F.M. (1987) *Mergers, Sell-offs, and Economic Efficiency*, The Brookings Institution, Washington, DC.

Rhee, Y.W., Ross-Larson, B. and Pursell, G. (1984) *Korea's Competitive Edge: Managing the Entry into World Markets*, Johns Hopkins University Press, Baltimore.

Safford, J.J. (1985) 'The United States merchant marine in foreign trade, 1800–1939' in Committee for the International Conference on Business History, *Business History of Shipping: Strategy and Structure*, University of Tokyo Press, Tokyo, pp. 91–118.

Salter, M.S. and Weinhold, W.A. (1979) *Diversification through Acquisition: Strategies for Creating Economic Value*, The Free Press, New York.

Salter, W.E.G. (1966) *Productivity and Technical Change*, 2nd edn, Cambridge University Press, Cambridge.

Sanjeeva Rao, T.S. (1965) *A Short History of Modern Indian Shipping*, Popular Prakashan, Bombay.

Savary, J. (1984) *French Multinationals*, St Martin's Press, New York.

Scherer, F.M. (1970) *Industrial Market Structure and Economic Performance*, Rand McNally, Chicago.

—— (1975) *The Economics of Multi-plant Operation: an International Comparisons Study*, Harvard University Press, Cambridge, Mass.

Schmidt, K-D. (1984) 'West Germany: another industrial policy victim' in T.E.

Petri, W.F. Clinger, N.L. Johnson and L. Martin (eds), *National Industrial Policy: Solution or Illusion*, Westview, Boulder, Col., pp. 63–9.

Schönknecht, R., Lüsch, J., Schelzel, M. and Obenaus, H. (1983) *Ships and Shipping of Tomorrow*, MacGregor Publications, Hounslow.

Sharpe, R. (1988) *Jane's Fighting Ships 1988–89*, Jane's Publishing, London.

Sinha, N.C. and Khera, P.N. (1962) *Indian War Economy: Supply, Industry and Finance*, Orient Longman, New Delhi.

Smith, C.H. (1981) *Japanese Technology Transfer to Brazil*, UMI Research Press, Ann Arbor, Michigan.

Smith, J.W. and Holden, T.S. (1946) *Where Ships are Born: Sunderland 1346–1946*, Thomas Reed, Sunderland.

Spruill, C.R. (1982) *Conglomerates and the Evolution of Capitalism*, Southern Illinois University Press, Carbondale.

Stråth, B. (1987) *The Politics of De-industrialisation: the Contraction of the West European Shipbuilding Industry*, Croom Helm, London.

Swann, D. (1983) *Competition and Industrial Policy in the European Community*, Methuen, London.

Taylor, G.W. (1986) *Shipyards of British Columbia: the Principal Companies*, Morriss Publishing, Victoria, BC.

Todd, D. (1983) 'Technological change, industrial evolution, and regional repercussions: the case of British shipbuilding', *Canadian Geographer*, vol.27, pp. 345–60.

—— (1983) 'Area development or sectoral conflict? An example of the discriminatory effects of regional policy in Britain', *Environment and Planning C: Government and Policy*, vol.1, pp. 153–62.

—— (1985) *The World Shipbuilding Industry*, Croom Helm, London.

—— (1988) *Defence Industries: a Global Perspective*, Routledge, London.

—— (1988) 'Technology transfer and naval construction: part 2', *Naval Forces*, vol.10, pp. 53–8.

—— (1990) *The World Electronics Industry*, Routledge, London.

Tregonning, K.G. (1967) *Home Port Singapore: a History of Straits Steamship Company Limited 1890–1965*, Oxford University Press, Singapore.

Trezise, P. and Suzuki, Y. (1976) 'Politics, government, and economic growth' in H. Patrick and H. Rosovsky (eds), *Asia's New Giant: How the Japanese Economy Works*, The Brookings Institution, Washington, DC, pp. 753–811.

Trivedi, H.M. (1980) *Indian Shipping in Perspective*, Vikas Publishing House, New Delhi.

Uriu, R.M. (1984) 'The declining industries of Japan: adjustment and reallocation', *Journal of International Affairs*, vol.38, pp. 99–111.

Utton, M.A. (1979) *Diversification and Competition*, Cambridge University Press, Cambridge.

Vernon, R. (1966) 'International investment and international trade in the product cycle', *Quarterly Journal of Economics*, vol.80, pp. 190–207.

Walker, F.M. (1984) *Song of the Clyde: a History of Clyde Shipbuilding*, Patrick Stephens, Cambridge.

Watson, B.W. and Dunn, P.M. (eds) (1986) *The Future of the Soviet Navy: an Assessment to the Year 2000*, Westview, Boulder, Col.

Whitehurst, C.H. (1986) *The US Shipbuilding Industry: Past, Present and Future*, Naval Institute Press, Annapolis.

Wray, W.D. (1984) *Mitsubishi and the NYK, 1870–1914: Business Strategy in the Japanese Shipping Industry*, Harvard University Press, Cambridge, Mass.

Yip, G.S. (1982) *Barriers to Entry: a Corporate Strategy Perspective*, D.C. Heath, Lexington.

Yoo, Y. (1984) 'Industrial policy of South Korea: past and future' in R.E. Driscoll and J.N. Behrman (eds), *National Industrial Policies*, Oelgeschlager, Gunn & Hain, Cambridge, Mass., pp. 167–76.

Young, A.K. (1979) *The Sogo Shosha: Japan's Multinational Trading Companies*, Westview, Boulder, Col.

Yui, T. (1985) 'Introduction' in Committee for the International Conference on Business History, *Business History of Shipping: Strategy and Structure*, University of Tokyo Press, Tokyo, pp. ix–xxix.

Glossary

AESA Astilleros Españoles SA, the principal state-owned ship-builder in Spain.

AFNE Astilleros Y Fabricas Navales Del Estado, the main Argentine shipbuilder with yards at Rio Santiago and Buenos Aires.

AIC advanced-industrial country.

ASRY Arab Shipbuilding and Repair Yard Company, a VLCC repair yard in Bahrain owned by the governments of Bahrain, Saudi Arabia, Kuwait, Libya, Iraq, Qatar and the United Arab Emirates.

AWES Association of West European Shipbuilders, the Hamburg-based lobby group speaking on behalf of the shipbuilders of 12 European countries.

B&V Blohm & Voss AG, a West German shipbuilder and member of the Thyssen steel-based conglomerate.

B&W Burmeister & Wain Skibsvaerft A/S, a Danish shipbuilder and (formerly) marine engine builder owning a yard in Copenhagen.

BHP Broken Hill Proprietary Co. Ltd, an Australian mining and steel group currently engaged in shipowning and formerly involved in shipbuilding.

bhp brake horse power, the conventional means of measuring the maximum performance (i.e. size) of a marine diesel engine.

BS British Shipbuilders.

bulker abbreviated term for bulk carrier, a vessel specially designed to handle bulk cargoes of grain, coal, ores and sugar.

CAD/CAM computer-aided design, computer-aided manufacturing.

CCN–Maua Companhia Comercio E Navegacao-Estaleiro Maua, a major Brazilian shipbuilder located in Rio de Janeiro.

cgrt	compensated gross register tonnage, a means of deducing ship size and shipbuilding activity levels that depends on the amount and complexity of the effort expended in building the vessel. Of late, it has been used as a basis of comparison for different shipbuilding industries, although some question its validity on this score.
chaebōl	South Korean conglomerates which, aided and abetted by the government, have spearheaded the country's drive to industrialisation. Shipbuilding has been a major preoccupation of them. In this respect they are best represented by DHI, HHI, SSHI, and Hanjin Heavy Industries (the former KSEC).
CMN	Constructions Mécaniques de Normandie, a Cherbourg shipbuilder concentrating on small naval vessels.
CNIM	Constructions Navales et Industrielles de la Méditerranée, a French shipbuilder at La Seyne which eventually merged with the Empain-Schneider yards to form NORMED.
CNR	Cantieri Navali Riuniti SpA, an Italian shipbuilder with yards at Genoa, Ancona, Muggiano, Palermo and Riva Trigoso. Now absorbed into the Fincantieri organisation.
COMECON	an acronym for the Council for Mutual Economic Assistance, the East Bloc trading association.
COSCO	China Ocean Shipping Company, the state shipping arm of the People's Republic.
CSBC	China Ship Building Corporation, the principal Taiwan shipbuilder.
CSEL	Canadian Shipbuilding and Engineering Limited, a shipbuilder with headquarters at St Catherines, Ontario.
CSSC	China State Shipbuilding Corporation, the controlling organisation for shipbuilding in China.
CSSRA	Canadian Shipbuilding and Ship Repairing Association, the industry's trade body in Canada, now renamed Canadian Maritime Industries Association.
DBS	Development Bank of Singapore.
DFDS	Det Forenede Dampskibsselskab A/S, a Danish shipping firm and member of the Lauritzen Group.
DHI	Daewoo Heavy Industries, a core unit of the Daewoo chaebōl, earmarked to absorb DSHM.
disp	displacement tonnage, the conventional yardstick for measuring warships. It equates the mass of water displaced by the ship.

DKB	Dai-Ichi Kangyo Bank, a major Japanese bank and centre of an industrial group.
DSHM	Daewoo Shipbuilding and Heavy Machinery Ltd, a South Korean shipbuilder with yards at Okpo.
dwt	deadweight tonnage, a measure of ship size determined by its carrying capacity or the difference between the light and loaded displacement of a ship.
ECU	European Currency Unit.
EDB	Economic Development Board (Singapore).
EEC	European Economic Community.
EMAQ	Engenharia e Máquinas S/A, a Brazilian shipbuilder sited at the Ilha Do Governador, Rio de Janeiro.
FELS	Far East-Levingston Shipbuilding Ltd, a Singapore shipbuilder concentrating on offshore platforms.
GE	General Electric, the US conglomerate which counts marine engines among its many lines of business.
GEC	General Electric Company, the British conglomerate, owner of the Yarrow yard as well as marine engine interests.
GMT	Grandi Motori Trieste SpA, engine building division of Fincantieri with works in Trieste. Formerly half owned by Fiat.
grt	gross register tonnage, a measure of ship size established from combining the volume of the underdeck spaces with the enclosed spaces above deck.
gt	gross tonnage, a less precise measure than grt for determining the internal carrying capacity of a ship and, hence, its size.
H&W	Harland and Wolff PLC, the Belfast shipbuilders.
HDW	Howaldtswerke-Deutsche Werft AG, a German shipbuilder, part of the government-owned Salzgitter Group, founded in 1967 from the merger of Howaldtswerke and Deutsche Werft. The former bequeathed yards in Hamburg and Kiel while the latter contributed a Hamburg facility.
HHI	Hyundai Heavy Industries Co. Ltd, the principal South Korean shipbuilder with yards at Ulsan.
HUD	Hong Kong United Dockyards Ltd, ship repairers located on Tsing Yi Island.
IBJ	Industrial Bank of Japan, a large bank which also functions as the centre of an industrial group.
IHI	Ishikawajima–Harima Heavy Industries Co. Ltd, a major

	Japanese shipbuilder conceived in 1960 from the combination of the Ishikawajima Shipyard with Harima Shipbuilding and Engineering.
JDB	Japan Development Bank.
JSEA	Japan Ship Exporters' Association.
KHI	Kawasaki Heavy Industries Ltd, a large Japanese shipbuilder.
KHIC	Korea Heavy Industries and Construction, a Changwon manufacturer of machinery, including marine diesel engines.
KMPA	Korea Maritime and Ports Administration.
KMS	Vlissingen yard Koninklijke Maatschappij 'de Schelde', the shipbuilding arm of the Dutch Royal Schelde Group.
KSEC	Korea Shipbuilding and Engineering Corporation. Now known as Hanjin Heavy Industries.
LNG	liquid natural gas.
LPG	liquefied petroleum gas.
MAN/B&W	Maschinenfabrik Augsburg–Nürnberg/Burmeister and Wain, engine builders divided, for the purposes of supplying marine diesel engines, into two operating divisions: Augsburg and Copenhagen.
MCI	Ministry of Commerce and Industry (South Korea). Latterly, it has assumed the style of MTI.
MES	Mitsui Engineering and Shipbuilding Co. Ltd, the shipbuilding and heavy engineering arm of Mitsui of Japan.
MHI	Mitsubishi Heavy Industries Ltd, a leading Japanese shipbuilder.
MIL	Marine Industries Limitée, a Quebec shipbuilder with sites at Lauzon, Montreal and Sorel.
MISC	Malaysian International Shipping Corp. Behrad, the leading Malaysian shipping line.
MITI	Ministry of International Trade and Industry (Japan).
MOL	Mitsui OSK Lines Ltd, a major Tokyo-based shipping company.
MoT	Ministry of Transport (Japan).
MSE	Malaysia Shipyard and Engineering Sdn Bhd, the principal Malaysian shipbuilder and repairer.
MTI	Ministry of Trade and Industry (South Korea), the former MCI.
NASSCO	National Steel and Shipbuilding Company, a San Diego, California, builder and repairer.

NESL	North East Shipbuilders Ltd, the defunct BS subsidiary located in Sunderland.
NIC	abbreviation standing either for newly industrialising country or for newly industrialised country.
NKK	Nippon Kokan KK, a Japanese shipbuilder and steel manufacturer.
NOL	Neptune Orient Lines Ltd, a Singapore government-owned shipping firm and major container line, founded in 1967.
NORMED	Chantiers du Nord et de la Méditerranée, the group formed in 1983 from the merger of Ateliers et Chantiers de France-Dunkerque, Chantiers Navals de La Ciotat and CNIM.
NYK	Nippon Yusen Kabushiki Kaisha, a large Japanese shipping company founded in 1885.
O&K	Orenstein & Koppel AG, engineers of Dortmund, West Germany, with a shipbuilding branch located in Lübeck.
OBO	ore/bulk/oil, or combination carrier.
OECD	Organisation for Economic Co-operation and Development.
OPEC	Organisation of Petroleum Exporting Countries.
P&O	Peninsular & Oriental Steam Navigation Company, a leading British shipping firm.
R&D	Research and Development.
RDM	Rotterdamsche Droogdok Mij, or the Rotterdam Dry-dock Company, now specialising in submarine construction.
Reefer	refrigerated cargo ship specially designed to carry perishable food products.
Ro-Ro	roll-on/roll-off ship, a vessel designed for the carriage of cars, trucks and unitised cargo.
RSV	Rijn–Schelde–Verolme Machinefabrieken en Scheepswerven NV, a large Dutch shipbuilding group, now defunct.
SAJ	Shipbuilders' Association of Japan.
SCI	The Shipping Corporation of India.
SHI	Sumitomo Heavy Industries Ltd, one of the major Japanese shipbuilders.
SIMA	the acronym for Peruvian state shipbuilder and repairer Empresa Publica Servicios Industriales de la Marine.
SSE	Singapore Shipbuilding and Engineering Ltd, a state-owned builder concentrating on small warships and container vessels.

SSHI   Samsung Shipbuilding and Heavy Industries Co., Ltd, a South Korean shipbuilder sited on Koje Island.

TMMC   Taiwan Machinery Manufacturing Corporation, a state-owned engineering firm involved in the production of marine diesels and, to a minor extent, ships.

UIE   Union Industrielle et d'Enterprise, a major French supplier of offshore rigs which acquired the Clydebank shipyard in 1980.

ULCC   ultra large crude carriers, the biggest tankers in the 400,000 dwt class and over.

UNCTAD   United Nations Conference on Trade and Development.

VLCC   very large crude carrier, a large tanker of 200,000 dwt or more.

VSEL   Vickers Shipbuilding and Engineering Ltd, a UK shipbuilder located at Barrow-in-Furness.

Y–S   Yamashita–Shinnihon Steamship Company Ltd, a large Tokyo shipping line which merged with Japan Line in 1989 to form Navix Line.

zaibatsu   Japanese business groups, usually centred on banks, which link diversified manufacturing and trading activities. The modern groups are outgrowths of the pre-war zaibatsu which accomplished so much in laying the groundwork for Japan's future shipbuilding dominance. MHI, KHI and IHI remain major forces in world shipbuilding.

Index